Compendium

Volume Three

to

Commentary

on

The Book of Mormon

Philip M. Hudson

The Book of Mormon speaks for itself, and its principles bear their own witness. May this book cultivate your interest to dig deeper into the themes woven into the tapestry of the gospel, as it invites you to turn to the scriptures for guidance. As you do so, the Spirit will bless you with insight, intuition, inspiration, and will sweep you up in quickening currents of direct revelatory experience with God.

Copyright 2024 by Philip M. Hudson.
Published 2024.
Printed in the United States of America.
All rights reserved.

No portion of this book may be reproduced,
stored in a retrieval system, or transmitted
in any form or by any means, mechanical,
electronic, photocopy, recording, scanning,
or other, except for brief quotations in
critical reviews or articles, without
the prior written permission
of the author.

ISBN 978-1-957077-75-8
Illustrations - Google Images.

This book may be ordered from
online bookstores.

Publishing Services
by BookCrafters, Parker, Colorado.
www.bookcrafters.net

In The Book of Mormon, we take our bearings on eternity, and we get a fix on the stars in the heavens. For it is there that our telestial tendencies are transformed into celestial sureties. This process is not one of maturation, but of generation, as we are "born again" as we are ushered into a delivery room we call the baptistry.

Index
to
Compendia
Volumes 3-7

When the Nephite prophets spoke to their people,
they did so with decisiveness and precision, but they
knew that to do so without love unfeigned would be cruel. If
they backed their people into corners, the only way they could
come out would be swinging. Accompanied by love, however,
their candor manifest itself with a sense of integrity that
shined as a light in their eyes. They possessed the most
sought-after of all the character traits; to be known
not only for their forthrightness, but also for
their tender hearts, benevolent blindness,
and for their willingness to quickly
and unconditionally extend their
forgiveness to others for their
perceived faults and
shortcomings.

Volume 3 Essays

Abstinence in a Permissive World
Additional Scripture
Addressing Deity
Agency
Agency and Opposition
Agency and Youth
Age of Accountability
Alma's Discourse on Faith
And it Came to Pass
And Thus We See
Angels
Are Mormons Christian?
Are We Alone in The Universe?
(The) Atonement
Bah Humbug!
Baptism
Batteries are Not Included
Become as Little Children
Before a Wound Can Heal
Behold
Being Well Grounded
(The) Bible
(The) Biggest Loser
Blood, Covenant, and Land Israel
(The) Book of Mormon as History
Book of Mormon Strengths

(The) Book of Mormon was Preserved for our Day
Born Again Christians
Brevity)
Buddy Can You Spare a Dime?
Caesar
(A) Change of Heart
(The) Character of God
Choose the Harder Right
Choose ye This Day
Christians
(A) Christmas Miracle
Christ's Church is Restored
(The) Church
(The) Church of Jesus Christ in Former Times
Circle of Knowledge
Citizenship in The Church and Kingdom
Civil Liberties
(A) Coat of Many Colors
Cogito Ergo Sum
Cognates in The Book of Mormon
Combatting Evil
Commitment
Conditional Sentences in The Book of Mormon
Connections
Construction Zone: Proceed with Caution
Conversion

People think
that they can be
happy if they wander
and play, forgetting that
a key feature of the Plan is
to ponder and pray, as Moroni
beseeched in Moroni 10:3. Only
then will they have the necessary
tools to find the happiness that's
been prepared for the Saints
in the household of
faith.

Volume 4 Essays

- Courage
- Covenant Consciousness
- Covenants
- (The) Creation of The World
- Dancing With the Stars
- (The) Desert Shall Rejoice
- Diversity
- Doctrine – The Meaning of
- (The) Door Swings Both Ways
- Dry Humor in The Book of Mormon
- (The) Dust of The Earth
- (The) Duty of The Priest
- Education
- (The Best) Education
- Enduring to The End
- Entropy in The Physical and Eternal Worlds
- Environmental Concerns: An Eternal Perspective
- Establishing the Word
- (Our) Eternal Nature
- Eternal Progression in a Dynamic Universe
- Everyone Wants to Go to Heaven
- Evidences of God
- Faith and Knowledge
- Faith Building
- Faith is a Principle of Power
- (The) Fall
- Fasting
- Fate
- Father Forgive Them
- Finding Balance in Our Lives
- Friendship
- Focus
- Follow the Prophet
- Forgiveness
- For Unto Us a Child is Born
- (The Importance of) Friends
- Friendship
- Gathering of Israel
- General Conference
- (The) Germination of our Faith
- Gifts of The Spirit
- God is NowHere
- Godly Qualities
- God's Tactical Flashlight
- Gold – The Appearance of
- Grace
- Gratitude

When the laws that relate to the ordinances of salvation, sanctification, justification, and exaltation, that are alluded to by the prophets in The Book of Mormon, have been woven into the sinews of our souls, that they become essential elements of the tapestry of our lives and become central to the very pattern upon which we trace our progress along the path of progression, our "minds become single to God, and the days will come that (we) shall see him, for he will unveil his face unto (us)."
(D&C 88:68).

Volume 5 Essays

Happiness
Happiness and Sharing the Gospel
Happiness / Wickedness
Having Been Commissioned of Jesus Christ
Heaven Can Wait
Heavenly Father Knows Us
(The) Heavens Were Opened
Higher Dimensional Realities
(The) Holy Ghost
(The) Holy Grail of Religious Doctrine
Honesty
(The) Hourglass of Life
How Does God Get Things Done?
Huckleberries and Chokeberries
Humility
Hypocrisy
I am a Child of God
I Have Fought a Good Fight
I Have Overcome the World
Isaiah in The Book of Mormon
Is Heaven Hotter Than Hell?
It's Our Book
Joseph Smith: A Rough Stone Rolling
Joseph Smith History
Joseph Smith's World

Jumping Out of Our Skin
Just Get Back on The Bike
Justice
Justice and Mercy
Keep Smiling
Labels
Lamanites by The Waters of Sebus
(The) Last Judgment
Life is a Three Act Play
Life or Death?
Life's Greatest Questions
Life's Important Decisions
Light
Light and Darkness
Light and Truth
(The) Light of Christ
(The) Light of The World
Limiting Beliefs
Living Water
Look Who's Coming to Town
Lost Books of The Bible
(The) Lost Manuscript
(The) Lost Ten Tribes
Lucifer

Nothing stifles the guiding Spirit faster than the stubborn self-confidence that has mutated into vanity, unbridled pride, selfishness, and haughtiness. These are the character crippling traits that are antithetical to the expansion of understanding that can be found in the revelatory atmosphere within the pages of The Book of Mormon.

Volume 6 Essays

(A) Mailbox Marked With an "X"
Management by The Spirit
(The) Manifestation of Spirits
May the 4th Be With You
(The) Millennium
(The) Mind of God
Missing Scripture
Missionary Work
Moral Discipline
Mothers
Multi-tasking
(The) Name of Christ in The Book of Mormon
(The) Nature of God and Our Covenants
(Our) Neighbors
No Greater Call
(The) Number of Disciples Was Multiplied
Obedience
One Lord, One Faith, One Baptism
Persecution
Personal Revelation
(The) Plan of Salvation
(The) Plan of Salvation 15 Names
(A) Positive Mental Attitude
Power: The Ultimate Test of Character
Pragmatism in The Book of Mormon
Premortal Life
Preparation
Pride

(The) Priests of Baal in Our Lives
(The) Prime Directive
Professors
Proper Prior Preparation
(The) Prophet Joseph Smith
Prophet, Seer, and
(The) Q Continuum
Quorum Sensing
Receiving Revelation
Recognizing the Church of Christ
Removing the Barnacles of Life
Restoration – The Early Days
Revelation
Reverence
(The) Sabbath
(The) Sacrament
Sacramental Waters
Satan
(The) Scope of Our Decisions
(The) Second Mile
Service
Set Apart
Sharing the Gospel
Sharper Than a Two-edged Sword
(The) Sons of Mosiah
Speak Kind Words to Each Other
(The) Spirit of Revelation

Of all the sanctuaries that have been created by God to be safe havens from the follies of the world, it is The Book of Mormon that stands out as one of the least understood. It reminds us that the natural man does not receive the things of the Spirit of God, for they are foolishness unto him. He cannot know them, for they are discerned spiritually.

Volume 7 Essays

Spiritual Calisthenics
Spiritual Gifts
Spiritual Identity Theft
(A) Standard of Excellence
Strangers in The Land
Strengths and Weaknesses
Studying the Scriptures
Success Strategies
Symbols
Talents
Teaching in The Church
Teaching Key Doctrine
Technological Traps
(A) Testimony of Christ
(A) Thirty Day Spiritual Fitness Program
Thou Hast Done Wonderful Things
(The) Thrill of Victory / Agony of DeFeet
Tithing
Too Good to Be True
(The) Tools of The Trade
Touching His Garment
Tough Questions
Travel at The Speed of Thought
(The) Twelve Tribes of Israel
Types, Rites, Ceremonies, and Symbols (Alma Unity
Updates are Ready
Walk in The Light of The Lord
(Our) Weaknesses
Were There Two Cumorahs?
What Think Ye of Christ?
Wherefore and Therefore in The Book of Mormon
(A) Whirlwind into Heaven
Who is Packing Your Parachute?
Why We Laugh
Words of Mormon
Work and Personal Responsibility
Worship in Music
Writing on Metal Plates Was a Pain
Zion

Those who persist in
stubbornly refusing Heavenly Father's
invitation to come in out of the cold, instead
will often seek refuge in the fortress of what is only
a perceived satisfaction in their own accomplishments.
(See Alma 30:17). In order to maintain their outward
appearance, the fabrication of a façade that would
demand inordinate attention to trivial detail
and to continual cosmetic reconstruction
would be required. But in the end,
it is all nothing but smoke
and mirrors.

Compendium Volume 3-7 Scriptures

Introduction - Look Who's Coming to Town
1 Nephi 1:20 - Follow the Prophet
2 Nephi 1:30 - Friendship
1 Nephi 2:1-3 - Life's Important Decisions
1 Nephi 3:7 - Obedience
1 Nephi 3:15-16 - Just Get Back on The Bike
1 Nephi 8:2 - Cognates in The Book of Mormon
1 Nephi 8:20 – (The) Hourglass of Life
1 Nephi 8:24 & 11:25 - Being Well Grounded
1 Nephi 9:5-6 – (The) Lost Manuscript
1 Nephi 11:6 & 8 - Jumping Out of Our Skin
1 Nephi 11:25 - Living Water
1 Nephi 13:26 – (The) Lost Books of The Bible
1 Nephi 14:7 - Book of Mormon Strengths
1 Nephi 14:10 – (The) Church
1 Nephi 15:14 - Teaching Key Doctrine
1 Nephi 15:20 - Gathering of Israel
1 Nephi 15:30 - God's Tactical Flashlight
1 Nephi 17:22 - Speak Kind Words
1 Nephi 17:50-51 - Multi-tasking
1 Nephi 19:12 - Environmental Concerns
1 Nephi 20:6 - Circle of Knowledge
1 Nephi 21:25 - Combatting Evil
2 Nephi 1:30 - Friendship
2 Nephi 2:4 – (The) Fall
2 Nephi 2:11 - Entropy
2 Nephi 2:15-16) - Work & Responsibility
2 Nephi 2:16 & 27 - Agency
2 Nephi 2:2 &, Alma 42:8 - Why We Laugh
2 Nephi 2:27 - Fate
2 Nephi 2:28 - Cogito Ergo Sum
2 Nephi 3:7 - Joseph Smith: A Rough Stone
2 Nephi 3:7 & 15 – (The)Prophet Joseph Smith
2 Nephi 31:16 & 18, & Moroni 10:5 - Joseph Smith

2 Nephi 4:35 - Life's Greatest Questions
2 Nephi 9:13 - Plan of Salvation Names
2 Nephi 9:13 - Holy Grail of Religious Doctrine
2 Nephi 9:18 - (The) Church in Former Times
2 Nephi 9:29 - Agency and Opposition
2 Nephi 9:29 - Education
2 Nephi 11:7 – (The) Creation of The World
2 Nephi 12:5 - Walk in The Light
2 Nephi 15:20 - Light and Darkness
2 Nephi 21:6-9 – (The) Millennium
2 Nephi 21:22-23 – (The) Desert Shall Rejoice
2 Nephi 21:31 - Quorum Sensing
2 Nephi 21:31 - (The Meaning of) Doctrine
2 Nephi 24:1 - Strangers in The Land
2 Nephi 24:12 - Lucifer
2 Nephi 25:23 - Grace
2 Nephi 25:1 - Are Mormons Christian?
2 Nephi 26:14 - (The) Church in The Last Days
2 Nephi 26:16 - Book of Mormon Preserved
2 Nephi 26:16 - Establishing the Word
2 Nephi 26:29 – (The) Priests of Baal
2 Nephi 27:10-11 - Receiving Revelation
2 Nephi 27:26 - Wonderful Things
2 Nephi 28:3-4 – (The Best) Education
2 Nephi 28:12 - Pride
2 Nephi 28:20 - God is NowHere
2 Nephi 28:26 - Power: Ultimate Test of Character
2 Nephi 28:30 - Christ's Church is Restored
2 Nephi 28:30-32 - Updates are Ready
2 Nephi 29:3 – (The) Bible
2 Nephi 29:6 - For Unto Us a Child is Born
2 Nephi 29:7-8 - Additional Scripture
2 Nephi 30:2 & 2 Nephi 24:1-2 - Blood,
   Covenant, and Land Israel

Although The
Book of Mormon record doesn't mention
it, the Nephite prophets must have urged their
people to lengthen their stride, for they must have
known that by doing so, their spirituality would be
intensified. The Savior urged those in bondage of
any kind to go the second mile, to double their
stride. "The second mile is a gift of spiritual
independence that removes the veil of
insensitivity to a divine destiny."
(Richard L. Gunn).

2 Nephi 31:16 & 18, & Moroni 10:5 - Joseph Smith History
2 Nephi 31:17-18 - Eternal Progression
2 Nephi 31:19-20 - (The) Prime Directive
2 Nephi 31:20 - Spiritual Calisthenics
2 Nephi 32:5-6 - Faith and Knowledge
2 Nephi 33:4 – (The) Second Mile
Jacob 1:6 - Revelation
Jacob 1:13-14 – (Our) Neighbors
Jacob 2:31 - Abstinence in a Permissive World
Jacob 4:6 – (The Spirit of) Revelation
Jacob 4:8 – (The) Mind of God
Jacob 4:11 - Faith Building
Jacob 4:13 - Too Good to Be True
Jacob 5:10 - Is Heaven Hotter Than Hell?
Enos 1:27 - Spiritual Identity Theft
Jarom 1:4 - Godly Qualities
Jarom 1:5 – (The) Sabbath
Jarom 1:20 - Plan of Salvation
Omni 1:26 - Fasting
Words of Mormon 1:3 - Words of Mormon
Words of Mormon 1:5 - Brevity
Mosiah 2:1 - General Conference
Mosiah 2:17 – Service
Mosiah 2:25 – (The) Dust of The Earth
Mosiah 3:12-13 - Proper Prior Preparation
Mosiah 3:15 - Symbols
Mosiah 3:19 - (The) Atonement
Mosiah 4:9 - Are We Alone in The Universe?
Mosiah 4:19 - Buddy Can You Spare a Dime?)
Mosiah 4:20-21 - Batteries are Not Included
Mosiah 4:27 - Finding Balance in Our Lives
Mosiah 5:7 - I am a Child of God
Mosiah 5:7 - Born Again Christians
Mosiah 5:7 - A Change of Heart
Mosiah 5:8-10 - Huckleberries and Chokeberries
Mosiah 8:13 & 16-17 – Heavens Were Opened
Mosiah 8:16 - Prophet, Seer, and
Mosiah 15:14-18 – (The) Thrill of Victory &
   The Agony of DeFeet
Mosiah 18:20 - Before a Wound Can Heal
Mosiah 18:21 – (A) Positive Mental Attitude
Mosiah 23:16-17 & 25:29 - Having Been
   Commissioned of Jesus Christ
Mosiah 25:19-20 - (The) Duty of The Priest

Mosiah 26:22 - Father Forgive Them
Mosiah 27:3 - Teaching in The Church
Mosiah 27:8-9 - Agency and Youth
Mosiah 27:11 - Angels
Mosiah 29:2 - Caesar
Mosiah 29:12-13 - Citizenship
Alma 5:7 - Set Apart
Alma 5:26 - Worship in Music
Alma 5:46 - Personal Revelation
Alma 7:20 - How Does God Get Things Done?
Alma 9:19-23 - Talents
Alma 11:43 – (The) Biggest Loser
Alma 12:27 – (The) Last Judgment
Alma 13:3 - Life is a Three Act Play
Alma 13:3 - Premortal Life
Alma 17:2-3 – (The) Sons of Mosiah
Alma 17:4 - Sharing the Gospel
Alma 17:34-36 – Lamanites by The Waters of Sebus
Alma 22:18 - Removing the Barnacles of Life
Alma 26:8 - Gratitude
Alma 27:27 - Honesty
Alma 26:23-24 – (The) Scope of Our Decisions
Alma 29:1 - Happiness and Sharing the Gospel
Alma 29:1-2 - No Greater Call
Alma 29:4 - Life or Death?
Alma 30:7-9 - Choose Ye This Day
Alma 30:13 - Everyone Wants to Go to Heaven
Alma 30:13 - Evidences of God
Alma 30:41 – (A) Testimony of Christ
Alma 30:44 - Dancing With the Stars
Alma 31:5 - Studying the Scriptures
Alma 31:5 - (Spiritual Fitness Program
Alma 32:5 - Limiting Beliefs
Alma 32:27 - Alma's Discourse on Faith
Alma 32:28 – (The) Germination of Our Faith
Alma 32:35 - Light
Alma 32:42-43 – (The) Tools of The Trade
Alma 34:32 - Preparation
Alma 36:12-14 - Bah Humbug!
Alma 36:19 - I Have Overcome the World
Alma 37:45 - Types, Rites, Ceremonies,
   and Symbols
Alma 40:20 - Construction Zone

The Nephites
were happiest when they
observed the summons to gather
in their synagogues and churches,
to partake of the companionship of
the Spirit, where they would receive
health in their navels and marrow
in their bones. Their gatherings
must have reverberated with the
sounds of the anticipation of
an even more enthralling
reunification in heaven
with their Father,
Who was their
God.

Alma 40:23-24 – (Our) Eternal Nature
Alma 41:10 - Happiness
Alma 41:13 - Justice
Alma 42:13-15 - Justice and Mercy
Alma 42:26 – (The) Character of God
Alma 46:12 - A Coat of Many Colors
Alma 46:15 - Christians
Alma 46:20 - May the 4th Be With You
Alma 48:7 - Courage
Alma 48:19 - Choose the Harder Right
Alma 50:23 - Happiness / Wickedness
Alma 51:5-6 - Civil Liberties
Alma 56:47-48 - Mothers
Alma 60:6-7 - Focus
Helaman 3:25-28 - The Number of Disciples Was Multiplied
Helaman 3:33 - Professors
Helaman 3:35 - Touching His Garment
Helaman 3:35 - Humility
Helaman 5:12 - Covenant Consciousness
Helaman 6:37 - Missionary Work
Helaman 10:6 - Heavenly Father Knows Us
Helaman 12:7-10 - Sharper Than a Two-edged Sword
Helaman 16:23 - Satan
Helaman 18:19-20 - Missing Scripture
Helaman 13:38 - Heaven Can Wait
3 Nephi 1:12-13 - (A) Christmas Miracle
3 Nephi 9:33 - Conversion
3 Nephi 11:10-11 – (The) Light of the World
3 Nephi 12:2 - What Think Ye of Christ?
3 Nephi 12:10 - Persecution
3 Nephi 12:48 - Nature of God and Covenants
3 Nephi 13:9 - Addressing Deity
3 Nephi 13:14 - Forgiveness
3 Nephi 13:14-15 - Door Swings Both Ways
3 Nephi 13:22 – (The) Q Continuum
3 Nephi 14:5 - Hypocrisy
3 Nephi 14:11 - Spiritual Gifts
3 Nephi 14:22-23 – (A) Mailbox Marked With an "X"
3 Nephi 15:9 - Enduring to The End
3 Nephi 16:1-3 – (The) Twelve Tribes of Israel
3 Nephi 17:4 – (The) Lost Ten Tribes
3 Nephi 19:30 - Keep Smiling
3 Nephi 23:1 - Isaiah in The Book of Mormon

3 Nephi 24:8-10 - Tithing
3 Nephi 26:14 - Become as Little Children
3 Nephi 27:5 – (The) Name of Christ in The Book of Mormon
3 Nephi 27:8 - Recognizing the Church of Christ
3 Nephi 27:13-20 - Baptism
3 Nephi 27:22 – Restoration, The Early Days
3 Nephi 27:28-29 - Tough Questions
3 Nephi 28:6 - Travel at The Speed of Thought
3 Nephi 28:13-15 - Higher Dimensional Realities
3 Nephi 28:13-15 – (A) Whirlwind into Heaven
3 Nephi 29:3 - Covenants
4 Nephi 1:17 - Labels
4 Nephi 1:17-18 - Unity
Mormon 1:3-4 – Book of Mormon as History
Mormon 3:20-22 - It's Our Book
Mormon 6:2 - Were There Two Cumorahs?
Mormon 8:5 – (The Importance of) Friends
Mormon 8:8 - Age of Accountability
Mormon 8:35 - Connections
Mormon 8:35 - Joseph Smith's World
Mormon 8:38 – (Our) Neighbors
Mormon 8:38 - Technological Traps
Mormon 9:6 - Who is Packing Your Parachute?
Mormon 9:32-33 - And it Came to Pass
Ether 4:12 - Light and Truth
Ether 12:24-25, Jacob 4:1 & Mormon 8:17 - Writing on Metal Plates Was a Pain
Ether 12:26 – (Our) Weaknesses
Ether 12:27 - Strengths and Weaknesses
Ether 15:11 - Gold – The Appearance of
Moroni 2:2 – (The) Holy Ghost
Moroni 4:1 – (The) Sacrament
Moroni 5:1-2 - Sacramental Waters
Moroni 6:9 - Reverence
Moroni 7:13 - Management by The Spirit
Moroni 7:19 – (The) Light of Christ
Moroni 7:24 - Diversity
Moroni 7:33 - Moral Discipline
Moroni 7:41 - Success Strategies
Moroni 7:44 - Faith is a Principle of Power
Moroni 8:8 - Commitment
Moroni 8:25-26 - One Lord, One Faith, One Baptism

Samuel the Lamanite possessed the meekness to become an instrument in His Father's hand. (See Helaman Chapter 13). As Boanerges, he went forth to the city of Zarahemla to preach the word of truth to the people. He was as a Son of Thunder among them, and was armed with power, might, mind, and strength (see Mosiah 2:11), to say nothing save that which was the God's will.

Moroni 10:8 - Gifts of The Spirit
Moroni 10:8 – (The) Manifestation of Spirits
Moroni 10:31 - Zion

Moroni 10:31 – (A) Standard of Excellence
Moroni 10:34 - I Have Fought a Good Fight

The only desire of
Samuel the Lamanite was
to set the people free from sin,
uncertainty, and ignorance, and
to liberate them to make thoughtful
choices, to receive priesthood ordinances,
and to serve others with more charity and
influence; to more fully enjoy the blessings
of the Plan, as they recommitted themselves
to obedience to gospel principles, that they
might repent and move steadily forward
along a path that would lead back
to their heavenly home and the
warm embrace of God.

If you don't find what you are looking for in the Index of Volumes 3 – 7, check out this list of topics with related essay references.

Abstinence – Abstinence in a Permissive World
Accountability – Age of Accountability
Adaptivity – Updates are Ready
Apocrypha – Additional Scripture
Apocrypha – Lost Books of The Bible
Apocrypha – Missing Scripture
Apostolic Church – (The) Church of Jesus Christ in Former Times
Are We Alone in The Universe? – Dancing With the Stars
Attitude – Just Keep Smiling
Authority – Having Been Commissioned of Jesus Christ
Born Again – A Change of Heart
Ceremonies - Types, Rites, Ceremonies, and Symbols
Character – Our Eternal Nature
Charity – Buddy Can You Spare a Dime?
Charity – A Mailbox Marked With an X
Chastity - Abstinence in a Permissive World
Christians – Are Mormons Christians
Christ – What Think Ye of Christ?
Church – Recognizing The Church of Christ
Consequences – The Scope of Our Decisions
Corrections – Writing on Metal Plates Was a Pain
Covenants – Covenant Consciousness
Covenants – The Nature of God and Our Covenants
Cumorah – Were There Two Cumorahs?
Darkness – Light and Darkness
Death – Everyone Wants to Go to Heaven
Dependency – Who is Packing Your Parachute?
Devil – Lucifer
Discipline – Moral Discipline
Doctrine – Teaching Key Doctrine
Evangelicals – Born Again Christians
Evil – Combatting Evil
Excellence – A Standard of Excellence
Faith – Alma's Discourse on Faith
Faith – The Germination of our Faith
Faith – Alma's Discourse on Faith
Feet – The Thrill of Victory / The Agony of DeFeet

Forgiveness – The Door Swings Both Ways
Forgiveness – Father Forgive Them
Freedom of Choice - Agency
Free Will – Agency
Gathering of Israel – The Desert Shall Rejoice
Gifts of The Spirit – Spiritual Gifts
Government – Caesar
Government – Management by The Spirit
Great Apostasy – Apostasy
Heaven – Higher Dimensional Realities
Holy Ghost – Batteries are Not Included
Holy Ghost – God's Tactical Flashlight
Humility – The Dust of The Earth
I Am a Child of God – Spiritual Identity Theft
Immorality - Abstinence in a Permissive World
I Think, Therefore I Am – Cogito, Ergo Sum
Joseph's Technicolor Dream Coat – A Coat of Many Colors
Kindness – Speak Kind Words to Each Other
Knowledge – The Circle of Knowledge
Last Days – The Church in The Last Days
Laughter – Why We Laugh
Light – Walk in The Light
Mercy – Justice and Mercy
Missionary Work – Happiness and Sharing The Gospel
Missionary Work – No Greater Call
Missionary Work – The Number of Disciples Was Multiplied
Missionary Work – Sharing The Gospel
Missionary Work – The Sons of Mosiah
Missionary Work – Strangers in The Land
Music – Worship in Music
Non-members – Strangers in The Land
Omniscience – (The) Q Continuum
One Way – One Lord, One Faith, One Baptism
Opposition – Agency and Opposition
Opposition – Lamanites by The Waters of Sebus
Optimism – Huckleberries and Chokeberries

Samuel hoped that the people of Zarahemla would search out wisdom and even flowing fountains of knowledge. His ministry was to help the Nephites find the spirit of truth in secret places. In his mind, there was no hidden thing that could escape the attention of a people who were determined to follow the guidance of the Spirit and to know and do the will of God.

Peer Pressure – (The) Priests of Baal in Our Lives
Permissiveness - Abstinence in a Permissive World
Perseverance – Just Get Back on The Bike
Personal Responsibility – Work and Personal Responsibility
Plan of Salvation – (The) Hourglass of Life
Plan of Salvation – Life is a Three Act Play
Plates – Writing on Metal Plates Was a Pain
Power – May the 4th Be With You
Preaching the Gospel – Establishing the Word
Preparedness – Spiritual Calisthenics
Priest's Duty – (The) Duty of The Priest
Primitive Church – (The) Church of Jesus Christ in Former Times
Pseudepigrapha – Additional Scripture
Repentance – Before a Wound Can Heal
Repentance – Removing the Barnacles of Life
Responsibility – Work and Personal Responsibility
Restoration – Christ's Church is Restored
Revelation – The Heavens Were Opened
Revelation – Personal Revelation
Revelation – (The) Spirit of Revelation
Revelation – Receiving Revelation
Rites – Types, Rites, Ceremonies, and Symbols
Satan – Lucifer
Scripture Not in The Bible – Additional Scripture

Scriptures – Studying the Scriptures
Speed of Light / Thought – Travel at The Speed of Thought
Spirits – (The) Manifestation of Spirits
Spiritual Fitness – (A) Thirty Day Spiritual Fitness Program
Spiritual Gifts – Gifts of The Spirit
Symbols – Types, Rites, Ceremonies, and Symbols
Technology – Technological Traps
Telestial / Celestial – Jumping Out of Our Skin
Ten Tribes – (The) Lost Ten Tribes
Translation – (A) Whirlwind into Heaven
Truth – Light and Truth
Types – Types, Rites, Ceremonies, and Symbols
Unity – Quorum Sensing
Weakness – Strengths and Weaknesses
Why Things Fall Apart – Entropy in The Physical and Eternal Worlds
Wickedness – Happiness and Wickedness
Wishful Thinking – Too Good to Be True
Word of God – Sharper Than a Two-edged Sword
Work in Progress – Construction Zone: Proceed With Caution
Worship – Worship in Music
Youth – Agency and Youth

As the seasons of our lives unfold before us, we realize just how much we need the influence of The Book of Mormon, as we engage the Plan of Salvation. "For life is a sheet of paper white, where each of us may write a line or two, and then comes night. Greatly begin! If thou hast time for but a line, make that sublime. Not failure, but low aim, is crime." (James Lowell).

Table of Contents

*"Scripture consists not in what we read,
but in what we understand."
(St. Hilary).*

The endowment soften our telestial tendencies and creates an impenetrable shield of faith. The Plan of Salvation, of which it testifies, provides a sounding board against which we may discern between the polarized opposites that seek our attention. The Atonement lies at the doctrinal center of the book, and strikes familiar chords within our heartstrings as it describes the difference between joy and its worldly counterfeits.

Author's Note...1

Introduction..3

Essays..11

The Book of Mormon replenishes the power cells that fuel our actions, giving our sight infinite perspective in the flow of a pulsing stream of inspiration that has no temporal or spatial boundary. As we are swept up by quickening currents into the direct experience of a holy communion with God, the heady appeal of the enticements of Satan fades in the brilliant light of day.

Observations

Observations..249

Commentary, Compendia, & Observations Index

Commentary, Compendia, & Observations Index...365

We take for granted
that prophets, seers, and
revelators receive revelation.
But isn't it amazing when the
sound of the voice of the Lord
that is so familiar to them is
for us a continuous melody
and a thunderous appeal,
as we read The Book
of Mormon?

Author's Note

These Compendia have taken on a life of their own, expanding into a collection of eight volumes of detailed information about The Book of Mormon that supplement my three volumes of Commentary. In essence, they are a distillation of my feelings that relate to The Book of Mormon. Their content is more visceral that that of the Commentary, and perhaps it more accurately reflects my personal feelings about the monumental themes that run throughout all of scripture. They summarize the more comprehensive body of work in my Commentary and showcase my feelings, in the hope that they might become living documents that not only reflect my present understanding of The Book of Mormon, but also the paradigms that expand with the utilization of new tools of discovery. It's a good bet that there is more to come. As the adage encourages, we need to "Think ourselves empty, read ourselves full, write ourselves clear, pray ourselves hot, and let ourselves go!"

When
Adam and
Eve were driven
from the Garden,
they were "punished"
with the very thing that
would later prove to bring
them the greatest happiness.
(See 2 Nephi 2:11-13). The Sufi
poet Rumi echoed Lehi, when he
wrote that our wounds become the
portals that allow light to enter us.
A Savior would be provided for God's
children, but in the interim, cherubim
and a flaming sword were set in place to
keep the way of the Tree of Life, to observe
the doctrines of Justice and of Mercy and
to initialize the principle of repentance
that is founded upon the doctrine of
the Atonement. In the Garden, after
their fall from grace, our first
parents were commanded
to have faith in all
these things.

Introduction

When
a faithless society has
been weighed in the balances
and is found wanting, it can be
traced all the way back to spiritual
bankruptcy on an institutional scale;
simply to its denial of the power of the
doctrine within The Book of Mormon.
Its motto seems to be: 'Eat, drink,
and be merry, for tomorrow we
will surely die'. (See
Luke 12:19).

Cicero wrote: "The first law for the historian is that he shall never dare utter an untruth. The second is that he shall suppress nothing that is true. Moreover, there shall be no suspicion of partiality or of malice in his writing." The accounts in The Book of Mormon written by the prophets Nephi, Jacob, Alma, Mormon, Moroni, and others, and abridged by the prophet-historian Mormon, were true to the mandate given by Cicero. Although, as Washington Irving brooded: "It is the rule that history fades into fable; fact becomes clouded with doubt and controversy; the inscription moulders, and columns, arches, and pyramids are but heaps of sand, and their epitaphs, nothing but characters written in the dust," yet The Book of Mormon stands as a shining example of the divine model.

It "is the witness that testifies to the passing of time. It illuminates reality, vitalizes memory, provides guidance in daily life, and brings us tidings of antiquity." It is the "evidence of time, the light of truth, the life of memory, the directress of life, committed to immortality." (Cicero, "De Oratore," ii, 36). In its pages, "the centuries roll back to the ancient age of gold." (Horace, "Odes," IV, ii, 39).

In one of the beautiful simplicities of the gospel, we are taught that the Plan allows all of us to enjoy the same access to the simplest, and yet most powerful, witness to the truth. In an inarticulate voice softer than the faintest whisper of sweet breath on the cheek, the Holy Ghost gently testifies, or bears witness, of truth. As Moroni 10:5 teaches (in a verse that is often overlooked, in favor of the previous verse): "By the power of the Holy Ghost ye may know the truth of all things."

The Holy Ghost has revealed all that is true, and has illuminated every eternal principle that has guided the minds of men and women since the dawn of history. We constantly benefit from that which He reveals. In the Last Days, when the Spirit is "poured out upon all flesh, and when "young men see visions, and old men dream dreams," (Joel 2:28), it will be the Holy Ghost Who provides the creative drive. The irony is that many will fail to recognize the source of their inspiration. Job did not. He wrote: "For God speaketh once, yea twice, yet man perceiveth it not. In a dream, in a vision of the night, when deep sleep falleth upon men, in slumberings upon the bed; then he openeth the ears of men, and sealeth their instruction." (Job 33:14-16). We cannot help but think of the experience of Joseph Smith in his bedchamber, when we read Job's description of how, at certain times, Heavenly Father chooses to communicate with His children.

All who desire to have a sure personal witnesses must carefully and prayerfully read The Book of Mormon, and then ask in faith if what they have studied is true. They will then receive the testimony of the Holy Ghost to motivate them to seek out the Priesthood and to enter into sacred covenants with God. It will be as it was on the Day of Pentecost, when Peter and others were preaching to a multitude whose hearts and minds were open and receptive to the truth. The words of the Apostles carried the weight of authority, and penetrated the hearts of their listeners to the end that they asked: "Men and brethren, what shall we do? Then Peter said unto them, Repent, and be baptized every one of you in the name of Jesus Christ for the remission of sins, and ye shall receive the gift of the Holy Ghost." (Acts 2:37-38). And on that day, there were about 3,000 souls added to the kingdom of God on earth. (See Commentary Reference to 3 Nephi 15:21-24).

A similar scenario exists today. Since the restoration of the gospel, there has been a Pentecostal outpouring of the Spirit, and those with a sincere desire to understand the will of God bring the same humble petition to the doorstep of the missionaries: "Now that we have heard your message, have put it to the test of prayerful inquiry, and have received a witness of the Spirit, what shall we do?" The response of the servants of the Lord is unequivocal: "You must exercise saving faith that leads to the waters of baptism and to continuing commitment, dedicated discipleship, selfless service, and sustained spirituality."

Shakespeare wrote: "The past is prologue." ("The Tempest," Act 2, Scene 1). The phrase was intended to imply that our

The Book of Mormon emphasizes that we must never allow ourselves to squander precious energy by becoming preoccupied with what is missing. Focusing our attention on what we lack could become a paralyzing fear. It's a flawed strategy that will ultimately defeat us. We must concentrate on the resources that are available, be they large or small, capitalize on them, and turn them into forces for positive, substantive, and significant change. We must pray as if everything depended upon the will of God, as it surely does, but then work as if it all depended upon us.

past is merely a prologue, or an introduction, to the great adventure upon which we will embark if we follow through on our plans. This original interpretation teaches that what has come before on our journey through life doesn't matter in the grand scheme of things, because a new future lies before us, subject to the choices we will yet make. The human condition does not change much over time, which is one reason why the Lord has revealed The Book of Mormon in the Last Days, so that we might profit from the experiences of the Nephites who are distant from us in time and yet are so like us.

Hugh Nibley observed: "Men fool themselves, when they think for a moment that they can read scripture without ever adding something to the text or omitting something from it." Therein lies the power inherent in its study. We glean insight and understanding every time we investigate the word of God. I have learned to love the scriptures, and I often think of St. Hilary, who wrote: "Scripture consists not in what we read, but in what we understand." In these Compendia, I have consistently tried to anchor to the scriptures the ideas swirling around in my head.

Utilization of commentaries and compendia does not replace personal scripture study. The spiritual awakening that accompanies prayerful efforts to understand the mysteries of God through the study of His word cannot be achieved through another person's interpretation. Perhaps, though, my own perspectives on the eternal themes expressed within The Book of Mormon will be helpful to you as you read and seek your own guidance. It is my hope that you will use these compendia only to assist you in your own personal journey to Christ.

Our challenge is to enlist the aid of the Holy Ghost as we undertake that journey. Many years ago, Dallin Oaks wrote: "Latter-day Saints know that learned or authoritative commentaries (and compendia) can help us with scriptural interpretation, but we maintain that they must be used with caution. (They) are not substitutes for the scriptures any more than a good cookbook is a substitute for food. When I refer to "commentaries," I mean everything that interprets scripture, from the comprehensive book-length commentary to the brief interpretation embodied in a lesson or an article, such as this one."

"One trouble with commentaries," he continued, "is that their authors sometimes focus on only one meaning to the exclusion of others. As a result, commentaries, if not used with great care, may illuminate the author's chosen and correct meaning but close our eyes and restrict our horizons to other possible meanings. Sometimes, those other less obvious meanings can be the ones most valuable and useful to us as we seek to obtain answers to our own questions. This is why the teaching of the Holy Ghost is a better guide to scriptural interpretation than is even the best commentary." ("Ensign," 1/1985).

Harold B. Lee taught: "We are convinced that our members are hungry for the gospel undiluted, with its abundant truths and insights. There are those who have seemed to forget that the most powerful weapons the Lord has given us against all that is evil are His own declarations – the plain and simple doctrines of salvation as found in the scriptures." (Regional Representatives Seminar, 10/1/1970).

Bruce R. McConkie explained that "revelation is necessary because ... each pronouncement in the holy scriptures is so written as to reveal little or much, depending on the spiritual capacity of the student." ("A New Witness for The Articles of Faith," p. 71).

And so, as President Oaks continued, "the scriptures are not the ultimate source of knowledge, but what precedes the ultimate source. The ultimate source comes by revelation. We encourage everyone to make careful study of the scriptures and of prophetic teachings ... and to prayerfully seek personal revelation to know their meaning for themselves ... If we seek and accept revelation and inspiration to enlarge our understanding, we will have the mysteries of God unfolded to us by the power of the Holy Ghost."

We are at
risk of falling
into transgression
in consequence of our
shallow understanding of
the principles of the gospel as
they are found on nearly every
page of The Book of Mormon. As
Alma declared to the wicked people
of Ammonihah, "The scriptures are
before you. If ye will wrest them it
shall be to your own destruction."
(Alma 13:20). Picking apart the
scriptures can distort dogma
into meaningless fragments
without any coherent
connection.

Elder McConkie also said: "I sometimes think that one of the best kept secrets of the kingdom is that the scriptures open the door to the receipt of revelation." ("Doctrines of The Restoration," p. 243). And President Oaks reaffirmed: "We do not overstate the point when we say that the scriptures can be a Urim and Thummim to assist each of us to receive personal revelation."

President Oaks enlarged upon the perspective of the young prophet: "Joseph was, by his own admission, no writer. He felt imprisoned by what he called the 'total darkness of paper, pen, and ink." (Joseph Smith to William W. Phelps, 11/27/1832, B.Y.U. Press, 2002, p. 287). He thus considered it 'an awful responsibility to write in the name of the Lord'. (Joseph Smith Papers, 1:367).

He did not suppose that he could receive the revelations perfectly, nor did the Lord ever set that standard. Joseph and his appointed brethren edited the revelations (see D&C 70:1-4) based on (that) same premise ... namely, that he represented the voice of God as he spoke in what he characterized as his own 'crooked, broken, scattered, and imperfect language'. (Joseph Smith to William W. Phelps, 11/27/1832, quoted in "Making Sense of the Doctrine & Covenants, a Guided Tour Through Modern Revelation," Steven Harper. "Personal Writings of Joseph Smith," p. 186-187).

President Oaks concluded his own epistle by stating a simple truth: "Latter-day Saints know that true doctrine comes by revelation from God, and not by worldly wisdom." (See Moses 5:58). He was in good company, for the Apostle Paul wrote that we are not capable of thinking any thing of ourselves; but we look to God for our wisdom. (See 1 Corinthians 3:5).

I could not agree more heartily with these wise words of counsel. As a matter of fact, every time I proofed my compendium (and I did this many times) I found myself scribbling additional notes in the margins and thinking to myself, "Why didn't I see that before?." That is precisely what I hope will be the experience of everyone who takes the time to read my compendia. I trust the process will motivate you to search the scriptures more carefully and to be instructed by the Spirit, as you do so, that you might be led in directions that will prove to be personally illuminating.

I would expect that my older grandchildren who read this compendium will be impacted in ways that are different from my adult children or my contemporaries. I hope that my observations will touch you differently each time you read them. When I am long-gone, perhaps the considerable thought that went into its production will generate a palpable bond that will span the years separating us. Maybe, the gulf that then divides us will not be as great, and our shared energies will pave the way to an eventual joyous reunion.

When
we sink our
roots down in
the earthy loam
of covenants and
ordinances, and the
foundation of life is
grounded in the ideals
of The Book of Mormon,
we find the Savior's love
and encouragement to be
just the underpinning that
we'll need, in order for us to
firmly establish our footings
well beneath the frost lines of
faithlessness and far beyond
every conceivable limitation
to our progression, such as
selfishness, greed, pride,
immorality, and
dishonesty.

Essays

The Book of Mormon illustrates our interesting relationship with God as He brings to pass our immortality and eternal life within a biological broth whose secret spice is our unbridled free will. It is unthinkable that He would focus His attention and concentrate His energies on an endeavor that was doomed to failure because of flaws in the instruments that are not only critical to its success but are also the very center of His attention. The little boy's exclamation that "God don't make junk!" betrays a keen wisdom beyond his years. It may be that Victor Hugo also heard the majestic clockwork when he wrote: "Be like a bird that pausing in her flight a while on boughs to light, feels them give way beneath her and yet sings, knowing that she has wings."

Abstinence in A Permissive World

"I, the Lord have seen
the sorrow, and heard the
mourning of the daughters
of my people in … all the lands
of my people, because of the
wickedness and abominations
of their husbands."
(Jacob 2:31).

What are those who are slinging condoms at our youth really thinking? Certainly, abstinence is not on their minds. When individuals and organizations cater to the lowest common denominator, however, do they really think that the results will be stratospheric? When the bar is lowered so drastically that even the most morally challenged individual can easily step over it, should we really expect an Olympian outcome? When the stage is set for mediocre acts, should we be looking for Oscar-worthy performances? What does society think will be the result of government-sponsored programs that promote safe sex within our adolescent population?

Adolescence is already as bewildering as it needs to be, without adding to the confusion. Beginning with puberty, the teenage years can be a rough passage. Already, too few of our youth evolve into socially responsible, moral, and mature adults. Even flirting with sin can be an insidiously dangerous practice, because once the lifestyle has been established, the unwary are surprised to find that they have sacrificed their power to act independently and are bound under the yoke of sin in habit patterns that are very difficult to break.

Better to light a candle than curse the darkness, say well-meaning individuals and organizations that are confronted with rising teen pregnancy rates and higher and higher incidences of S.T.D.s. But you cannot light a candle in a raging windstorm. If we really want our youth to learn to engage their agency wisely, successfully, and with demonstrably positive results, they need shelter and security. A context of abstinence from sexual activity is the foundation of that shelter and the framework of that security.

N. Eldon Tanner observed: "The craving for praise and popularity too often controls actions, and as a people succumb, they find themselves bending their character, when they think they are only taking a bow." ("Ensign," 11/1975, p. 76). Abstinence requires a measure of faith since the lifestyle of self-restraint is almost universally disparaged by the few who do not totally dismiss it as an anachronism. But the more that young people indulge, the more they have to lose. The more they abstain, the more they have to gain. The raw sewage that has permeated our culture in the last generation has contaminated the basic understanding of these principles, and a raging current of filth has undermined the foundations of their appreciation. With every gift of power comes the temptation to abuse it, and unbridled freedom to indulge in every whim has led to a very real tyranny. Of that class of individuals who cannot control their appetites, Edmund Burke declared: "Their passions forge their fetters." ("Letter to a Member of the National Assembly, in "The Works of the Right Honorable Edmund Burke," 4:51-52).

If there is security in abstinence, then its adherents must have the satisfaction of a freedom that others do not enjoy. Self-mastery releases us from the bondage of bad habits, compulsion, and sin that cloud our vision with an opacity that obstructs our ability to see what is really there. Abstinence becomes a medium of clarity through which we are able to grasp reality.

Will and Ariel Durant wrote: "A little knowledge of history stresses the variability of moral codes, and concludes that they are negligible because they differ in time and place, and sometimes contradict each other. A larger knowledge stresses the universality of moral codes, and concludes to their necessity." ("The Lessons of History," p. 37).

The rising generation faces unprecedented challenges as Satan makes a frontal assault on virtue and chastity. The youth need to understand that "the new morality is a fad - it ignores history, it denies the physical and mental composition of human beings, it is intolerant, exploitive, and is oriented toward intercourse, not life. The unity and community that couples seek cannot be accomplished at the pelvic level." (Robert Collins, M.D., "A Physician's View of College Sex," J.A.M.A., 4/28/1975).

We live in a world where the distinctions between good and evil are blurred and idolatry takes an ephemeral form, like a will-o-the-wisp. We try to focus on something, anything that will provide the stability that eludes us. Whether it is a sex goddess, eternal youth, free love, or the siren song of enchantment from a glossy magazine cover, it is all the same. Many years ago, one of our most popular periodicals was "Life." Then came "People," and then "Us." Next was "Self." Where do we go from there? "Indulgence?"

The gospel of Jesus Christ is the only sure way to avoid the compromises that assault morality. It teaches absolutely and unequivocally that sexual relationships outside of marriage cannot provide the celestial coordinates that are required to stay on course.

Post-script: This essay, written in the 1970s, seems ridiculously naive fifty years later. Today, it is clear that we have sown the wind and have reaped the whirlwind. (See Hosea 8:7).

Additional Scripture

"Know ye not
that there are more nations than
one? Know ye not that I, the Lord your
God, have created all men, and that I remember
those who are upon the isles of the sea; and that I rule
in the heavens above and in the earth beneath; and I bring
forth my word unto the children of men, yea, even upon all the
nations of the earth? Wherefore murmur ye, because that ye shall
receive more of my word? Know ye not that the testimony of
two nations is a witness unto you that I am God, that I
remember one nation like unto another? Wherefore, I
speak the same words unto one nation like unto
another. And when the two nations shall
run together the testimony of the two
nations shall run together also."
(2 Nephi 29:7-8).

"What is its meaning?" an angel asked Nephi of the Bible. (See 1 Nephi 13:21). "The book that thou beholdest is a record of the Jews, which contains the covenants of the Lord, which he hath made unto the house of Israel, and it also containeth many of the prophecies of the holy prophets ... wherefore they are of great worth unto the Gentiles. (For) when it proceeded forth from the mouth of a Jew, it contained the fulness of the gospel of the Lord." (1 Nephi 13:22-24). In older editions of The Book of Mormon, this verse was rendered "the plainness of the gospel of the Lord." The fulness of the gospel is the Plan of Salvation, which is a more accurate description of the Bible before the plain and most precious parts were removed.

What is missing from the K.J.T. of the Bible, and equally importantly, why is it missing, does it matter that it is missing, and if so, what should be done about it? The "great and abominable church, which is most abominable above all other churches, (has) taken away from the gospel of the Lamb many parts which are plain and most precious; and also, many covenants of the Lord have they taken away." (1 Nephi 13:26).

Sometimes knowingly, and at other times unwittingly, the world has changed the covenant, and has effectively eliminated the Old Testament as a witness for Christ. This is an abomination because such an action stops the progression of those caught in its snares and destroys our knowledge of the purpose of mortality within the context of great Plan of Salvation. With this in mind, in 1966 the "Church News" reported, "the witness for Christ was the most important thing in that ancient record." Without the testimony of Christ, the Old Testament loses much of its purpose and power.

Paul had prophesied of a coming apostasy from the faith. He wrote to the Thessalonian Saints: "Be not soon shaken in mind, or be troubled, neither by spirit, nor by word, nor by letter as from us, as that the day of Christ is at hand. Let no man deceive you by any means: for that day shall not come, except there come a falling away first." (2 Thessalonians 2:2-3).

In the Third Century A.D., the early church historian Eusebius provided a glimpse of the falling away that had been spoken of by Paul. He wrote: "But with our greater freedom a change came over us. We yielded to pride and sloth (and) to mutual envy and abuse. We warred upon ourselves as occasion offered, and we used the weapons and the spears of words. Leaders fought with leaders, and laity formed factions against laity. Unspeakable hypocrisy and dissimulation traveled to the farthest limits of evil." (Colm Luibheid, "The Essential Eusebius," p. 177). Later, during the Age of Chivalry, Charlemagne urged his churchmen to faithful gospel scholarship. "In a letter to abbots and bishops he complained of illiterate monks. 'What pious devotion had faithfully prompted in their hearts, their uneducated tongues could not put into words without stumbling.' Hardly a Bible existed that was not riddled with the gross errors of untutored copyists." (Will Durant, "The Age of Chivalry," p. 61).

An English-born theologian, minister, and leader of the Reformation in America, Roger Williams, wrote: "There is no regularly constituted church on earth, nor any person authorized to administer any church ordinance, nor can there be until new apostles are sent by the Great Head of the Church, for Whose Coming I am seeking." (William Cullen Bryant, "Picturesque America," p. 502).

Finally, Thomas Jefferson fumed: "The religion builders have so distorted and deformed the doctrines of Jesus, so muffled them in mysticisms, fancies, and falsehoods, have caricatured them into forms so inconceivable, as to shock reasonable thinkers. Happy in the prospect of a restoration of primitive Christianity, I must leave to younger persons to encounter and lop off the false branches which have been engrafted into it by the mythologists of the middle and modern ages." ("Jefferson's Complete Works," 7:210 & 257).

There is a prolonged negative consequence associated with any doctrinal dilution of the gospel. "Because of the things which are taken away out of the gospel of the Lamb, an exceedingly great many do stumble, yea, insomuch that Satan hath great power over them." (1 Nephi 13:29). This verse warns that without the iron rod, wandering off into mists of darkness is a very real possibility, but conversely it underscores the power of the word of God to help us to conduct ourselves righteously and to resist the temptations of the devil.

Why is additional scripture important? By divine investiture of authority, an angel promised Nephi that the Lamb of God would visit the remnant of the House of Israel represented by the seed of Lehi, saying: "I will bring forth unto them, in mine own power, much of my gospel, which shall be plain and precious, saith the Lamb." (1 Nephi 13:34). The reason for the preservation of this unambiguous record was made clear to Nephi. "For behold, saith the Lamb: I will manifest myself unto thy seed, that they shall write many things which I shall minister unto them, which shall be plain and precious; and after their seed shall be destroyed, and dwindle in unbelief, and also the seed of thy brethren, behold, these things shall be hid up, to come forth unto the Gentiles, by the gift and power of the Lamb. And in them shall be written my gospel, saith the Lamb, and my rock and my salvation." (1 Nephi 13:35-36).

"And after it had come forth unto them I beheld other books, which came forth by the power of the Lamb. These last records, which thou hast seen among the Gentiles, shall establish the truth of the first, which are of the twelve apostles of the Lamb, and shall make known the plain and precious things which have been taken away from them, and shall make known to all kindreds, tongues, and people, that the Lamb of God is the Son of the Eternal Father, and the Savior of the world; and that all men must come unto him, or they cannot be saved." (1 Nephi 13:39-40). The simple truth is that the Christian world today needs more than ever a witness that Jesus is the Christ and the Savior of the world.

The concern of our Father is not only for the Jews, but also for all nations. Therefore, He speaks to whomever He will, and His recorded words become scripture, or holy writ. When His prophets "speak when moved upon by the Holy Ghost," their words also assume "the power of God unto salvation." (D&C 68:4). The Savior taught: "These words are not of men nor of man, but of me; wherefore, ye shall testify they are of me and not of man; For it is my voice which speaketh them unto you; for they are given by my Spirit unto you, and by my power you can read them one to another; and save it were by my power you could not have them; Wherefore, you can testify that you have heard my voice, and know my words." (D&C 18:34-36).

Additional scriptures satisfy the requirements of the Law of Witnesses, wherein by two or three independent sources shall every word of God be established. The Book of Mormon, Another Testament of Jesus Christ, is an additional and necessary second witness. The Lord told the Pharisees: "It is also written in your law, that the testimony of two men is true." (John 8:17). Whenever Christ or His messengers have ministered on the earth, "he left not himself without witness, in that he did good." (Acts 14:17).

Most importantly, the scriptures are the foundation upon which God will judge the world. "Therefore, having so great witnesses, by them shall the world be judged, even as many as shall hereafter come to a knowledge of this work. And those who receive it in faith, and work righteousness, shall receive a crown of eternal life. But those who harden their hearts in unbelief, and reject it, it shall turn to their own condemnation." (D&C 20:13-14). Of The Book of Mormon, Ezra Taft Benson declared: "Every Latter-day Saint should make the study of (this text) a lifetime pursuit. Otherwise, he is placing his soul in jeopardy and neglecting that which could give spiritual and intellectual unity to his whole life." (C.R., 4/1975).

In the Last Days, God is performing a work of unprecedented importance and scale among the people, and He remembers the Abrahamic Covenant He made with our forefathers. "I shall proceed to do a marvelous work among them, that I may remember my covenants which I have made unto the children of men, that I may set my hand again the second time to recover my people, which are of the house of Israel." (2 Nephi 29:1). All who qualify by the Lord's Own standard will once again receive the blessings and ordinances particular to the Covenant. These include baptism, that is a covenant of salvation, the companionship of the Holy Ghost, that is a covenant of justification, the Sacrament, that is a covenant of sanctification, and celestial marriage, that is a covenant of exaltation. These blessings also include an inheritance in the various lands of inheritance. All are available because of the ministry and Atonement of Christ, Who came through the lineage of Abraham.

The Covenant has the power to gather scattered Israel the second time and to fulfil the promises made to the Nephites of old, as His words "hiss forth unto the ends of the earth." (2 Nephi 29:2). But at the same time, many will deny its reality and its necessity, even though Paul taught: "If ye be Christ's, then are ye Abraham's seed, and heirs according to the promise" or the Covenant. (Galatians 3:29). Some lack faith in the universal application of the Covenant, while others do not understand that true believers may join with Israel through adoption. Many have closed their minds to the possibility that God has an interest in His scattered people. In response to the bold declaration that The Book of Mormon is another testament of Jesus Christ, such individuals will cry: "A Bible! A Bible! We have got a Bible and there cannot be any more Bible." (2 Nephi 29:3). These are the same people who deny the power of God, who do not feel the need to receive more heavenly instruction, who reject his Covenant, and who rebel against His light and truth. (2 Nephi 28:26-28).

There are eleven direct references to the "Bible" in The Book of Mormon. (Found only in 2 Nephi 29:3, 4, 6 & 10). Understandably, the word is not found in the Old Testament or the New Testament, since the Bible as we know it was not gathered into one book, or "Biblos," until hundreds of years after the close of the Apostolic Ministry. We do not know what the Nephite word for "Bible" was, but Joseph Smith freely used this term that is familiar to us in his translation.

2 Nephi 29:3 is really an indictment of the spiritual state into which Christianity had fallen by the time of the Restoration, and is an indication that just as the first war waged against Satan was ideological, so too will be the last one. The Lord expressed His displeasure with those who have the Bible but fail to give thanks to "the Jews, (His) ancient covenant people," for providing it for the Gentiles. He asked: "Do they remember the travails, and the labors, and the pains of the Jews, and their diligence in bringing forth salvation unto the Gentiles?" (2 Nephi 29:4). He has made a terrifying statement to those who have "cursed (the Jews), and have hated them, and have not sought to recover them. "Behold," He said, "I will return all these things upon your own heads." (2 Nephi 29:5). "Thou fool!" exclaimed Nephi, "that shall say: A Bible, we have got a Bible, and we need no more Bible." (2 Nephi 29:6). "Fool" is translated from the Chaldean as "Raca," which means "worthless" or "a wicked and reprobate person." (See Matthew 5:22). Those who believe they need no more Bible, and who yet hold that imperfect and imprecise text as their ultimate authority, deny themselves refreshment from the fountain of living waters that continues to flow freely from the Source of all truth.

The Book of Mormon provides a wealth of doctrine imbedded in a historical matrix that touches on reality in a thousand different ways. On all these points, it can be tested. Joseph Smith placed it before the world without a single reservation. Those who hastily reject it, and pass judgment on its value without having paid the price to discover its merits or its treasures, do so dangerously.

When the scriptures encourage us to find wisdom and great treasures of knowledge, even hidden treasures, they are suggesting the need to search for those pearls that may not be readily discernible after only a cursory glance. (D&C 89:19). It is dangerous to summarily dismiss as a thing of no consequence a book that so boldly declares that it is the word of God. "And all they who receive the oracles of God, let them beware how they hold them lest they are accounted as a light thing, and are brought under condemnation thereby, and stumble and fall when the storms descend, and the winds blow, and the rains descend, and beat upon their houses." (D&C 90:5). Those who have access to the revelations through the prophets, but who do not take them seriously, will not be able to withstand the trials of this life.

In 2 Nephi 29:7, we find what could be a reference to the party of Hagoth, who led a group of Nephites into the "west sea," that was never heard from again: "I remember those who are upon the isles of the sea." (See Alma 63:5). In any event, the assurance is given here that God "rules in the heavens above and in the earth beneath" wherever His children might be. The Law of Witnesses establishes God's word, proving that He is I Am, "the same yesterday, today, and forever." He speaks according to His "own pleasure. Wherefore," asked the Lord, "murmur ye, because that ye shall receive more of my word? Know ye not that the testimony of two nations is a witness unto you that I am God, that I remember one nation like unto another?" (2 Nephi 29:8-9).

God has caused much to be written in order to prove that He "is the same yesterday, today, and forever." (1 Nephi 10:18). Just because He has spoken to one people we need not suppose that He cannot speak to others, because His work among His children has not yet been completed. "If you will bring together all the written records of man's past, you will find that the overwhelming mass of materials is religious in nature, and that the primary purpose to which writing has been put through the ages has been for keeping a remembrance of God's dealing with men." (Hugh Nibley, "The World and The Prophets," p. 189). The striking exception to this rule has been the profusion of profane material that has cascaded like an avalanche from the press in the past 200 years. The secular humanists have finally found a forum to present their case in print and on social media. It is no wonder that Jacob cautioned that it is good to be learned, but only if we hearken to the counsels of God. (2 Nephi 9:29).

He commands all men, wherever they might live, to write the words that He speaks to them. "Because that I have spoken one word ye need not suppose that I cannot speak another; for my work is not yet finished ... Wherefore, because that ye have a Bible ye need not suppose that it contains all my words; neither need ye suppose that I have not caused more to be written. For I command all men, both in the east and in the west, and in the north, and in the south, and in the islands of the sea, that they shall write the words which I speak unto them; for out of the books which shall be written I will judge the world, every man according to their works, according to that which is written." (2 Nephi 29:9-11).

"The scriptures overcome time and are the common meeting ground of all the prophets. Here they all speak a common tongue, and all bear witness to each other. The prophets constantly and characteristically quote each other. The Book of Mormon was meant as a sign and a wonder to an unbelieving world. It was meant to give instruction to those who should believe in the Last Days. It is a book for hard times and for great times." (High Nibley, "The World and The Prophets," p. 190 & 195). It is a book that has the power to focus our thoughts on issues of real substance that should occupy our attention, but that often do not, because worldly concerns get in the way.

The language of The Book of Mormon is simple, yet lofty, and can carry us to new heights and solid plateaus of understanding. It is unpretentious, yet momentous, as it grapples with the significant issues of our time. It is clear and concise, yet expansive, and far-reaching in its content.

"The English language Book of Mormon, when it quotes the Bible, follows the English of the King James Translation whenever possible, because this happened to be the one official version of the scriptures known to the people for whom it was translated. In short, today, as in ancient times, people are always taught from their own Bible." (Hugh Nibley, "Of All Things," p. 76). In The Book of Mormon, we find a second witness of Jesus Christ, and we learn that the record of the Lost Ten Tribes is a third witness, and that there may yet be additional scripture of which we are unaware, that also testify of Christ. "For behold, I shall speak unto the Jews, and they shall write it; and I shall also speak unto the Nephites, and they shall write it; and I shall also speak unto the other tribes of the house of Israel, which I have led away, and they shall write it; and I shall also speak unto all nations of the earth, and they shall write it." (2 Nephi 29:12).

2 Nephi 29:13 chiastically reinforces for us that the Covenant Children of Israel, no matter where they are, will ultimately share their sacred scriptures with each other. "And it shall come to pass that the Jews shall have the words of the Nephites, and the Nephites shall have the words of the Jews; and the Nephites and the Jews shall have the words of the lost tribes of Israel; and the lost tribes of Israel shall have the words of the Nephites and the Jews."

2 Nephi 29 begins and ends with God's declared commitment to Israel, whom He specifically addressed as His Covenant "people" in five of the fourteen verses. Ultimately, the words of God will be incorporated into one body of scripture for their benefit, and they will be gathered into one unified congregation of the faithful. "And I will show unto them that fight against my word and against my people, who are of the house of Israel, that I am God, and that I covenanted with Abraham that I would remember his seed forever." (2 Nephi 29:14).

The witness of Christ found on nearly every page of The Book of Mormon gives every thread in the fabric of our faith the vim, vigor, verve, vitality, & vivacity unique to holy vestments, whose steadfast colors will never fade, save it be thru neglect or unbelief. They will remain impervious to blemishes, but for the stubborn stains of unresolved sin.

Addressing Deity

(D&C 109)

"After
this manner
therefore pray ye."
(3 Nephi 13:9).

This prayer was "offered at the dedication of the temple at Kirtland, Ohio, March 27, 1836. According to the Prophet's written statement, this prayer was given to him by revelation." (Superscript to D&C 109). In the 80 verses of this prayer, Deity is addressed 42 times by at least 14 different name-titles, including once as the "Lord God of Israel, as the "Most High," as "God," as the "Mighty God of Jacob," as the "Lord God Almighty," as "Jesus Christ the Son of thy bosom," as the "Holy Father," as "the Son of Man," as "God and the Lamb;" three times as "Jehovah;" six times as the Holy Father;" and no fewer than nineteen times as "Lord."

"Latter-day Saints believe that Elohim is our God and Father, and Jehovah is Jesus Christ. (See D&C 110:1-4). Although these titles may not have always been used in this way anciently, Latter-day prophets have reinforced this belief, for example, the following statement by President Joseph F. Smith: "Among the spirit children of Elohim the firstborn was and is Jehovah or Jesus Christ to whom all others are juniors." ("Improvement Era," 8/1916).

These titles may be thought of as a naming convention used in the modern church for clarity and precision. Since Christ may appropriately be spoken of as "the Father" in many situations, Latter-day Saints use these name-titles to avoid ambiguity, regardless of the role in which a divine Personage has been characterized.

Since this terminology was not standardized for convenience and clarity prior to the Twentieth Century, readers are cautioned not to expect the early writings of the church to always reflect a practice that arose only decades later. Likewise, attempting to read the Bible as if its writers followed the same modern protocols is anachronistic, and may lead to confusion and misinterpretation.

Latter-day Saints also believe that Jesus often spoke for the Father by right of divine investiture. "Since he (Jesus) is one with the Father in all of the attributes of perfection, and since he exercises the power and authority of the Father ... the Father (sometimes) puts his own name on the Son and authorizes him to speak in the first person as though he were the Father." (Bruce R. McConkie, "Mormon Doctrine," p. 130-31).

There are numerous examples of divine investiture in scripture. The clearest biblical examples involve angels speaking on behalf of God or Christ (see Genesis 22:11-12, Exodus 3:2 & 6, 23:20-21, Revelation 1:1, 19:9-13 & 22:8-16), although Christ also spoke as though he were the Father on many occasions throughout the Old Testament. (See, for example, Genesis 17:1 & 35:11, & Exodus 6:3). Christ is also referred to in scripture as "the Almighty." (See Revelation 1:8 & 18, 4:8, & 11:17). It is for this reason that many Christians mistakenly identify Elohim and Jehovah as the same deity.

The concept of Christ as the Father is clearly set forth in a 1916 statement entitled, "The Father and the Son: A Doctrinal Exposition by the First Presidency and the Twelve." Additional support for the LDS differentiation in the use of divine titles is found in New and Old Testament scriptures, as cited above. Matthew and Mark reported that, while on the cross, Jesus cried out to his Father using the name Eli (See Matthew 27:46) or Eloi (see Mark 15:34). Both of these names are regarded by scholars as the Aramaic equivalents of El or Elohim.

Although references to Christ's sonship are somewhat rare in the Old Testament, they nevertheless exist. Daniel 3:25 describes a fourth individual in Nebuchadnezzar's furnace whose form was like a "Son of God (Elah)." Proverbs 30:4 speaks of the "son" of the creator, and Daniel 7:13 refers to the glorious coming of the "Son of man." (Compare John 3:13, & Moses 6:57). Hosea 11:1 was quoted by Matthew, in chapter 23 verse 15, as a prophecy that God's "son" would be called out of Egypt, and we should not forget that Isaiah's famous messianic prophecy foretold the birth of a son who would also be known by the titles "everlasting Father" and "mighty God." (Isaiah 7:14 & 9:16). All of these scriptures provide evidence that, as Nephi stated, many do now "stumble exceedingly" because of the "plain and precious thing which have been taken away" from the scriptures." 1 Nephi 13:26-30, 34 & 40).

Verse 1: "Thanks be to thy name, O Lord God of Israel."
Verses 3, 4, 31, 33, 43, 44, 46, 47, 48, 49, 50, 51, 54, 60, 68, 69, 71, 72, & 78): "O Lord"
Verse 4: Heavenly Father is addressed as "Holy Father in the name of Jesus Christ, the Son of thy bosom."
Verse 5: Jesus Christ is referenced as "the Son of Man."
Verse 6: The Prophet addresses Heavenly Father and refers to a revelation given by Him. (D&C 88:117-120). However, D&C Section 88 is clearly a revelation given to Joseph Smith by Jesus Christ.
Verses 10, 14, 22, 24, 29, & 47: "Holy Father."
Verse 13: The temple is referred to as both "the Lord's house," and as "thy house."
Verse 16: The temple is referred to as "a house of glory and of God."
Verse 17-19: The Prophet prayed "that all the incomings of thy people, into this house, may be in the name of the Lord; That all their outgoings from this house may be in the name of the Lord; And that all their salutations may be in the name of the Lord, with holy hands, uplifted to the Most High."
Verse 22: "Holy Father" is again addressed, and then in the same verse the Prophet asks "that thy name may be upon them." (The name is commonly accepted as "Jesus Christ").
Verses 34, 42, and 56: "O Jehovah" (A name title of Jesus Christ).
Verse 47: In this verse, the Prophet address God as both "Holy Father" and as "Lord."
Verse 68: The Prophet refers to God as both "Lord" and as the "Mighty God of Jacob."
Verses 71 – 73: The Prophet refers to the church as "thy church."
Verse 75: The Prophet pleads for the day when "we shall be caught up in the cloud to meet thee, that we may ever be with the Lord."
Verse 77: "O Lord God Almighty."
Verse 79: The Prophet first prays for acceptance of "this church, to put upon it thy name." Then he references "God and the Lamb."

Agency

"The Lord God gave
unto man that he should act
for himself. Wherefore, man could not
act for himself save it should be that he was
enticed by the one or the other, Wherefore, men are
free according to the flesh; and all things are given
them which are expedient unto man. And they are
free to choose liberty and eternal life, through
the great Mediator of all men or to choose
captivity and death, according to the
captivity and power of the devil."
(2 Nephi 2:16 & 27).

The term "agency" is used only six times in the scriptures, in D&C 29:36, 64:18, 93:31, 107:78, Moses 4:3 & 7:32. It is interesting that such an important principle is so infrequently referenced by this term, and yet we incessantly talk about it in gospel discussions. Then again, the term "free agency" is never found in the scriptures, although in years past, the term was in common usage. "More recently, we have taken note of our being "free to choose" and "free to act" (2 Nephi 2:27 & 10:3, see Helaman 14:30), and of our opportunity to do many things of our own "free will." (D&C 58:27, & Mosiah 18:28). When we use the term "moral agency," found just once in the scriptures, in D&C 101:78, we appropriately emphasize accountability. We have the capacity for free will, but are moral beings who are responsible for not only our decisions, but also for the consequences of our actions.

We have purchased our agency at great cost and sacrifice. Knowing what we do about the War in Heaven, it is no wonder that our youth are so zealous regarding the exercise of their agency. They were among the most valiant in the pre-earth existence, and during the ideological War in Heaven, that was fought by Lucifer for mind control, they were zealous in their defense of agency.

During that conflict, agency did prevail, and when the victorious spirits came to the earth clothed in bodies of flesh and bone, they did so with a passion for the freedom to choose their own destiny. Therefore, when those embodied spirits are controlled by compulsion, "in any degree of unrighteousness," it is ingrained within their nature to resist. It is helpful to understand why they feel as passionately as they do, and to be very cautious when questions arise that involve their exercise of agency.

The most powerful weapons used in warfare today utilize chemical, nuclear, and biological agents. But the most coldly efficient way to kill another's spirit is through the manipulation of ideology.

Agency is the lynchpin of the Plan of Salvation. The righteous application of this principle, that is fundamental to the operation of the Plan, is difficult to master. All one has to do is read or listen to the "News" to see how the battle is going, and to see who seems to be winning. But here's the really amazing thing about agency: The more it is exercised with responsibility, the more of it there is to use. The less wisely it is used, the less of it there is to use.

Making correct choices very subtly increases our power to make more correct choices. "You may know me," said this personality trait. "I'm your constant companion. I'm your greatest helper; I'm your heaviest burden. I will push you onward or drag you down to failure. I am at your command. Half the tasks you do might as well be turned over to me. I'm able to do them quickly, and I'm able to do them the same every time if that's what you want. I'm easily managed; all you have to do is be firm with me. Show me exactly how you want it done; after a few lessons I'll do it automatically. I'm the servant of all great men and women, and the servant of failures, too. But I work with all the precision of a marvelous computer. You may run me for profit, or you may run me to ruin; it really makes no difference to me. Work with me. Be easy with me and I will destroy you. Be firm with me and I'll put the world at your feet. Who am I? I'm Habit!" (Anonymous).

It only takes about three to four weeks of conscious and consistent use of agency to create a "good" habit. That's also about how long it takes to break "bad" habits. Consistently attending church services is a good example of the creation of a good habit.

Following Satan limits our choices and substantially hobbles our freedom to make good choices. Anyone who has suffered the consequences of bad choices knows firsthand what it means to be snared in Satan's strong cords and feel the downward drag of the weight of the chains of hell.

This begs the obvious question: Why, then, do we seem to find it so easy to follow Satan? There are always two voices operating, "two voices are calling, one coming out from the swamps of selfishness and force, where success means death, and the other from the hilltops of justice and progress, where even failure brings glory. Two lights are seen on your horizon, one, the last fading marsh light of power, and the other the slowly rising sun of human brotherhood. Two ways lie open for you, one leading to an ever lower and lower plane, where are heard the cries of despair and the curses of the poor, where manhood shrivels and possessions rot down the possessor, and the other leading to the highlands of the morning, where are heard the glad shouts of humanity, and where honest effort is rewarded with immortality." (John P. Altgeld).

The kicker is that we can we use agency, the very principle that Satan uses to get us to follow him, to withstand His temptations. The correct application of moral agency can be used to set us free from enslavement to self-defeating behaviors. At the end of the day, agency is both the beginning and the end of the Plan. Finally, the Judgment will hinge upon how we exercised our agency.

Contemporary prose illustrates the principle: "My father focuses heart-gripping flashes across the wall screen. Family slides. I am small, my brother is smaller, and my sister is smallest. Days now dead re-open like old storybooks from memory's heaped box. Pulling out pictures of cooking in Grandfather's Dutch oven; playing cheetah on our backyard monkey-jungle; being beautifully Easter-bested with my coat buttoned wrong; hugging a mommy minus grey hair. Soberly, I think of another Father, Who someday shall open my mind, and flash reeling remembering of every day's minute across my soul, across the heavens, and kindly ask me to narrate." (Lora Lyn Stucker, "New Era," 8/1973).

Perhaps we can start now to make a conscious effort to be aware of the number of times we exercise our agency, and make mental notes relating to its righteous application. We can then thank God each time, not only for the gift, but also for our power to make correct choices, and for the ripple effect it will have in our lives.

Agency is the lynchpin of the Plan of Salvation. Its righteous application is fundamental to the sucessful operation of the Plan, but it is difficult to master. All one has to do is read the "News" to see how the battle is going, and who seems to be winning. But there is a really remarkable thing about agency: The more it is exercised with responsibility, the more of it there is to use. The less wisely it is used, the less of it there is to use.

Agency and Opposition

"It must needs be, that there is (the contrary of)
opposition in all things." (2 Nephi 9:29).

When agency, or free-will, is exercised, two conditions become immediately obvious: the opportunity to make choices in an atmosphere of opposition, and the necessity of facing consequences that are associated with those choices. The urgency of reconciliation to the laws of heaven through atonement is not so apparent, but is equally important. Chapters 2 and 9 of the Second Book of Nephi forthrightly address these issues, and comprise the theological core of The Book of Mormon. In fact, these chapters could be studied independently to capture these essential elements of the gospel plan.

In a patriarchal blessing given to his son Jacob, Lehi taught the fundamental truth that "men are instructed sufficiently that they know good from evil." (2 Nephi 2:5). It is for this purpose that the Spirit of Christ is given. The Light of Christ is intrinsic within each of us, and we were created with inherent goodness and the capacity to recognize and cleave to truth. This is why Joseph Smith was able to confidently say of the Saints: "I teach them correct principles, and they govern themselves." ("Messages of the First Presidency," compiled by James R. Clark, 3:54). Such knowledge is powerful. It "will forever govern ignorance," declared James Madison, "and a people who mean to be their own governors must arm themselves with the power which knowledge gives."

But even in the best of circumstances, no one is undeviatingly obedient to eternal law. This is why Lehi taught: "No flesh is justified." (2 Nephi 2:5). That is to say, no-one keeps the laws and commandments of God in perfection, for to be justified means to stand uncondemned before the Lord. Lehi emphasized that without a Redeemer, our plight is hopeless. But, as he explained to his son, and as Jacob would later teach his own family, the requirements or demands of the Law of Justice were satisfied by the Redeemer's infinite Atonement.

His mortal ministry, His agony in the Garden of Gethsemane, and His reconciliation with the will of His Father on the Cross of Calvary constitute the evidence that Christ qualifies as an acceptable sacrifice for the sins of mankind. In return, He only asks that we approach Him with the sacrifice of a broken heart and contrite spirit. So, our indebtedness to God is completely beyond our ability to pay. But He does not ask us to settle our account with Him; He only asks that we keep His commandments. The marvel of His love is that the more we try to serve Him, the more He blesses us. Therefore, we become even more deeply indebted to Him and will remain so forever. We can only show how we feel about the Savior by expressing our gratitude, which is much deeper than thanks. Thankfulness is the beginning of gratitude and may consist merely of words, but gratitude is shown in action. It is independent of circumstances, penetrates the deepest undercurrents of life, and is founded upon God.

Because of His intercession on our behalf, we will all be briefly redeemed from spiritual death, which is alienation or estrangement from God. We will be allowed to come into His presence, some for the last time, to see how much intrinsic light we have lost through wicked behavior. If we have not repented, the soul-stains of sin will disqualify us from making a legitimate claim on eternal life. The judgment that is ultimately rendered will be based on the legal demands of Justice, and will dispassionately examine how completely we have met the conditions of our probation during mortality.

Fourteen parenthetical verses in 2 Nephi 2 grow out of Lehi's remarks on the Atonement, and are set apart at beginning and end by aphorisms that are foundation scriptures in the liturgy of the church. (See 2 Nephi 2:11-25). This section begins with Lehi's oft-quoted observation: "It must needs be that there is opposition in all things." (2 Nephi 2:11). The verses that follow demonstrate why that is so, illuminate the principle with examples, and caution that because of the exercise of agency in an atmosphere of opposition, both desirable and undesirable consequences are likely to follow.

Happiness, for example, is the opposite of misery and is one of the natural consequences of resistance to negative influences. As a matter of fact, it is the very "object and design of our existence," this purpose having been agreed upon in the Council in Heaven before the world was, "and will be the end thereof, if we pursue the path that leads to it, and this path is virtue, uprightness, faithfulness, holiness, and keeping all the commandments of God." (Joseph Smith, "Teachings," p. 255). Virtue has its opposite in vice, uprightness in slothfulness and indolence, faithfulness in secular humanism and self-reliance, holiness in carnality and worldliness, and obedience in wanton defiance of God's laws. Someone once wisely wrote that happiness is like a butterfly. The more we chase it, the more it eludes us. But if we turn our attention away from self-gratification and self-indulgence to the determination to love and serve God, it will come and sit softly on our shoulder.

An appreciation of true happiness ("the object and design of our existence") requires an understanding of the Fall of Adam. This can only come through inspired instruction. As Joseph Smith declared: "We shall at last have to come to this conclusion, whatever we may think of revelation, that without it we can neither know nor understand anything of God, or the devil." ("Teachings," p. 205).

Without revelation, we cannot comprehend the two great opposites that are at work in the universe, nor can we create order in the seeming chaos of existence. We cannot enjoy the holy and exalted state of happiness unless we are in harmony with gospel principles and in opposition to satanic forces, and so Lehi provided a wealth of information on this subject. He taught that there was opposition from the beginning, and that notwithstanding the idyllic state in Eden, Adam and Eve could not have had true moral agency leading to happiness until they had accepted the enticements of one who had been allowed by God to invade the sanctity, albeit morally static atmosphere, of that Garden.

By pointing out that there is opposition in all things, Lehi also implied that had Adam not transgressed the Law in the Garden, he would have vegetated there forever. Life in Eden before the Fall was not an ideal existence. Father knew that Adam must fall as a critically operative part of the Plan of Salvation, but Satan had no such knowledge, and so he pressured Eve to partake of the forbidden fruit, which was the very action necessary to bring about mortality and the opportunity for personal growth and eternal happiness that were critical to the successful implementation of the Plan.

Not knowing the mind of God, that opposition is necessary for the enjoyment of eternal happiness, Satan sought what he thought would be the misery of all mankind, and with his congenital short-sightedness and his typical stratagem of promoting half-truths, he offered the forbidden fruit to Eve. "Ye shall be as God," he unwittingly but presciently promised, "knowing good and evil." (2 Nephi 2:18).

The Savior Himself explained: "It must needs be that the devil should tempt the children of men, or they could not be agents unto themselves; for if they never should have bitter they could not know the sweet. Wherefore, it came to pass that the devil tempted Adam, and he partook of the forbidden fruit and transgressed the commandment, wherein he became subject to the will of the devil, because he yielded unto temptation." (D&C 29:39-40). But Adam was not deceived. His was an intelligent, conscious decision, the result of a clear understanding of the requirements of the gospel Plan. Adam fell that his family might come to know true happiness. Without understanding all the ramifications of his decision to partake of the fruit of the Tree of Knowledge of Good and Evil, he still believed that the change to a mortal condition was necessary, even though it might come like a flash of lightning and a clap of thunder. In the end, though, he knew the storm would pass and that flowers would bloom. (See "I Ching," The Chinese Book of Changes).

The Fall set the stage for the creation of "the family of all the earth." (2 Nephi 2:20). The Doctrine & Covenants clearly teaches that Adam and Eve were the first of Heavenly Father's children to live on this earth. They are characterized as "Father Adam, the Ancient of Days, and father of all, and our glorious Mother Eve." (D&C 138:38-39). The Lord Himself commissioned them: "Teach it unto your children, that all men, everywhere, must repent, or they can in nowise inherit the kingdom of God. That by reason of transgression cometh the fall, which fall bringeth death, and inasmuch as ye were born into the world by water, and blood, and the spirit, which I have made, and so became of dust a living soul, even so ye must be born again into the kingdom of heaven, of water, and of the Spirit, and be cleaned by blood, even the blood of mine Only Begotten that ye might be sanctified from all sin, and enjoy the words of eternal life in this world, and eternal life in the world to come, even immortal glory." (Moses 6:57 & 59).

Spencer W. Kimball observed: We often try to "expel from our lives physical pain and mental anguish and assure ourselves of continual ease and comfort, but if we were to close the doors upon such sorrow and distress, we might be excluding our greatest friends and benefactors. Suffering can make saints of people as they learn patience, long-suffering, and self-mastery." ("Faith Precedes the Miracle," p. 98). These are the very emotions that Adam and Eve must have appreciated, and which may actually have sustained them as they forged new lives in the lone and dreary world outside the overly protective influences of the Garden.

He continued: "If we looked at mortality as the whole of existence, then pain, sorrow, failure, and short life would be calamity. But if we look upon life as an eternal thing stretching far into the premortal past and on into the eternal post-death future, then all happenings may be put in proper perspective." ("Faith Precedes the Miracle," p. 97). This longitudinal view must also have been our first parents' perspective on life, for it explains why they cherished the opportunity to become mortal. "Blessed be the name of God," Adam declared, "for because of my transgression my eyes are opened, and in this life I shall have joy, and again in the flesh shall see God. And Eve, his wife, heard all these things and was glad, saying: Were it not for our transgression we never should have had seed, and never should have known good and evil, and the joy of our redemption, and the eternal life which God giveth unto all the obedient." (Moses 5:10-11).

President Kimball pointed out: "If all the sick for whom we pray were healed, if all the righteous were protected and the wicked destroyed, the whole program of the Father would be annulled and the basic principle of the gospel, (agency), would be ended. No man would have to live by faith. If joy and peace and rewards were instantaneously given the doer of good, there could be no evil – all would do good and not because of the rightness of doing good. There would be no test of strength, no development of character, no growth of powers, no (agency), only satanic controls." ("Faith Precedes the Miracle," p. 97-98). Oh, the wisdom of Lehi, when he declared: "It must need be that there is opposition in all things!" (2 Nephi 2:11). Thanks be to our Father in Heaven and to Adam and Eve for making it possible to have posterity in the stimulating environment of mortality! It is for our benefit that we become acquainted with evil as well as with good, with darkness as well as with light, with error as well as with truth, with sorrow as well as with happiness, and with punishment for the infraction of eternal laws as well as with the blessings that follow obedience.

The Plan was carefully crafted to create the conditions to come unto Christ within the crucible of mortal experience. Perhaps there is sense, after all, in the seeming chaos of existence, and there is a common thread underlying all experience. "For my thoughts are not your thoughts, neither are your ways my ways, saith the Lord. For as the heavens are higher than the earth, so are my ways higher than your ways, and my thoughts than your thoughts." (Isaiah 55:8-9).

In one of the few references in scripture to Lucifer's banishment from the presence of God for rebellion, Lehi described how an angel "had fallen from heaven; wherefore, he became a devil, having sought that which was evil before God. And because he had fallen from heaven, and had become miserable forever, he sought also the misery of all mankind." (2 Nephi 2:17-18). Joseph Fielding Smith, Jr. taught that the devil and his angels were cast out because they had "lost the power of repentance, for they chose evil after having had the light." ("Doctrines of Salvation," 2:218-219). Once again, through the example of contraries, we can see why cleanliness founded on the power of the Atonement is a central theme in the scriptures, because its opposite, filthiness or the failure to repent, is a form of rebellion against God that has eternally damaging consequences. Satan is the quintessential "rebel without a cause." All of his efforts will come to naught, and as Perdition his counterfeit proposal is utterly ruined when we look to God, and live.

To this end, Lehi next taught Jacob that since gaining experience and walking by faith are part of the mortal condition, "the days of the children of men were prolonged, according to the will of God, that they might repent while in the flesh." Lehi knew that he and every member of his own family would fail to keep the commandments with exactness, "wherefore, their state became a state of probation, and their time was lengthened, according to the commandments which the Lord God gave unto the children of men: For he gave commandment that all men must repent." (2 Nephi 2:21).

Mortality would thus become a time of testing and of putting to the proof. Agency and opposition are powerful forces that constantly refine us by pushing, pulling, and tearing at us in the crucible of experience. We can never eliminate the consequences that hang over our heads as the dangling Sword of Damocles. Always at issue is the question whether we will repent and take advantage of the Atonement of the Savior, so that we might enjoy eternal happiness in the Kingdom of God. If not, we must be lost because of the transgression of Adam and Eve, which brought temporal and spiritual death to mankind; temporal death because of the separation of the body from the spirit at the close of mortal existence, and the first spiritual death at the time we first sin after the age of accountability. Since the Law of Justice cannot be compromised, we will experience not only physical death, but also suffer a spiritual death, which is alienation from God.

Alma taught that spiritual death occurs when we die "as to things pertaining unto righteousness." (Alma 12:16). For when Satan came among the children of Adam, they "loved him more than God. And men began from that time forth to be carnal, sensual, and devilish." (Moses 5:13). In the scriptures, this alienation from God is called "the first spiritual death." (D&C 29:41). This is why after repentance and baptism of water, we must be spiritually born again through the cleansing action of the Holy Ghost. "By the water ye keep the commandment; by the Spirit ye are justified, and by the blood ye are sanctified." (Moses 6:60). The second spiritual death comes in the absence of Atonement, at the time of the Judgment. It is an eternal separation from the presence of God, that occurs if we pass from mortality without having participated in the ordinances of the Priesthood, or if we later willingly decline the vicarious ordinances performed on our behalf in the temples of the Lord.

But from the beginning, we have possessed the capacity to repent and have received instruction regarding how to do so. The Lord Himself told Adam: "Wherefore, teach it unto your children, that all men, everywhere, must repent, or they can in nowise inherit the kingdom of God, for no unclean thing can dwell there, or dwell in his presence." (Moses 6:57). Thus, the parenthetical aside begun in 2 Nephi 2:11 ends in verse 25 with a completely logical aphorism providing eloquent closure to the principle: "Adam fell that men might be, and men are that they might have joy." It is a grand summary of Lehi's discourse on opposition and the Fall of Adam, speaks volumes, and is one of the basic messages of the Restoration. When the Fall of Adam is considered in conjunction with the Atonement of Christ, it is clear that both are part of God's Plan of Progression, for we can only attain eternal happiness in a personal, tangible, reunification of our body and spirit. "For man is spirit, the elements are eternal, and spirit and element, inseparably connected, receive a fullness of joy." (D&C 93:33).

In 2 Nephi 2:26, Lehi returned to his original discussion. He wanted to impress upon Jacob that it is Christ's way for us to act for ourselves and to use our agency with responsibility, while it is Satan's way for us to be acted upon, or to forfeit our agency in exchange for the fleeting pleasures of the world. Whether we do this consciously or unwittingly, the consequences are the same. The 'perfect law of liberty' allows us to do as we wish and to be free according to the flesh. The exercise of agency in an atmosphere of diametrically opposed alternatives comes down to a choice between liberty and eternal life, or captivity and spiritual death. But for agency to operate successfully with a positive outcome, all action must be carried out within the context of the gospel and its laws. Otherwise, unbridled freedom leads to tyranny. We are free to choose, but we cannot choose to escape the unfortunate consequences of poor choices.

Of all God's creations, Satan is most miserable, and his tactics and plan would have made us equally unhappy by denying agency, requiring obedience, relying on compulsion, and preventing progression. Although the plan he proposed in heaven was counterfeit, a fraud, inoperable, and ultimately rejected by the Council, basic elements have been transferred to the mortal battlefield, where a last-ditch effort for their acceptance is underway. Elements of its ideology can be seen in social, political, cultural, and economic programs that pander to the natural man's innate insecurity, lack of initiative, and desire for undeserved entitlements. Those who voluntarily or involuntarily give up their agency in exchange for whatever transient pleasures that poor choices may provide, are snared by Satan and bound by his strong chains. When they feel the heavy cords of oppression around their necks, they realize too late that their choices have limited their options, restricted their actions, and fettered their self-expression. Habitual sin is a quicksand that mires us in a monotonously repetitive underwhelming convention and mind-numbing conformity that are the opposites of imaginative spontaneity and refreshingly distinctive artistic individuality. If we allow it to limit our choices, often all that is left is the cold reality of concession, conciliation, and compromise that can leave us as empty shells with a very bad taste in our mouths.

Sometimes all too quickly, and sometimes agonizingly slowly, those who have sold their birthright are dragged down to a hell on earth that they themselves have fashioned. It is very hard to break the bad habits that are the result of repetitive poor choices precisely because agency must be surrendered in order to acquire them, and ironically, "you can never get enough of what you don't need, because what you don't need won't satisfy you." (Dallin Oaks, "Ensign," 11/1991).

Heavenly Father does not operate this way. He always honors the eternal principle of agency. "Nevertheless," He counseled Adam, "thou mayest choose for thyself, for it is given unto thee." (Moses 3:17). It is riskier, but it is the only way that eternal progress can be possible. "Behold," He declared in the Garden after the Fall, "the man is become as one of us to know good and evil." (Moses 4:28). Choices and opposites are necessary if we are to achieve immortality and eternal life through the Atonement of Christ. In the process, rather than enslaving us in good habits, God repeatedly gives us the opportunity to voluntarily recommit ourselves to covenants of obedience to true and eternal principles. Thus, church membership and activity are vital to our spiritual well being, as is the renewal of covenants we have made through the ordinances.

"The Spirit is pure," declared Brigham Young, "and is under the special control and influence of the Lord, but the body is of the earth, and is subject to the power of the devil, and is under the mighty influence of that fallen nature that is of the earth. If the Spirit yields to the body, the devil then has power to overcome the body and spirit of that man, and he loses both." ("Discourses of Brigham Young," p. 69-70). At the end of the journey, all will "reap their rewards according to their works, whether they were good or whether they were bad, to reap eternal happiness or eternal misery, according to the spirit which they listed to obey, whether it be a good spirit or a bad one. For every man receiveth wages of him whom he listeth to obey." (Alma 3:26-27).

Lehi closed his blessing to Jacob by declaring that he had "chosen the good part," meaning that he had wisely elected to use his agency to yield himself to the redeeming power of the Atonement. (2 Nephi 2:30). "All things which pertain to our religion are only appendages" to the Atonement, declared the Prophet Joseph Smith. ("Teachings," p. 127). The truths that are fundamental to our understanding of the purpose and potential of life have to do with the Fall of Adam, the Divine Sonship of the Lord, and His Atonement. How appropriate it is that Lehi would address these concepts in such a personal way, via a patriarchal blessing to his son.

Jacob must have carefully studied and pondered his blessing many times, for a number of years later he expounded upon it in an address to his brethren. He reiterated many of its elements by approaching each subject in terms of God's goodness and greatness, and by relating the covenants of God to all the house of Israel. He began by affirming that it is a great gift to have a body. With our knowledge of the War in Heaven and its consequences, we know that some of Heavenly Father's children have forfeited the privilege to obtain a body. With the gift of mortality for those who remained faithful in the pre-earth existence, however, come grave liabilities, and so the Plan required the Creator to "become subject unto man in the flesh, and die for all men." (2 Nephi 9:5).

2 Nephi 9:6-15 contains one of the most important discussions to be found in all scripture of the necessity of the Resurrection and the power of the Atonement as it relates to the Resurrection and the principles of agency and opposition. Death, taught Jacob, is a natural part of the "merciful plan of the great Creator." (2 Nephi 9:6). Life is sometimes short, and yet all that is required may be accomplished. Death, which from a mortal perspective is the opposite of life, is essential to the Plan of Salvation. Jacob would later write: "Our lives passed away like as it were unto us a dream, we being a lonesome and a solemn people, wanderers, cast out from Jerusalem, born in tribulation, in a wilderness, and hated of our brethren ... wherefore we did mourn out our days." (Jacob 7:26). Yet, in a larger view and with an opposing perspective, he looked forward to a joyful reunion with his brethren, to whom he optimistically wrote: "I shall meet you before the pleasing bar of God." (Jacob 6:13).

The transgression of Adam, Jacob knew, was a necessary and integral part of the Plan, inasmuch as it gave Adam's posterity the opportunity to be born into this world, to live, and to die. He had learned that Adam did not sin in the Garden of Eden, in the classical sense, for he did not have true moral agency. The scriptures refer only to his "transgression," and the Second Article of Faith makes a specific distinction between it and our "sins." Mortality, the opposite, the mirror, or the contrary of immortality, was the consequence of his transgression, but it was not a punishment for sin. As Lehi firmly asserted: "Adam fell that men might be, and men are that they might have joy." (2 Nephi 2:25).

In any event, an Atonement was required to activate the Plan and to address the two other contraries, or opposites: Mercy and Justice. The Atonement removes the permanent effects of physical death and gives all the opportunity to have the effects of spiritual death removed through repentance. The Atonement can save us from our natural state of carnality, sensuality, and devilish inclinations. It does this by triggering the Law of Mercy, which mitigates for those who conform to its requirements the effects of the first Law, which demands Justice. It lifts us to a state of holiness, spirituality, and angelic innocence. Having explained this to his brethren, Jacob was enraptured by the mercy and the grace of God as was the Apostle Paul, who confirmed: "By grace ye are saved, thru faith, and that not of ourselves; it is the gift of God." (Ephesians 2:8).

The alternative to, or the opposite of, grace is frightening. Jacob was familiar with Isaiah's prophecy that darkness should "cover the earth, and gross darkness the people." (Isaiah 60:2). Without the Atonement, we would be subject to the devil, "to rise no more." (2 Nephi 9:8). Satan is Perdition, (meaning "loss," "destruction," or "utter ruin"), and we would become his subjects had no Atonement been made, for we would never have had the opportunity to repent. We would be carried down to hell in the grasp of the "awful monster" physical and spiritual death. (2 Nephi 9:10). But the Holy One of Israel overcame both by the power of the Resurrection.

He has the power to exercise the priesthood keys of authority relating to the resurrection. He Who lived a perfect life and atoned for our sins, acted in complete obedience to law in bringing into play His control over Justice through Mercy. Because His power legitimately conformed to the principle of agency, He was able to buy our sins with the legally recognized currency of the Atonement. His voluntary act of sacrifice was perfectly balanced and attuned to the task at hand, to overcome death and hell, which are the eternal opposites of life in the Kingdom of God.

Joseph Fielding Smith, Jr. taught that it is contrary to the law of God for the heavens to be opened and messengers to come and do anything for us that we can do for ourselves. Since we cannot redeem ourselves, a Savior had to be provided. The Lamb of God was slain from before the foundation of the world in the sense that it was in the Grand Council in Heaven that it was determined that He would be the Savior of the world. Mention has been made that Lucifer was also present in that Council. He too was free to exercise his agency to promote his counterfeit plan that was the exact opposite of the Plan of Salvation proposed by the Father. (Joseph Fielding Smith, "Doctrines of Salvation," 1:196).

In 2 Nephi 9:13, Jacob explained that "the paradise of God" in the spirit world is the abode of the righteous. Its opposite is the Spirit Prison of the Unjust where the unrighteous go to await their day of redemption. That day will come only when they have paid the penalty for their own sins, or when they accept the gospel of Jesus Christ and when necessary priesthood ordinances have been vicariously performed for them. This is one reason why the dead, who have been taught and who have accepted the gospel in the Spirit World, who did not have the opportunity to join the church while in mortality, are so anxious for us to do their family history research, so that the ordinances can be done for them vicariously. By so doing, we can literally become "saviors on Mount Zion" to our kindred dead, in the sense that they will be able to experience the opposite of spiritual death. (See Obadiah 1:19).

Those in the Spirit Prison of the Unjust, who reject the gospel and thus deny both the power of the Atonement and salvation through Jesus Christ, will have to pay for their sins themselves, since they are not at-one, or in harmony, with the Savior. (See D&C 76:73, 138:8 & 28, Isaiah 61:1, 1 Peter 3:19 & Moses 7:57). They will not be redeemed from the Fall until they have personally "paid the uttermost farthing" to satisfy the demands of Justice. (Matthew 5:26).

Jacob then explained that because of the resurrection of Christ, all will pass from physical death to immortality, which is the condition of the body when reunited eternally with the spirit. Because of the resurrection of Christ, this will come as a free gift to all who have ever lived on the earth. In addition, for the moment, all will pass from spiritual death, and will have the opportunity to meet God at the Judgment Bar. Thus, the Resurrection will totally overcome the effects of the Fall, which are physical and spiritual death. God is eminently fair, and the principle of agency will put responsibility squarely on the shoulders of the individual. At least briefly, all will come back into the presence of God to be judged. The nature of those who have refused to repent will be incompatible with His Holy Being, and so they will be banished from His presence, for in their filthy state they could not long endure His glory.

Those who have not been cleansed in the blood of the Lamb, who have not taken the opportunity to rely on the merits of Christ and the power of His Atonement through the first principles and ordinances of the gospel, are described as being "filthy." For them, the Atonement does not have the power to pay the penalty for their sins. Therefore, the Law of Mercy is of no effect for them. These individuals must live with the consequences of their poor choices. They must submit themselves to the demands of Justice, as if there had been no Atonement made, and the torment that follows is symbolically described "as a lake of fire and brimstone, whose flame ascendeth up forever and ever and has no end." (2 Nephi 9:16). But for the righteous, the place of judgment will be "the pleasing bar of the great Jehovah." (Moroni 10:34). For them, the Last Judgment will be reconciliation through the Atonement between two opposites: damnation on the one hand and eternal life on the other.

In spite of the horror that is the fate of the unrepentant, we must give God credit for even-handedness. His justice is affirmed, "for he executeth all his words, and they have gone forth out of his mouth, and his law must be fulfilled." (2 Nephi 9:17). His mercy is also validated, for "he delivereth his saints from that awful monster the devil, and death, and hell, and that lake of fire and brimstone, which is endless torment." (2 Nephi 9:19).

Consistent with Psalms 149:1, wherein ancient Israel was described as a congregation of "Saints," Jacob used that term to describe the righteous who believe in the Holy One of Israel. (2 Nephi 9:18). Implied is its opposite, unrighteous and unbelieving sinners who go about busily constructing the crosses of the world. The Saints are those who have endured these crosses. Christ identified what this means: "For a man to take up his cross is to deny himself all ungodliness, and every worldly lust, and keep my commandments." (J.S.T. Matthew 16:25-26). The opposite of the path to Calvary is the road to indulgence, self-gratification, and idolatry.

Paul used the "cross of Christ" to impress upon the mind the doctrine of the Atonement. Book of Mormon prophets also used the symbolism of the cross to focus on the ordinance of the Sacrament, where we take upon ourselves the name of Christ, and promise to always remember Him and to keep His commandments.

God understands opposition. He appreciates the powerful force of temptation on the exercise of agency. But He also knows everything. He sees the end from the beginning, for He is not only Alpha, but also Omega. If He were not omniscient, He would cease to be God, and we could not have faith in Him. God progresses by increasing His creations, and by bringing to pass the immortality and eternal lives of these creations. His holiness puts Him beyond the power of the adversary. Thus, He has spiritual life, proven virtue, unimpaired innocence, unimpeachable honesty, complete unity of purpose and harmony with eternal laws, and total victory over the tempter who is the antithesis, the contrary, or the diametrical opposite, of these qualities.

Because He knows what is best for us, and understands our divine potential to develop His nature, God gives the commandments to repent, to be baptized, and to develop perfect faith. These are the basic requirements for entrance into His Kingdom. Perfect faith impels us to action as though we had God's perfect knowledge. The principles of the gospel draw us to divine characteristics and change our nature so that we are repelled by sin. The gospel is the only weapon we need to vanquish Satan.

Jacob explained that the Law of Mercy satisfies the demands of Justice for those who do not have knowledge of God's laws. "Wherefore, he has given a law; and where there is no law given there is no punishment; and where there is no punishment there is no condemnation; and where there is no condemnation the mercies of the Holy One of Israel have claim upon them because of the atonement; for they are delivered by the power of him. For the atonement satisfieth the demands of his justice upon all those who have not the law given to them, that they are delivered from that awful monster, death and hell, and the devil." (2 Nephi 9:25-26). Nevertheless, all those who have reached the age of accountability have the light of Christ, which allows them to have a foundation of understanding of what is good and what is evil.

Because of the Atonement, all have equal opportunity before the Lord. All "have the privilege, living or dead, of accepting the conditions of the great plan of redemption provided by the Father, thru the Son, before the world was." (John Taylor, "Mediation and Atonement," p. 181). But "wo" unto those who have the law if they transgress. (2 Nephi 9:27). They will experience the deep suffering, misfortune, affliction, grief, and calamity that accompany personal accountability for misdeeds.

Jacob then warned his brethren that an appeal to vanity is the devil's way of turning our minds against the Plan of Salvation. "O that cunning plan of the evil one!" He lamented. "O the vainness, and the frailties, and the foolishness of men! When they are learned they think they are wise, and they hearken not unto the counsel of God, for they set it aside, supposing they know of themselves, wherefore, their wisdom is foolishness and it profiteth them not. And they shall perish." (2 Nephi 9:28). Jacob's counsel is a warning against the pitfalls of intellectual apostasy. It posts notice that education alone offers no protection against the forces of opposition that are always operating in the theater of life. Too much self-assurance is a dark contrast, or contrary, to the illumination of the mind that can come through learning when it is accompanied by meekness and humility. Jacob then employed an aphorism to drive home the point: "But to be learned is good, if they hearken unto the counsels of God." (2 Nephi 9:29).

From 2 Nephi 9:29 to the end of the chapter, we find a parallel to Isaiah 50:11 and 2 Nephi 7:11. These verses concern the final judgment, and were written as much for the Latter-day Saints as for Jacob's Nephite brethren.

Satan uses telestial trash, or the corruptible treasures of the earth, as counterfeits for God. They are the opposites of celestial sureties and the incorruptible riches of eternity. Jeremiah asked the question: "Shall a man make gods unto himself, and they are no gods?" (Jeremiah 16:20). In His Preface to the Doctrine and Covenants, the Lord declared of those who lived at the time of Joseph Smith: "They seek not the Lord to establish his righteousness, but every man walketh in his own way, and after the image of his own god, whose image is in the likeness of the world, and whose substance is like that of an idol, which waxeth old and shall perish in Babylon, even Babylon the great, which shall fall." (D&C 1:16).

"Wo unto the rich, who are rich as to the things of the world," wrote Jacob. (2 Nephi 9:30). Satan's Golden Question is and always has been: "Do you have any money? You can have anything in this world for money." (See Hugh Nibley, "Zeal Without Knowledge," and also "Educating the Saints"). "Wo unto the deaf that will not hear," Jacob continued. (2 Nephi 9:31). Those who will not see, or hear, or who are uncircumcised of heart, are of terrestrial and telestial quality. Those who are so focused on selfish pleasures, the things of the world, and the honors of men, cannot see beyond the horizon of their limited vision, and are fettered by their self-inflicted blindness. Without the perspective of the gospel, they "tend to fill space, as if what they have, what they are, is not enough. Being affluent, they strangle themselves with what they can buy, things whose opacity obstructs their ability to see what is really there." (Greta Erlich, "Under Wyoming Skies," "The Atlantic Monthly," 5/1985).

Verse 34 parallels Proverbs 19:9: "Wo unto the liar, for he shall be thrust down to hell." Those who bear false witness qualify only for the telestial kingdom. If we view the forces operating in the vortex of life as naturally occurring opposites, false witness is a particularly damaging sin, since it poisons the atmosphere in which correct choices might otherwise be made. Its fiction may compellingly distort the facts, in a way that makes the righteous application of agency very difficult.

"Wo unto the murderer who deliberately killeth, for he shall die." (2 Nephi 9:35). The sin of deliberately killing another robs that individual of agency and self-determination with abrupt, total, and irreversible finality. Such a brutal act of selfishness places the transgressor beyond the power of the Atonement, and so the doctrine of Blood Atonement, wherein the transgressor must atone with his own blood for his sins, was taught among the Nephites.

"Wo unto them who commit whoredoms, for they shall be thrust down to hell." (2 Nephi 9:36). A "whore" can be "a corrupt or idolatrous community" or individual. (O.E.D.). Thus, the worship of idols of any kind is a whoredom, and is adulterous in a figurative sense. Our worship of idols, when we turn our backs on the sacred covenants of the Priesthood, is akin to infidelity. It is the diametrical opposite of those who come to the marriage supper of the Lamb with their lamps of oil filled to overflowing.

"Wo unto those that worship idols, for the devil of all devils delighteth in them." (2 Nephi 9:37). In the final analysis, the devil can only rule in the earth if he is able to seductively manipulate those who worship idols. His followers have traded their birthright for a mess of pottage. They have given up their agency for the rush that accompanies carnality and sensuality. The opposite of counterfeit sensory stimulation is priesthood power, which "is the legitimate rule of God and is the only legitimate power that has a right to rule upon the earth. When the will of God is done on the earth, as it is done in heaven, no other power will bear rule." (John Taylor, J.D., 5:187).

"O my beloved brethren," Jacob implored, "remember the awfulness in transgressing against that Holy God, and also the awfulness of yielding to the enticings of that cunning one." (2 Nephi 9:39). The devil's bribery stands in sharp contrast and in opposition to the blessings that follow obedience to God's will. Satan costumes his wares in gaudy paraphernalia that attract the curious yet demand no commitment. As moths that are drawn to fire, if they venture too closely, they will wither and die due to the radiant heat of brimstone. His powerful lures are attractive because they offer pleasure and advantage, but they are insidious and adroit, for he is, after all, a tempter. In the end, however, his impoverished and malnourished disciples are left destitute and helpless with rescue a near impossibility. The insolvency of Satan's seduction cannot be mitigated by a third-party bailout. The only solution to his nepotism is to throw the bums out, wipe the slate clean, kill all the lawyers, as Shakespeare urged, and begin anew with an Elector who truly represents our best interests.

The Plan that was provided for us considers the reality that we would exercise our agency to yield in varying degrees to temptation even as we learn to deal with opposition and experience consequences. Repentance is like a fuel rod that energizes the Atonement in our behalf. It allows us to make mistakes, to learn from them, and to then grasp the horns of sanctuary so that at the end of the day we may be justified by the grace of God. Mortality is a wonderful learning laboratory; indeed, as Henri Bergson so astutely observed, "the universe is a machine for the making of Gods." ("The Two Sources of Morality and Religion"). With the gospel as its mainspring, it is a majestic clockwork. Without it, it can be an improvised explosive device, an evil trap, and a snare of Satan. Agency and opposition are always before us.

"Remember," cautioned Jacob, "to be carnally minded is death, and to be spiritually minded is life eternal." (2 Nephi 9:39). His message was intended to pierce the hearts of unconfronted individuals who had not yet made a commitment. These he urged to "come unto the Lord," acknowledging that the way is narrow, meaning that there are no worthy alternatives. (2 Nephi 9:41). He taught that agency must be exercised with great sensitivity and selectivity. Once committed, however, he promised that the way lies in an easily "identifiable straight course" in contrast and in opposition to Satan's alternative program that is twisted, deceptive, unreliable, and is indifferent to our needs.

Opportunities for recommitment and rededication are critical to spiritual well being, because disciples of Christ are painfully aware that two choices lie constantly before us. "Two forces are operating, two voices are calling, one coming out from the swamps of selfishness and force, where success means death, and the other from the hilltops of justice and progress, where even failure brings glory. Two lights are seen on your horizon, one, the last fading marsh light of power, and the other the slowly rising sun of human brotherhood. Two ways lie open for you, one leading to an ever lower and lower plane, where are heard the cries of despair and the curses of the poor, where manhood shrivels and possessions rot down the possessor, and the other leading to the highlands of the morning, where are heard the glad shouts of humanity, and where honest effort is rewarded with immortality." (John P. Altgeld). Boyd Packer simply stated: "The choice in life is not between wealth and poverty, or between fame and obscurity. It is between good and evil." ("Ensign," 11/1980).

Jacob summarized his teachings by exhorting his people: "And whoso knocketh, to him will he open; and the wise, and the learned, and they that are rich, who are puffed up, because of their learning, and their wisdom, and their riches – yea, they are they whom he despiseth; and save they shall cast these things away, and consider themselves fools before God, and come down in the depths of humility, he will not open unto them." (2 Nephi 9:42).

Blessings are predicated upon obedience to law, and when we observe the statutes, we will surely experience the "happiness which is prepared for the saints." (2 Nephi 9:43). Jacob had fulfilled the commandments of God from his childhood and now had taken to heart the patriarchal blessing given him so many years earlier. As a responsible adult and priesthood leader, and perhaps as a patriarch himself, he had taught his brethren boldly and with plainness, and so, even though he had solemn responsibilities as their priest and teacher, he was free from their sins.

Nevertheless, he was concerned that the "chains" of the devil might shackle the Nephites and darken their minds. Hundreds of years later, the prophet Alma explained what these chains are. "And they that will harden their heart, to them is given the lesser portion of the word until they know nothing concerning his mysteries; and then they are taken captive by the devil, and led by his will down to destruction. Now this is what is meant by the chains of hell." (Alma 12:11).

This warning applies equally to members of The Church of Jesus Christ of Latter-day Saints. When our hearts are hardened against the message of salvation, it is as though our portion is diminished further and further, until we are left defenseless against the aggressive tactics of the devil. Left to ourselves, we are influenced by the lies of the Deceiver, rather than by the illuminating truths of the Spirit, and we will be dragged down to hell. In the harsh light of day, the exercise of agency in the midst of difficult choices and opposition can lead to devastating consequences.

The Day of Judgment will be glorious for the righteous, however, because the Holy Ghost will justify them. Repentance, made possible by the Atonement, will have removed all traces of impurity from the tapestry woven into the sinews of the souls of the righteous. As John Taylor wrote: "That record is written by the man himself in the tablets of his own mind. It cannot lie, and will in that day be unfolded before God and angels." (J.D., 11:79).

Contemporary prose illustrates the principle: "My father focuses heart-gripping flashes across the wall screen. Family slides. I am small, my brother is smaller, and my sister is smallest. Days now dead re-open like old storybooks from memory's heaped box. Pulling out pictures of cooking in Grandfather's Dutch oven; playing cheetah in our backyard monkey-jungle; being beautifully Easter-bested with my coat buttoned wrong; hugging a mommy minus grey hair. Soberly, I think of another Father, Who someday shall open my mind, and flash reeling remembering of every day's minute across my soul, across the heavens, and kindly ask me to narrate." (Lora Lyn Stucker, "New Era," 8/1973).

The conclusion of Jacob's address begins in 2 Nephi 9:47. "Ye look upon me as a teacher," he said, and so "it must needs be expedient that I teach you the consequences of sin. Behold, my soul abhorreth sin, and my heart delighteth in righteousness." (2 Nephi 9:48-49). Only a fully committed individual, speaking with power and authority, could make this bold statement. In the church, the greatest qualifications required of teachers are that they have faith in the principles of the gospel, believe revealed truth, and exercise their privileges in the spirit of prayer and of faith.

After explaining the great Plan of Redemption to his people, that solved the dilemma created by God's demand for perfection coupled with our inability to lead sinless lives, Jacob simply stated: "O be wise; what can I say more?" (Jacob 6:12). 2 Nephi Chapters 2 & 9 illustrate why Joseph Smith said: "The Book of Mormon was the most correct of any book on earth, and the keystone of our religion, and a man would get nearer to God by abiding by its precepts than by any other book." ("Introduction to The Book of Mormon"). As Hugh Nibley has said: "We are not laying down ground rules for taste, or saying that The Book of Mormon is good because some people like it or bad because others do not. What we are saying is that The Book of Mormon, whatever one may think, is one of the great realities of our time, and that what makes it so is that certain people believe it. Its literary or artistic qualities do not enter into the discussion. It was written to be believed. Its one and only merit is truth. Without that merit, it is all that nonbelievers say it is. With it, it is all that believers say it is." ("Of All Things").

Agency and Youth

"The Sons of Mosiah were numbered among the unbelievers; and also one of the sons of Alma ... And he was a man of many words, and did speak much flattery to the people; therefore, he led many of the people to do after the manner of his iniquities. And he became a great hinderment to the prosperity of the church of God; stealing away the hearts of the people; causing much dissention among the people; giving a chance for the enemy of God to exercise his power over them."
(Mosiah 27:8-9).

Latter-day prophets have consistently taught that our youth were among the most valiant spirits in the pre-earth existence. During the War in Heaven, those who stood with the Savior sought to preserve agency as a foundation principle of the Plan of Salvation, while those who rebelled and fought with Lucifer sought control of the minds of men, through the devious manipulation of ideology. Those who were zealous in the defense of their freedom of expression kept their first estate, and were added upon. They were blessed to be able to come to earth, to fill the measure of their creation.

During the pre-mortal conflict that pitted contrasting ideologies against each other, the principle of free will, together with the natural consequences related to its expression, prevailed, and when the victorious spirits were given their opportunity to experience mortality, they grasped it with a passion for the freedom to choose their own destiny, that had become ingrained within their nature. Consequently, when those spirits who have come to earth to dwell in mortal clay sense that they are being controlled by compulsion, "in any degree of unrighteousness" whatsoever, their innate tendency is to resist with the same tenacity they exhibited in their pre-mortal life.

Therefore, we need to be very careful how we relate with our youth in every situation that involves the exercise of agency. It is helpful to appreciate and to put into context "where they are coming from," because that helps us to understand why they act as they do, and to give us an appreciation of where they are going.

When we exercise our agency, or our free will, two conditions become obvious: our opportunity to make decisions within an atmosphere of opposition, and the necessity of facing consequences that are related to those choices. The urgency of reconciliation to the laws of heaven through atonement is not so apparent, but is equally important.

Age of Accountability

"Little children are whole, for they are not capable of committing sin; wherefore, the curse of Adam is taken from them in me, that it hath no power over them." (Moroni 8:8).

"For all men must repent and be baptized, and not only men, but women, and children who have arrived at the years of accountability." (D&C 18:42). "Little children also have eternal life." (Mosiah 15:25). They are "redeemed from the foundation of the world through (the) Only Begotten." (D&C 29:46). "All children who die before they arrive at the years of accountability are saved in the l of heaven." (D&C 137:10).

In other words, provision for their exaltation was made at the Grand Council in Heaven, even before the world was. "Little children cannot (or need not) repent; wherefore, it is awful wickedness to deny the pure mercies of God unto them, for they are all alive in him because of his mercy." (Moroni 8:19).

As children advance in years, however, they "become accountable." This suggests developing accountability, as, with maturity, children gradually assume complete responsibility for their actions. "Heaven lies about us in our infancy," wrote William Wordsworth. "Shades of the prison house begin to close upon the growing boy, but he beholds the light and whence it flows. He sees it in his joy. The youth, who daily farther from the east must travel, still is nature's priest, and by the vision splendid, is on his way attended. At length, the man perceives it die away, and fade into the light of common day." ("Ode: Intimations of Immortality").

"Since "children shall be baptized for the remission of their sins when eight years old," it seems that this is the age of accountability. (D&C 68:27). J.S.T. Genesis 17:11 reads: "And I will establish a covenant of circumcision with thee, and it shall be my covenant between me and thee, and thy seed after thee, in their generations; that thou mayest know for ever that children are not accountable before me until they are eight years old."

The practice of infant baptism in the various sects in the last days, and the differences of opinion regarding the correct method of baptism in Joseph Smith's day, in particular, made the restoration of the gospel administered by the true church even more necessary. It is critically important that the ordinance that would admit applicants into the fold of Christ be carried out according to His explicit instruction, for there is "one Lord, one faith, (and) one baptism."

(Ephesians 4:5). "Except a man be born of water and of the Spirit," declared the Savior, "he cannot enter into the kingdom of God." (John 3:5).

Mormon had a correct understanding of the mission of the Redeemer, and knew that the Savior had come "into the world not to call the righteous but sinners to repentance. The whole need no physician," he taught, "but they that are sick; wherefore little children are whole, for they are not capable of committing sin." (Moroni 8:8). Therefore, he said, "it is solemn mockery before God, that ye should baptize little children," because to do so denies the power of the Atonement. (Moroni 8:9).

The doctrine of infant baptism is an implicit denial that Jesus Christ atoned for the "original sin" of Adam, and it neutralizes the concept of individual accountability. It asks us to believe that little children who die without baptism cannot enter heaven. But the simple fact is that the Atonement did redeem them from the Fall. It is true that children are capable of actions that are inconsistent with obedience to gospel principles, but they are not counted against them as sins. Children are not culpable.

Rather, Mormon wrote: "This thing shall ye teach - repentance and baptism unto those who are accountable and capable of committing sin; yea, teach parents that they must repent and be baptized, and humble themselves as their little children, and they shall all be saved with their little children." (Moroni 8:10). Then, for added emphasis, he declared: "Little children need no repentance, neither baptism. Behold, baptism is unto repentance to the fulfilling the commandments unto the remission of sins. But little children are alive in Christ, even from the foundation of the world." (Moroni 8:11-12).

It was an integral part of the Plan of Salvation, ordained in the Grand Council in heaven before the world was, that little children who died before the age of accountability would be saved in the Celestial Kingdom by the far reach of the power of the Infinite Atonement. "If not so, God is a partial God, and also a changeable God, and a respecter of persons; for how many little children have died without baptism!" Those who labor under the burden of a belief in infant baptism are "in the gall of bitterness," for how could a just and loving Father in Heaven consign so many of His innocent children to an eternal fate that, on their own merits, they did not deserve? (Moroni 8:14).

Such unenlightened individuals are "in the bonds of iniquity" in the sense that they must experience despair, or a sense of hopelessness regarding their little ones who have died without baptism. (Moroni 8:14). "Despair cometh because of iniquity," because when sin clouds vision, unrepentant sinners can see no way out of their miserable situations. (Moroni 10:22). Apostate teachings leave no alternative but to suggest that "if little children could not be saved without baptism, these must have gone to an endless hell." (Moroni 8:13).

Mormon would have us recognize the doctrine of infant baptism for the damnable heresy that it is. Those who persist in this practice "must go down to hell." (Moroni 8:14). "For awful is the wickedness to suppose that God saveth one child because of baptism, and the other must perish because he hath no baptism. We be unto them that shall pervert the ways of the Lord after this manner, for (after they understand the role of accountability, its effects on the fall of Adam, and the necessity of the Savior's redemption) they shall perish except they repent." (Moroni 8:15-16).

Whereas those who teach the doctrine of infant baptism believe that those children who die without the ordinance will go to hell, the truth is that "they (the professors of the doctrine, are the ones who) are in danger of death, hell, and an endless torment." (Moroni 8:21). Mormon knew that he was speaking boldly, but God had commanded him to do so. Our eternal welfare depends upon our correct understanding of this doctrine. (Moroni 8:21).

Alma's Discourse on Faith

(Alma Chapter 32)

"If ye will awake and arouse your faculties, even to an experiment upon my words, and exercise a particle of faith, yea, even if ye can no more than desire to believe, let this desire work in you, even until ye believe in a manner that ye can give place for a portion of my words." (Alma 32:27).

Those who read this chapter on faith must remember that Alma was not speaking to members of the church who had a sound understanding of basic gospel principles, but to a people who had been living in a state of apostasy and all their lives had been taught only false doctrine. Therefore, his spiritually immature listeners were capable of processing the details of only the initial steps that we must take to develop faith. Alma explained only the first steps, and not all there is to understand about faith. It is important for members of the church who have a firm foundation in gospel principles to keep this in mind when reading his oft-quoted discourse on faith.

Alma was on solid ground when he invited the Zoramites to test the truths of the gospel. The Apostle James also challenged: "If any of you lack wisdom, let him ask of God, that giveth to all men liberally, and upbraideth not; and it shall be given him." (James 1:5). Joseph Smith put this promise to the test with spectacular results. (See J.S.H. 1:17). So have countless others who have prayed with the desire to know of the divine authenticity of the latter-day Restoration.

Alma first taught the people in their synagogues. (V. 1-2). Evidence of the depth of apostasy of the Zoramites is revealed by the designation of their places of assembly as "synagogues" and not as "churches." The Book of Mormon invariably uses "synagogue," that is a Greek word, to designate early Jewish assemblies, and "church," from the Greek "ecclesia," to designate such assemblies after they had become Christian. It is hard to think of more appropriate terms, bearing in mind that this is a translation, and the purpose of the words is not to convey what the Nephites called their communities, but only how they invited us to picture them in our own minds.

The wealthy Zoramites, who likely wore "fine-twined linen" (1 Nephi 13:7), scorned their poorer brethren "because of the coarseness of their apparel." (V. 2). The temporally disadvantaged Zoramites were "poor as to the things of the world, (but) also they were poor in heart." (V. 3). In other words, their straightened circumstances fostered humility, and in turn, teachability. They came to Alma expressing a common concern of those who seek the truth but do not know where or how to find it: "We have no place to worship our God," they lamented, "and behold, what shall we do?" (V. 5). They did not understand their true relationship to God and His Son but thought that they could only worship within the structured setting of their synagogues.

Alma was overjoyed that the poor Zoramites had come to him, for he "beheld that their afflictions had truly humbled them, and that they were in a preparation to hear the word." (V. 6). Immediately, he clarified two basic principles that they had grossly misunderstood. First, he explained that God can be worshipped wherever we may be, and secondly that every day is a day of worship. (V. 10-11).

Alma realized that the Zoramites had been blessed because circumstances had compelled them to be humble. He knew that with proper gospel instruction, their humility would lead them through faith and repentance, to mercy and forgiveness via the ordinances of the gospel, and finally to salvation by the grace of God. (V. 13). The guiding lights of correct principles would lead them to even greater humility and meekness "because of the word." (V. 14). Alma understood that, as seeds planted in fertile soil, gentleness, modesty, and mildness would be nurtured. (V. 15). He wanted the Zoramites to enjoy the blessings related to enduring to the end in the light of the gospel. Although endurance is often cast in a negative light, as in "enduring pain" or "enduring persecution," it can ultimately be positive and pleasant. However, it always carries a performance cost.

If we wish to have physical endurance, for example, we must pay the price. Good diet and mental and physical discipline are essential ingredients to achieve new heights that would otherwise have been beyond our reach. With sound bodies, we can choose from a wider variety of options and our opportunities to do so seems to have no bounds. Walk all day without fatigue? Participate in consecutive endowment sessions? Ski in the mountains? Hike to a lake for a day of fishing? Play three sets of tennis or a round of golf? Given the natural limitations of age and individual temporal circumstances, when we possess physical endurance there are many worthwhile and uplifting activities from which we may choose.

Nor does spiritual fitness, or endurance, come without effort. A testimony of the gospel and its exalting principles must be earned. We read such things as: "Behold, you have not understood; you have supposed that I would give it unto you, when you took no thought save it was to ask me. But, behold, I say unto you, that you must study it out in your mind." (D&C 9:7-8). Lorenzo Snow declared: "It is impossible to advance in the principles of truth, to increase in heavenly knowledge, except we exercise our reasoning faculties and exert ourselves." (J.D., 18:371. Discourse delivered in the St. George, Utah Temple, 4/5/1877). Agency is not free but is purchased at a substantial price.

If we desire a testimony of family home evening, we must understand and obey the laws of the gospel associated with that principle. "For all who will have a blessing at my hands shall abide the law which was appointed for that blessing, and the conditions thereof." (D&C 132:5, see D&C 130:20-21). If we want to know that The Book of Mormon is the word of God, we must read with a desire to receive a witness. (See Moroni 10:4). If we want to know that obedience to the gospel Plan is the path to happiness, we need to try the virtue of the word of God. (See Alma 31:5).

God has promised us "knowledge by (the) Holy Ghost, yea, by the unspeakable gift of the Holy Ghost." (D&C 121:26, see D&C 1:38). When this happens, we become the lucky recipients of testimony that is the intrinsic knowledge of the truth of a principle. No one can rob us of that testimony. It can only be forfeit by embracing lifestyle behaviors that alienate the confirming Spirit.

The scriptures teach with clarity and finality: "All saints who remember to keep and do these sayings, walking in obedience to the commandments, shall receive health in their navel and marrow to their bones; and shall find wisdom and great treasures of knowledge, even hidden treasures; and shall run and not be weary, and shall walk and not faint. And I, the Lord, give unto them a promise, that the destroying angel shall pass them by, as the children of Israel, and not slay them. (D&C 89:18-21).

During his ministry among the Zoramites, Alma's exhausting confrontation with Korihor must have been fresh in his mind. Perhaps he was thinking of that antichrist when he told the Zoramites: "There are many who do say: If thou wilt show unto us a sign from heaven, then we shall know of a surety; then we shall believe." (V. 17). He wanted to teach the Zoramites about saving faith without being reduced to giving them a sign in order to satisfy the need for theological titillation required by faithless apostates, and so he was meticulous to carefully establish a foundation for the lesson to follow.

Every discussion of faith must distinguish it from its caricatures. It is not naiveté or gullibility, nor is it wishful thinking. It is more than confidence and greater than optimism. Faith and positive thinking go hand in hand, but faith is more than an attitude. Within the Zoramite framework, receiving heavenly signs cannot generate faith. In fact, Alma told the Zoramites that they should not desire a sign, because faith precedes the miracle. He explained that during the genesis of faith, it is necessary to take a few steps into the darkness, and then the spiritual strong searchlight will illuminate the way. Only after the trial of our faith will it be confirmed by direct experience and will the Spirit validate God as its Author and Finisher.

This is why Alma carefully taught the Zoramites: "If a man knoweth a thing he hath no cause to believe (or exercise faith), for he knoweth it." (V. 18). That is to say, in its initial stages of development, faith is not knowledge. If a sign were to be given before our transformation through faith, we might have a sure knowledge of the principle, but it would have come to our undisciplined mind without the necessary expenditure of faith. This was Korihor's fatal flaw. He demanded a sign from heaven without the appropriate and necessary exercise of faith.

Under proper circumstances, though, as we gain spiritual maturity "by doing our duty, faith increases until it becomes perfect knowledge." (Heber J. Grant, C.R., 4/1934). Certainly, God Himself is full of faith, and yet He is omniscient. There is nothing that He does not know. For our part, as imperfect mortals struggling to believe what we do not see, the reward of our maturing faith is to see what we believe. Some things just have to be believed to be seen.

Heavenly Father has not left us destitute, and He has not abandoned us to blindly tap our way through a lone and dreary world. "Faith in Christ is not a leap in the dark. It is, instead, trust in what the spirit learned eons ago; and religious recognition is just that, a re-cognition, a re-knowing, the sum of existence. If we thwart or suppress that instinctive response, we are accountable, and to a degree, we condemn ourselves. We knew Christ before this life, we know Him here, and we will know Him hereafter. His sheep do indeed know His voice. And thus, the impact of truth on man is a test of man" and not of God. (Truman Madsen, Commentary on "B.H. Roberts, The Way, The Truth and The Life").

Thus, Alma taught: "How much more cursed is he that knoweth the will of God and doeth it not, than he that only believeth, or only hath cause to believe, and falleth into transgression?" (V. 18). Belief is a mental assent to the truth or actuality of a concept without the moral element of responsibility that we call faith. (V. 21). To those to whom much is given, however, much is expected. The gift of faith demands action. Therefore, when we exercise our moral agency, "without works (it) is dead, being alone." (James 2:17). Faith is an action verb.

"Without faith, we are free, and that is a pleasant feeling at first. There are no questions of conscience, no constraints, except the constraints of custom, convention, and the law, and these are flexible enough for most purposes. It is only later that the terror comes. We are free in chaos, in an unexplained and unexplainable world, in a desert from which there is no retreat but inward toward our hollow core." (Morris West, "The Devil's Advocate"). Agency is meaningful when faith drives us to purposeful performance.

Therefore, Alma told the Zoramites: "Now of this thing ye must judge. Behold, I say unto you, that it is on the one hand even as it is on the other; and it shall be unto every man according to his work." (V. 20). He was asking the Zoramites, poised to make life's most important decisions, to cast aside their fears and take a tremendous step as they stood at a crossroads. (See Joshua 24:15). As Robert Frost wrote: "I shall be telling this with a sigh somewhere ages and ages hence: Two roads diverged in a wood, and I, I took the one less traveled by, and that has made all the difference." ("The Road Not Taken").

Alma hoped the Zoramites would develop faith unto salvation, knowing full well that Heavenly Father does not expect us to exercise faith in things for which there is insufficient evidence. As this sermon unfolded, Alma would give the Zoramites a formula for the development of justifiable faith that would be the key to their liberation from enslavement to apostate religious dogma. The next move would be theirs to make.

In matters of faith, it is we, and not the Lord, who are on trial. At the bar of justice, the evidence will be presented, and our previous conformity with or rejection of eternal law will determine our reward or punishment. The trial we call mortality is eminently fair because of our capacity, even our innate tendency, to develop faith.

Because they had neither a doctrinal nor an experiential foundation, the Zoramites were told: "Faith is not to have a perfect knowledge of things; therefore, if ye have faith ye hope for things which are not seen, which are true." (V. 21, see Hebrews 11:1). This is correct in the ultimate sense. The important point that Alma illustrated was that faith is unnecessary if the object of our faith is demonstrable to the physical senses. In Alma's usage, verse 21 might more clearly read: "Faith is not to have a perfect knowledge of things gained through our own experiences." Remember that Korihor's demand for a sign had been the condition for his faith, since he trusted only his physical senses. This rational approach is the enemy of faith. Thus, secular humanism and other similar ideologies destroy faith and are devilish doctrines, subtle though they may be. They are abominable to God because they thwart the successful execution of a Plan that requires us to live by faith.

Truth is at the very foundation of faith. Heavenly Father will not lead people to have faith in that which is false; for example, in professional faith healers. In these cases, Satan is responsible for the healing, for he has limited power over life and death. (See Job 2:6). Nevertheless, God sanctions those evincing pure and simple faith. Hence, we are familiar with examples of healing by those without the priesthood.

Faith may lead us to believe the truth "in the first place," to obtain mercy. (V. 23). It is a motivating catalyst, for the horizon of our faith extends only as far as our deeds. This is why works are an important companion to vital, active faith. (See James 2:17 & Matthew 5:16). Faith without action or without good works has no life generating or sustaining power, because alone it is impotent since it leads to no purposeful performance. It is the sizzle without the steak.

Even Martin Luther understood faith to be more than intellectual assent. It is "vital, personal self-committal to a practical belief. He heartily approved of good works. What he denied was their efficacy for salvation. 'Good works,' he said, 'do not make a good man, but a good man does good works.' And what makes a man good? Faith in God, and Christ." (Will Durant, "The Lessons of History: The Reformation," p. 374-375).

After the aside in verses 22-25, Alma returned to his subject in verse 26: "Now, as I said concerning faith - that it was not a perfect knowledge (in its infancy) - even so it is with my words. Ye cannot know of their surety at first, unto perfection, any more than faith is," at first, "a perfect knowledge." (V. 26). Therefore, in verses 27-43, Alma proposed an experiment to generate incipient faith. He asked the Zoramites to "awake and arouse (their) faculties, even to an experiment upon (his) words." (V. 27). The experiment involved desire (V. 27), planting a seed (V. 28), nourishing it (V. 37-41), and harvesting fruit. (V. 42-43).

They were to "exercise a particle of faith" even if it was no more than the "desire to believe." (V. 27). The principle that the Zoramites were asked to believe was that the Son of God would come and atone for the sins of the world. (See Alma 33-35). Alma was counting on the fact that "truth as well as untruth may be recognized by its effects. Rendering obedience to its principles of action may test the claims of the gospel. Practicing our religion is the most direct method of gaining a testimony of the truth." (John Widtsoe, "Evidences and Reconciliations").

Comparing the word to a seed, Alma asked the Zoramites to "give place," or study, pray and commit themselves to a specific plan of action. Consequently, they would feel the word enlarge their souls and enlighten their understanding. (V. 28). As Brigham Young said: "Every gospel principle carries within it a witness that it is true." (J.D., 9:149). It is in the economy of the gospel that "we often catch a spark from the awakened memories of the immortal soul, which lights up our whole being as with the glory of our former home." (Joseph F. Smith, "Gospel Doctrine," p. 14).

In the Last Days, the missionaries often ask those who are introduced to the church to engage in the experiment suggested by Alma, to determine for themselves the validity of the message of The Restoration and of the divine origin of The Book of Mormon itself. As Hugh Nibley has said: "We are not laying down ground rules for taste, or saying that The Book of Mormon is good because some people like it or bad because others do not. What we are saying is that The Book of Mormon, whatever one may think, is one of the great realities of our time, and that what makes it so is that certain people believe it. Its literary or artistic qualities do not enter into the discussion. It was written to be believed. Its one and only merit is truth. Without that merit, it is all that nonbelievers say it is. With it, it is all that believers say it is." ("Of All Things," p. 93).

It is important to reiterate the very narrow sense in which Alma proposed the experiment to the Zoramites. After its completion, their knowledge of that specific principle would be perfect, and the faith required to accept it would have been profitably expended, and so would become "dormant." (V. 34, see V. 21).

Thus, the successful completion of the experiment would result in a budding testimony of a gospel principle. Testimony is composed of three essential ingredients. First is recognition of an eternal principle. Second is an understanding of the Lord's counsel concerning the principle, and third is direct experience with the principle, that is the fruits of faith. The Zoramites had been asked to experiment only on the words of Alma, whose objective was to bring them to direct experience with a specific principle of the gospel. He recognized that they would first have to build on a desire to believe, and then establish the groundwork of knowledge that would only then provide a solid foundation for their newfound faith.

As he explained: "Neither must ye lay aside your faith, for ye have only exercised your faith to plant the seed that ye might try the experiment to know if the seed was good." (V. 36). As the seed was nurtured, it would "grow up, and bring forth fruit." (V. 37). In other words, additional knowledge would be added to the expanding foundation of faith.

But if the seed were neglected, Alma cautioned: "Behold, it will not get any root; and when the heat of the sun cometh and scorcheth it, because it hath no root it withers away." (V. 38). This, he explained, is "because your ground is barren, and ye will not nourish the tree." (V. 39). There is no revelation where there is no student and as long as we ask the wrong questions, we will be at odds with Biblical faith. Our rational mind will never bridge the gap between the secular and the divine. "As humanity continues to struggle with death, despair, hopelessness, fear, and anxiety, the scriptures speak a far more relevant message to society than any rational explanation." ("Newsweek," 11/1980).

"If you will not nourish the word," cautioned Alma, you must not think that the experiment failed. We "can never pluck of the fruit of the tree of life" if we have not accepted the fact that perspiration must precede inspiration. (V. 40). If we choose mediocrity, rationalization, selfish pleasures, things of the world, the honors of men, or willful disobedience, our priorities are out of order, and the experiment will fail. As long as we remain in this state, we can never partake of the fruit of the tree of life. The world before us will appear as a barren desert, devoid of refreshing oases, the welcome shade of trees, and the abundance of well-watered and fruited gardens.

"But if ye will nourish the word," explained Alma, "it shall take root; and behold it shall be a tree springing up unto everlasting life," reminiscent of the tree in Lehi's dream that represented the love of God and its ultimate expression of eternal life. (V. 41, see 1 Nephi 8:10-12). Alma cautioned the Zoramites that it would take diligence and patience to "reap (the) rewards of (their) faith." (V. 42-43). We call these efforts "enduring to the end in righteousness," in a process wherein faith is multiplied unto us.

This message from Alma to the poor Zoramites is as relevant today as it was two thousand years ago, because our world faces the same temporal problems and is in the same spiritual predicament. In materialistic western societies that reflect the conditions found so long ago among the more affluent Zoramites, the challenges are even greater.

We seem to be in a quandary from which there is no escape. Latter-day Zoramites "tend to fill space, as if what we have, what we are, is not enough. Being affluent, we strangle ourselves with what we can buy, things whose opacity obstructs our ability to see what is really there." (Gretel Erlich, "Under Wyoming's Skies," "The Atlantic Monthly," 5/1985).

We can learn from the account of Alma's missionary efforts among the Zoramites that we should take specific measures to avoid the pitfalls associated with seeking "for things (we cannot) understand." (Jacob 4:14). In their spiritual immaturity, the Zoramites required milk, and not meat, to nourish the quality of their belief. (See 1 Corinthians 3:2, & Hebrews 5:12). The tender shoots that would spring from their young testimonies would be carefully nurtured in accordance with Alma's wise formula, without the ecclesiastical embroidery that often needlessly complicates simple gospel messages.

And it Came to Pass

In all probability, Joseph Smith likely would
not have employed the phrase at all in The Book of
Mormon, or at least not consistently, had he created the
record himself. Thus, the discriminating use of the Hebraic
phrase "and it came to pass" in The Book of Mormon is
further evidence that the record is what it says it
is - a translation from reformed Egyptian
with ties to the Hebrew language.
(See Mormon 9:32-33).

Some have quite legitimately asked the question: Why was the phrase "and it came to pass" so frequently employed by the authors of The Book of Mormon? Mark Twain wondered this very thing, and famously joked that if the phrase were omitted from the text, the church could have instead published "The Pamphlet of Mormon." ("Roughing It," p. 33). As it turns out, however, the joke is on him. This much-maligned phrase actually provides strong evidence of the authenticity of the record.

Donald W. Parry, an instructor in biblical Hebrew at BYU, wrote in the "Ensign" (12/1992, p. 29): "The English translation of the Hebrew word wayehi, often used to connect two ideas or events, is "and it came to pass," and appears some 452 times in the King James Version of the Bible. The expression is rarely found in Hebrew poetic, literary, or prophetic writings. Most often, it appears in Old Testament narratives, such as the books by Moses that recounted the history of the children of Israel.

As in the Old Testament, the expression in The Book of Mormon (where it appears some 1,424 times) occurs only in the narrative selections, and is clearly missing in the more literary parts, such as the psalm of Nephi (see 2 Ne. 4:20-25); the direct speeches of King Benjamin, Abinadi, Alma, and Jesus Christ; and in the epistles.

But why does the phrase "and it came to pass" appear in The Book of Mormon so much more often, page for page, than it does in the Old Testament? The answer is twofold. First, The Book of Mormon contains much more narrative material, chapter for chapter, than does the Bible. Secondly, but equally important, the translators of the King James Version did not always render "wayehi" as "and it came to pass." Instead, they chose to draw from a multitude of similar expressions, such as "and it happened," "and it became," or "and it was."

The word "wayehi" is found about 1,204 times in the Hebrew Bible, but it was translated only 727 times as "and it came to pass" in the King James Version. Joseph Smith did not introduce that variety into the translation of The Book of Mormon. Rather, he retained the precision of "and it came to pass," which better performs the transitional function of the Hebrew word.

In all probability, the Prophet Joseph Smith likely would not have used the phrase at all in The Book of Mormon, or at least not consistently, had he created that record himself. Thus, the discriminating use of the Hebraic phrase "and it came to pass" in The Book of Mormon is further evidence that the record is what it says it is - a translation from reformed Egyptian with ties to the Hebrew language. (See Mormon 9:32-33).

As an afternote, there is also a New World connection to the phrase. Experts confirm that an element translated "and it came to pass" functioned in at least four ways in Mayan texts: (1) As a posterior date indicator in a text that meant "to count forward to the next date," and (2) as an anterior date indicator that signified "to count backward to the given date." Additionally, the phrase could also function (3) as a posterior or (4) anterior event indicator, meaning "counting forward or backward to a certain event."

There are instances of all four functions of "and it came to pass" in The Book of Mormon, as well as combined date and event indications in both posterior and anterior expressions. For example, "and it came to pass that the people began..." is a posterior event indicator (3 Nephi 2:3), whereas "and it had come to pass..." is an anterior event indicator. (3 Nephi 1:20)."

And Thus We See

In total, the phrase "and thus we see" is used over fifty times in The Book of Mormon, (depending on how picky you get about exact terminology) with the record keeper Mormon using the phrase or one of its variants in nearly every one of those instances.

The phrase "and thus we see" is unique to The Book of Mormon; it is not found in any other book of scripture. Other related phrases that are also unique to that ancient text include "thus we see," "thus we may see," and "we can see," as well as "and thus we can plainly discern."

"And thus we see" has received attention in the following presentations, to name a few: "And Thus We See," "Ensign," August 2008, p. 40-43; Helaman 12. "And Thus We See," "Book of Mormon Seminary Student Study Guide," p. 152-153; Henry B. Eyring, "And Thus We See: Helping a Student in a Moment of Doubt," address to religious educators, Temple Square Assembly Hall, Salt Lake City, 5 February 1993; and David A. Bednar, "Come unto Christ," BYU - Idaho religion symposium address, 29 January 2000.

Thirteen variants of "and thus we see" are found over 50 times in The Book of Mormon. "And thus we see" – in 1 Nephi 16:29, 1 Nephi 17:3, Alma 12:21-22 (twice), Alma 24:19 (twice), Alma 28:13-14 (three times), Alma 30:60 (twice), Alma 42:4, 7 & 14 (three times), Alma 50:19, Helaman 6:34-36 & 40, Helaman 12:3, and Ether 14:25.

"Thus we see"- in Alma 24:27 and Alma 46:8. "Now we see" – in Alma 12:22, and Helaman 3:29. "We can also see – in Alma 46:9. "We can also see" – in Alma 46:9. "And we may see" – in Helaman 12:3. "And we may see" – in Helaman 12:3. "Thus we may see" – in Helaman 3:27. "We ca behold" – in Alma 50:19, Helaman 12:1, and Ether 2:9. "We can see" – in Helaman 12:1. "And thus we can plainly discern" – in Alma 24:3, Alma 44:4, & Alma 46:8. "And now ye see" – in Alma 44:4. "And thus" – in Alma 42:26 and Alma 52:14. "We see" – in Alma 9:14, Alma 12:24, Alma 19:23, Alma 26:37, Alma 29:8, Alma 37:26, Alma 42:3, and Alma 50:21. "We may see" – in 2 Nephi 15:9 and Helaman 12:2. "And thus it is"- in Helaman 12:26.

There are 2 other similar phrases in The Book of Mormon that are also found in other scriptures, but these phrases in the other scriptures don't convey the same significance as those in The Book of Mormon. The first is "we see," found in Alma 9:14, 12:24, 19:23 & 36, 26:37, 29:8, 37:26, 42:3, & 50:21, in Helaman 3:29, as well as in the Old Testament in Psalms 36:9 & 74:9, Jeremiah 5:12, and in the New Testament in John 9:41, Romans 8:25, 1 Corinthians 13:12, and in Hebrews 2:8 & 3:19. The second is "we may see," that is found in 2 Nephi 15:9 and Helaman 12:2, and in the Bible in Isaiah 5:19, Mark 15:32 and in John 6:30. Other variations include "we saw" and "we shall see." A similar phrase that is unique to the Doctrine and Covenants is "and thus we saw," found in D&C 76:89, 91, & 92.

In total, the phrase "and thus we see" is used over fifty (depending on how picky you get about exact terminology) with the record keeper Mormon using the phrase or one of its variants in nearly every one of those instances.

As we continue our spiritual education, The Book of Mormon will help us to expand our spiritual capacity, and to see as God sees, and to know and understand as He does. When we turn our attention to the interesting phrase "and thus we see," that is used by the prophets, and to its related variants, we open our minds to pearls of great price and hidden treasures of knowledge.

Angels

"The angel of the Lord
appeared unto them; and he
descended as it were in a cloud;
and he spake as it were with a voice
of thunder, which caused the earth
to shake upon which they stood."
(Mosiah 27:11).

Angels are the Lord's messengers, who are spoken of by Paul as "ministering spirits." (Hebrews 1:14). Latter-day revelation teaches that angels may be spirits that have not yet obtained a body, or those who are awaiting the resurrection. They may also be those who have been resurrected or have been translated.

"There are two kinds of beings in heaven, namely: Angels who are resurrected personages, having bodies of flesh and bones. For instance, Jesus said: Handle me and see, for a spirit hath not flesh and bones, as ye see me have. Secondly: the spirits of just men made perfect, they who are not resurrected, but inherit the same glory. When a messenger comes saying he has a message from God, offer him your hand and request him to shake hands with you. If he be an angel he will do so, and you will feel his hand. If he be the spirit of a just man made perfect he will come in his glory; for that is the only way he can appear. Ask him to shake hands with you, but he will not move, because it is contrary to the order of heaven for a just man to deceive; but he will still deliver his message. If it be the devil as an angel of light, when you ask him to shake hands he will offer you his hand, and you will not feel anything; you may therefore detect him. These are three grand keys whereby you may know whether any administration is from God." (D&C 129:1-9).

In the Old Testament, the "angel of the Lord" speaks as the voice of God. (Genesis 22:11-12). Angels may be human messengers (JST Genesis 19), or may be those who serve God in heaven. (1 Kings 22:19, see also Alma 36:22). Or they may minister to those on the earth. (See Genesis 28:12 & 32:1, 2 Samuel 24:16, 2 Kings 1:15 & 19:35, & Psalms 91:1). Some angels are mentioned by name. (Daniel 8:16, 9:21, 10:13 & 21, & 12:1, Luke 1:19 & 26). In latter-day revelation we learn that the angel Michael is Adam, and the angel Gabriel is Noah. (H.C., 3:386).

In the New Testament, there are many references to the ministry of angels, but no clear statement as to their nature or their relation to mankind in general. Angels attended the Savior during His mortal ministry. (Matthew 1:20, 2:13 & 19, 4:11 & 28:2-8, Luke 1:11-20 & 26-30, 2:9-15 & 22:43). He often spoke of angels. (Matthew 13:14-30, 37-41, 16:27, 18:10, 22:30 & 24:36, & Luke 15:10). Other New Testament references can be found in Acts 7:53, 1 Corinthians 4:9, 6:3 & 11:10, Galatians 1:8 & 3:19, (where we are warned against worship of angels), and throughout the Revelation of John. There are references to fallen angels in 2 Peter 2:4, & Jude 1:6. The scriptures speak of the devil's angels who are spirits who followed Lucifer and were thrust out in the war in heaven and cast down to the earth. (Revelation 12:1-9, D&C 29:36-38, Moses 4:1-4, & Abraham 3:27-28).

Latter-day revelation speaks of the nature, ministry, and identification of angels. (2 Nephi 32:2-3, Alma 12:28-29 & 13:24-26, Moroni 7:29-31, D&C 7:6-7, 13:37, 76:21, 110:11, 128:21 & 132:160-18). In H.C., 3:392, we learn that angels do not have wings.

The word angel is used in various ways. A person who is a divine messenger is called an angel. Thus Moroni, John the Baptist, Peter, James, John, Moses, Elijah, and Elias all ministered to Joseph Smith as angels. These all shall be exalted and inherit celestial glory. The scriptures also speak of another class of persons who, because of failure to obey the gospel, will not be exalted and will become angels in eternity. These are spoken of as angels in Matthew 22:29-30, & 22:29-30, & D&C 132:16-18. This latter designation should not be confused with the use of the term angels having reference to the heavenly messengers sent forth to minister to the inhabitants of the earth.

A 1994 Gallup poll found that 72% of all Americans believe angels exist. (That number has remained relatively constant for the past 30 years. In 2024, 69% believed in angels, and about 65% in aliens.) For Christians, the figure is 83%. Anyone who has seen the Christmas classic "It's a Wonderful Life" is familiar with angels. Most can tell you the name of the angel in the movie, and they know that every time a bell rings, another angel has gotten his wings, including Clarence.

Our church is familiar with heavenly messengers, and many of us can recite from memory the revelatory passage: "I saw another angel fly in the midst of heaven, having the everlasting gospel to preach unto them that dwell on the earth, and to every nation, and kindred, and tongue, and people." (Revelation 14:6). We do not know how many angels there are, but the Bible reads: "Ye are come unto mount Sion, and unto the city of the living God, the heavenly Jerusalem, and to an innumerable company of angels." (Hebrews 12:22). In the Protestant Bible, the named angels are Michael, Gabriel, and Satan, the fallen angel. The Catholic Apocryphal books also include Raphael.

Angels are usually so awesome that when they appear their first words are often, "Fear not." For example, in "the end of the Sabbath, as it began to dawn toward the first day of the week, came Mary Magdalene and the other Mary to see the sepulchre. And, behold, there was a great earthquake: for the angel of the Lord descended from heaven, and came and rolled back the stone from the door, and sat upon it. His countenance was like lightning, and his raiment white as snow: And for fear of him the keepers did shake, and became as dead men. And the angel answered and said unto the women, Fear not." (Matthew 28:1-4).

Angels are ministering spirits sent to serve those who believe, and they are God's messengers. (Hebrews 1:14). In fact, the word "angel" in the original languages of both the Old and New Testaments means "messenger." Some of the heavenly hosts are assigned to be guardian angels (Psalm 91:11). They carry out God's will by protecting and delivering their charges from harm. Angels were present at the giving of the Ten Commandments (Deuteronomy 33:2), and they carry out God's justice. (Acts 12:23). Jesus taught that at the time of death, angels accompany believers to heaven. (Luke 16:22).

Angels may be any of the following: 1) pre-earth existent spirits (Revelation 12:7, D&C 130:5), 2) translated beings (J.S.T. Genesis 14:26-36, Teachings, p. 170), 3) spirits of just men made perfect, awaiting the resurrection (D&C 76:66-69), 4) resurrected beings (D&C 129), or, 5) righteous mortal men (Genesis 19 & J.S.T. Genesis 19).

Latter-day Saints often speak "with the tongue of angels," and priests are entitled to the ministering of angels. (D&C

84:26). "The power and authority of the lesser, or Aaronic Priesthood, is to hold the keys of the ministering of angels, and to administer in outward ordinances, the letter of the gospel, the baptism of repentance for the remission of sins, agreeable to the covenants and commandments." (D&C 107:20).

"Joseph Smith was called by the "ministering servants" of God. (D&C 136:37). "There are no angels who minister to this earth but those who do belong or have belonged to it. (D&C 130:5. "Therefore, when they are out of the world they neither marry nor are given in marriage; but are appointed angels in heaven, which angels are ministering servants, to minister for those who are worthy of a far more, and an exceeding, and an eternal weight of glory." (D&C 132:16).

During the pre-
mortal conflict pitting contrasting
ideologies against each other, the principle
of free will prevailed, together with natural
consequences that are related to its expression.
When the victorious spirits were given their
opportunity to experience mortality, they
grasped it with a passion for the
freedom to choose their
own destiny.

Are Mormons Christians?

"We talk of Christ,
we rejoice in Christ, we preach of
Christ, we prophesy of Christ, and we write
according to our prophecies, that our children
may know to what source they may look
for a remission of their sins."
(2 Nephi 25:26).

Many of our friends view us as likeable and trustworthy, but nevertheless "peculiar." We are like the converted Jews of Seville, who during the Spanish Inquisition paraded through the streets eating pork as a demonstration of their "Christianity." They were still found guilty of heresy and burned at the stake. We are definitely "peculiar" (from the Hebrew "Segullah," meaning "One's very own, exclusive, or special"). That's okay, because it's not important that some other faiths don't regard us as "Christian." "How we regard ourselves is what is important. We acknowledge without hesitation that there are differences between us. Were this not so there would have been no need for a restoration of the gospel." (Gordon B. Hinckley, C.R., 4/1998).

"We have a clear and present answer to the nature of God and of our Savior," he continued. "We are Christians as followers of Him, regardless of what others say, and the more they talk the more certain it becomes that a restoration was necessary if the work of the Lord were to succeed and move forward. We are the beneficiaries of that great restoration." Consequently, "we can't afford to be tawdry people."

If we are "tawdry" we are ragged around the edges, ill defined, indistinct, sloppy, and even slovenly. "We ought to stand a little taller," President Hinckley said, and "be a little better for the great inheritance which we have. We must be as the Saints of God, a good people, a righteous people, and a faithful people, loving our neighbors who are not of our faith, helping them in whatever problems arise. Yes, by all means, with tolerance and love and respect for them, but at the same time going forward in our faith, the faith of the living God, the truth of the restoration." (Springville, Utah, Kolob 2nd and 4th Wards chapel rededication, 3/1/1998).

Even as we champion the cause of Zion, we are tolerant of the religious views of those who do not share our beliefs. "All is well between me and the heavens," said Joseph Smith. "I have no enmity against anyone, and as the prayer of Jesus ... so I pray. 'Father, forgive me my trespasses as I forgive those who trespass against me,' for I freely forgive all men. If we would secure and cultivate the love of others, we must love others, even our enemies, as well as our friends. The Saints can testify whether I am willing to lay down my life for my brethren. If it has been demonstrated that I have been willing to die for a Mormon, I am bold to declare before heaven that I am just as willing to die in defending the rights of a Presbyterian, a Baptist, or a good man of any denomination, for the same principles that would trample upon the rights of the Latter-day Saints would trample upon the rights of the Roman Catholic, or of any other denomination who may be unpopular and too weak to defend themselves." (H.C., 5:498).

Such tolerance notwithstanding, some exclude us from the body of Christ because we do not fit their definition of "Christian." If we define "Christian" as "one who believes in Jesus Christ and whose life conforms to His doctrine, we create a problem. Just what is the doctrine of Christ?

If we define "Christian" generically and tolerate doctrinal differences, then Latter-day Saints are Christian. But if "Christian" is more narrowly understood to mean "those who believe as I believe," then Latter-day Saints, with others, might be regarded as non-Christian. The very Articles of Faith to which we point in defense of our "Christianity," might actually position us outside the standard frames of reference used by others to define "Christian."

The First Article of Faith pits us against those who believe in the Holy Trinity. The Second Article of Faith denies original sin. The Third acknowledges the Atonement but ties its power to laws and ordinances that might not be recognized by others as efficacious. The Fourth precisely identifies the ordinances necessary for salvation, but does so more narrowly than might others. The Fifth argues that authority, in addition to the Holy Spirit, qualifies a man for the priesthood. The Sixth defines the church in historical, rather than traditional, terms. The Seventh declares that the heavens are still open, and the Eighth denies the infallibility of the Bible. The Ninth states that we believe, with other Christians, that God has spoken to His children. But we take a quantum leap forward by declaring that He continues to do so. The Tenth should be familiar to Evangelicals, when it alludes to the Rapture, but it does so in very literal terms when it mentions the Gathering of Israel and the rest of the Ten Tribes, the Holy City of the New Jerusalem, and the ultimate destiny of the earth. And so, it goes.

Some exclude us by misrepresentation, fabricating and perpetuating lies about our beliefs, or distorting and twisting our doctrines. We have all heard: "Oh, no, that's not what Mormons believe. This is what they believe." The vitriolic literature discrediting the church tells the world that "Mormons aren't allowed to dance." "Mormons in Utah have more than one wife." "Mormons worship Joseph Smith." "Mormon elders have horns." "Mormons believe what is portrayed in 'The God Makers'." "Mormons believe we are saved by works, and not by grace." "Mormons carry out secret rituals in their temples." "Mormons wear magical underwear." "Mormon leadership is autocratic." "Mormon women are subjugated by men."

Sometimes, we are the guilty party who perpetuates doctrinal misunderstandings: "Eight-year-old children are clean and pure when they come out of the waters of baptism, and all their sins are washed away." "Only Mormons can go to heaven." "My church is true; therefore, your church must be false." "One third of Heavenly Father's children in the pre-earth existence were cast out of heaven for disobedience." "Mormons can't drink coke." "If you don't get married in the temple, you are going to spend eternity as a single person." "Except for Mormons, everyone is going to hell." "If you don't accept the invitation of the missionaries to join the church in this life, your progression stops." "There is no progression between kingdoms of glory." "We are saved by our good works." Only Mormons have the companionship of the Holy Ghost."

B.H. Roberts clarified our doctrinal foundations, explaining: "The church has confined the sources of doctrine by which it is willing to be bound before the world to the things that God has revealed, and which the church has officially accepted, and those alone. These would include the Bible, The Book of Mormon, the Doctrine and Covenants, and the Pearl of Great Price; these have been repeatedly accepted and endorsed by the church in General Conference assembled, and are the only sources of absolute appeal for our doctrine."

There is nothing wrong with the practice of Latter-day Saints to write books or articles, or to otherwise express their opinions on doctrinal matters. "Nevertheless, until such opinions are presented to the church in general conference and sustained by vote of the conference, they are neither binding nor the official doctrine of the church. Critics of LDS doctrine seldom recognize this vital distinction. Rather, if any Latter-day Saint, especially one of the leading Brethren, ever said a thing, these critics take it to represent "Mormonism," regardless of whether any other Latter-day Saint ever said it or believed it. Often the Latter-day Saints themselves are guilty of this same error and search through the Journal of Discourses as if it were some sort of Mormon Talmud, looking for 'new' doctrines not found in the standard works and not taught in the church today."

"Such anomalies do not define Latter-day Saint beliefs. Each is a glitch in the doctrinal dissemination of truth by a church that values individual scholarship and prides itself on a lay ministry. The most confusing anomalies are widely disseminated statements by leaders of the church that are doctrinal distortions that can neither be reconciled to the official doctrines of the church nor clearly nor logically understood." (Stephen Robinson, "Are Mormons Christians?" p. 15).

Some exclude us simply by calling us names. They figuratively and literally cast sticks and stones with the intention of breaking our bones, and their names really do hurt us. Name-calling can be both emotionally and physically damaging. Protestants have called Catholics "Papists." Catholics have called Protestants "Heretics." Both have called Jews "Christ Killers" and Muslims have called all three "Infidels." Our religion is often labeled as a cult, which is an emotionally charged word that sometimes evokes images of "Druids burning captives alive in wicker baskets, of painted priests flinging virgins into volcanoes, or of satanic rituals performed in the dark of the moon." ("Are Mormons Christians?" p. 24). It serves no useful purpose, is intentionally inflammatory, and is a major roadblock to mutual understanding and tolerance.

Throwing out the word "cult" as if it were an epithet is the equivalent of saying "I don't understand you, I am uncomfortable with you, and I am afraid of you. My only defense, therefore, is a strong offense." Too many people, when they are burdened with ignorance become anti-enemy rather than pro-gospel. We are in good company, however. Christianity itself was initially characterized as a cult shortly after the time of the ministry of Jesus.

"Cults are organizations that were started by strong and dynamic leaders who are in complete control of their followers. They possess scripture that is either added to or which replaces the Bible as God's Word. They have rigid standards for membership often recruiting members from other "cults." They are actively evangelistic and proselytize new converts. They have leaders who are not professional clergymen. They have a system of doctrine and practice that is in a state of flux, and they believe there is continual, ongoing communication from God. Such communication can contradict or supersede God's revelation as found in the Bible. As such, they have truth not available to any other group or individuals. They have an initiate vocabulary by which they describe the truths of their revelations. They may even coin new words or phrases. Any objective definition of 'cult' that can be applied to The Church of Jesus Christ of Latter-day Saints can also be applied to the Christian church of the New Testament, and to most of today's mainline denominations when they were in their infancy." ("Are Mormons Christians?" p. 25).

Some exclude us because we do not accept both Biblical Christianity and the Traditional or Historical Christianity that grew out of it. Historical Christianity sprang from the councils, creeds, customs, theologians, and philosophers who, without the benefit of the Apostles' instruction and continuing revelation, attempted to interpret the teachings of Christ with limited spiritual light and insight.

Therefore, Latter-day Saints somewhat abrasively characterize Historical Christianity as the "Apostasy." They feel that Historical Christianity necessitated the Restoration. They look to the very writings of the Apostles in the New

Testament for substantiation of their interpretation of the Apostasy and suggest that if a Christian is someone who accepts both Biblical and traditional Christianity, then neither Jesus nor the Apostles would qualify as Christians, since they lived centuries before traditional or historical Christianity evolved.

Some exclude us because we have scripture in addition to the Bible. The fact is, however, that there is no single canon of scripture accepted by all Christian denominations. In Joseph Smith's day, there were thousands of textual variants among the popular versions of the New Testament. There are even references in the King James Translation to books that are not found within its pages. For example, the following fourteen: The Book of The Covenant (Exodus 24:7), The Book of The Wars of the Lord (Numbers 21:14), The Book of Jasher (Joshua 10:13), The Book of The Acts of Solomon (1 Kings 11:41), The Books of Nathan and Gad (1 Chronicles 29:29), The Prophecy of Ahijah and Visions of Iddo (2 Chronicles 9:29), The Book of Shemaiah (2 Chronicles 12:15), The Book of Jehu (2 Chronicles 20:34), The Acts of Uzziah (2 Chronicles 26:22), The Sayings of The Seers (2 Chronicles 33:19), an earlier Epistle of Paul to the Ephesians (Ephesians 3:3), an Epistle of Paul from Laodicea (Colossians 4:16), a former Epistle of Jude (Jude 3), and Prophecies of Enoch (Jude 14).

Even today, the Vulgate Bible used by Catholics differs from King James Translation used by Protestants, and the interpretations of the Bible used by Protestants differ from one denomination to another. For example, we have not just the K.J.T., but also the American Standard Version, The Revised Standard Version, the New English Bible, the New American Standard Version, the New International Version, the New King James Version, the New Revised Standard Version, and over 450 other versions. Doctrinal understanding seems to be going through an evolutionary process, as man seeks to clarify God's word. It would seem that it will only end when God Himself intervenes and personally reveals His will. But this is a development that most Christians are unwilling to accept as a viable possibility, our Ninth Article of Faith notwithstanding.

Instead, "critics cite Revelation 22:18-19 as evidence that the Bible forbids addition to or subtraction from the canon of scripture. In these verses, John curses those who would add to or take away from 'this book.' But when John wrote Revelation, the Bible in its present form did not yet exist. He was simply referring to his own book, the Book of Revelation, rather than to the whole Bible." ("Are Mormons Christians?"). After all, God had said the same thing to Moses 1,200 years earlier: "Ye shall not add unto the word which I command you, neither shall ye diminish ought from it, that ye may keep the commandments of the Lord your God which I command you." (Deuteronomy 4:2).

"The Bible itself never claims to be perfect, never claims to be sufficient for salvation, and never claims to grant its readers authority to speak or act for God. Rather, such claims are made by those who have lost priesthood authority and have lost direct revelation, and, instead of trying to find them again, are trying desperately to maintain that their loss doesn't matter." ("Are Mormons Christians?" New Era, 5/1998, p. 44).

Some exclude us because we do not interpret the Bible as other Christians do, because we believe the Bible to be the word of God only as far as it is translated correctly. Our concept of some of the basic tenets of faith is distinct from other Christian traditions. For example, we view the Trinity differently. In contrast to our biblical perspective, the Catholic concept was formulated by church councils hundreds of years after the apostolic ministry closed, at Nicaea in 325 A.D., and Chalcedon in 451 A.D.

Some exclude us because we differ in our concept of God the Father. God is love (1 John 4:8), light (1 John 1:5), and the way, the truth, and the life (John 14:6), but we do not restrict His person to these qualities. He is more than these divine attributes.

Those who attack the church rarely address the issue of whether we accept Jesus Christ as the Son of God, as our

Redeemer and as the Savior of the world. The fact is that we do believe in Christ. We do characterize the church as His. The Book of Mormon is Another Testament of Jesus Christ. We are Saints and the children of Abraham. Each member of the church who has received a testimony may declare: "Behold, for mine own part I have reached the interview, and through the spirit thou has placed within me, come to know Thee, my God." (The Eleventh Hymn of The Dead Sea Covenanters, at ancient Qumran).

We speak and testify of His ante-mortal existence and of His foreordination to be the Redeemer of the world. The scriptures speak of His relationship with the Father and of His divine investiture of authority. His appearances to His servants throughout history were many. The Book of Mormon, particularly, explains His condescension in taking a mortal body. Thus, we can better understand not only His temptations, but also the power, might, dominion, and authority that typified His experience on the earth.

In His baptism, He demonstrated by example the way for all to follow. In His ministry, He taught with simplicity the truths of the gospel. In the Garden of Gethsemane, He demonstrated His strength and compassion. The crucifixion, then, was only an apostrophe; His death was but a pause to allow us to re-focus our attention on His resurrection and ascension into heaven. When He comes again, it will be in the clouds. The Church of the Firstborn will accompany him, and His Second Coming will usher in His Millennial Reign. For a thousand years, His gospel will penetrate every soul and burn brightly in every bosom. He is our Advocate with the Father, the Bread of Life. He is the Cornerstone of our creation, the foundation of our existence, the Creator of worlds without number, and the Deliverer of the Covenant to all the children of the Father.

He is Emmanuel, for truly, God is with us. The Firstborn of the Spirit Children of the Father, He is perfect in every detail. He is the Good Shepherd and the Judge of both the quick and the dead. As Lord, King, and Jehovah, He has all power to act as the Mediator and as the Messenger of the Covenant. The Lamb of God, He is the Messiah, the Anointed One, and the anticipated Redeemer of all mankind. He is our Rock and our Savior, the Only Begotten Son of God in the flesh. He is the Son of Man of Holiness, and will be the Second Comforter to those who trust completely in His Holy Name.

When critics are asked: "With which of our teachings about Christ do you disagree?" most will find only the following of our claims objectionable: 1) Joseph Smith was His prophet. 2) The Book of Mormon is another testament of Christ. 3) His gospel has been restored through His divine intervention in the Last Days. These are the very teachings that must be proclaimed because of the Apostasy. These are the restored truths that must be put to the test suggested by Moroni: "And when ye shall receive these things, I would exhort you that ye would ask God, the Eternal Father in the name of Christ, if these things are not true; and if ye shall ask with a sincere heart, with real intent, having faith in Christ, he will manifest the truth of it unto you, by the power of the Holy Ghost." (Moroni 10:4). As the signboard in front of the Baptist church so famously put it: "Don't pray about The Book of Mormon. That's how they get you!"

Some years ago, there appeared in the Spokesman Review an article entitled: "Shaping a Word: Church people at odds over the meanings the word "Christian" should carry with it." The article described "a widespread feeling that the word 'Christian' has been taken over by a particular community, namely evangelicals and other religious conservatives." On the other side of the coin, these same evangelicals "who have recently entered into theological dialogue with Roman Catholics are at times suspicious of Catholic references to the 'one true church.'

"Then there are the 'Mormons,' who reportedly are "grappling more and more with what it means to be Christian even as some Christian groups continue to describe the 17-million-member Church of Jesus Christ of Latter-day Saints as non-Christian. Some even claim "the word 'Christian' would be more acceptable if we gave up our theological idea that the only way to salvation is through the cross of Christ. Of course, the ecumenical movement has long sought to open up the word 'Christian' to every church that confesses Jesus Christ, from the Roman Catholics to the Southern Baptists." Finally, the article sidestepped the entire issue with a concluding cop-out, claiming, "only God ultimately knows who a true Christian is." (Saturday, July 13, 1996). Truly, "the Lord looketh on the heart, and seeth not as man seeeth, for man looketh on the outward appearance, but the Lord looketh on the heart." (1 Samuel 16:7).

Latter-day Saints agree with Samuel and have confidence in God's ability to stir a man's heart to action. On the Day of Pentecost, after Peter and his companions had preached the gospel, the scriptures record: "Now when they heard this, they were pricked in their heart, and said unto Peter and to the rest of the apostles, Men and brethren, what shall we do? Then Peter said unto them, Repent, and be baptized every one of you in the name of Jesus Christ for the remission of sins, and ye shall receive the gift of the Holy Ghost." (Acts 2:37-38).

Latter-day Saint scriptures speak plainly about the need to develop a covenant relationship with Christ, proclaiming, "we talk of Christ, we rejoice in Christ, we preach of Christ, we prophesy of Christ, and we write according to our prophecies, that our children may know to what source they may look for a remission of their sins." (2 Nephi 25:26).

The doctrine of our church emphatically teaches that "there is no other name given whereby salvation cometh." (Mosiah 5:8). "Yea, come unto Christ, and be perfected in him," wrote the Prophet Moroni, "and deny yourselves of all ungodliness; and if ye shall deny yourselves of all ungodliness, and love God with all your might, mind and strength, then is his grace sufficient for you, that by his grace ye may be perfect in Christ." (Moroni 10:32). Replete with such counsel, The Book of Mormon becomes a powerful witness of Jesus Christ, Who is referred to by name or inference 3,925 times within its pages. Since there are a total of 6,607 verses in The Book of Mormon, it follows that some form of Christ's name is mentioned an average of every 1.7 verses.

Those who enter into the ordinance of baptism "are born of him." (Mosiah 5:7). This covenant is a binding contract, and since God is a party to every gospel covenant, it must come through revelation. No person may enter into such a covenant except on the basis of direct revelation from God. A "Born Again Christian" is one who is in a covenant relationship with the Lord, something that only members of Christ's true church can do through the authority of His priesthood. It might then be argued that the only real Born-Again Christians are Latter-day Saints!

In The Book of Mormon, King Benjamin told his people that because of their covenant with God, they would "be called the children of Christ, his sons and his daughters." (Mosiah 5:7). With such powerful scriptural affirmation, we cannot afford to trivialize the term "Christian." We recognize that "Jesus Christ (is) the Son of God, the Father of heaven and earth, the Creator of all things." (Mosiah 3:8). And so, we proudly take His name upon us.

Just as we are known by the name of our mortal parents, so too are we called by the name of Christ in a familial way. We are Christ's children in the sense that He united our body and spirit through the Resurrection: "For this day He hath spiritually begotten you," explained Benjamin. (Mosiah 5:7). This special family relationship is reserved for the faithful and is in addition to the reality that we are all spirit children of the Father.

As the Lord revealed to Joseph Smith, the "greater priesthood administereth the gospel and holdeth the key of the mysteries of the kingdom, even the key of the knowledge of God. Therefore, in the ordinances thereof, the power of godliness is manifest. And without the ordinances thereof, and the authority of the priesthood, the power of godliness is not manifest unto men in the flesh." (D&C 84:19-21).

Only by making covenants with God and Christ is the power of heaven unleashed. "There is no other name given whereby salvation cometh," said Benjamin; "therefore, I would that ye should take upon you the name of Christ, all you that have entered into the covenant with God." (Mosiah 5:8). Is it any wonder that the Church of Jesus Christ of Latter-day Saints is a missionary oriented church, and that the Lord Himself proclaims that it "is the only true and living church upon the face of the whole earth, with which I, the Lord, am well pleased?" (D&C 1:30). When non-members better understand the pure motives of our missionaries, they will be less inclined to judge them harshly, regard them superficially, or dismiss their message.

The reality of the apostasy and the subsequent restoration of priesthood authority are well documented in the scriptures and in the history of the church. Today, no other church has the authority of the priesthood, which is necessary to bind and ratify the covenants made with God. The priesthood, in fact, has the power to break the death grip of Satan, who would drag the souls of all mankind down to hell in an instant, if he were given the opportunity to do so.

The attitude of King Benjamin's subjects following his discourse was the same as that of true believers 50 years later, who "took upon them, gladly, the name of Christ, or Christians, as they were called, because of their belief in Christ who should come." (Alma 46:15). They recognized the source of the only legitimate authority on earth with the power to bring men into the presence of God. In fulfillment of Benjamin's promise, they were no longer "the people of Zarahemla" or "the people of Nephi," but "Christians." Those who took upon themselves the name of Christ would be found at the right hand of God, for they would know the name by which they were called; for they would be called by the name of Christ. (See Mosiah 5:9). As the Savior said: "My sheep hear my voice, and I know them, and they follow me." (John 10:27). In the latter days, when God's children come unto Him, they are no longer Baptist, or Presbyterian, or Methodist, or Catholic, Buddhist, or Muslim, but members of the Church of Jesus Christ.

Benjamin pointed out that those who would dig in their heels and decline to take upon themselves the name of Christ would find themselves in His disfavor, for their misplaced fealty would be manifest. "Whosoever shall not take upon him the name of Christ," Benjamin declared, "must be called by some other name; therefore, he findeth himself on the left hand of God." (Mosiah 5:10).

Alma asked: "If ye will not hearken unto the voice of the good shepherd, to the name by which ye are called, behold, ye are not the sheep of the good shepherd. And now if ye are not the sheep of the good shepherd, of what fold are ye? Behold, I say unto you, that the devil is your shepherd, and ye are of his fold; and now, who can deny this? ... Whosoever bringeth forth evil works, the same becometh a child of the devil, for he hearkeneth unto his voice, and doth follow him." (Alma 5:38-41). Benjamin also warned that through transgression the name of Christ would be blotted out of their hearts, for the heart is the repository of feeling. They would no longer feel like Christians (or Latter-day Saints). (Mosiah 5:11).

Every missionary extends this simple invitation to those who are pure in heart: Deny the cares of the world and respond to a nobler calling. Such discipline to follow the Royal Law is alien to the natural man. After all, "urging self-restraints on hedonists is like asking Dracula to avoid hanging around the blood bank." (Neal Maxwell, C.R., 4/1995). But Christians know that it is only the precious redeeming blood of Jesus Christ that sanctifies the soul.

It is important to both hear and know "the name by which (Christ) shall call you." (Mosiah 5:12). Many hear, yet do not comprehend, "for how knoweth a man the master whom he has not served, and who is a stranger to him, and is far from the thoughts and intents of his heart?" (Mosiah 5:13).

Baptism alone assures no-one of eternal life. All need to be "steadfast and immovable, always abounding in good works." (Mosiah 5:15). All must be sealed by the ratifying power of the Holy Spirit of Promise that is the Holy Ghost. (See D&C 88:3-4). No matter who we are, our calling and election is made sure only after the Lord has fully proven us. Then, when we receive "the other Comforter," Christ will appear and personally teach us the visions of eternity.

What, then, is a Christian? No Latter-day Saint who is founded on the bedrock of faith, and is schooled in the grammar of the gospel, need grapple with this question. It is this very question in the minds of many that opens the way to serious inquiry and leads to the waters of baptism.

Are We Alone in The Universe?

"Believe in God;
believe that he is, and
that he created all things,
both in heaven and in earth."
(Mosiah 4:9).

If you hold up a grain of sand at arm's length against the night sky, hidden behind the blocked-out area are roughly 2,000 galaxies, each of which might contain 100 billion stars. (200 trillion stars, in total). The Hubble telescope and the James Webb Telescope are able to "see" these galaxies. They are so powerful that, were it in New York City, they would be able to distinguish between two fireflies in Tokyo that were just 10 feet apart.

But have these telescopes, or any other man-made instruments for that matter, taken us any closer to the resolution of the question: "Are we alone in the universe?" Their reach has taken us back in spacetime over 4 billion light years (1/3 of the distance back to the Big Bang itself) and have identified among other wonders a nondescript cluster of some 73 galaxies, each containing perhaps 100 billion stars, found below the bowl of the Big Dipper. These galaxies are so densely packed that a thousand trillion stars all fit within an area of sky smaller than the size of a postage stamp.

On a scale so large, it seems reasonable that within the cosmic laboratory the building blocks of life would be easily and endlessly created. For example, the laws of physics tell us that every heavy element in our bodies, the calcium in our bones, and the iron in the hemoglobin of our blood, was created during the cataclysmic explosions of supernova.

"The very molecules that make up our bodies are traceable to the crucibles that were once the centers of high-mass stars that exploded into the galaxy, seeding pristine gas clouds with the chemistry of life. We are all connected to each other biologically, to the earth chemically, and to the rest of the universe atomically. We are part of the universe." (Neil deGrasse Tyson).

So, in our efforts to comprehend the universe, we come to a greater understanding of ourselves. When we ask: "What is the origin of the universe?" or "Why do its disparate elements behave as they do?" or "What is its ultimate destiny?" what we are really asking is "Where did we come from, and where are we going?" Perhaps it is the seething background radiation from the Big Bang that makes our blood hot to the touch.

Astronomers consider the possibility that there are one hundred thousand million (one hundred billion) galaxies.

They also calculate that, in a typical galaxy, there may be on the order of one hundred thousand million (one hundred billion) stars. This means that there could be ten billion trillion total stars in the universe.

If only one in a thousand of those stars has a solar system, that is still ten million trillion stars. If only one in a thousand of those stars with solar systems actually has planets capable of supporting life, that is still ten million billion stars. If only one in a thousand of those stars that have solar systems with planets that are capable of supporting life, have planets that do support life, that is still ten thousand billion stars. If only one in a thousand of those stars that have solar systems that have planets that support life, in fact support life as we know it, that is still ten billion planets. Looking at it another way, if only one in one thousand billion stars in our known universe supports a planet just like Earth, that is still ten thousand million (ten billion) "earths."

If you tried to number these worlds at the rate of one per second, it would take over 300 years. If you spent just an hour finding out everything you could about each of these worlds and their inhabitants, you would be at it for over 1,000,000 years. If God spent 6 "days" creating each of these worlds, it would take Him around 200,000,000 years to do so. Dumbing it down for us, and by divine investiture of authority, the Lord simply said: "And worlds without number have I created; and I also created them for mine own purpose; and by the Son I created them, who is mine Only Begotten." (Moses 1:33).

Are we alone in the universe? In 1977, the United States of America launched the cosmic equivalent of the slogan: "Kilroy was here" when it sent Voyager 1, like a bottle in the cosmic ocean, out into space. After forty-seven years (as of 2024), it has traveled 14.5 billion miles at a constant velocity of 36,387 miles per hour, or just over 10 miles per second. Light, traveling at 186,200 miles per second, takes over 22 hours to reach the probe that is now in interstellar space.. (Learn about Voyager 1 in real time at Voyager.jpl.nasa.gov/mission/status/). In about 40,000 years, Voyager 1 will be as close as it's going to get to another star: (AC+79 3888 in the Ophiuchus Constellation.) The Golden Record it carries describes life on earth. Electroplated upon its surface is a sample of the isotope uranium-238 that has a half-life of 4.51 billion years. It is possible that, one day in a far-distant future, a civilization that stumbles upon the record will be able to calculate its decay to determine the age of the probe. It is unsettling to consider that they might also be able to track its trajectory, and plot a course to Earth.

Are we alone in the universe? Movies with catchy titles like "Close Encounters of The Third Kind," "E.T. The Extra-Terrestrial," "Contact," and "Interstellar" stimulate our imagination. The stated mission of S.E.T.I., the Search for Extra Terrestrial Intelligence, is to "explore, understand and explain the origin, nature and prevalence of life in the universe."

In New Mexico, a "Very Large Array" of independent antennas that are each 82 feet in diameter is positioned along thirteen-mile-long arms in the shape of a Y. In essence, the 27-dish group acts as a single antenna with a 22-mile-wide diameter whose sole purpose is to detect an artificial electromagnetic signal from space. It hopes to resolve the Fermi Paradox that asks, if there is a such strong statistical probability of technologically advanced extra-terrestrial civilizations, why is there no evidence of them?

Are we alone in the universe? The mind-boggling distances involved in the search make it difficult for science to answer the question. The nearest star to earth (other than our Sun) is one of the three in the Alpha Centauri system, 4.27 light years away. Light travels about 6 trillion miles in one year. This places the system about 25.62 trillion miles distant. (Voyager 1 would take 80,376 years to make the journey from earth, at its current velocity of 36,387 mph).

Even in our own local neighborhood of the Milky Way Galaxy, if only one in a thousand of its 100 billion stars has planets, and if one in a thousand of those has planets like earth, that is still 100,000 indigenous planets that could support life as we know it. Perhaps the surest sign that intelligent life exists elsewhere in the universe, and even in our own galaxy, is that none of it has tried to contact us. This has spawned another question: Is there intelligent life on earth? (But that is the subject of another essay).

"Are we alone in the universe?" may be the wrong question. When our inquiry is rephrased, and we ask: "Where did we come from? Why are we here? Where are we going?" the power of creation itself is unleashed in our behalf. The power "to become" is released from the bondage of our ignorance and our arrogance. The genesis of the universe falls into perspective, and our reality expands to mind-boggling proportion.

When Joseph Smith rephrased the question, he asked: "O God, where art thou? And where is the pavilion that covereth thy hiding place?" (D&C 121:1). To all who study the scriptures, the Lord responded: "Do not I fill heaven and earth?" (Jeremiah 23:24).

During times of frailty, it may seem that the easier way out is to adopt the ways of the world, and we may find that it is harder to acknowledge that there is an autobiographical thread within each of us that leads all the way back to heaven. Sometimes, we cannot see the forest for the trees, or that we are as the acorns of mighty oaks. Because of our distractions, we lose focus on the things that are most important in life, just as did those in Lehi's dream who lost their grip on the Rod of Iron, and were then lost in mists of darkness.

(The) Atonement

"The natural man is
an enemy to God, and has
been from the fall of Adam, and
will be forever and ever, until he yields
to the enticings of the Holy Spirit, and
putteth off the natural man and becometh
a saint through the atonement of Christ, the
Lord, and becometh as a child, submissive
meek, humble, patient, full of love, willing
to submit to all things which the Lord
seeth fit to inflict upon him, even as
a child doth submit to his
father." (Mosiah 3:19).

With great clarity, The Book of Mormon prophets taught principles, such as the Atonement, that are elsewhere in scripture dealt with incompletely; Alma Chapter 7 leaves little room for confusion.

Verse 11 suggests that part of the Atonement was accomplished during the three years that the Savior labored among the Jews. "And he shall go forth, suffering pains and afflictions and temptations of every kind; and this that the word might be fulfilled which saith he will take upon him the pains and the sicknesses of his people." The description of the suffering of the Savior is particularly poignant in light of Alma's own suffering. (See Alma 36:14 & 21). It seems that the work in which the Savior was engaged followed a natural progression, and was built "line upon line, and precept upon precept," until His preparation was complete, and every necessary detail had been worked out. Early in His ministry, Jesus said, "My time is not yet come." (John 7:6). But later, when all had been accomplished, He confirmed, "My time is at hand." (Matthew 26:18).

Verse 12 concerns the aspect of the Atonement that was completed upon the Cross. "And he will take upon him death, that he may loose the bands of death which bind his people; and he will take upon him their infirmities, that his bowels may be filled with mercy, according to the flesh, that he may know according to the flesh how to succor his people according to their infirmities." The crucified Christ is the primary focus of Christianity today, but if one fails to understand the Mortal Messiah, one risks receiving only a one-dimensional view that ignores the wonderful harmony of His humanity and His divinity. In the context of this verse, it is well to remember that people who have known hardship are usually much better able to help others to meet adversity. This principle may help to explain why so many church members, even after living Christ-like lives, are not spared such challenges in their mortal experiences.

However, it would be wrong to assume that the more righteous one is, the less one will suffer. The promise is that one will be blessed even though the blessing may be the strength to endure suffering. All suffer. The difference is that the wicked must suffer the consequences of sin, in addition to the suffering that is a part of the mortal experience. (See D&C 121:7). Marion G. Romney once said, "If we can bear our afflictions with understanding, faith, and courage, we shall be strengthened and comforted and spared the torment which accompanies the mistaken idea that all suffering comes as a chastisement for transgression." (C.R., 10/1964).

Verse 13 focuses on the dimension of the Atonement that was fulfilled in Gethsemane. "Now the Spirit knoweth all things; nevertheless, the Son of God suffereth according to the flesh that he might take upon him the sins of his people, that he might blot out their transgressions according to the power of his deliverance." Latter-day Saints tend to emphasize Gethsemane as the pivotal experience attendant to the Savior's sacrifice, but we can see that it was really a many-faceted drama played out on different stages. It began even before the creation of the earth, for the scriptures identify Jesus Christ as "the Lamb slain from the foundation of the world." (Revelation 13:8). It will only end when the last repentant sinner has received intercession by the Redeemer, and forgiveness by the Father.

Bah! Humbug!

"I was racked with eternal torment, for my soul was harrowed up to the greatest degree and racked with all my sins. Yea, I did remember all my sins and iniquities, for which I was tormented with the pains of hell; yea, I saw that I had rebelled against my God, and that I had not kept his holy commandments. Yea, I had murdered many of his children, or rather, led them away unto destruction; yea, and in fine so great had been my iniquities, that the very thought of coming into the presence of my God did rack my soul with inexpressible horror." (Alma 36:12-14).

"Marley was dead, to begin with. There is no doubt whatever about that. The register of his burial was signed by the clergyman, the clerk, the undertaker, and the chief mourner. Scrooge signed it. Old Marley was as dead as a doornail." (Charles Dickens, "A Christmas Carol," p. 1).

In the seven years since Marley's death, Ebenezer Scrooge had become even more cold-hearted; a miser who despised Christmas and everything for which it stood. He was the embodiment of winter, bringing to mind images of darkness, despair, sadness, and death. As Dickens put it: "The cold within him froze his old features, nipped his pointed nose, made his eyes red, his thin lips blue, and spoke out shrewdly in his grating voice." He was "a squeezing, wrenching, grasping, scraping, clutching, covetous old sinner!" He had been transformed by the inexorable erosion from endless waves beating upon his cold, pinched heart.

One fateful Christmas Eve, Scrooge was visited by Marley and the ghosts of Christmas Past, Present, and Future. In a memorable exchange, he told Marley's ghost: "But you were always a good man of business, Jacob!" "Business," cried the ghost, wringing its hands again. "Mankind was my business. The common welfare was my business; charity, mercy, forbearance, and benevolence were all my business. The dealings of my trade were but a drop of water in the comprehensive ocean of my business."

And then, there was remorse in his voice, for opportunities missed, and potential denied: "At this time of the rolling year," the spectre said, "I suffer most. Why did I walk through crowds of fellow beings with my eyes turned down, and never raise them to that blessed Star which led the Wise Men to a poor abode? Were there no homes to which its light would have conducted me?"

Over the course of the night, like the Prodigal Son, Ebenezer Scrooge first hit rock-bottom, and only then was able to change his nature. We are encouraged to realize that there were no boundaries or restrictions put upon him as he dragged himself back out of his misery to face the better angels of his nature. In the process, he regained the opportunity to restore the nurturing atmosphere of hearth and home to the benefit of others, particularly the Cratchit family, including Tiny Tim.

The ghosts that appeared to him on Christmas Eve gave him a chance to be "born again," to recommit himself to obey the higher standard from which he had strayed. In a larger sense, the spiritual transformation of Ebenezer Scrooge teaches us that our Heavenly Father's Plan is designed to save even the worst of His children, but only after they have changed their nature. With renewed confidence, we feel a glimmer of hope, inasmuch as we sometimes feel equally undeserving of His unconditional love and grace.

My own conversion was less dramatic than that of Ebenezer Scrooge, and yet my feelings relating to my journey cannot be easily expressed in words. I do know that by the grace of our Heavenly Father, my eyes have been opened. The Savior helps me to forget my bad days and to focus on becoming better; to love my family, to be more responsible towards others, and to help them, to sacrifice myself through His love, to be a willing participant in the creation of a little bit of heaven on earth, to make a small contribution to the spirit of Christmas throughout the year, and to assist others on their journey to Christ.

Dickens wrote of Scrooge after his transformation: "It was always said of him, that he knew how to keep Christmas well." May that be said of each of us, as well! As Tiny Tim observed: "God Bless us, every one!"

Baptism

"This is the gospel which I have given unto you - that I came into the world to do the will of my Father, because my Father sent me. And my Father sent me that I might be lifted up upon the cross; and after that I had been lifted up upon the cross, that I might draw all men unto me ... And it shall come to pass, that whoso repenteth and is baptized in my name shall be filled.
(3 Nephi 27:13-20).

Baptism serves a number of purposes, including the following: 1) We are baptized to demonstrate our obedience, and 2) to follow in the footsteps of the Savior. 3) We are baptized to fulfil all righteousness. 4) Baptism allows us to receive a remission of our sins if we have reached the age of accountability. 5) Baptism enables us to gain admission to the Lord's church, "the only true and living church upon the face of the whole earth" with which He is pleased. (D&C 1:31). 6) Baptism provides us with the opportunity to be personally sanctified through fire and the Holy Ghost. 7) It is outwardly symbolic of our re-birth, as we pass through a portal in the similitude of the grave. 8) It is the gateway ordinance leading to the blessings reserved for the faithful that are found in the other ordinances of the gospel, and 9) it sets us squarely on the path that leads to the Celestial Kingdom of God.

Even in the days of the patriarchs, there was confusion among the ancients concerning the proper administration of the ordinance. "And it came to pass, that Abram fell on his face, and called upon the name of the Lord. And God talked with him, saying, My people have gone astray from my precepts, and have not kept mine ordinances, which I gave unto their fathers. And they have not observed mine anointing, and the burial, or baptism wherewith I commanded them; but have turned from the commandment, and taken unto themselves the washing of children, and the blood of sprinkling; And have said that the blood of the righteous Abel was shed for sins; and have not known wherein they are accountable before me." (J.S.T. Genesis 17:3-7).

In Book of Mormon times, Mormon considered the procedural dispute regarding baptism to be of such magnitude that immediately upon learning of it, he went and "inquired of the Lord concerning the matter." (Moroni 8:7). The ecclesiastical counsel that he then gave came by direct revelation from the Lord, "by the power of the Holy Ghost." (Moroni 8:7). The reason that a correct understanding of baptism is essential is that it is a foundation ordinance that lies at the very heart of the gospel of Jesus Christ.

As the Savior taught the Nephites: "This is the gospel which I have given unto you - that I came into the world to do the will of my Father, because my Father sent me. And my Father sent me that I might be lifted up upon the cross; and after that I had been lifted up upon the cross, that I might draw all men unto me ... And it shall come to pass, that whoso repenteth and is baptized in my name shall be filled. (3 Nephi 27:13-20).

It is critically important that the ordinance admitting supplicants into the fold of Christ be carried out according to His specific and pointed instruction, for there is "one Lord, one faith, one baptism." (Ephesians 4:5). "Except a man be born of water and of the Spirit," declared the Savior, "he cannot enter into the kingdom of God." (John 3:5).

Because God is a party to every gospel covenant, those who make sacred promises with Him at the waters of baptism will be visited "with fire and with the Holy Ghost." (3 Nephi 11:36). Fire and smoke have always been symbolic of the presence of the Lord and the glory of God. They are frequently used to depict the glory of celestial realms. In the language of Joseph Smith: "God Almighty Himself dwells in eternal fire. Our God is a consuming fire." ("Teachings," p. 367, see Deuteronomy 4:24, & Hebrews 12:24). The Spirit of God is like a burning fire.

One of the responsibilities of the Holy Ghost is to bear the most sacred witness of the validity of every gospel ordinance. Because there can be no greater witness, with the baptism of fire and the unimpeachable witness of the Holy Ghost, the Atonement is complete, Mercy satisfies Justice, and the penitent faithful receive a remission of sins in a symbolic rite of purification. (See 2 Nephi 31:17).

Stephen Robinson wrote: "Faith and repentance lead us to the strait gate of baptism. Those who pass through this gate, will obtain a remission of sins, gain membership in the church, and open the door leading to personal sanctification through repentance and receipt of the Holy Ghost. We may then find ourselves on the path of eternal progression leading to the Celestial Kingdom. The way is strait and narrow. The gospel standard is undeviating, with no room for rationalization or compromise." ("Ensign," 6/2001).

The authority restored by John will "never be taken again from the earth until ..." (D&C 13:1). "Until" is used in this phrase in a continuing sense; for example, "God be with you until we meet again." In the footnote to J.S.H. 1:71, "Oliver Cowdery describes these events thus: "What joy filled our hearts, and with what surprise we must have bowed ... when we received under his hand the Holy Priesthood as he said, 'Upon you my fellow-servants, in the name of Messiah, I confer this Priesthood and this authority, which shall remain upon earth, that the Sons of Levi may yet offer an offering unto the Lord in righteousness.'"

"The sons of Levi (will) offer again an offering unto the Lord in righteousness." (D&C 13:1). The sons of Levi are "the sons of Moses and also the sons of Aaron (who) shall offer an acceptable offering and sacrifice in the house of the Lord." (D&C 84:31). Joseph taught that "the sons of Moses and of Aaron shall be filled with the glory of the Lord, upon Mount Zion in the Lord's house, whose sons are ye, and also many whom I have called and sent forth to build up my church. For whoso is faithful unto the obtaining these two priesthoods of which I have spoken, and the magnifying their calling, are sanctified by the Spirit unto the renewing of their bodies." All who are faithful and obtain these two priesthoods "become the sons of Moses and of Aaron, and the seed of Abraham, and the church and kingdom, and the elect of God." (D&C 84:32-34).

It is ordained that the Gentile nations of the earth are to receive the gospel, and the elect among them are to be converted by the power of the Holy Ghost. Peter, who first brought the gospel to the Gentiles, wrote: On them "also was poured out the gift of the Holy Ghost." (Acts 10:45). These gifts of the Spirit are sufficient to carry us along the path leading to eternal life, and so the Word was given to Israel in both the Old and the New World. As Peter said: "Of a truth I perceive that God is no respecter of persons: But in every nation, he that feareth him, and worketh righteousness, is accepted with him." (Acts 10:34-35).

By obedience to the covenant, we who have been born again through baptism make "an offering to the Lord in righteousness." (D&C 13:1). We are valiant in the testimony of Jesus, and make our offering on the altar of faith. We "take the Lord's side on every issue. We think what He thinks, believe what He believes, say what He would say, and do what He would do." (Bruce R. McConkie, C.R., 10/1974). Fulfilling the requirements of our stewardship, or magnifying our calling, means to build it up in dignity and importance, to make it honorable and commendable in the eyes of all, to enlarge and strengthen it, to simply perform the service that pertains to it. John Taylor taught: "If you do not magnify your calling, God will hold you responsible for those whom you might have saved had you done your duty." (J.D., 20:23).

Even after the appearance of the resurrected Lord to the Apostles, Peter resumed his former occupation, and announced to the others, "I go a fishing." (John 21:3). When the Savior appeared on the shore, and after He had instructed the Apostles, he said to Peter: "Follow me." (John 21:19). We are assured by the accounts of Peter's subsequent ministry that he did just that. The dawning of recognition came to him that he was "elect according to the foreknowledge of God the Father, through sanctification of the Spirit, unto obedience and sprinkling of the blood of Jesus Christ." (1 Peter 1:2). He obtained "precious faith," and became a partaker "of the divine nature." (2 Peter 1:1 & 4).

The principles of true conversion point us in the direction of a clear recognition of iniquity, and then to a deep godly sorrow for our sins. Next comes inescapable suffering and torment that stimulates an appeal to the Savior, together with our awakening understanding of the power of the Atonement. From Him comes forgiveness, spiritual enlightenment, and great joy. This motivates us to a lifestyle of righteousness and service. Because of the Atonement, all have equal opportunity before the Lord. All "may have the privilege, living or dead, of accepting the conditions of the great Plan of Redemption provided by the Father, through the Son, before the world was." (John Taylor, "Mediation and Atonement," p. 181).

All those who have reached the age of accountability have the light of Christ to give them a foundation of understanding of what is good and what is evil. (2 Nephi 9:25-26). As Parley P. Pratt declared: "I have received the Holy Anointing and I can never rest until the last enemy is conquered, death destroyed, and truth reigns triumphant." ("Deseret News," 4/30/1853).

Those of us who read
Alma's explanation of faith to the
poor Zoramites must remember that he was not
speaking to members of the Church who had a sound
understanding of basic Gospel principles, but rather to a
people who had been living in apostasy and had been taught
only false doctrine. Therefore, his spiritually immature listeners
were capable of processing the details of only the initial steps that we
must take to develop faith. Alma explained only the first steps, and
not all there is to understand about faith. It is important for
members of the Church who have a firm foundation
in Gospel principles to keep this in mind
when studying his oft-quoted
discourse on faith.

Batteries Are Not Included

"He has poured out his Spirit upon you, and has caused that your hearts should be filled with joy, and has caused that your mouths should be stopped that ye could not find utterance, so exceedingly great was your joy. And … God, who has created you, on whom you are dependent for your lives and for all that ye have and are, doth grant unto you whatsoever ye ask that is right, in faith, believing that ye shall receive." (Mosiah 4:20-21).

We have been sent to earth with just enough power to keep our pulse rate steady, our breathing normal, and our body temperature hovering around 37o C. But, when it comes right down to it, batteries are not included. We need to get our energy, power, drive, motivation, zeal, and inspiration elsewhere. The sooner we come to the realization that it is God upon whom we are utterly dependent to move us from stasis to higher planes of achievement, the sooner He will breathe new life into our dead batteries. God is, after all, "the light which is in all things, which giveth life to all things, which is the law by which all things are governed." (D&C 88:13).

It's worse for those who don't recognize the need for God's influence, for although man may "have power to do many mighty works, yet if he boasts in his own strength, and sets at naught the counsels of God, and follows after the dictates of his own will and carnal desires, he must fall." (D&C 3:4). Whatever power he may have had will be sucked right out of him as his inertia evaporates.

Therefore, knowing that batteries are not included, the Lord has revealed the formula designed to energize man's potential. "Let thy bowels also be full of charity towards all men," He counseled, "and to the household of faith, and let virtue garnish thy thoughts unceasingly; then shall thy confidence wax strong in the presence of God; and the doctrine of the priesthood shall distil upon thy soul as the dews from heaven. The Holy Ghost shall be thy constant companion, and thy scepter an unchanging scepter of righteousness and truth; and thy dominion shall be an everlasting dominion, and without compulsory means it shall flow unto thee forever and ever." (D&C 121:45-46). God thus promises an unlimited flow of power to all who obey His counsel.

Because the process of building the infrastructure of energy dependency can take a while, the power that comes from knowing the Creator and the Holy Scriptures is frequently ignored. But we can be confident that the Lord will fulfil

His promises. When we finally get around to reading His instruction manual of life, we recognize our complete and utter dependence upon God as He who quickens our spirits, and with Moses we acknowledge: "Now ... I know that man is nothing, which thing I never had supposed." (Moses 1:10).

This perspective permits us to grasp our potential to know, understand, and apply the instructions that teach us how to assemble our lives so they may function properly, even though batteries have not been included. The Lord's manual contains instructions sufficient to the task, which are not of man. "For it is my voice," He explained, "which speaketh them unto you; for they are given by my Spirit unto you, and by my power you can read them one to another; and save it were by my power you could not have them; Wherefore, you can testify that you have heard my voice, and know my words." (D&C 18:34-36).

When we tap into His power source, even if we set the outflow of energy to trickle charge, amazing change takes place. By the power of the same Spirit that is accessible to the rest of us, Joseph Smith wrote: "Our eyes were opened ... so as to see and understand the things of God." (D&C 76:12). His comprehension was possible because he prepared himself to "listen to the voice of Jesus Christ ... whose word is quick and powerful." (D&C 27:1). He holds out to each of His children the promise of purposeful performance. For example, to His missionaries, he promises: "Ye shall go forth in the power of my Spirit, preaching my gospel, two by two, in my name, lifting up your voices as with the sound of a trump, declaring my word like unto angels of God." (D&C 42:6).

The fact that batteries are not included is inconsequential when the potential of the Holy Ghost is unleashed, for as the newly called Twelve found: "Whatsoever they shall speak when moved upon by the Holy Ghost ... shall be the will of the Lord, shall be the mind of the Lord, shall be the word of the Lord, shall be the voice of the Lord, and the power of God unto salvation." (D&C 68:4). The Holy Ghost thus becomes an inexhaustible source of clean, green, and renewable energy.

God is no respecter of persons, and esteems all flesh as one. It makes no difference to Him to what station in life one may have been born. Wealth and poverty are of equal unimportance. Neither beauty, fame, sickness nor health exerts lasting influence. The Lord Himself explained the great equalizing and environmentally friendly principle: "Every soul who forsaketh his sins and cometh unto me, and calleth on my name, and obeyeth my voice, and keepeth my commandments, shall see my face and know that I am." (D&C 93:1). He is the consummate external power supply Who replaces the supposedly missing batteries. "For there is no power but of God," wrote Paul. (Romans 13:1). In his letter to the Ephesians, he further explained: "whereof I was made a minister, according to the gift of the grace of God given unto me by the effectual working of his power." (Ephesians 13:7). Just as Paul experienced illumination of the Spirit, so too can all men when "the mysteries of God (are) unfolded unto them, by the power of the Holy Ghost." (1 Nephi 10:19). John's "Go Green" message was utterly contemporary when he wrote: "As many as received Jesus Christ, to them gave he power to become the sons of God." (John 1:12).

A good place to go, when we realize that batteries are not included, is the House of The Lord. His temples are characteristically "filled with smoke from the glory of God, and from his power." (Revelation 15:8). It is in the temple where we learn that "the rights of the priesthood are inseparably connected with the powers of heaven, and that the powers of heaven cannot be controlled nor handled only upon the principles of righteousness." (D&C 121:36). "And without the ordinances thereof, and the authority of the priesthood, the power of godliness is not manifest unto men in the flesh." (D&C 84:21).

When we complain about weakness because for whatever reason our batteries have been drained of power, it is because we lack energizing faith. "And now I speak unto all the ends of the earth," warned Moroni, "that if the day cometh that the power and gifts of God shall be done away among you, it shall be because of unbelief." (Moroni 10:24).

We must not "dispute the power of God." (Mosiah 27:15). Instead, when we feel the current coursing through our bodies, we are moved to exclaim, as did Nephi: "O Lord, I have trusted in thee, and I will trust in thee forever. I will not put my trust in the arm of flesh" nor in its ineffectual counterfeit for real power. (2 Nephi 4:34).

Because batteries are not included, God gives us a privileged opportunity to draw upon His intrinsic strength. "The power and authority of the higher, or Melchizedek Priesthood," after all, "is to hold the keys of all the spiritual blessings of the church … The power and authority of the lesser, or Aaronic Priesthood, is to hold the keys of the ministering of angels, and to administer in outward ordinances." (D&C 107:18 & 20).

We fortify ourselves against the adversary by utilizing the external power supply provided by God, and we rely upon His promise that the "redemption of Zion must needs come by power." (D&C 103:15). This was the miracle of ancient Israel, a nomadic people of little consequence who came out of the desert of Sinai and changed the world: "So the people shouted when the priests blew with the trumpets: and it came to pass, when the people heard the sound of the trumpet, and the people shouted with a great shout, that the (walls of Jericho) fell down flat, so that the people went up into the city, every man straight before him, and they took the city." (Joshua 6:20).

The young shepherd David later drew upon that same power when "he took his staff in his hand, and chose him five smooth stones out of the brook, and put them in a shepherd's bag which he had, even in a scrip; and his sling was in his hand: and he drew near to the Philistine" and slew Goliath by the valley of Elah. (1 Samuel 17:40).

In The Book of Mormon account of Ammon by the Waters of Sebus, "every man that lifted his club to smite Ammon, he smote off their arms with his sword; for he did withstand their blows by smiting their arms with the edge of his sword, insomuch that they began to be astonished, and began to flee before him; yea, and they were not few in number; and he caused them to flee by the strength of his arm." (Alma 17:37). Alma may have included this episode in his abridgment because he knew that in our day we would face our own "Lamanites by the waters of Sebus." We all have the same primal needs, and the focus of our concern should be on the potential loss of our energy, vitality, and ultimately our eternal lives. King Lamoni's people were astonished at Ammon's performance because in the Land of Nephi batteries were nowhere to be found, and the Lamanites had not yet learned how to draw upon the power of God. When the king's servants testified to him of the things they had seen Ammon do, "he was astonished exceedingly, and said: Surely, this is more than a man. Behold is this not the Great Spirit?" (Alma 18:1-2). They knew that God was capable of mighty works, but they had never considered that He might transfer His power to man so that he might also perform miracles. They did not know that the power was in them, for they were free agents. (See D&C 58:28).

Some people never do figure out that batteries are not included. For them, life is nothing more than a night in a second-class hotel with no heat and just the flickering glow from a bare bulb hanging at the end of a frayed cord from the ceiling.

In a moving account from The Book of Mormon, after the missionaries Alma and Amulek had been cast into prison in The Land of Nephi, "Alma cried, saying: How long shall we suffer these great afflictions, O Lord? O Lord, give us strength according to our faith which is in Christ, even unto deliverance. And they broke the cords with which they were bound." The failure of the chief judge, the lawyers, and the priests and teachers who smote upon Alma and Amulek, to recognize legitimate power when it was staring them right in the face cost them their lives, for "the earth shook mightily, and the walls of the prison were rent in twain, so that they fell to the earth; and (they) were slain by the fall thereof." Simply inserting batteries with properly oriented polarity would have set the stage for a miraculous display of power at the simple flick of a switch.

Ultimately, the Lord manifests His power as a testimony to the world. Batteries are not included, but at the same time, "the earth rolls upon her wings, and the sun giveth his light by day, and the moon giveth her light by night, and the stars also give their light … they roll upon their wings in their glory, in the midst of the power of God. Unto what shall I liken these kingdoms," asked the Lord, "that ye may understand? Behold, all these are kingdoms, and any man who hath seen any or the least of these hath seen God moving in his majesty and power." (D&C 88:45-47).

Emerson declared: "The man who has seen the rising moon break out of the clouds at midnight has been present like an archangel at the creation of light and of the world." Truly, when God said, "Let there be light," it was a simple statement of fact as much as a command. It was an invitation to His works to embrace the light, to celebrate it, and to revel in it. As are most of His entreaties, the formula is simple. To again quote Emerson: "How does nature deify us with a few and cheap elements! Give me health and a day, and I will make the pomp of emperors ridiculous."

Truly, "earth is crammed with heaven, and every bush with fire of God. But only those who see take off their shoes. The rest stand around picking blackberries." (Elizabeth Barrett Browning, "Aurora Leigh," Book Seven, 1856).

Become as Little Children

"Children are the living messages
we send to a time we will not see."
(Anonymous).

"And it came to pass
that he did teach and minister
unto the children … and he did
loose their tongues, and they did
speak unto their fathers great and
marvelous things, even greater than
he had revealed unto the people,
and he loosed their tongues
that they could utter."
(3 Nephi 26:14).

We all know that "little boys are made of frogs and snails and puppy dog tails, and that little girls are made of sugar and spice and everything nice." (Attributed to Robert Southey). But did you also know that "little girls are made of daisies and butterflies and soft kitty cat purrs, and all the precious memories of times that once were. Little girls are made of angel's wings and giggles and a firefly's glow, and all the happy feelings, deep inside, that we all know. Little girls are made of cinnamon and bubbles and fancy white pearls, and snowflakes and rainbows and ballerina twirls. Little girls are made of sunshine and cupcakes and fresh morning dew, and these are the reasons, little one, why everyone loves you." (Anonymous).

Because Jesus loved all little children, He taught us to have the child-like qualities of innocence, trust, virtue, purity, and curiosity, to treat all people with humility, gentleness, and kindness, and to view the world enthusiastically, energetically and with wide-eyed wonder, awe, and anticipation. When His disciples asked Him: "Who is the greatest in the kingdom of heaven?" they were seeking approval and validation as do our own children, but they were thinking as adults whose mature perspective can be a double-edged sword. When we put away childish things, we view life more dispassionately, but at the same time we sacrifice, to some degree our ability to express ourselves naturally with unrestrained spontaneity. We can lose our "joie de vivre." Let's face it; adults can be boring. So, in His response to His disciples, the Savior emphasized: "Except ye be converted, and become as little children, ye shall not enter into the kingdom of heaven." (Matthew 18:1-2).

Two things, then, are necessary in order to regain our heavenly home. First is conversion, and inseparably related to it is the capacity to become as little children. The world teaches us to be as "grown-up" as possible in order to succeed in life. Children are inundated with adult-themed messages: "Act your age!" "Don't be a baby!" and "Grow up!" as if the process of maturation could be hastened. Later, we are told how to gain a competitive edge as adults: "It's not what you know, it's who you know." "You don't get what you deserve, you get what you negotiate." "Watch your back." Even: "Do as I say, not as I do." Those who have learned to roll with the punches are characterized as "seasoned veterans" and yet the process, far from tenderizing us, gives us a mental toughness and a thick skin with few sensory nerve endings. Daddy Warbucks, reflecting on his life in the business world, told Annie: "You don't have to be nice to those you step on or climb over, on your way up the ladder of success, if you don't plan on coming back down again." To put it even more bluntly: "He who has the gold makes the rules." But, as Brigham Young taught: "If we go on lusting after the groveling things of this life which perish with the handling, we shall surely remain fixed with a very limited amount of knowledge and like a door upon its hinges, move to and fro from one year to another without any visible advancement or improvement." (J.D., 10:266-267).

When Adam and Eve were introduced to the lone and dreary world outside the Garden, they were told they would have to earn their bread by the sweat of their brow. This was not a curse, but was instead God's own formula for success that would enable them to live in a telestial world and make their mark in business without compromising their celestial standards. As Gretel Erlich observed, with material prosperity comes the temptation "to fill space, as if what we have, what we are, is not enough. Being affluent, we strangle ourselves with what we can buy, things whose opacity further obstructs our ability to see what is already there. "("The Solace of Open Spaces").

In a sense, we must return to the secret garden of our childhood in order to fully mature because, as Wordsworth wrote: "Heaven lies about us in our infancy. Shades of the prison house begin to close upon the growing boy, but he beholds the light and whence it flows. He sees it in his joy. The youth, who daily farther from the east must travel, still is nature's priest, and by the vision splendid, is on his way attended. At length the man perceives it die away, and fade into the light of common day." ("Intimations of Immortality from Recollections of Early Childhood"). Fortunately, the organization of the church "detoxifies us from the cares and conditioning influences of the world and from the homogenization process that occurs as we are worn down by the vicissitudes of life. When we are born again, we are re-vitalized, as we are re-introduced to a magical kingdom that is the place where dreams come true.

In between the sights and sounds, rides and attractions, and thrills and spills of our earthly theme-park experience, we'll need to pay attention to personal spiritual hygiene. The Plan for our preservation includes regular bathing to remove the grit and grime that fouls our inner-workings. It mandates the need to make frequent changes out of soiled clothing into clean garments, and even requires occasional physical therapy appointments for relief from the bumps and bruises that we'll surely receive along the way. But the "buildings" we have fitly framed and into which we retreat for sanctuary will have drafty windows and doors, leaky pipes, faulty fixtures, and hot water heaters that are overwhelmed with calcium deposits. We cannot hope to attend to our personal needs so successfully that ideal form and function are maintained. Grandma's home remedies will not be equal to the task, and although we may eagerly embrace the elixirs peddled by snake-oil salesmen, we are just grasping at straws.

So, we must embrace the Plan and the organization of the church to provide the gurneys upon which we will be given transfusions of the spiritual element to keep us going, at least until it's time to repeat the process. When we frequent the blood-bank, we will be on both the receiving and the giving end. Those who go to dialysis centers have similar experiences where contaminants are removed from their blood because their kidneys cannot accomplish the task on their own. But there will be some who will not seek help, because they are so caught up in the celebration of their so-called autonomy. The Lord characterized such as "the natural man" who "is an enemy to God, and has been from the fall of Adam, and will be, forever and ever, unless he yields to the enticings of the Holy Spirit … and becometh as a child, submissive, meek, humble, patient, full of love, willing to submit to all things which the Lord seeth fit to inflict upon him, even as a child doth submit to his father." (Mosiah 3:19). It's great to strike out on our own, get our own apartment, earn a living, and pay our own bills. But eventually we'll all pack our bags and return Home to move back in with our Heavenly Parents and live under one roof as we did at first. We'll be one big happy family again. He is forever our Father, and we are His children.

As His offspring, we are now and ever will be "in progress either to an endless advancement in eternal perfections, or back to dissolution. There is no period in all the eternities wherein we will become stationary, that we cannot advance in knowledge, wisdom, power, and glory." (Brigham Young, J.D., 1:349). Our child-like nature reflects the enduring qualities that characterize our Parents' nurturing influence that is less judgmental, less suspicious, and more friendly. It is more accepting of others, often without reservation. It sees others as neighbors and not as strangers. It is more trusting and speaks without guile. It is more transparent and less prejudicial. It has no pretensions and is more genuine. It is less prone to rationalization and is quicker to forgive. It is more honest, true, benevolent, chaste, and virtuous. Its faith is more pure, its hope is more comprehensive, and its charity knows no bounds.

When we were born again, we were given the promise of a new lease on life. Few of us would care to repeat high school, and yet when the gospel Plan reintroduces us to our childhood, we are literally given a second chance to get it right. We enthusiastically welcome the opportunity, and it never enters our mind to throw a tantrum or lie on the floor with our arms and legs flailing.

No matter what life may have thrown at us the first time around, we are given a clean slate and invited to re-write our life's story. We can not only start today and make a new ending, but we can also go back and re-write our beginning. We can preplay before we replay. As little children, we can role-play just as grown-ups do. We can sit in the director's chair, edit the script, and orchestrate our own extreme home makeover. The ordinance symbolizing our rebirth may have taken only a few seconds to perform, but its butterfly effect is boundless and experienced forever. When we are born again, the influence of the Lord's presence is felt, as if it were the omnipresent background radiation from the Big Bang that accompanied the creation of our universe. No matter the direction we are facing, because we are new creatures in Christ, He is always and forever before our faces. There is no path we may follow and no hiding place to which we may flee where we cannot feel His profound influence. Why would we want to? We have learned to grasp the horns of sanctuary whenever our yoke seems too heavy for us to bear alone. Every time we do a reality-check, we find Him there. He is "Jesus Christ, the Great I Am, Alpha and Omega, the beginning and the end, the same which looked upon the wide expanse of eternity, and all the seraphic hosts of heaven, before the world was made. The same which knoweth all things, for all things are present before (His) eyes." (D&C 38:1-2).

We cannot avoid our duty any more than could Jonah, nor would we choose to do so. If we were to try to shirk our responsibilities, we would be swallowed up by a leviathan no less real and eventually spit out on the shoreline of our obligations. It makes no difference if we turn to the right or to the left, because He will be there. When we lift our eyes to the heavens, He will be watching us from above. No matter that we may be weighed down by sin or sorrow with downcast eyes, He is always beneath us, to lift us up and carry our burdens. Every time we knock, He will answer. Every time we ask, we will receive. When petty concerns distract us, He is patiently waiting in the wings until we regain our senses. When we act foolishly, He looks past our behavior into our core. He is the Father of our spirits, and like the parent we all want to be, He is there to bind up and heal our wounds every time we stumble and fall. If we regard ourselves as His spiritual offspring and internalize His divine characteristics, how it will change our lives for the better!

Latter-day revelation teaches that angels may be spirits that have not yet obtained a body, or those who are awaiting the resurrection. They may also be those who have been resurrected or have been translated.

Before a Wound Can Heal

"Repentance is the first pressure we feel
when we are drawn to the bosom of God."
(Jeffrey R. Holland).

"He commanded them
that they should preach nothing
save it were repentance and faith on
the Lord, who had redeemed his people."
(Mosiah 18:20).

"The first condition of happiness is a clear conscience." (David O. McKay, "Gospel Ideals," 1976). In physical terms, before a wound can heal, it has to be clean. Anyone who has had a physician vigorously scrub out a wound knows how carefully and thoroughly the task must be accomplished before sterile dressings may be applied to allow the healing process to begin. The same principle applies to character development. There is no room for dry rot when building character. A noble character has no skeletons lurking in the closet. The Savior called the Scribes and Pharisees hypocrites, for they were "like unto whited sepulchres, which indeed appear beautiful outward, but are within full of dead men's bones, and of all uncleanliness." (Matthew 23:27).

The purpose of earth life is to grow and progress in stature, until we have developed the image and likeness of our Heavenly Father. During the process, we will fail again and again. This creates a problem because "no unclean thing can dwell with God," and yet it is human nature to repeatedly violate eternal law. (1 Nephi 10:21). Unfortunately, sin stops our progress. God, however, provided the principle of repentance so that we may yet become holy. Therefore, we are commanded: "All men, everywhere, must repent." (Moses 6:57).

David O. McKay taught: "Spirituality is the consciousness of victory over self, and of communion with the infinite. (C.R., 10/1969). The invitation of the Spirit leads us to sainthood through repentance and forgiveness because of the Atonement of Christ. As we submit to His will, we develop His nature and character. His gentle counsel is: "All that I have, I could give to you, but what I am, you must earn for yourself, line upon line, and precept upon precept.

The great blessing of repentance is that it allows us to become clean in the sight of God, and to get moving again on the pathway to perfection. After repentance, God will remember our sins no more. It is true that we might retain a remembrance of them, insofar as they increase our testimonies and strengthen us to become more stalwart as soldiers in the army of Christ. But we will no longer feel the guilt or suffer the consequences of disobedience that include withdrawal of the Spirit.

Repentance, then, can satisfy a two-fold purpose. First, it allows us to be justified by the Spirit, become holy or sanctified, and qualified to enter the Presence of the Lord. Secondly, it serves to strengthen existing testimony, which makes it more unlikely that we will yield to temptation in the future. For example, after his exhortation to them, King Benjamin's people "cried with one voice, saying … the Spirit of the Lord Omnipotent … has wrought a mighty change in us, or in our hearts, that we have no more disposition to do evil, but to do good continually." These people made a covenant to forsake their sins, and to keep the commandments, in order to be able to avoid the otherwise inevitable consequences of disobedient behavior. (Mosiah 5:2 & 5).

They knew that their repentance was complete when the Spirit of the Lord fell upon them, they were filled with joy, and they had peace of conscience. In his last hours of mortality, Joseph Smith was similarly able to declare: "I have a conscience void of offense towards God, and towards all men." (D&C 135:5). He gave us all the confidence to walk in the valley of the shadow of death and yet to fear no evil. "Life actually has no significance except as a preparation for the ultimate goal of death," wrote Carl Jung. "In Christianity, the meaning of existence is consummated in its end." For Latter-day Saints, "one of the greatest contributions of Joseph Smith was his knowledge of what is to come after death. He did much to clarify our understanding of heaven, and to make it seem worth working for." ("My Religion and Me Lesson Manual").

The sons of Mosiah had a similar effect on those whom they taught in the Land of Nephi. (See Alma 23). Their Lamanite converts left behind their former lives, giving up all their sins to know the Savior. They changed their names and became Saints, promising to never again return to their wicked ways. They embraced the cultural lifestyle and traditions of the Nephite missionaries, and opened up a lasting correspondence with them. As the scales of darkness began to fall from their eyes, they become a pure and delightsome people. This remarkable transformation was accomplished in a very short time under the cleansing influence and power of the gospel of Jesus Christ. Given the opportunity, it does the same thing today for all the people of the earth, for it is "the power of God unto salvation." (Romans 1:16).

Repentance that brings about such change requires great courage, much strength, many tears, unceasing prayers, and untiring efforts. It also requires a Redeemer to provide an Atonement to satisfy the demands of Justice. "There is no royal road to repentance, no privileged path to forgiveness. Every man must follow the same course whether he is rich or poor, educated or untrained, tall or short, prince or pauper, king or commoner. There is only one way. It is a long road spiked with thorns and briars and pitfalls and problems." (Spencer W. Kimball, "The Miracle of Forgiveness," p. 149). It may require that we travel a path leading to our own personal Gethsemane, on to Calvary, and then to a quietly empty Garden Tomb. But reaching our destination makes the journey worth the effort.

In order to repent, we must recognize our sins. This might at first sound like a trivial point, but we should remember Alma's wise counsel to his son that applies to us all: "Let your sins trouble you," he urged Corianton, "with that trouble which shall bring you down unto repentance. Do not endeavor to excuse yourself in the least point." (Alma 42:29-30).

We must feel sorrow for our sins. We must feel terrible about them. We must feel profoundly filthy. We must want to unload and abandon them. We must be almost obsessive-compulsive about cleansing our souls. We must be broken in heart, and have the spirit of contrition. A broken heart is softened to receive the things of the Spirit, and is teachable. It is "to be broken down with deep sorrow for sin, to be humble and thoroughly penitent." (Bruce R. McConkie, "Mormon Doctrine," p. 161). At that level of spiritual preparation, when our faith has convicted us of our sins, we must be prepared to ask, as did those on the Day of Pentecost: "What shall we do?" The answer is straightforward: "Repent and be baptized every one of you in the name of Jesus Christ for the remission of sins." (Acts 2:37-38).

We must confess and forsake our sins. "By this ye may know if a man repenteth of his sins - behold, he will confess them and forsake them." (D&C 58:43). Confession removes a heavy burden from the sinner. The Lord has promised, "I, the Lord, forgive sins, and am merciful unto those who confess their sins with humble hearts." (D&C 61:2).

All sins must be confessed to God, but those that might affect our standing in the church should be confessed to the proper priesthood authority, as well. In our day, the bishop and others in comparable positions can forgive in the sense of waiving the penalties. In this capacity, the bishop represents the Lord. This is why it is proper that members confess their sins to the bishop, when those sins might jeopardize their standing in the Kingdom. Church judicial action as it relates to members is required for three reasons: to preserve the good name of the church, to help the sinner on the pathway to repentance and forgiveness, and to ensure impartiality when priesthood leaders deal with church members.

However, only the Lord "hath power on earth to forgive sins." (Matthew 9:6). But He recognizes that even the righteous do not become perfect overnight. Therefore, He has promised: "As often as my people repent will I forgive them their trespasses against me." (Mosiah 26:30). Of those who will not repent, however, He said: "The same shall not be numbered among my people." (Mosiah 26:32). Excommunication is the extent of the penalty.

"We believe that all religious societies have a right to deal with their members for disorderly conduct, according to the rules and regulations of such societies; provided that such dealings be for fellowship and good standing; but we do not believe that any religious society has authority to try men on the right of property or life, to take from them this world's goods, or to put them in jeopardy of either life or limb, or to inflict any physical punishment upon them. They can only excommunicate them from their society, and withdraw from them their fellowship." (D&C 134:10).

We must make restitution, if possible. Wrongs must be righted, and fences mended. The truth is that restitution can be therapeutic for the transgressor, for "that which ye do send out shall return unto you again." (Alma 41:15).

We must forgive others. "Wherefore, I say unto you, that ye ought to forgive one another; for he that forgiveth not his brother his trespasses standeth condemned before the Lord; for there remaineth in him the greater sin." (D&C 64:9). We may find that "enduring to the end" simply involves mastery of two principles: repentance for our own sins, and forgiveness of others. The Savior obtained forgiveness for the sins of mankind only after the most excruciating suffering on His part. Is it, then, too much for Him to ask us to forgive each other? He recognized that the Plan of Redemption breaks down without our forgiveness, and so its quality is really a celestial barometer that measures our testimony temperature. Christ requires forgiveness by those who would be obedient to the Laws of His Kingdom simply because they must do so in order to feel comfortable living there. He commanded Joseph Smith: "I, the Lord, will forgive whom I will forgive, but of you it is required to forgive all men." (D&C 64:10). Brigham Young put it a little more bluntly, when he declared: "He who takes offense when none was intended is a fool, and he who takes offense when one was intended is usually a fool."

When we withhold our love, we repudiate the Spirit of Christ in a brazen confirmation that we never really knew Him, and that for us He lived in vain. It means that His teachings suggested nothing to us, and that in all our thoughts we were never really near enough to Him to be seized with the spell of His compassion for the world. We are only fully repentant when we have charity or the pure love of Christ, and are strictly obedient to the principle of forgiveness, and that door swings both ways.

When the process of repentance has been completed, the Atonement becomes fully effective. In our lives. "My soul was harrowed up to the greatest degree and racked with all my sins, "Alma recalled. "Yea, I did remember all my sins and iniquities, for which I was tormented with the pains of hell; yea, I saw that I had rebelled against my God, and that I had not kept his holy commandments. So great had been my iniquities, that the very thought of coming into the presence of my God did rack my soul with inexpressible horror. It came to pass that as I was ... harrowed up by the memories of my many sins, behold, I remembered also to have heard my father prophesy ... concerning the coming of one Jesus Christ, a Son of God, to atone for the sins of the world. Now, as my mind caught hold upon this thought, I cried within my heart: O Jesus, thou Son of God, have mercy on me. And now, behold, when I thought this, I could remember my pains no more. And oh, what joy, and what marvelous light I did behold; yea, my soul was filled with joy as exceeding as was my pain! There can be nothing so exquisite and sweet as was my joy." (Alma 36:12-14, 17-21).

What a great Plan of our Father! Live your life, push the envelope, and dare to take risks. After the Plan has been explained to you, if you fail to abide by its laws, Jesus Christ will take the heat. The beauty of the Plan is that if you Recognize your mistakes, if you experience Remorse for having made them, if you attempt to make Restitution if your behavior has wronged others, if you learn from the mistake and Reform your ways, and Resolve to Refrain from repeating. It, you will be free to continue the path of progress, with a complete Resolution of what would have otherwise been an incapacitating short-coming.

The unique source of that peace is our complete and all-encompassing repentance, the power of the Savior's Atonement that transforms us, and Heavenly Father's consequent forgiveness of our sins. Such is our cleansing that we may "manifest unto the people," as did Alma, that we have "been born of God." (Alma 36:23). As Parley P. Pratt declared: "I have received the holy anointing, and I can never rest until the last enemy is conquered, death destroyed, and truth reigns triumphant." ("Deseret News," 4/30/1853). Each of us may share that intensity of feeling when we have conquered those self-defeating behaviors and character traits that limit our progression. The Prophet Joseph Smith said: "Salvation consists in a man's being placed beyond the power of his enemies, meaning the enemies of his progression, such as dishonesty, greediness, lying, immorality, and other vices."

We should repent now, in order "to prepare to meet God." (Alma 34:32). It is difficult to learn a skill all at once, but it is easy if we repetitively practice each day until we gain mastery. We are past repentance when we no longer have the will or the desire to repent. As Spencer W. Kimball wrote: "It is true that the great principle of repentance is always available, but for the wicked and rebellious there are serious reservations to this statement. For instance, sin is intensely habit forming, and sometimes moves us to the tragic point of no return. Without repentance there can be no forgiveness, and without forgiveness all the blessings of eternity hang in jeopardy. As the transgressor moves deeper and deeper in his sin, and the error is entrenched more deeply and the will to change is weakened, it becomes increasingly near hopeless and he skids down and down until either he does not want to climb back, or he has lost the power to do so." ("The Miracle of Forgiveness," p. 117).

The Savior said that we must be perfect, for otherwise we cannot inherit the kingdom of God. Perhaps He meant that we must be perfect in our repentance. After explaining to his people the great Plan of Redemption that solved the dilemma created by God's demand for perfection coupled with our inability to live sinless lives, the prophet Jacob simply stated:" O be wise; what can I say more?" (Jacob 6:12). Moroni offered the same message: "Be wise in the days of your probation: strip yourselves of all uncleanness ... Ask with a firmness unshaken, that ye will yield to no temptation, but that ye will serve the true and living God." (Mormon 9:28).

Behold

At
the end of the
day, Joseph Smith
said that he translated
The Book of Mormon by the
gift and power of God, and he
let it go at that. And that's pretty
much all we can say about it. It
stands on its own merits and
that alone. But all things
considered, its quite
clear that he did
very well.

The word "behold" appears 1,669 times in the King James Translation of the Bible, and 1,275 times in The Book of Mormon, so Another Testament of Jesus Christ has scored anther bulls-eye when it comes to being true to authentic ancient grammar usage, syntax, and gospel terminology. Because it is a phrase that is encountered so often, though, the casual reader frequently passes right over it without thinking about what the word means and why it appears so often. The fact is that are good reasons why the word "behold" is used so many times, and these are linked to its different nuances, depending on the context.

The King James Translators encountered the Hebrew word "hinneh "in the Old Testament and the Greek word "idou" in the New Testament, and since no single word in English adequately conveyed its shades of meaning, they tended to leave the word as is, retaining the word "behold," because they could not find a suitable substitute. However, some modern English translations of the Bible have spurned the archaic phrasing in the King James Version in favor of more contemporary expressions.

Nevertheless, in a valiant attempt to retain the original meaning of the word "hinneh," the preface to the English Standard Version of the Bible explains: "Although 'Look!' and 'See!' and 'Listen!' would be workable in some contexts, in many others these words lack sufficient weight and dignity. Given the principles of 'essentially literal' translation, it is important not to leave "hinneh" and "idou" completely untranslated, for to do so would sacrifice the intended emphasis in the original languages. The older and more formal word 'behold' has usually been retained, therefore, as the best available option for conveying the original sense of meaning."

In the KJT, the word "behold" was translated from the Hebrew הִנֵּה, which translates into one of three meanings: First, the word is used to call attention to a person, object, principle, or doctrine. For example, Exodus 24:8 reads: "And Moses took the blood, and sprinkled it on the people, and said, Behold the blood of the covenant, which the Lord hath made with you concerning all these words."

Secondly, the word can be employed to introduce or reassert a principle, truth, or doctrine, as in Genesis 1:29, where God says to Adam and Eve, "Behold, I have given you every herb bearing seed, which is upon the face of all the earth, and every tree, in the which is the fruit of a tree yielding seed; to you it shall be for meat."

Thirdly, the word may dramatize a concept. Genesis 1:31 reads: "And God saw every thing that he had made, and, behold, it was very good."

Each of the three different variations of meaning of the word depends upon who is being addressed. "Behold" can be directed to persons in in the narrative, but in other cases, it reaches outside of time and space to draw the reader in, either to ensure that attention is given to a particular detail of the narrative, or to instill a sense of excitement within the reader.

But what about the cultural and literary milieu that surrounded the translation of The Book of Mormon? By the 1820s, these classical distinctions relating to the use of the word "behold" had become blurred. In the 1828 edition of Webster's Dictionary, "the word "behold was defined as: "to fix the eyes upon; to see with attention; to observe with care." In other words, the Nineteenth Century definition focused only on directing one's attention to a particular event or person, and completely ignored the other definitions that had classically been related to the introduction of new truth and to dramatization. But, as one would expect from the inspired translation of an ancient text, the word "behold" in The Book of Mormon remains true to the pattern of the Hebrew Bible, rather than to its contemporary 1828 definition.

Examples from The Book of Mormon illustrate how this literary feat is accomplished.

1). When "behold" is employed to instill enthusiasm:

"For behold, it came to pass that the Lord spake unto my father, yea, even in a dream, and said unto him…" (1 Nephi 2:1). In this instance, Nephi used the term "behold" to instill enthusiasm in the mind of his readers, relating to his father's dream. That he would do so is reasonable, because Nephi recognized the dream's beautiful symbolism and meaning that would resonate with readers throughout the rest of his narrative, and in fact, throughout the entire Book of Mormon.

"And now, because thou hast done this with such unwearyingness, behold, I will bless thee forever; and I will make thee mighty in word and in deed, in faith and in works; yea, even that all things shall be done unto thee according to thy word, for thou shalt not ask that which is contrary to my will. Behold, thou art Nephi, and I am God. Behold, I declare it unto thee in the presence of mine angels, that ye shall have power over this people, and shall smite the earth with famine, and with pestilence, and destruction, according to the wickedness of this people. Behold, I give unto you power, that whatsoever ye shall seal on earth shall be sealed in heaven; and whatsoever ye shall loose on earth shall be loosed in heaven; and thus shall ye have power among this people." (Helaman 10:5-7). With the term "behold" used 4 times in these verses, three new concepts are introduced with its use: 1) Nephi will be blessed forever, 2) God reasserts who Nephi is, and Who He is, in an interesting parallel statement, and 3) Nephi is given the sealing power.

2). When "behold" is used for added emphasis, to encourage the reader to "see" what is written, and as an introduction to newly discovered truth:

"And when Amulek saw the pains of the women and children who were consuming in the fire, he also was pained; and he said unto Alma: How can we witness this awful scene? Therefore, let us stretch forth our hands, and exercise the power of God which is in us, and save them from the flames. But Alma said unto him: The Spirit constraineth me that I must not stretch forth mine hand; for behold the Lord receiveth them up unto himself, in glory; and he doth suffer that they may do this thing, or that the people may do this thing unto them, according to the hardness of their hearts, that the judgments which he shall exercise upon them in his wrath may be just; and the blood of the innocent shall stand as a witness against them, yea, and cry mightily against them at the last day. Now Amulek said unto Alma: Behold, perhaps they will burn us also. And Alma said: Be it according to the will of the Lord. But behold, our work is not finished; therefore, they burn us not." (Alma 14:10-13).

3). When "behold" is used to introduce new truth:

"Behold, I speak unto you as if ye were present, and yet ye are not. But behold, Jesus Christ hath shown you unto me, and I know your doing." (Mormon 8:35

Behold, I speak unto you as though I spake from the dead; for I know that ye shall have my words." (Mormon 9:30).

These verses beautifully capture all three meanings of the word "behold," that calls attention to a principle, introduces a truth, and dramatizes a concept. Near the conclusion of the thousand-year history of the Nephites, Moroni reached out through time and space to lift our gaze, and as an experienced teacher, and with renewed energy, he redirected us to a startling truth. We are figuratively stopped in our tracks, lest we breeze past the final pages of the book without consciously recognizing the importance and intent of what we've read. It's a final plot twist that leaves us wanting more. As is the case many times in The Book of Mormon, new truth is adroitly emphasized and reasserted in such a way that the intent of the message cannot be overlooked.

The bottom line is that The Book of Mormon follows Hebraic patterns such as its faithfully accurate use of the word "behold." This is yet another example of the miraculous nature of the translation. Joseph Smith did not initiate his study of Hebrew until 1835, five years after The Book of Mormon was published, and due to his belated efforts, an independent translation of The Book of Mormon would have been impossible. As some antagonists purport, he could never have created such a neat, tidy, and entirely appropriate narrative as the product of his own wild imaginations.

In accordance with Occam's Razor, the most likely explanation is the simplest one: The Book of Mormon is what it says it is: "An abridgment of the record of the people of Nephi, and also of the Lamanites - Written to the Lamanites, who are a remnant of the house of Israel; and also to Jew and Gentile - Written by way of commandment, and also by the spirit of prophecy and of revelation - Written and sealed up, and hid up unto the Lord, that they might not be destroyed - To come forth by the gift and power of God unto the interpretation thereof - Sealed by the hand of Moroni, and hid up unto the Lord, to come forth in due time by way of the Gentile - The interpretation thereof by the gift of God." (Book of Mormon: "Introduction").

One could not do better than to employ the testimony of our Lord and Savior Jesus Christ: "And (Joseph Smith) translated the book, even that part which I have commanded him, and as your Lord and your God liveth, it is true." (D&C 17:6).

If critics are asked: "With which of our teachings about the Savior do you disagree?" most find only the following claims objectionable: 1) Joseph Smith was His prophet. 2) The Book of Mormon stands as another testament of Christ. 3) His Gospel has been restored thru divine intervention in the Last Days. These are the very teachings that must be proclaimed because of the Apostasy. These are the restored truths that must be put to the test suggested by Moroni.

Being Well-Grounded

"And they did press
forward through the mist of
darkness, clinging to the rod of
iron, even until they did come forth
and partake of the fruit of the tree ... The
rod of iron ... was the word God, which led to
the fountain of living waters, or to the tree of
life; which waters are a representation of the
love of God; and (Nephi) also beheld that
the tree of life was a representation
of the love of God." (1 Nephi
8:24 & 11:25).

My grandson Parker Edwards and I went for a motorcycle ride at Priest Lake, Idaho, during the summer of 2009. From East Shore Road, we started up the trail at Cavanaugh Bay, heading to the fire lookout high above Coolin, atop Sundance Mountain.

It was a steep and technical climb, but 10-year-old Parker made it without a problem. When we got to the top of the rocky trail, we were startled to see a pickup truck in the parking lot, and even more surprised to be greeted by a man standing atop the lookout itself. He was a volunteer firefighter who served on that lonely and windswept mountaintop, primarily monitoring for wildfires the rugged terrain that stretched out before him in a 360o panorama.

I'd been to the top of Sundance several times, but had never before had the chance to see inside, and so we were thrilled when he invited us to climb the rickety stairs for a tour of the lookout itself. He showed us his propane stove and refrigerator, his bed and table, his binoculars, maps, and triangles, and the basic comforts of home that he'd created. But most interestingly, he pointed out how the entire living quarters was surrounded by a copper grid, with connected lightning rods extending 60 feet down to the ground. Curiously, outside one window a large nail dangled from a wire. He explained that, during thunderstorms, when the nail glowed with a bluish ball surrounding it, it was a warning that a lightning strike was about to occur.

At that moment, he said, he had been trained to jump onto the bed or the chair, both of whose legs rested within large glass insulators. Then he would raise his feet off the floor and wait for the imminent strike. A clap of thunder and flash of blinding light always occurred simultaneously when the tower took a direct hit, and he said the feeling was as if he were inside the bolt itself as it enveloped the copper grid in blinding light, streaked down the rods, and then dissipated into the ground.

As he described his intimate relationship with a primal force of nature, I thought how important it is to be "well-grounded." His physical ground was a direct connection to the earth, designed to protect not only property but also himself from injury or death due to excessive voltage. (By the way, cloud-to-ground lightning strike voltage tends to range up to 1 billion volts. Lightning temperatures typically reach 50,000 degrees Fahrenheit, which is about four times the temperature of the surface of the sun.)

As I looked at the glass insulators on the floor of the lookout, I thought of their scriptural equivalents and there came to my mind accounts of those who, in the Last Days, are not so "well-grounded." Isaiah wrote of such: "Stay yourselves, and wonder; cry ye out, and cry: they are drunken, but not with wine; they stagger, but not with strong drink." (Isaiah 29:9). His was an accurate description of the consequences we all face when we are not well-grounded in gospel principles.

Similarly, the Psalmist wrote of those who "reel to and fro, and stagger like a drunken man, and are at their wits' end." (Psalms 107:27). Daniel described his king, whose "thoughts troubled him, so that the joints of his loins were loosed, and his knees smote one against another." (Daniel 5:6). When we are not well-grounded, the very fibers of our being fail to hold us together coherently, and we lose our physical, emotional, and spiritual co-ordination. Within our central nervous systems, synaptic activity fires sporadically, and we respond to our environment inappropriately and ineffectively, without synchronization.

Sometimes, those who are not well-grounded need to be jolted out of their complacency, in the same way that defibrillator paddles are used to restore normal cardiac rhythm in a heart attack patient. Remember the Lord's instruction to Nephi: "Stretch forth thine hand again unto thy brethren, and…I will shock them, saith the Lord, and this will I do, that they may know that I am the Lord their God." (1 Nephi 17:53).

The spiritual equivalents to being "well-grounded" are powerful. Nephi described those who were "pressing forward, and they came forth and caught hold of the end of the rod of iron; and they did press forward through the mist of darkness, clinging to the rod of iron, even until they did come forth and partake of the fruit of the tree. (1 Nephi 8:24). The rod of iron was for them a lightning rod, firmly grounding them to unchanging principles, so that they would "henceforth be no more children, tossed to and fro," like flotsam and jetsam on the sea of life, "and carried about with every wind of doctrine," (Ephesians 4:14)

"The rod of iron … was the word of God, which led to the fountain of living waters, or to the tree of life; which waters are a representation of the love of God; and (Nephi) also beheld that the tree of life was a representation of the love of God." (1 Nephi 11:25). Being well-grounded, the faithful need not fear, although they "see signs and wonders, for they shall be shown forth in the heavens above, and in the earth beneath. And they shall behold blood, and fire, and vapors of smoke." (D&C 45:40-41). The spiritual equivalents of lightning may strike all around them, but they will be protected from harm by the "copper grid" that surrounds them and grounds them to truth.

Even though the "proud and they that do wickedly shall be as stubble; and (are) burn(ed) up" (D&C 64:24), those who are well-grounded are like the "man which built an house, and digged deep, and laid the foundation on a rock: and when the flood arose, the stream beat vehemently upon that house, and could not shake it: for it was founded upon a rock." (Luke 6:48). When we are well-grounded, we "are no more strangers and foreigners, but fellowcitizens with the saints, and of the household of God, and are built upon the foundation of the apostles and prophets, Jesus Christ himself being the chief corner stone." (Ephesians 2:19-20).

By the way, if you were wondering how thunder and lightning occur, it happens when relatively warm air clashes with cold air, and the lighter, warmer air rises into the upper atmosphere, creating thunderheads. On the way up, warm water molecules rub against cold water molecules in clouds, causing all the molecules to shed electrons that collect at the bottom of the cloud. When enough electrons are buzzing around the base, they're attracted to the ground, which temporarily has an opposite charge. Then, lightning streaks to the earth, breaking the sound barrier and creating thunder. God does work in mysterious ways.

On a scale so large,
it seems reasonable that within
the cosmic laboratory the building blocks
of life would be easily and endlessly created.
For example, the laws of physics tell us that every
heavy element in our bodies, the calcium in our bones,
and the iron in the hemoglobin of our blood, was created
during the cataclysmic explosions of supernova. "The
very molecules that make up our bodies are traceable to
the crucibles that were at one time the centers of high-
mass stars that exploded into the galaxy, seeding
pristine gas clouds with the chemistry of life. We
are all connected to each other biologically,
to the earth chemically, and to the rest
of the universe atomically. We are
part of the universe." (Neil
deGrasse Tyson).

(The) Bible

Basic Information
Before Leaving Earth

"And it came to pass
that he did teach and minister
unto the children ... and he did
loose their tongues, and they did
speak unto their fathers great and
marvelous things, even greater than
he had revealed unto the people,
and he loosed their tongues
that they could utter."
(3 Nephi 26:14).

Does the Bible stand alone as the definitive word of God? At the end of his Book of Revelation John declared: "If any man shall take away from the words of the book of this prophecy, God shall take away his part out of the book of life, and out of the holy city, and from the things which are written in this book." (Revelation 22:19). But Moses had written roughly the same thing 1,200 years earlier: "Ye shall not add unto the word which I command you," he cautioned Israel, "neither shall ye diminish ought from it, that ye may keep the commandments of the Lord your God which I command you. (Deuteronomy 4:2).

What does the Bible contain that is of worth? The Book of Nephi provides some insight: "Knowest thou the meaning of the book?" an angel had asked. "The book that thou beholdest is a record of the Jews, which contains the covenants of the Lord, which he hath made unto the house of Israel, and it also containeth many of the prophecies of the holy prophets ... wherefore they are of great worth unto the Gentiles. (For) when it proceeded forth from the mouth of a Jew it contained the fulness of the gospel of the Lord." (1 Nephi 13:23).

Does the King James Translation contain the fullness of the gospel? The "great and abominable church, which is most abominable above all other churches, (has) taken away from the gospel of the Lamb many parts which are plain and most precious; and also many covenants of the Lord have they taken away." (1 Nephi 13:26). God's instruction to His people should contain clear and concise counsel regarding His Plan. What is the consequence of the removal of these things? "Because of the things which are taken away out of the gospel of the Lamb, an exceedingly great many do stumble, yea, insomuch that Satan hath great power over them" to thwart the divine purpose of the Plan. (1 Nephi 13:29). Why is additional scripture so important? "I beheld the book of the Lamb of God, which had proceeded forth from the mouth of the Jew, that it came forth from the Gentiles unto the remnant of the seed of my brethren. And after it had come froth unto which came forth by the power of the Lamb. These last records, which thou hast seen among the Gentiles, shall establish the truth of the first, which are of the twelve apostles of the Lamb, and shall make known the plain and precious things which have been taken away from them, and shall make known to all kindreds, tongues, and people, that the Lamb of God is the Son of the Eternal Father, and the Savior of the world; and that all men must come unto him, or they cannot be saved." (1 Nephi 13:38-40).

These additional scriptures testify of the divinity of Jesus Christ and create a richly endowed palette from which we may select the appropriate paints to create a comprehensive portrait of His mission on earth and His Atonement for the sins of mankind.

In the Last Days, "many of the Gentiles shall say: A Bible! A Bible! We have got a Bible, and there cannot be any more Bible." (2 Nephi 29:3). But God is interested in other nations, besides the Jews. "Know ye not that there are more nations than one?" he asked. "Know ye not that I, the Lord your God, have created all men, and that I remember those who are upon the isles of the sea; and that I rule in the heavens above and in the earth beneath; and I bring forth my word unto the children of men, yea, even upon all the nations of the earth? Know ye not that the testimony of two nations is a witness unto you that I am God, that I remember one nation like unto another. Wherefore, I speak the same words unto one nation like unto another. And when the two nations shall run together the testimony of these two nations shall run together also." (2 Nephi 29:7-8).

This comprehensive body of scriptures is the basis upon which God shall judge the world. "For I command all men, both in the east and in the west, and in the north, and in the south, and in the islands of the sea, that they shall write the words which I speak unto them; for out of the books which shall be written I will judge the world, every man according to their works, according to that which is written." (2 Nephi 29:11, see verse 12).

The Savior said of the scriptures: "I leave these sayings with you to ponder in your hearts, with this commandment which I give unto you, that ye shall call upon me while I am near. Draw near unto me and I will draw near unto you." (D&C 88:62-63). God, Who cannot lie, has promised us that our eyes may be opened by the power of the Spirit, and our understandings enlightened, so as to see and understand the things of God. (D&C 76:12).

Furthermore, He made an amazing promise to those who would read the scriptures: "These words are not of men, nor of man, but of me; wherefore, you shall testify they are of me and not of man. For it is my voice which speaketh them unto you; for they are given by my Spirit unto you, and by my power you can read them one to another; and save it were by my power you could not have them. Wherefore, you can testify that you have heard my voice, and know my words." (D&C 18:34-36).

(The) Biggest Loser

"The spirit and the
body shall be reunited again
in its perfect form, both limb
and joint shall be restored
to its proper frame."
(Alma 11:43).

Just like the food that those on Weight Watchers eat, every action in life has "points" related to it. When we live our lives in moderation and in harmony with gospel principles, the sum of our behaviors doesn't exceed the acceptable number of "points" associated with those activities. We stay fit and trim, and able to fulfil the measure of our creation.

In the style of Weight Watchers, provident living requires our attendance at regular gatherings of like-minded individuals. We call these "Sacrament Meeting," "Relief Society Meeting," and "Priesthood Meeting," to name a few. The peer pressure generated is a powerful positive reinforcement to encourage us to conform to the prescribed program and helps us to develop the discipline to deter deviation, expand our energies in constructive directions, cultivate fortitude, and build mental toughness.

Weight-Watchers helps us to be aware of our lean body mass index, the sum of everything in our bodies except fat. Likewise, in life we need to be able to recognize the immaterial element that influences our spiritual nature, namely the sin that weighs us down. Then, we can develop a program to shed those offensive pounds and get back to our optimal weight, to fit into the clothes in which we were baptized. For at that time, when we were "born again," we were at our ideal form because we weren't yet weighed down with sin.

Alma, whom you might recall was an early Weight-Watcher motivational speaker, encouraged all who would listen to adhere to the program: "The spirit and the body shall be reunited again in its perfect form," he promised, "both limb and joint shall be restored to its proper frame." (Alma 11:43). Much later, Joseph Fielding Smith, Jr., a vocal proponent of Weight-Watchers, taught: "All deformities and imperfections will be removed, and the body will conform to the likeness of the Spirit." ("Doctrines of Salvation," 2:289). Moreover, he asserted "in the restoration of all things, there shall come perfection." ("Answers to Gospel Questions," 4:185-189). In neither case was there significant objection from the scientific community. It seems the claims of both Alma and Joseph have withstood the tests of time.

No matter how heavy we have allowed ourselves to become, no matter how many pounds of sin have begun to pile on, no matter how ponderous a burden we have created from our own inattention to our spiritual health, Christ, the mediator of the Weight-Watcher Program, will still lift us up. No matter how weak we have become, no matter that our spiritual muscles have turned to flab, no matter that we are for all intents and purposes "dead weight," He has the strength to carry us until, revitalized, we can once again walk and run on our own.

"Heaven lies about us in our infancy," wrote William Wordsworth. "Shades of the prison house begin to close upon the growing boy, but he beholds the light and whence it flows. He sees it in his joy. The youth, who daily farther from the east must travel, still is nature's priest, and by the vision splendid, is on his way attended. At length the man perceives it die away, and fade into the light of common day." And then, perhaps only when he has hit rock-bottom, he hears an awful noise ringing in his ears as "the whole earth groans under the weight of its iniquity." (D&C 123:7). This motivates him to drag his battered and beaten body to the local chapter of Weight Watchers.

The Weight-Watcher Program can give us the resolve to avoid food that is not nutritious. Our covenant-consciousness helps us to avoid the highly caloric snacks of sin, the empty calories of confusion that do not really satisfy our hunger, the enticements of excess that blind us to temperance, the hydrogenated oils of overindulgence that clog our avenues of intuition, the bribery of bewilderment that clouds our vision and makes acceptable choices difficult, the cupcakes of confusion that are little more than the spiritual equivalents of refined sugar, and the unwholesome processed factory food that is mechanically dispensed by the devil's dieticians at the automat of life. As Elder Dallin Oaks remarked: "You can never get enough of what you don't need, because what you don't need won't satisfy you."

In a scenario similar to that of Weight-Watchers, inattention allows the weight of sin to slowly creep up on us. We compensate for its added pounds by unconsciously working just a little harder to move around. Because we are exhausted by ordinary efforts to stabilize our behavior, we become passive participants rather than active combatants in the arena of life, where sin, Satan's tag-team partner, is always our enemy. We would rather be a couch potato, than a determined disciple. We never even notice our poor spiritual fitness, because our neglect fogs the mirror on our soul when we step out of the shower. Our conscience, the calorie-counter provided by our Father, is pushed aside. Thus, we avoid the only certifiably reliable scale that would alert us to our condition.

The burden of unresolved sin makes it seem as if we are carrying the weight of the world on our shoulders, and our hearts are heavy as they pump ever harder just to keep our circulation going. We become familiar with after-hours emergency centers, and our loved ones become alarmed that life-support could become a real possibility. Our congestive heart failure is a sign that our worldliness has worsened. The only solution offered by the Lord's Weight-Watcher Program is to change our own heart. Technology can provide no alternative because there are no donor hearts available even if a transplant were possible. How wonderful it would be in these circumstances to say of us: "This day he hath spiritually begotten you, for … your hearts are changed." (Mosiah 5:7).

We don't notice the increase in our resting heart rate or its inability to absorb compassion. As our respiration rate increases, we are short of spiritual breath after mechanically performing even routine tasks. The exercise and lifestyle changes that would have remedied our condition seem too difficult, and we're too busy to even think about these alterations to our routines anyway.

If only we could participate in the spiritual equivalent of Weight-Watchers, we would have less trouble sleeping, less difficulty focusing, and less of a problem concentrating on the tasks at hand. We wouldn't have that nagging angina in our chest that is aggravated every time we neglect our responsibilities.

At Weight-Watchers, we learn that we burn protein at a rate of 4 calories per gram, and fat at 9 calories per gram. Unfortunately, sin is purged in the same way. It takes over twice as much energy to eliminate it as it does to retain righteousness. It's far better to resist the urge to sin, because we have to pay for it later, and in spades. It's harder to lose a pound of sin than it is to retain our classic form with righteousness. It's far less expensive to be clothed in righteousness than it is to be burdened down with sin. Sin might look fashionable at the moment, but styles change quickly. . Righteousness is always modest in its appearance, and its value is enduring. It has a certain "timelessness" about it, perhaps because it is always "on sale," while we always pay a premium for sin. Sin is never the bargain it is purported to be, while righteousness always retains its value. Weight-Watchers costs $16.95 per month, with a one-time sign-up fee of $29.95, while righteousness costs nothing. It only has a performance cost, not including tithing and fast offering. As Isaiah wrote: "He that hath no money; come ye, buy" a lifetime membership in the Lord's equivalent of the Weight-Watcher Program "without money and without price." (Isaiah 55:1).

Obedience to principles that mirror the Weight-Watcher Program will yield results that are evident when we study the mirror on the soul. With our finger on the pulse of our spirits, we will avoid behavioral binge-eating. We will distain the artificial sweetener of sin. The midriff bulge of poor spiritual nutrition will melt away before our eyes, and we will feel the satisfaction of being able to take in our priesthood pants a few inches because we are in such good shape. We "shall renew (our) strength; (we) shall mount up with wings as eagles; (we) shall run, and not be weary; and (we) shall walk, and not faint." (Isaiah 40:31). Through the church-sanctioned Weight-Watcher Fitness Program, we will become and remain lean, mean, fighting machines, able to fulfil the measure of our creation.

Nevertheless, even Joseph Smith admitted that, from time to time, he lost his resolve. He recalled that he "was left to all kinds of temptations; and mingling with all kinds of society, (he) frequently fell into many foolish errors, and displayed the weakness of youth, and the foibles of human nature." He was guilty of "levity, and sometimes associated with jovial company." (J.S.H. 1:28). In fact, he acted much as we all do. In the next few years, however, he helped to establish Weight Watcher Programs that ultimately would be franchised throughout the world.

Just as he did, we have the ability to reset our spiritual appestat when we notice it is out of whack. We can learn not to splurge on "food" that has no nutritional value and we can condition ourselves to habitually resist temptation. We can train ourselves to recognize the sticky and glistening qualities that are characteristic of the appearance of high fructose corn syrup telestial treats.

When we learn that "evils and designs (do) exist in the hearts of conspiring men in the last days," we will realize that low calorie beer is still beer. (D&C 89:4). Reduced fat Haagen Dazs ice cream still has 17 grams of fat in a half-cup serving (290 calories, and 153 of those from fat). Pizza that is on-sale is still pizza. Too much of that, and we may as well don a hospital gown and climb up on a gurney in preparation for a procedure, because we are headed for the liposuction of laziness. Better to be anxiously engaged in a good cause and to do many things of our own free will than to let someone hiding behind a mask suck out a couple of quarts of fat from our tummies with a straw designed by the Marquis de Sade, because we've been unwilling to sweat through a few crunches, and unable to resist the temptation to throw a few packages of Twinkies into our shopping cart every time we go to the market.

Years of spiritual neglect take drastic action to reverse. The plastic surgery of repentance is always necessary. When a cancerous growth is removed, it has to have clean borders, but when it is gone, so too will be the soul scars that accompanied the surgery. These procedures need to be performed by a member of the American Society of Plastic Surgeons, just as bishops need to monitor the Lord's Weight Watcher Program.

The Stair Master of day-to-day perseverance can not only keep us in shape, but it can also be the mechanism to carry us to new heights. We can be "re-newed" to "re-gain" our former spiritual stature, to "re-fresh" ourselves to begin once again, as we "re-double" our efforts, and "re-turn" to our roots. As in the Weight-Watchers Program, we learn that "love-handles" don't really express love at all, that spiritual obesity is at epidemic levels, that Wonder Bread isn't what Jesus was talking about, and that a sedentary lifestyle is antithetical to the concept of eternal progression. We need to be moving along the path and making steady progress. When we feel ourselves in bondage to the excess weight of unresolved sin, we need to increase our metaphysical metabolism, to go the second mile in order to burn as much fat as possible in the crucible of contrition, to double our stride. When we move forward at this increased tempo, we will receive "a gift of spiritual independence that removes the veil of insensitivity to a destiny." (Richard L. Gunn).

We recall that in the Sacred Grove, Heavenly Father and Jesus Christ appeared to Joseph Smith as identical personages. One was indistinguishable from the other. We wonder if this was because they didn't have an accumulation of the excess pounds that accompany improvident living and contribute to physical imperfection. We should not be surprised that when "the Savior shall appear, we shall see him as he is," a glorified, resurrected being of light. (D&C 130:1). The profound implication is, that if we are true to His Weight-Watcher Program, our appearance at that moment will reflect our true spiritual stature. Finally, we will be in both the image and the likeness of God. Sign me up now.

Blood, Covenant, and Land Israel

"As many of the Gentiles as will repent (shall become) the covenant people of the Lord; and as many of the Jews as will not repent shall be cast off; for the Lord covenanteth with none save it be with them that repent and believe in his Son, who is the Holy One of Israel." "For the Lord will have mercy on Jacob, and will yet choose Israel, and set them in their own land: and the strangers shall be joined with them, and they shall cleave to the house of Jacob. And the people shall take them and bring them to their place; yea, from far unto the ends of the earth; and they shall return to their lands of promise." (2 Nephi 30:2 & 24:1-2; see Isaiah 14:1-2).

In order to better understand Israel and her role in the events that are unfolding in the Last Days, she must be viewed from different perspectives, because she has both physical and spiritual qualities that influence her impact upon her neighbors. There is also the added element of adoption to be considered, that increases many-fold her capacity to change the world in preparation for the Second Coming. In one sense, Israel may simply be viewed as those in whom the blood of Israel flows. Another perspective explores the expanding influence of those within Gentile nations who have covenanted to forsake the world and to join latter-day Israel. As Paul taught the elect of God who had thereby become Israelites by adoption: "Ye are all the children of God by faith in Christ Jesus. For as many of you as have been baptized into Christ have put on Christ. There is neither Jew nor Greek, there is neither bond nor free, there is neither male nor female: for ye are all one in Christ Jesus. And if ye be Christ's, then are ye Abraham's seed, and heirs according to the promise." (Galatians 3:26-29).

A third point of view considers those whose ancestors have occupied the Holy Land since biblical times. Many of these are descendants of Abraham and have deeply rooted ties that will surely figure prominently in the events surrounding the fulfillment of prophecy in the Last Days, such as the gathering of Israel and preaching of the gospel. For a greater appreciation of the complex issues relating to Arab-Israeli relations in the Promised Land, see: "Of The House of Israel," by Daniel Ludlow, in the "Ensign," 1/1991, "How Should Latter-day Saints View the Conflict in Israel?" by Kelly Ogden, in "Meridian Magazine," 9/6/2013, and "Peace in the Holy Land," by Kelly Ogden and David B. Galbraith, published in the "Liahona," 12/1997.

Some voices are silent, and some are vocal, but all the world stands as a witness, as Israel is "gathered home to the lands of (her) inheritance, and (is) established in all (her) lands of promise." (2 Nephi 9:2). That process has been going on long enough for us to acknowledge that there are many lands of inheritance, and many lands of promise, all of which reflect the broad strokes with which Heavenly Father paints His portrait of the children of the covenant.

In the first Area Conference of the church held in Mexico City, in August 1972. Bruce R. McConkie stated: "Of this glorious day of restoration and gathering, a Nephite prophet said: 'The Lord … has covenanted with all the house of Israel,' that 'the time comes that they shall be restored to the true church and fold of God'; and that 'they shall be gathered home to the lands of their inheritance, and shall be established in all their lands of promise.' (2 Nephi 9:1-2).

Now I call your attention to the facts, set forth in these scriptures, that the gathering of Israel consists of joining the true church; of coming to a knowledge of the true God and of his saving truths; and of worshiping him in the congregations of the Saints in all nations and among all peoples. Please note that these revealed words speak of the folds of the Lord; of Israel being gathered to the lands of their inheritance; of Israel being established in all their lands of promise; and of there being congregations of the covenant people of the Lord in every nation, speaking every tongue, and among every people when the Lord comes again.

The place of gathering for the Mexican Saints is in Mexico; the place of gathering for the Guatemalan Saints is in Guatemala; the place of gathering for the Brazilian Saints is in Brazil; and so, it goes throughout the length and breadth of the whole earth. Japan is for the Japanese; Korea is for the Koreans; Australia is for the Australians; every nation is the gathering place for its own people." (See also: "The Scattering and Gathering of Israel," Bruce Satterfield, B.Y.U. Idaho). Therefore, as we ourselves participate in the Gathering, it would help if we were clear about the following:

Blood Israel

The term "blood Israel" could be applied to those who are Israelites by lineage. Today, it is largely the Jews who are "blood Israel." They are of the lineage of Abraham, Isaac, Jacob, and primarily his son Judah. They are the modern-day personification of the ancient covenant people of the Lord.

An angel had asked Nephi, who considered himself a Jew: "Rememberest thou the covenants of the Father unto the House of Israel?" (1 Nephi 14:8). He was speaking of the Abrahamic Covenant that was familiar to Nephi. This covenant has been only imperfectly preserved in the Book of Genesis: "Behold, my covenant is with thee, and thou shalt be a father of many nations. Neither shall thy name any more be called Abram, but thy name shall be Abraham; for a father of many nations have I made thee. And I will make thee exceeding fruitful, and I will make nations of thee, and kings shall come out of thee. And I will establish my covenant between me and thee and thy seed after thee in their generations for an everlasting covenant, to be a God unto thee, and to thy seed after thee." (Genesis 17:4-7).

The full force of the covenant promised to Abraham was that he would have numberless descendants who would be entitled to receive the gospel, the priesthood, and the ordinances of exaltation. He would establish the same covenant with all the generations of Abraham's children. They would ultimately carry the gospel to the nations of the earth and, through them, extend the blessings of God to all mankind. It is the intent of the Abrahamic Covenant to give all of Heavenly Father's children an equal opportunity to participate in and receive the blessings of the Plan of Salvation.

Covenant Israel

There are also those who, by accepting Christ and His covenants, become adopted members of the House of Israel, and who thus have equal claim upon the blessings of Abraham. These individuals could be termed "covenant Israel." Today, "covenant Israel" is in a position to recognize and understand its relationship with God because of the clarification of principles and doctrines that have accompanied the restoration of the gospel. We learn that the Savior had originally explained to his servant Abraham: "My name is Jehovah, and I know the end from the beginning; therefore, my hand shall be over thee. And I will make of thee a great nation, and I will bless thee above measure, and make thy name great among all nations, and thou shalt be a blessing unto thy seed after thee, that in their hands they shall bear this ministry and Priesthood unto all nations … And I will bless them that bless thee, and curse them that curse thee; and in thee (that is, in thy Priesthood) and in thy seed (that is, thy Priesthood), for I give unto thee a promise that this right shall continue in thee, and in thy seed after thee (that is to say, the literal seed, or the seed of the body) shall all the families of the earth be blessed, even with the blessings of the gospel, which are the blessings of salvation, even of life eternal." (Abraham 2:8-11).

Adoption is a process whereby Heavenly Father accepts with a sacred covenant (the Abrahamic Covenant) the parenting rights and responsibilities relating to His righteous children. Because of His determination to honor all of the provision of the covenant, His offspring are empowered to enjoy the status that had formerly defined the relationship between them and their biological parents. Adoption enlarges the scope of their potential so that it may exponentially expand to eternal proportions. It has the power to bring us, the spirit children of our Heavenly Father, back into the fold so that we may, once again, bask in the light of truth.

When we are converted to the gospel, we do not need to be the literal descendants of Abraham in order to qualify to receive from God the blessings of the Abrahamic Covenant. Literal descendants of Abraham are not the only people whom He calls His covenant people. Speaking to Abraham, God said: "As many as receive this gospel shall be called after thy name, and shall be accounted thy seed and shall rise up and bless thee, as their father." (Abraham 2:10). Thus, the two groups of people cited above who are included in the covenant made with Abraham are: (1) Abraham's righteous literal descendants and (2) those who have been adopted into his lineage by accepting and living the gospel of Jesus Christ. (See 2 Nephi 30:2).

In the Last Days, "as many of the Gentiles as will repent (shall become) the covenant people of the Lord; and as many of the Jews as will not repent shall be cast off; for the Lord covenanteth with none save it be with them that repent and believe in his Son, who is the Holy One of Israel." (2 Nephi 30:2). These are God's covenant people.

As a result of my exposure to the church beginning with a short film ("Man's Search for Happiness") at Flushing Meadows during the 1964 World's Fair, I learned about the covenants God wishes to make with me. For example, I learned about God's morality and the Covenant of Chastity. I learned about His charity and His commandment to love Him and each other. I learned about the principle of consecration as I studied the example of His Son. I learned about His compassion and the Law of the Fast. When I humbled myself, and learned about His perfection, I better understood the importance of the Word of Wisdom. As I sought to become more like Him, His commandment to seek knowledge made more sense to me. As I pondered the gift of His Son, I began to understand the Law of Sacrifice. As I tried to honor the Law of the Sabbath, my thoughts turned to His creation of the world, and how He had rested from His labors on the seventh day.

As I considered my covenant relationship with God, I thought about specific blessings, including my right to guidance from the Holy Ghost. I thought about the priesthood, and women's privileges, blessings, rights, and responsibilities relating to femininity. I thought about eternal family life in the celestial kingdom.

I learned that the covenants we make with God have the ability to place us beyond the reach of the adversary, and that obedience gives us the priesthood and spiritual power necessary to overcome evil and obtain exaltation. The teachings of the Prophet Joseph Smith snapped into sharp focus, that "salvation consists of a man's being placed beyond the power of his enemies, meaning the enemies of his progression, such as dishonesty, greediness, lying, immorality, and other vices." (Nauvoo, May 21, 1843, see also "Teachings," p. 297-298).

As I continued to make covenants, I learned more and more about my responsibilities relating to my relationship with God. I was promised that the gates of hell would not prevail against me, and that the Lord God would disperse the powers of darkness from before me, and cause the heavens to shake for my good and His name's glory. (See D&C 21:6). I learned about my duty to keep His commandments. When I realized the Lord had promised Abraham that through his descendants the gospel would be taken to all the earth, I learned something about my sacred duty to share my new-found faith with others.

The beauty of my adoption into the House of Israel has been to claim the privileges associated with His rights and responsibilities, and to be continually learning about The New and Everlasting Covenant, including the covenants made at my baptism, with my ordination to the Melchizedek Priesthood, during the sacrament, and in the temple. I know that these covenants are everlasting and have been ordained by His authority. I know that although His covenants may have been new to me, they will never be changed, for He has given them to His children each time He has dispensed the gospel. (See Ezekiel 37:26). I know by personal example that He is no respecter of persons. (See Acts 10:34).

I am the lucky recipient of the new covenant made with the House of Israel and with the House of Judah, and I will put His law in my inward parts, and write it in my heart. He will be my God, and I will be counted among His people. (See Jeremiah 31:31-34). Because of His love for me, I have learned how to personalize the "contract provisions" of the New and Everlasting Covenant. I have agreed to repent, be baptized, receive the Holy Ghost, the endowment, the covenant of marriage in the temple, and to follow and obey Christ to the end of my life. Heavenly Father has promised, in turn, that I will receive exaltation in the celestial kingdom. (See D&C 132:20-24). The potential of that promise is hard for me to understand. I only know that the commandments were designed with me in mind, that they are for my benefit, and that if I am faithful, I may have a part in sharing the beauties and the blessings of both heaven and earth. One day, I may live once again in His presence, to partake of His love, compassion, power, greatness, knowledge, wisdom, glory, and dominions.

I am overjoyed that my Father in Heaven established His Covenant to release me from my bondage to sin, and to set me free to take advantage of every feature of the Plan of Salvation. Without His Covenant in my behalf, I realize that the Plan would have been frustrated. I am thrilled to know that covenants have set me free from the bands of death. I believe the words of King Benjamin, who said: "There is no other name given whereby salvation cometh, therefore, I would that ye should take upon you the name of Christ, all you that have entered into the covenant with God." (Mosiah 5:8).

My covenants have set me free to reach my potential. I have learned to know the truth of Benjamin's words, that those who enter into the Covenant "are born of him." (Mosiah 5:7). I understand what it means to be a "Born Again Christian," to be in a covenant relationship with the Lord.

As the Lord revealed to Joseph Smith, so have I learned that the "greater priesthood administereth the gospel and holdeth the key of the mysteries of the kingdom, even the key of the knowledge of God. Therefore, in the ordinances thereof, the power of godliness is manifest. And without the ordinances thereof, and the authority of the priesthood, the power of godliness is not manifest unto men in the flesh." (D&C 84:19-21).

Land Israel

As great as are the blessings of "blood Israel" and "covenant Israel," there are those who have inhabited and worked the land since ancient times, and who have been included by the Lord to be counted among those who will receive the blessings of Abraham. These are those whom we might identify as "land Israel."

Leviticus taught: "And if a stranger sojourn with thee in your land, ye shall not vex him. But the stranger that dwelleth with you shall be unto you as one born among you, and thou shalt love him as thyself; for ye were strangers in the land of Egypt." (Leviticus 19:33-34).

Perhaps dualistically, Isaiah prophesied: "For the Lord will have mercy on Jacob, and will yet choose Israel, and set them in their own land: and the strangers shall be joined with them, and they shall cleave to the house of Jacob." (Isaiah 14:1).

Heaven's admission policy will welcome Blood Israel, Covenant Israel, and Land Israel. Persons of any race, creed, color, or national origin are accepted for admission to heaven provided they maintain ideals and standards in harmony with those of The Church of Jesus Christ of Latter-day Saints, and meet heaven's requirements. These are baptism, and the ordinances of the Melchizedek Priesthood.

It may come as a surprise to some, to realize that Israel comes in many different colors. It speaks Arabic, Dutch, Fijian, Mandarin, Russian, and dozens of other languages. It lives in well over 3,000 stakes, in practically every country in the world, from Algeria to Zimbabwe. It has over 15 million members who are red, yellow, brown, black, and white. Israel wears a sarong, a grass skirt, a blue collar, a tupeno, a business suit, and a kilt. It lives in igloos, huts, and high-rise condominiums. Most important of all, it shares a common destiny, and a testimony that Jesus is the Christ, and that His love, indeed, makes the world go round. Today, it is more important than ever to remember that there is no United States of America in heaven. The great equalizer in the sight of God is obedience by His children to His will.

The key to Israel's liberation from bondage to her freedom to become, is an adjustment in her attitudes reflected in her desire to be born again. To paraphrase Helen Keller, the real tragedy is not the Israelite who is born without sight, but those of blood, covenant, and land Israel who do not have vision.

"The role of Israel as the depository of true religion is almost self evident: the freeing of mankind from the idolatry which obstructs its salvation. For as Isaiah understood, there can be no redemption for man unless he conquers self-deification. He must abandon the worship of his own creations, and liberate himself from his lust for power, avarice, domination, and the cult of the state. There can be no redemption until man recognizes his moral obligations as transcendent and divine.

No form of government, no level of material well-being, will save man. He will be redeemed only when 'towers fall, and Jerusalem triumphs over Babylon.' What is at stake, finally, is not only intelligence, but feeling. Man has to change his heart. Salvation, the prophets tell us, is preconditioned by repentance. The redeeming act of God waits upon Israel's initiative." (Abba Eban, "My People: The Story of The Jews," p. 59-60).

Baptism serves a number of purposes:
1) We are baptized to demonstrate our obedience, and 2) to follow in the footsteps of the Savior. 3) We are baptized to fulfill all righteousness. 4) Baptism allows us to receive a remission of our sins if we have reached the age of accountability. 5) Baptism enables us to gain admission to the Lord's church, "the only true and living church upon the face of the whole earth" with which He is pleased. (D&C 1:31).6) Baptism provides us with the opportunity to be personally sanctified through fire and the Holy Ghost. 7) It is outwardly symbolic of our re-birth, as we pass through a portal in the similitude of the grave. 8) It is the gateway ordinance leading to the blessings reserved for the faithful that are found in the other ordinances of the gospel, and 9) it sets us squarely on the path that leads to the Celestial Kingdom of God.

(The) Book of Mormon as History

"Remember the things that ye have observed concerning this people; and ... go to the land Antum, unto a hill which shall be called Shim; and there have I deposited unto the Lord all the sacred engravings concerning this people. And behold, ye shall take the plates of Nephi unto yourself, and the remainder ye shall leave in the place where they are; and ye shall engrave upon the plates of Nephi all the things that ye have observed concerning this people."

Cicero wrote: "The first law for the historian is that he shall never dare utter an untruth. The second is that he shall suppress nothing that is true. Moreover, there shall be no suspicion of partiality or of malice in his writing." The accounts abridged by Mormon were true to the mandate given by Cicero. Although, as Washington Irving brooded, it is the rule that "history fades into fable; fact becomes clouded with doubt and controversy; the inscription moulders from the tablet; the statue falls from the pedestal," and that "columns, arches, pyramids are but heaps of sand, and their epitaphs, nothing but characters written in the dust," yet The Book of Mormon stands as a shining example of the divine model.

Truly, it "is the witness that testifies to the passing of time; it illumines reality, vitalizes memory, provides guidance in daily life, and brings us tidings of antiquity." It is "the evidence of time, the light of truth, the life of memory, the directress of life, the herald of antiquity, committed to immortality." (Cicero, "De Oratore," ii, 36). In its pages, "the centuries roll back to the ancient age of gold." (Horace, "Odes," IV, ii, 39)

To read The Book of Mormon is to embark upon an incredible journey through thousands of years of history, as the pages of a most profound text unfold before the panorama of great civilizations. Within its pages lie the intrigue of ancient Asia, as warlords battle for supremacy, the tension in Jerusalem as rival empires of the Near East struggle for power, the thrill of those whose eyes were fixed on a Land of Promise beyond the horizon of their vision, and the exhilaration of prophets of God counseling all mankind. Those who truly appreciate it will feast upon the word of God and devour this book as if it were literally the bread of life. They will seek, and yearn, and strive, and wrestle for their blessing, for "unto some it is given by the Holy Ghost to know that Jesus Christ is the Son of God, and that he was crucified for the sins of the world. To others it is given ... the word of knowledge." (D&C 46:13 & 18).

The Book of Mormon makes the bold claim that its pages contain "the fulness of the gospel." (D&C 42:12). Even members of The Church of Jesus Christ of Latter-day Saints sometimes misinterpret this. It does not mean that there will be found on its pages detailed instruction regarding every doctrinal principle, nor does it mean that the Nephites participated in every ordinance of the gospel as we know it. Today, we live in the Dispensation of The Fulness of Times, when all that has been revealed throughout the ages will be given. The members of the church in Book of Mormon times were given knowledge sufficient for their own salvation. More properly, this is the context in which the definition "the fulness of the gospel" makes sense.

The Title Page of The Book of Mormon is an overview of its history, and was written by the Prophet Mormon, who inserted it into the last leaf of the collection of plates. (See H.C., 1:71). It was then translated by Joseph Smith and included by him in The Book of Mormon. The Title Page explains that The Book of Mormon was written for doubters, "to the convincing of the Jew and Gentile" that Jesus is The Christ. It also makes the astounding admission that there might be mistakes included therein. These mistakes, however, refer to faults other than theology. Joseph Smith assured the Saints that "The Book of Mormon (is) the most correct of any book on earth, and the keystone of our religion, and a man (will) get nearer to God by abiding by its precepts, than by any other book." (H.C., 4:461).

Joseph Smith translated The Book of Mormon in around six weeks, between April 7, 1829, and the first week of June 1829. The translation was unlike that of any other text, because it was accomplished "through the mercy (and) power of God." (D&C 1:29). This is as specific an explanation as is found regarding just how Joseph Smith translated the plates and recorded a thousand years of history without editorial revision.

During his lifetime, he tended to let the record speak for itself. It was appropriate that he do so, because when one understands the revelatory process, the reader is drawn to the book itself rather than to any specific means of translation. Without distraction, then, one can focus on the challenge left by Moroni, for what other book of religious history suggests this test of authenticity: "And when ye shall receive these things, I would exhort you that ye would ask God, the eternal Father, in the name of Christ, if these things are not true; and if ye shall ask with a sincere heart, with real intent, having faith in Christ, he will manifest the truth of it unto you, by the power of the Holy Ghost." (Moroni 10:4). Such a wonderful promise cannot be taken lightly.

Jesus Christ Himself testified that The Book of Mormon is a historically and doctrinally accurate record. Joseph Smith "translated the book, even that part which I have commanded him, and as your Lord and your God liveth it is true." (D&C 17:6). It is interesting that the Savior used an ancient Hebrew oath in His witness. As Paul said, "because he could swear by no greater, he sware by himself." (Hebrews 6:13).

Sometimes, those who are learning about the restoration of the gospel ask why the church does not still have the plates from which the Nephite history was translated. The question is innocent enough. But as Hugh Nibley pointed out: "The presence of the plates would only prove that there are plates, and no more. It would not prove that Nephites wrote them, or that an angel brought them, or that they had been translated by the gift and power of God. A far more impressive claim is put forth when the whole work is given to the world as a divinely inspired translation." ("An Approach to The Book of Mormon," p. 17-18).

Thus, The Book of Mormon has always stood on its own merits, without significant editorial revision or modification over the years. Contrast this with the confusion that is intrinsic to biblical scholarship. For example, "There are so many Greek New Testament manuscripts (over 5,000) that effective management and citation of them in a critical text amounts to a highly selective and careful genealogical classification into families, so that over 150,000 variant readings can be grouped and profiled in a useful way. Also, the American Bible Society has counted over 24,000 differences among only six separate pre-1830 editions of the 1611 King James Version of the Bible." ("FARMS Report").

Today, there is remarkable unity in the church regarding the historical and religious dogma embedded within The Book of Mormon. Every day throughout the world, millions of Latter-day Saints open their translations of this scripture and explore the same doctrinal themes. Contrast this unity of the faith with the thousands of denominations who interpret with significant differences hundreds of variants of single biblical verses of scripture. It is far better for the church to proclaim that The Book of Mormon has been translated by the gift and power of God through the Prophet Joseph Smith. This leaves little room for doctrinal interpretation either within or outside the church.

Joseph Smith is listed in the first edition as the "author and proprietor" of the book. Consequently, enemies of the church have claimed that he wrote the book, but the truth is simply that in accordance with the copyright laws of the State of New York, an individual had to be listed as author and proprietor of a text, and Joseph Smith was the logical choice.

Elder Bruce R. McConkie wrote the Introduction in the 1978 edition of The Book of Mormon. Paragraph two invites misunderstanding, because Lamanites are identified as the "principal" ancestors of the American Indians. Current archaeological and anthropological research suggests that the civilizations whose histories are recorded in The Book of Mormon actually lived in rather narrowly defined geographical areas within Meso-America. Certainly, there are many Native Americans today who could trace their lineage to the indigenous peoples who co-inhabited the Americas with Nephites, Lamanites, and "Mulekites" two thousand years ago. (The earlier Jaredite civilization was eliminated through warfare, although Jaredite names are occasionally found among the Nephites).

Just how important is it for us to read, understand, and apply the principles contained in a book that was heralded by heavenly angels? Joseph Fielding Smith, Jr. stated that "no member of this church can stand approved in the presence of God who has not seriously and carefully read The Book of Mormon." (C.R., 10/1961). It may be impossible to be valiant in the testimony of Jesus without the witness of His Divinity gained through a study of The Book of Mormon. Often, we marvel at the care with which the foundation was laid for the restoration of the gospel and the translation and publication of The Book of Mormon. Sometimes, however, we are guilty of carelessness in the diligence with which we then study its pages. We all need to sharpen our scholarship.

We left our heavenly home with the assurance from our Father that, while on earth, we would have the Light of Christ and the influence of the Holy Ghost, and that heavenly power would help us to recognize the truth when we heard it. As Brigham Young declared: "Every gospel principle carries within it a witness that it is true." Joseph Fielding Smith, Jr. said on one occasion that the witness of the Holy Ghost is more powerful than a vision or the manifestation of heavenly messengers. Since he was at that time a Prophet, Seer, and Revelator, he was in a position to know.

This concept is one of the beautiful simplicities of the gospel. Heavenly Father organized our mortal experience so that all His children can enjoy the same access to the simplest, and yet most powerful, witness to the truth. In gentleness and in an inarticulate voice softer than the faintest whisper of sweet breath on the cheek, the Holy Ghost testifies, or bears witness, of truth. As Moroni 10:5 teaches (and this is a verse that is often overlooked when one is memorizing only the fourth verse): "By the power of the Holy Ghost ye may know the truth of all things."

The Holy Ghost has revealed all that is true and every eternal principle that has ever guided mankind since the dawn of history. Humanity constantly benefits from that which He reveals. In the Last Days, when the Spirit is "poured out upon all flesh," and when "young men see visions, and old men dream dreams," it will be the Holy Ghost Who provides the creative drive. (Joel 2:28). The irony is that many will fail to recognize the source of their inspiration.

Of course, Jesus Christ wants us to believe The Book of Mormon to be the word of God. It has come to us through thousands of years of effort on the part of ancient prophets and the personal sacrifice of countless individuals. The prophet Isaiah foresaw a "marvelous work and a wonder" that would not come to pass for 2,700 years (Isaiah 29:14), and in the apocalyptic vision of John, another angel was seen "in the midst of heaven, having the everlasting gospel to preach unto them that dwell on the earth, and to every nation, and kindred, and tongue, and people." (Revelation 14:6).

Precisely because The Book of Mormon is far more than just history, because it is another testament, or second witness, of Jesus Christ, missionaries use it to great effect as a principal tool of conversion. The organization of the book is divinely inspired to bring to pass the immortality and eternal life of man by teaching the principles of faith, repentance, baptism, and the ordinances of the priesthood. (See Moses 1:39). There was method to his madness when Mormon abridged the records with which Ammaron had entrusted him.

Anyone who desires to have a sure personal witness needs to carefully and prayerfully read The Book of Mormon, and then to ask in faith if it is true. They will then receive the testimony of the Holy Ghost, which will motivate them to seek out the Priesthood and to enter into sacred covenants with God.

Important, then, to comprehension of the monumental themes contained in The Book of Mormon is familiarity with the underlying structure of the text. It is not too difficult to understand, as long as one remembers that Mormon was the prophet who gathered all the records together, and who then abridged certain of these into the Plates of Mormon. (See Mormon 1:1). This is the main reason why the text is called The Book of Mormon. In a larger sense, though, it is not really his book alone.

The scope of its 531 pages is far-reaching, and its literary style is designed to focus the reader on the core material rather than on the various authors. It is remarkable, though, that 15 major writing styles and personalities survived both abridgment and translation. The working vocabulary of 1 Nephi alone has 23% more words than comparable Old Testament sections, and although there are only 2,696 root words, which is 10% of Shakespeare's working vocabulary, its depth is breathtaking.

Mormon said that he could not write "the hundredth part of the things of (his) people." (Words of Mormon 1:5). Even though Joseph wrote in his history that the plates on the Hill Cumorah were deposited in the earth in a box fashioned out of stone, other sources indicate that there were many more plates at that site. Brigham Young said that there was a whole room, with plates stacked high against the walls. Together, he said that they would comprise several wagon loads.

What we do have swells in significance when we realize that the fraction of the record that was included in the book is a condensation comprising that which was of most importance to Mormon. High Nibley rightly called the book a blueprint for survival in the Last Days. He said that "the events and situations that not many years ago seemed wildly improbable to some, and greatly overdrawn, have suddenly become the story of our times, and we see and shall see the words of the prophets who speak to us from the dust fearfully and wonderfully vindicated." ("The World and The Prophets," p. 196).

Nephi started writing 30 years after leaving Jerusalem, which might give solace to those of us who have trouble maintaining our own personal journals. He had plenty of time to distill in his mind just what he would include and how he would do it. He also wrote from the perspective of middle age, which might have been an advantage. Hindsight is always 20 / 20.

First, he abridged the writings of his father, that were collectively called The Book of Lehi, and then he made his own carefully constructed record. It took Nephi 10 years just to write the first 25 chapters, possibly because he wrote in a very stylized Hebraic pattern. The first nine chapters of 1 Nephi comprise a complex chiasm. Then, in chapters 10-22 he worked out a second, parallel chiasm. Note that chapter 9 and chapter 22 each end with a formal "Amen," signifying the end of a distinct literary process.

The Small Plates of Nephi in their entirety include The First Book of Nephi, The Second Book of Nephi, The Book of Jacob, The Book of Enos, The Book of Jarom, The Book of Omni, and The Words of Mormon. These plates were placed in the repository at Cumorah for a reason that was not clear to Mormon. Small Plates included a duplication of The Book of Lehi, an abridgement of which was written on The Large Plates of Nephi. The reason for their preservation became clear when Martin Harris lost the initial 116 pages of manuscript translation, forcing Joseph Smith to turn to The Small Plates of Nephi in order to translate a parallel history of the early Nephite record.

The Small Plates of Nephi are always called "these plates" in the text. They were translated in the first-person tense, inasmuch as they came, not from an abridgement, but directly from the record of Nephi and his descendants. The period of history covered by these plates is slightly less than half of the Nephite history, or 470 years out of a total of 1,021 years.

The Words of Mormon is an editorial insert placed in the record by Mormon. This short book helps to bridge the gap between The Small Plates of Nephi and The Plates of Mormon (his abridgement of The Large Plates of Nephi) that follow.

The literary labor of Mormon, called The Plates of Mormon, comprises The Books of Mosiah, Alma and Helaman, Third Nephi - The Book of Nephi, Fourth Nephi - The Book of Nephi, and The Book of Mormon chapters 1-7. These records were abridged onto The Plates of Mormon from The Large Plates of Nephi. When reading from the translation of The Plates of Mormon, the text is generally in the third person tense, inasmuch as it is an abridgement. When Mormon inserted editorial comments throughout his abridgement, however, it was written in the first-person tense. When reading 1 Nephi through Omni, "those plates" means The Large Plates of Nephi, which follow The Words of Mormon in our text of The Book of Mormon.

The Plates of Mormon also included writings of Mormon's son Moroni. These writings are found in The Book of Mormon chapters 8 & 9, and in The Book of Moroni.

The Book of Ether was written upon 24 gold plates found by the people of King Limhi in the days of King Mosiah. At least a portion of these plates were abridged by Moroni, either from Mosiah's earlier translation, or directly from the Plates of Ether. Moroni inserted editorial comments of his own, and included this record with the general history, under the title The Book of Ether.

Lehi's sons retrieved the Plates of Brass from Jerusalem at great expense and personal risk. They contained "the five books of Moses (or the first five books of the Old Testament), and also a record of the Jews from the beginning down to the commencement of the reign of Zedekiah, king of Judah; and also, the prophecies of the holy prophets." (1 Nephi 5:11-13). Consequently, the Plates of Brass included the writings of Isaiah. From both a historical and religious perspective, it is interesting to compare the writings of Isaiah in the Bible and The Book of Mormon.

"The version of Isaiah in the Nephite scripture hews an independent course for itself, as might be expected of a truly ancient and authentic record. It makes additions to the present text in certain places, omits material in others, transposes, makes grammatical changes, finds support at times for its unusual readings in the ancient Greek,

Syriac, and Latin Versions, and at other times no support at all. In general, it presents phenomena of great interest to the student of Isaiah." ("Book of Mormon Compendium," p. 512).

"The text of Isaiah in The Book of Mormon is not word for word the same as that of the King James Translation. Of 433 verses of Isaiah in the Nephite record, Joseph Smith modified 234. Some of the changes were slight, while others were radical. However, 199 verses are word for word the same as the K.J.T. We, therefore, freely admit that Joseph Smith may have used the K.J.T. when he came to the text of Isaiah on the gold plates. As long as the K.J.T. agreed substantially with the text on the gold plates, he let it pass; when it differed too radically, he translated the Nephite version and dictated the necessary changes." ("Book of Mormon Compendium," p. 507-508).

As Hugh Nibley has pointed out, "Resemblances between the Bible and The Book of Mormon are not hard to explain. Far from being evidence of fraud, they are rather confirmation of authenticity. If The Book of Mormon is what it pretends to be, we should expect to find a strong biblical influence in it. Its prophets sound like those of the Old Testament because they studied and consciously quoted the words of those prophets, and all prophets moreover are programmed to sound alike, being called for the same purpose under much the same conditions." ("Churches in The Wilderness").

The Plates of Brass were the Nephite scriptures and included the written record of their family histories and genealogies. That the Nephites revered them is evidenced by frequent quotations from and references to them throughout The Book of Mormon. As Nephi explained: "And I did read many things unto them which were written in the books of Moses; but that I might more fully persuade them to believe in the Lord their Redeemer I did read unto them that which was written by the prophet Isaiah; for I did liken all scriptures unto us, that it might be for our profit and learning." (1 Nephi 1:23).

The "books of Moses" referred to in 1 Nephi 19:23 concern the Pentateuch, Torah, or The Law. These are not to be confused with The Book of Moses in The Pearl of Great Price. Nephi's books of Moses were the principal scriptures of the Jews. From these books of The Law sprang an encyclopedic interpretation by the Jews at Jerusalem called the Talmud.

Readers of The Book of Mormon will repeatedly encounter direct references to Isaiah in the text. As a matter of fact, 32% of The Book of Isaiah is quoted in The Book of Mormon, while 3% is paraphrased. The New Testament follows the pattern established earlier in The Book of Mormon, for in that text there are more quotations attributable to Isaiah than to all other Old Testament prophets combined. It is little wonder then, that The Book of Mormon, which not only reflects Old World religious philosophy, but which also is a Latter-day Testament of Jesus Christ, should rely so heavily on this prophet.

Nephi delighted in the words of Isaiah, which proved the truth of Christ's coming and that save He should come, all men must perish. The writings of Isaiah that are recorded in 2 Nephi chapters 12-24 are illustrations of Nephi's efforts to do just that. Isaiah was what we call a "Messianic Prophet." His mission was principally to point us toward the Savior, His teachings, and to salvation that only comes through obedience to the principles of His gospel.

Nephi knew that the words of Isaiah would be a pearl of great price, particularly to Israel in the Last Days. He wrote: "In that day shall they understand them; wherefore, for their good have I written them." (2 Nephi 25:8). He considered the writings of Isaiah, who had lived just over a century earlier, to be Holy Scripture. Clearly, Nephi understood that whatsoever the prophets "shall speak when moved upon by the Holy Ghost shall be scripture, shall be the will of the Lord, shall be the mind of the Lord, shall be the word of the Lord, shall be the voice of the Lord, and the power of God unto salvation." (D&C 68:4).

Today, it is the clear responsibility of Covenant Israel to carefully study the prophecies of Isaiah, for he spoke to our generation. His language might be veiled in symbolism and shadows of meaning with which we are not superficially familiar; nevertheless, we have been commanded by the Savior Himself to "seek ye out of the best books words of wisdom; seek learning, even by study and also by faith." (D&C 88:118). "For you shall live by every word that proceedeth forth from the mouth of God." (D&C 84:44).

Nephi recognized Isaiah's witness of the Lord Jesus Christ to be pre-eminent among the testimonies of the prophets. It should be no surprise that the Savior Himself declared to the Nephite Saints: "And now, behold, I say unto you, that ye ought to search his teachings. Yea, a commandment I give unto you that ye search these things diligently; for great are the words of Isaiah." (3 Nephi 23:1).

The main reason for the scriptures, after all, is to persuade men to believe in Christ. This is why the prophets seem to sound alike. They all draw upon the same eternal truths to prove their points. Theirs is not vain repetition, but rather theatrical encore. "The prophets do have much the same message, and the now recognized practice of the prophets of giving out the words of their predecessors as their own receives its first clear statement and justification in The Book of Mormon." (Hugh Nibley). Shakespeare put it this way: "The past is prologue." ("The Tempest," Act 2, scene 1, 245). He intended to imply that our past is merely a prologue, or an introduction, to the great adventure upon which we will embark if we follow through on our plans. This original interpretation teaches us that what has come before on our journey through life doesn't matter in the grand scheme of things, because a new future lies before us, subject to the choices that we will yet make. That is to say, that which has transpired in the past is merely a foreshadowing of what is to come. The human condition does not change that much over the millennia. That is one reason why the Lord has revealed The Book of Mormon in the Last Days, that we might learn and profit from the Nephites, who are so distant in time and yet whose experiences were so similar to our own.

Nibley observed: "The tragedy of the Nephites, who brought destruction by war upon their own heads, was not what became of them, but rather what they themselves became." ("Since Cumorah," p. 425). "A man's character is his fate," wrote the Greek philosopher Heraclitus. In the scriptures, we can study human frailties within a historically accurate matrix, and in so doing we strengthen and clarify our moral and ethical values as the epic drama unfolds before our mind's eye.

In The Book of Mormon, "we are not laying down ground rules for taste, or saying that (it) is good because some people like it, or bad because others do not. What we are saying is that The Book of Mormon, whatever one may think of it, is one of the great realities of our time, and that what makes it so is that (millions of) people believe it. Its literary or artistic qualities do not enter into the discussion. It was written to be believed." It is true that its history is wonderfully symmetrical with a larger worldview, but that is incidental. "It's one and only merit is truth. Without that merit, it is all that non-believers say it is. With it, it is all that believers say it is." (Hugh Nibley, "Of All Things," p. 93).

But enough of historical perspective. Too often we spend more time in preparation for the journey than we do in the travel itself. Let us not make that mistake. Let us commit and re-commit ourselves to a lifetime of study of this keystone text.

In physical terms, before a wound can heal, it has to be clean. Anyone who has had a physician vigorously scrub out a wound knows how carefully and thoroughly the task must be accomplished before a sterile dressing may be applied to allow the healing process to begin. The same principle applies to the development of our character. There is no room for dry rot when building character, and nobility has no skeletons lurking in the closet.

Book of Mormon Strengths

"For the time cometh,
saith the Lamb of God, that I will
work a great and a marvelous work
among the children of men."
(1 Nephi 14:7).

The Book of Mormon is a blueprint for our survival in The Last Days. With this blueprint, under the direction of the Spirit, we can become the architects of our own fate and the masters of our destiny. We can be as "children coming down like gentle rain through darkened skies, with glory trailing from their feet as they go, and endless promise in their eyes. Strangers from a realm of light, who have forgotten all - the memory of their former life and the purpose of their call. And so, they must learn why they're here, and who they really are." (From "Saturday's Warrior," lyrics by Doug Stewart).

The Book of Mormon allowed the Restoration to move forward and the church to be organized. It gave us the gift of a fifth Gospel (3 Nephi) that summarizes Christ's ministry in the New World. It fulfilled the prophecies of Ezekiel and Isaiah. It empowered church members to stand out prominently among their Christian neighbors, and it endowed them with an element of singularity that distinguishes them from other Christian denominations, allowing the line in the sand separating the faithful from the world to be more clearly defined.

Because of The Book of Mormon, those who make their home in Idumea are differentiated from those who embrace the gospel. It gives us symmetry, balance, harmony, clarity, focus, and purpose, we have stories of inspiration that touch us personally and individually, and we have truth in its untarnished majesty that may be proclaimed to the world, while the Holy Ghost is unrestrained as the lives of millions are touched by invention and innovation whose catalyst is the Spirit.

Because of The Book of Mormon, we have a Second Witness of Christ, we learn to rely on Him not only as our protector but also as the generator of life itself, we have a standard by which we can judge the Bible, we have a weapon more powerful than military might, we have clear definitions of authority, the essential ordinance of baptism is re-defined, the army of God is equipped with superior firepower as it teaches the nations, from a unique perspective the missionaries confidently and strategically preach the gospel, and we can draw upon the life experiences of others and learn life-lessons from their similar challenges.

Because of The Book of Mormon, we have mentors, and we can understand the mysteries, the saving principles and ordinances of the gospel. With its profound spiritual insight, we can know who we are. Because we learn that we are accountable, we are not held hostage by guilt, but instead feel the sweet miracle of forgiveness. It guides us to refuge at the horns of sanctuary in a violent world, and shows us how to be born again. It gives us the confidence to feel the continuing mercies of God, find our way home, and obtain God's Rest.

It is intriguing to ask ourselves; "What would the face of the Restoration have been without The Book of Mormon?

Without The Book of Mormon, the church could not have been organized.

So important is The Book of Mormon, that The Church of Jesus Christ of Latter-day Saints was organized only after its publication. Fully ten years earlier, Joseph Smith had communed with The Father and The Son in the Sacred Grove. Three years later, he received several visits from the Angel Moroni. Between 1823 and 1830, he became personally acquainted with all of the important characters in The Book of Mormon, and enjoyed additional visits from Moroni. Still, so important was The Book of Mormon to the Restoration of the gospel, that the church could not be organized until it was hot off the press.

Without The Book of Mormon record, Christ could not have fulfilled, completely, His promise to feed His other sheep.

"Other sheep I have, which are not of this fold," He said. "Them also I must bring, and they shall hear my voice; and there shall be one fold, and one shepherd." (John 10:16).

"And if ye shall believe in Christ ye will believe in these words, for they are the words of Christ, and he hath given them unto me; and they teach all men that they should do good. And if they are not the words of Christ, judge ye - for Christ will show unto you, with power and great glory, that they are his words, at the last day; and you and I shall stand face to face before his bar; and ye shall know that I have been commanded of him to write these things." (2 Nephi 33:10-11).

Without The Book of Mormon, prophecy would not have been fulfilled.

The words of Christ were to be made known in The Book of Mormon, as well as in the Bible," and they were to be "established in one." (1 Nephi 13:41). As Ezekiel wrote: "Take thee one stick, and write upon it, For Judah, and for the children of Israel his companions: then take another stick, and write upon it, For Joseph, the stick of Ephraim, and for all the house of Israel his companions. And join them one to another into one stick; and they shall become one in thine hand." (Ezekiel 37:16-17).

2,500 years before Joseph's visit by Moroni, Isaiah prophesied of the Lord's ministry: "I will proceed to do a marvellous work among this people, even a marvellous work and a wonder." (Isaiah 29:14). And so, He did with the translation, publication, and distribution of The Book of Mormon.

Without The Book of Mormon, church members would stand out far less prominently as Christians.

The great Book of Mormon prophet Benjamin exhorted us: "I would that ye should take upon you the name of Christ, all you that have entered into the covenant with God that ye should be obedient unto the end of your lives. And it shall come to pass that whosoever doeth this shall be found at the right hand of God, for he shall know the name by which he is called; for he shall be called by the name of Christ." (Mosiah 5:8-10).

Without The Book of Mormon, the church would lose much of its prominence and singularity.

"Take away The Book of Mormon and the revelations, and where is our religion? We have none." (Joseph Smith, "Teachings," p. 71). The Book of Mormon sets us apart as a peculiar people. To be peculiar in a biblical sense is to be "one's very own, exclusive, or special." ("Bible Dictionary"). Moroni told Joseph Smith: "Wherever the sound (of the Restoration) shall go it shall cause the ears of men to tingle, and wherever it shall be proclaimed, the pure in heart shall rejoice." ("Joseph Smith & The Restoration," p. 14).

Without The Book of Mormon, the line in the sand would be far less clearly defined.

Mormon observed "that after a people have been once enlightened by the Spirit of God, and have had great knowledge of things pertaining to righteousness, and then have fallen away into sin and transgression, they become more hardened, and thus their state becomes worse than though they had never known these things." (Alma 24:30).

Joseph Fielding Smith, Jr. cautioned the Saints: "When you joined the church you enlisted to serve God. When you did that you left the neutral ground, and you can never get back on to it. Should you forsake the Master you enlisted to serve, it will be by the instigation of the evil one, and you will follow his dictation and be his servant." (C.E.S. Manual, p. 258).

Without The Book of Mormon, we would have fewer negative examples of those who embrace darkness rather than the gospel.

Mormon said of those who did not belong to the church, that they "did indulge themselves in sorceries, and in idolatry or idleness, and in babblings, and in envyings and strife, wearing costly apparel, being lifted up in the pride of their own eyes; persecuting, lying, thieving, robbing, committing whoredoms, and murdering, and all manner of wickedness." (Alma 1:32).

Without The Book of Mormon, we would have less symmetry, balance, harmony, clarity, focus, and purpose in our lives.

President Ezra Taft Benson told the Saints that if a church member does not study The Book of Mormon, "he is placing his soul in jeopardy and neglecting that which could give spiritual and intellectual unity to his whole life.

Without The Book of Mormon, we would have fewer stories of inspiration that touch us personally and individually.

From within its pages, we can almost hear Moroni's voice: "Behold, I speak unto you as if ye were present, and yet ye are not. But behold, Jesus Christ hath shown you unto me, and I know your doing." (Mormon 8:35).

Without The Book of Mormon, there would be less truth in the world.

The Book of Mormon "was written to be believed. Its one and only merit is truth. Without that merit, it is all that nonbelievers say it is. With it, it is all that believers say it is." (Hugh Nibley. "Of All Things," p. 93).

Although it is the rule, as Washington Irving observed, that "history fades into fable; fact becomes clouded with doubt and controversy; the inscription moulders from the tablet; the statue falls from the pedestal," and that "columns, arches, pyramids are but heaps of sand, and their epitaphs, nothing but characters written in the dust," yet The Book of Mormon stands as a shining example of the divine model.

Without The Book of Mormon, we would miss, terribly, its witness of many other truths.

The Book of Mormon "illumines reality, vitalizes memory, provides guidance in daily life, and brings us tidings of antiquity." It is "the evidence of time, the light of truth, the life of memory, the directress of life, the herald of antiquity, committed to immortality." (Cicero, "De Oratore," ii, 36). In its pages, "the centuries roll back to the ancient age of gold." (Horace, "Odes," IV, ii, 39).

Without The Book of Mormon, we would lack a Second Testament and perhaps the best witness of Jesus Christ.

"For behold, (The Book of Mormon) is written for the intent that ye may believe (the Bible); and if ye believe (the Bible) ye will believe (The Book of Mormon) also; and if ye believe (The Book of Mormon) ye will know concerning your fathers, and also the marvelous works which were wrought by the power of God among them." (Mormon 7:9).

Without The Book of Mormon, we would have fewer opportunities to learn how to rely on the Savior.

"No man of himself can lift himself to celestial glory. Our growth depends on the light of Christ, guidance of the Holy Ghost, and the power of the priesthood that is given us by God and his Son. The religion of Jesus Christ is not just a philosophy of life; it is the generator of life. If you go it alone, you cannot succeed. If you receive His power, you will increase and make it. There is no other way." ("Sunday School Course Manual").

Without The Book of Mormon, we would not have a standard by which to judge the Bible and other scriptures.

For example, we would not have the Lord's teachings to the Nephites that are similar to His Sermon on The Mount, and we would lack the powerful recitations of Isaiah and of Malachi that are reiterated in its pages. In fact, "The Book of Mormon is the keystone of our religion and the most correct book ever written, and a man can draw nearer to God by abiding by its precepts than any other book." (Joseph Smith).

Without The Book of Mormon, to what other body of scripture would we turn to emphasize the powerful premise that the pen is mightier than the sword?

President Benson said: "I urge you to recommit yourselves to a study of the scriptures. If you do so, you will find, as Alma did, (Alma 31:5) that 'the word (has) a great tendency to lead the people to do that which is just - yea, it (has) more powerful effect upon the minds of the people than the sword, or anything else which (has) happened to them." (C.R., 4/1986).

Without The Book of Mormon, where could we learn so clearly that one must have authority to administer the ordinances of the gospel?

Alma and his sons "preached the word, and the truth, according to the spirit of prophecy and revelation; and they preached after the holy order of God by which they were called." (Alma 43:2). If all churches were equal, then the true church would not exist anywhere. If, in education, any program were the equal of any other, then receiving any degree would be based upon an indiscriminate course of study that would qualify the recipient in all fields of study. But this is contrary to the order of God.

Without The Book of Mormon there would be confusion regarding the ordinance of baptism.

"The first fruits of repentance is baptism; and baptism cometh by faith unto the fulfilling the commandments; and the fulfilling the commandments bringeth remission of sins; and the remission of sins bringeth meekness, and lowliness of heart; and because of meekness and lowliness of heart cometh the visitation of the Holy Ghost, which

Comforter filleth with hope and perfect love, which love endureth by diligence unto prayer, until the end shall come, when all the saints shall dwell with God." (Moroni 8:25-26).

Without The Book of Mormon, the soldiers in the army of Christ could not so easily teach with power.

Mormon explained that The Sons of Mosiah "had given themselves to much prayer, and fasting; therefore, they had the spirit of prophecy, and the spirit of revelation, and when they taught, they taught with the power and authority of God." (Alma 17:3).

"God help all honest men," said Marion G. Romney, "to be born again and come to be of sound understanding and to know the word of God and maintain the spirit thereof by study, fasting, prayer, and work, that we may be blessed with His power and authority!" (C.R., 10/1941).

Without The Book of Mormon, we might well lack the confidence to proclaim the gospel.

Through Isaiah, the Lord said: "Then shall ye, who are a remnant of the house of Jacob, go forth among (the nations); and ye shall be in the midst of them who shall be many; and ye shall be among them as a lion among the beasts of the forest, and as a young lion among the flocks of sheep, who, if he goeth through both treadeth down and teareth in pieces, and none can deliver." (3 Nephi 20:16).

This mighty missionary army will be "clear as the moon, and fair as the sun, and terrible as an army with banners." (D&C 5:14). "The nations of the earth shall tremble because of her, and shall fear because of her terrible ones." (D&C 64:43). "And it shall be said among the wicked: Let us not go up to battle against Zion, for the inhabitants of Zion are terrible; wherefore we cannot stand." (D&C 45:70). "Fear may seize upon them, and they shall stand afar off and tremble. And all nations shall be afraid because of the terror of the Lord, and the power of his might." (D&C 45:74-75).

Without The Book of Mormon, we would know nothing of the life experiences of so many others of God's children who are much like ourselves.

"Behold, this is a choice land, and whatsoever nation shall possess it shall be free from bondage, and from captivity, and from all other nations under heaven if they will but serve the God of the land, who is Jesus Christ." (Ether 2:12). We would probably not know that "happiness is the object and design of our existence, and will be the end thereof, if we follow the path that leads to it, and this consists of faith, virtue, uprightness, and keeping all the commandments of God." (Joseph Smith).

Without The Book of Mormon, to whom would we turn for mentors?

"Yea, verily, verily I say unto you, if all men had been, and were, and ever would be, like unto Moroni, behold, the very powers of hell would have been shaken forever; yea, the devil would never have power over the hearts of the children of men." (Alma 48:17). We would never have known men like Nephi, Jacob, Benjamin, Alma, The Sons of Mosiah, Abinadi, Helaman, and Samuel the Lamanite. We would miss the anticipation of striking hands with them when we meet at the pleasing bar of Christ.

Without The Book of Mormon, there would be a conspicuously empty space on the bookshelf of time, instead of a prominently displayed chronicle written especially for our age.

Hugh Nibley observed: "It is an exciting thing to discover that the man Lehi was a real historical character ... but it is far more important and significant to find oneself in this (Twenty-First) Century standing as it were in his very shoes." ("The World and The Prophets," p. 196).

Without The Book of Mormon, we would less effectively cope with the mysteries of God.

These mysteries are the saving principles and ordinances of the gospel, received by the faithful only through personal revelation. They are sacred. "It is given unto many to know the mysteries of God; nevertheless, they are laid under a strict command that they shall not impart only according to the portion of his word which he doth grant unto the children of men, according to the need and diligence which they give unto him." (Alma 12:9). In other words, the faithful can benefit from spiritual insight while at the same time guarding pearls that might otherwise be cast before swine. (Matthew 7:6).

King Benjamin's discourse in the Book of Mosiah is a classic example of a General Conference type of address wherein the saving principles were unfolded to the membership of the church. When we read his words, faithfully recorded verbatim by Mormon, it is clear that he was concerned that his people might trifle with the words that he should speak. He recognized the serious nature of his topic, and wanted them to hearken to him or pay strict attention, and to open their ears to listen carefully, and their hearts to feel the Spirit of his message, and their minds to understand. (Mosiah 2:9).

This episode is one of many that illustrate how the mysteries of God may be unfolded to our view. We have the testimony of Christ Himself that The Book of Mormon contains a comprehensive body of doctrine, "even the fullness of (the) everlasting gospel." (D&C 27:5).

Armed with these scriptures, the Lord told Joseph Smith and Sydney Rigdon: "The time has verily come that it is necessary and expedient in me that you should open your mouths in proclaiming my gospel, the things of the kingdom, expounding the mysteries thereof out of the scriptures according to that portion of the Spirit and power which shall be given unto you." (D&C 71:1). Joseph described his subsequent experience in these words: "Our minds being now enlightened, we began to have the scriptures laid open to our understandings, and the true meaning and intention of their more mysterious passages revealed unto us in a manner which we never could attain to previously, nor ever before had thought of." (J.S.H. 1:74).

To the faithful, the Lord promised: "I will reveal all mysteries, yea, all the hidden mysteries of my kingdom from days of old, and for ages to come." (D&C 76:7). Nevertheless, there were certain points of doctrine that are not yet clear. To his son, Alma declared: "Now these mysteries are not yet fully made known unto me; therefore, I shall forbear." (Alma 37:11). He felt that it was always better to keep one's opinion to oneself, rather than to speculate without the foundation of fact or specific revelation. Sometimes it is better to remain silent and be thought a fool, rather than to speak and remove all doubt.

Without The Book of Mormon, we would know far less about the purpose of life.

"And now, I would commend you to seek this Jesus of whom the prophets and apostles have written, that the grace of God the Father, and also the Lord Jesus Christ, and the Holy Ghost, which beareth record of them, may be and abide in you forever." (Moroni, Ether 12:41). Because of this book, we know that "Adam fell that men might be, and men are, that they might have joy," (2 Nephi 2:25), that "wickedness never was happiness," (Alma 41:10), that we must "hold fast to the iron rod." (1 Nephi 8:30). We are counseled: "Watch yourselves, and your thoughts, and your words, and your deeds…" (Mosiah 4:30). But we also know: "By the power of the Holy Ghost, (we) may know the truth of all things," (Moroni 10:5), and that "when (we) are in the service of (our) fellow beings, (we) are only in the service of (our) God." (Mosiah 2:17).

Without The Book of Mormon, personal accountability would receive far less emphasis.

It teaches: "Men are free according to the flesh, and all things are given them which are expedient unto men. And they are free to choose liberty and eternal life, through the great Mediator of all men, or to choose captivity and death, according to the captivity and power of the devil." (2 Nephi 2:27)

Without The Book of Mormon, guilt would hold our future hostage.

"Do ye suppose that ye shall dwell with (God) under a consciousness of your guilt?" asked Moroni. "Do ye suppose that ye could be happy to dwell with that holy Being, when your souls are racked with a consciousness of guilt that ye have ever abused his laws?" (Mormon 9:3).

Without The Book of Mormon, the sweet miracle of forgiveness might be less tenderly treated.

"And as oft as they repented and sought forgiveness, with real intent, they were forgiven." (Moroni 6:8)

Without The Book of Mormon, we might be less likely to find peace in a violent world.

Its gift is His peace, "not the peace of the world, of ease, of luxury, idleness, absence of turmoil, and strife, but the peace born of the righteous life, the peace that lifts the soul, that day by day brings us closer to the home of Eternal Peace, the dwelling place of our Father." (J. Reuben Clark, Jr.).

Without The Book of Mormon, we might not understand that we have been born again.

Those who enter into the Covenant "are born of him." (Mosiah 5:7). "All mankind ... must be born again, yea, born of God, changed from their carnal and fallen state, to a state of righteousness, being redeemed of God, becoming his sons and daughters." (Mosiah 27:25). A "Born Again Christian" is one who is in a covenant relationship with the Lord, and since only members of Christ's true church can do that through the authority of the priesthood, if follows that the only real Born-Again Christians are Latter-day Saints!

Without The Book of Mormon, we might not recognize the signs that confirm we have been born again.

"And now behold, I ask of you, my brethren of the church, have ye spiritually been born of God? Have ye received his image in your countenances? Have ye experienced this mighty change in your hearts?" (Alma 5:14).

Without The Book of Mormon, finding our way home would be much more difficult.

"Think of stepping on shore, and finding it heaven. Of taking hold of a hand, and finding it God's hand. Of breathing a new air, and finding it celestial air. Of feeling invigorated, and finding it immortality. Of passing from storm and tempest to the unbroken calm of God's Rest. Of waking up, and finding it Home." (Anonymous).

Without The Book of Mormon, we could not attain God's Rest.

"We live in a day and in a world full of doubts and confusion, where people do not know what to believe, where tensions are high, where the pace is frantic and progress in terms of righteousness is not a popular goal. Violence and crudity are everyday patterns all around us. What a blessing it is to know there is a haven, a place of rest from the turmoil of the world. The prophets and the Savior have called upon us to enter into the rest of the Lord, where life has purpose and direction, and where priesthood power is possible." ("Gospel Doctrine Manual," p. 79)

Without The Book of Mormon, we might never know the truth of all things.

"He that will not harden his heart," taught Alma, "to him is given the greater portion of the word, until it is given unto him to know the mysteries of God until he know them in full." (Alma 12:10).

The Book of Mormon contains a unique promise, found nowhere else in scripture. Moroni's formula is given in Moroni 10:4-5: "And when ye shall receive these things, I would exhort you that ye would ask God, the Eternal Father, in the name of Christ, if these things are not true; and if ye shall ask with a sincere heart, with real intent, having faith in Christ, he will manifest the truth of it unto you, by the power of the Holy Ghost. And by the power of the Holy Ghost ye may know the truth of all things."

Moroni firmly believed in the power of God, that it works miracles in the lives of men. He knew that the Light of Christ, sometimes called the Spirit of God or the Holy Spirit, and the Holy Ghost have been provided by God to allow religious recognition leading to conversion to take place. Therefore, he urged those in the Last Days to "deny not the gifts of God, for they are many." (Moroni 10:8). All these gifts, he said, "are given by the manifestations of the Spirit of God unto men, to profit them." (Moroni 10:8).

Without The Book of Mormon, there would be less joy in the world.

Mormon said of those living after the ministry of the Savior among the Nephites: "Behold, there never was a happier time among the people of Nephi, since the days of Nephi, than in the days of Moroni." (Alma 50:23). Our day is also a wonderful time to be alive. The millennial day approaches. "How do you prepare for the Second Coming?" asked President Gordon B. Hinckley. "Well, you just do not worry about it. You just live the kind of life that, if the Second Coming were to happen tomorrow, you would be ready. Nobody knows what is going to happen. Our responsibility is to prepare ourselves, to live worthy of the association of the Savior, to deport ourselves in such a way that we would not be embarrassed if He were to come among us." (Weber State University, Institute Devotional, 4/15/1997, see B.Y.U. Devotional, 3/25/1979).

Without The Book of Mormon, there would be less hope in the world.

"Teenagers sometimes ask: "What's the use?" said Boyd K. Packer. "The world will soon be blown all apart and come to an end." That feeling comes from fear, not from faith. No one knows the hour or the day, but the end cannot come until all of the purposes of the Lord are fulfilled. Everything that I have learned from the revelations and from life convinces me that there is time and to spare for you to carefully prepare for a long life. One day you will cope with teenage children of your own. That will serve you right. Later, you will spoil your grandchildren, and they, in turn, will spoil theirs." (Boyd K. Packer, C.R., 4/1989).

The scripture may yet be written that there never was a happier time among the children of men, than in the days of Russell M. Nelson, Dallin H. Oaks, and Henry B. Eyring.

(The) Book of Mormon Was Preserved for Our Day

"Those who shall be destroyed shall speak unto them out of the ground, and their speech shall be low out of the dust, and their voice shall be as one that hath a familiar spirit; for the Lord God will give unto him power, that he may whisper concerning them, even as it were out of the ground; and their speech shall whisper out of the dust." (2 Nephi 26:16).

Mormon saw our day, and knew our needs. He knew that The Book of Mormon would help a world in need to "repent and prepare to stand before the judgment-seat of Christ. (Mormon 3:22). He also knew The Book of Mormon would help mankind to "believe the gospel of Jesus Christ." (Mormon 3:21). As Joseph Smith stated: "I told the brethren that The Book of Mormon was the most correct of any book on earth, and the keystone of our religion, and a man would get nearer to God by abiding by its precepts, than by any other book." ("Teachings," p. 194).

The Book of Mormon itself is a sign of the times and that we are living in the Last Days before the Second Coming of the Lord. With its publication, the world may know that "the covenant which the Father hath made with the children of Israel, concerning their restoration to the lands of their inheritance, is already beginning to be fulfilled." (3 Nephi 29:1). "In the Hellenistic age, the Jews had become dispersed over the whole Greek world. As early as 140 B.C.E., the author of the Sibylline Oracles testified 'that the whole land and seas are full of Jews.' Strabo, a contemporary of Herod, says, 'It would have been difficult to find a single place in the world where there are no Jews.' And Josephus added, 'There are no people in the world among whom part of our brethren is not to be found.' Philo spoke of the 'wide expansion of the Jews throughout the world,' and of Jerusalem as 'the center of the scattered nation.'" (Abba Eban, "My People: The Story of The Jews," p. 103-104). Clearly, in the last two or three millennia, the Jews, let alone the other tribes of Israel, have become scattered throughout the populations of the earth, and when Israel is gathered into identifiable bodies in the Last Days, they will have many lands of inheritance.

The Book of Mormon "would come forth in a day when, as Mormon said: "Ye need not imagine in your hearts that the words which have been spoken are in vain." (3 Nephi 29:3). All that the prophets have spoken, particularly the Messianic and Millennial prophets, is being fulfilled in the most marvelous ways.

The Book of Mormon would come forth in a day when many in the world "spurn at the doings of the Lord." (3 Nephi 29:4). To spurn something is to "ignore scornfully, to refuse, or to trample." Since its publication, the world has tried very hard to ignore The Book of Mormon. But President Ezra Taft Benson put great emphasis on it, and cautioned that if a church member does not carefully and prayerfully study that book, he is "placing his soul in jeopardy, and neglecting that which could give spiritual and intellectual unity to his whole life." (C.R., 4 1986). His counsel could have applied equally to non-members of the church. The world, quite simply, needs The Book of Mormon. It was "written to the Lamanites, who are a remnant of the house of Israel; and also to Jew and Gentile." ("Title Page" to The Book of Mormon). It was preserved for our day, and its publication came at great personal sacrifice because the world's people need, more than anything else in their lives, spiritual and intellectual unity.

"Where will you find another work remotely approaching The Book of Mormon in scope and daring? It appears suddenly out of nothing – not an accumulation of 25 years like the Koran, but a single staggering performance, bursting on a shocked and scandalized world like an explosion, the full-blown history of an ancient people, following them through all the trials, triumphs, and vicissitudes of a thousand years without a break, telling how a civilization originated, rose to momentary greatness, and passed away, giving due attention to every phase of civilized history in a densely compact and rapidly moving story that interweaves dozens of plots with an inexhaustible fertility of invention and an uncanny consistency that is never caught in a slip or a contradiction. As a sheer tour-de-force there is nothing like it." (Hugh Nibley, "Since Cumorah," p. 156-157).

The Book of Mormon would come forth in a day when Israel is commanding newfound respect among the nations of the earth. The Savior said: "Ye need not any longer hiss, nor spurn, nor make game of the Jews, nor any of the remnant of the house of Israel." (3 Nephi 29:8). After 2,000 years, the State of Israel is a reality of our times, and it is here to stay, the nefarious intentions of the Arab world notwithstanding.

Theodore Hertzl founded the Zionist movement in 1897, 57 years after Elder Orson Hyde, and acting on the instructions of Joseph Smith, traveled to Jerusalem to dedicate the Holy Land unto the gathering of the Jews. In substance, he offered a dedicatory prayer "on behalf of the Jews, that they would be moved upon by the spirit of the return; on behalf of the climate and soil, that they would be favorable to the support of a large population; and on behalf of the political governments of the world, that they would cooperate to make the Jewish settlement possible." ("Ensign," 5/1972, p. 94).

The Book of Mormon would come forth in a day when the Lord is showing His signs and wonders in heaven and on the earth. Mormon wrote: "Wo unto him that shall deny the revelations of the Lord, and that shall say the Lord no longer worketh by revelation, or by prophecy, or by gifts, or by tongues, or by healings, or by the power of the Holy Ghost!" (3 Nephi 29:6). "We testify to the world that revelation continues, and that the vaults and files of the church contain these revelations which come month to month, and day to day." (President Spencer W. Kimball, C.R., 4/1977).

"Yea, and wo unto him that shall say at that day, to get gain, that there can be no miracle wrought by Jesus Christ; for he that doeth this shall become like unto the son of perdition, for whom there was no mercy, according to the word of Christ!" (3 Nephi 29:7). It is not often in The Book of Mormon that the text is punctuated by exclamation points for emphasis, but these two verses are, and because of that, they should be studied with particular care.

It will be difficult for those who have lived a telestial life in the Last Days to justify their actions before God, in light of the many signs and wonders He has provided as warnings to mankind. "Behold, all these are kingdoms, and any man who hath seen any or the least of these hath seen God moving in his majesty and power." (D&C 88:47). In fact, the "earth is crammed with heaven, and every common bush with fire of God. But only those who see, take off their shoes. The rest stand around picking blackberries." (Elizabeth Barrett Browning, "Aurora Leigh," Book Seven, 1856). In 3 Nephi 30, Mormon turned his attention to the Gentiles of the Last Days, and gave them specific commandments of the Lord regarding behavior that should be avoided and conduct that should be encouraged. "Hear the words of Jesus Christ, the Son of the living God, which he hath commanded me that I should speak concerning you." (3 Nephi 30:1).

This message of the Lord, given through his prophet Mormon, is summarized in one verse that justifies the preservation of the book for the Last Days and makes perfect sense. It is literally His counsel to the Gentiles: "Turn, all ye Gentiles, from your wicked ways; and repent of your evil doings, of your lyings and deceivings, and of your whoredoms, and of your secret abominations, and your idolatries, and of your murders, and your priestcrafts, and your envyings, and your strifes, and from all your wickedness and abominations, and come unto me, and be baptized in my name, that ye may receive a remission of your sins, and be filled with the Holy Ghost, that ye may be numbered with my people who are of the house of Israel." (3 Nephi 30:2).

For the Gentile nations, The Book of Mormon is a second witness of Jesus Christ. As Nephi wrote: "We talk of Christ, we rejoice in Christ, we preach of Christ, we prophesy of Christ, and we write according to our prophecies, that our children may know to what source they may look for a remission of their sins." (2 Nephi 25:26). Nephi declared the Christian world needs to have a testimony of Christ as much as do the Jews. Since "the Gentiles (need to) be convinced also that Jesus is the Christ, the Eternal God," Christ will manifest "himself unto all those who believe in him, by the power of the Holy Ghost." (2 Nephi 26:12-13). Today, members and missionaries of The Church of Jesus Christ go about testifying publicly of their beliefs to a world that lacks both saving faith in Christ, and a testimony of the truths interwoven throughout the restored gospel.

The Book of Mormon was also preserved to stand as another witness to "the Jews, the covenant people of the Lord ... that Jesus, whom they slew, was the very Christ and the very God." (Mormon 3:21). As Nephi wrote, The Book of Mormon will be given to the Jews in the Last Days "for the purpose of convincing them of the true Messiah, who was rejected by them; and unto the convincing of them that they need not look forward any more for a Messiah to come ... for there is save one Messiah spoken of by the prophets, and that Messiah is he who should be rejected of the Jews." (2 Nephi 25:18).

The Book of Mormon was preserved for our day so "every soul who belongs to the whole human family of Adam (may) stand to be judged of (his or her) works, whether they be good or evil." (Mormon 3:20). Everyone will be redeemed from spiritual death, to stand, at least briefly, in the presence of God at the Judgment Bar of Christ. That experience will be akin to our father focusing "heart-gripping flashes across the wall screen. Family slides. I am small, my brother is smaller, and my sister is smallest. Days now dead re-open like old storybooks from memory's heaped box. Pulling out pictures of cooking in Grandfather's Dutch oven; playing cheetah in our backyard monkey-jungle; being beautifully Easter-bested with my coat buttoned wrong; hugging a mommy minus grey hair. Soberly, I think of another Father, Who someday shall open my mind, and flash reeling remembering of every day's minute across my soul, across the heavens, and kindly ask me to narrate." (Lora Lyn Stucker, "New Era," 8/1973).

Moroni described conditions in the Last Days, when The Book of Mormon would come forth. It would be revealed in a day when people would be rational and self-reliant, and when they would say "miracles are done away." (Moroni 8:26). But it would stir the soul and speak a language in harmony with the Spirit, "even as if one should speak from the dead." (Moroni 8:26). Joseph Fielding Smith once said: "The impressions on the soul that come from the Holy Ghost are far more significant than a vision. It is where spirit speaks to spirit, and the imprint upon the soul is far more difficult to erase." The Book of Mormon is such a powerful witness of Jesus Christ that it is one of the most effective missionary tools available, which is why Satan tried so hard to prevent its publication and distribution and why he now tries to discredit the work.

Nephi described the pride of the Gentiles, their churches established to get gain, and the secret combinations of the Last Days. He foresaw that many of these professors of Christianity would "put down the power and miracles of God, and preach up unto themselves their own wisdom and their own learning, that they may get gain and grind upon the face of the poor. And there are many churches built up which cause envyings, and strifes, and malice. And there are also secret combinations, even as in times of old, according to the combinations of the devil, for he is the founder of all these things, yea, the founder of murder, and works of darkness." (2 Nephi 26:20-22).

The Book of Mormon was to come forth "in a day when the blood of saints shall cry unto the Lord, because of secret combinations, and the works of darkness." (Moroni 8:27). These are the agents of Satan who "stare uncomprehendingly with slit eyed skepticism" as the work unfolds before them. (Neal Maxwell). These are they who tried fanatically to disrupt the Great Reformation that paved the way for the Restoration itself.

In the late Middle Ages in Europe, "theological rabies raged as seldom before or after in history. The Lutheran Pastor Nivander (1582) listed forty characteristics of wolves, and showed that these were precisely the distinctive marks of Calvinists. Said a Lutheran pamphlet of 1590: 'If anybody wishes to be told, in a few words, concerning which articles of the faith we are fighting with the diabolical Calvinistic brood of vipers, the answer is, all and every one of them!' 'These raging theologians,' mourned a Protestant writer in 1610, 'have so greatly aggravated and augmented the disastrous strife among the Christians who have seceded from the papacy, that there seems no hope of all this screaming, abusing, and anathematizing coming to an end before the advent of the Last Day.'" (Wil Durant, "The Age of Reason Begins," p. 552-553).

Interestingly, the Eleventh Article of Faith of the Church of Jesus Christ of Latter-day Saints states: "We claim the privilege of worshiping Almighty God according to the dictates of our own conscience, and allow all men the same privilege, let them worship how, where, or what they may." Free will or agency, the power to choose, is the crowning principle of creation. "Therefore, cheer up your hearts, and remember that ye are free to act for yourselves – to choose the way of everlasting death, or the way of eternal life." (2 Nephi 10:23). Mankind may choose, but it cannot escape the consequences of its choices.

The Book of Mormon would come in a day when the power of God would be denied and when churches would" become defiled and be lifted up in the pride of their hearts." (Moroni 8:28). Joseph Smith was given the following counsel in the Sacred Grove, in response to his astonishingly profound question: "Which church is right?" "I was answered that I must join none of them," he said, "for they were all wrong; and the Personage who addressed me said that all their creeds were an abomination in his sight, that those professors were all corrupt; that "they draw near to me with their lips, but their hearts are far from me, they teach for doctrines the commandments of men, having a form of godliness, but they deny the power thereof.'" (Joseph Smith History 1:19). Specifically, the abomination of their creeds was that they had form without substance. Insult was added to injury when hypocrisy became a part of humanized, spiritually impotent dogma, when people did not really believe, but were only professors of religion.

Religion had become "magical," when the power by which the church operated was transferred from God to those who professed to be His earthly representatives, but who were only competing for "market share." The Bible itself had become a magical book in the eyes of many, conveying power and knowledge without the aid of revelation. Priesthood had acquired the status of an office that automatically bestowed power and grace without any regard for the spiritual or moral qualifications of its possessor.

The Lord told Joseph Smith, in the Preface to The Doctrine and Covenants: The religious orders of the day have "strayed from mine ordinances, and have broken mine everlasting covenant. They seek not the Lord to establish his righteousness, but every man walketh in his own way, and after the image of his own god, whose image is in the likeness of the world, and whose substance is that of an idol." (D&C 1:15-16).

Moroni clearly saw in vision those in the Last Days who had "transfigured the holy word of God," or who would change the appearance and substance of the scriptures, and had so brought damnation upon their souls. (Moroni 8:33). For him, there was no better way to find "the way, the truth, and the life" than through the pages of The Book of Mormon. (John 14:6).

The Book of Mormon would come forth in a day when "there shall be heard of fires, and tempests, and vapors of smoke in foreign lands; and there shall also be heard of wars, rumors of wars, and earthquakes in divers places." (Moroni 8:29-30). These are the same conditions with which Moroni was intimately familiar. He knew that the wrath of God requires the destruction of the wicked, and that our day would be frighteningly similar to the last days of the Nephites. Perhaps it is because The Book of Mormon speaks to our common feeling that it is so convincing.

The Book of Mormon would come in a day when there would be "great pollutions upon the face of the earth." (Moroni 8:31). He was referring, not only to industrial or environmental pollutions, but also to those qualities that canker the soul and corrupt the expression of the Spirit. It is interesting that Moroni would call our attention to "pollution" when we find it fashionable to have an "environmental awareness," but when it is also common to ignore the welfare of our less fortunate neighbors.

The Book of Mormon would come forth in a day when the world desperately needs a blueprint for its survival. "And now I, Mormon, make a record of the things which I have both seen and heard, and call it The Book of Mormon." (Mormon 1:1). It is amazing that we actually have a record of a lost and fallen people, and that we can learn from both their successes and their mistakes. The Book of Mormon has come forth in a day when its relevance to our challenges is unquestionable. Nephi was talking about us, when he wrote: "I speak unto you as the voice of one crying from the dust." (2 Nephi 33:13).

The Book of Mormon would come forth as the record of an ancient people who should speak out of the ground, whose voice should be low out of the dust. 2 Nephi 16:16 parallels Isaiah 29:4, and reads: "For those who shall be destroyed shall speak unto them out of the ground, and their speech shall be low out of the dust, and their voice shall be as one that hath a familiar spirit; for the Lord God will give unto him power, that he may whisper concerning them, even as it were out of the ground; and their speech shall whisper out of the dust." "Out of the ground" and "low out of the dust" could also refer figuratively to the depths of humility.

There is an interesting account of the discovery of the Bar Kokhba Documents, which were hidden in caves near Ein Gedi on the western shores of the Dead Sea, about 3,000 B.C. These records were deliberately buried deeply in the dry earth of the cave floor, and when they came to light there were choking clouds of dust, so that the archaeologists had to wear masks in order to breathe.

The plates from which The Book of Mormon was translated were unearthed, as well. Brigham Young recorded in his journal that "when Joseph got the plates, the Angel instructed him to carry them back to the Hill Cumorah, which he did. Oliver says that when Joseph and Oliver went there, the hill opened, and they walked into a cave, in which there was a large and spacious room." Miraculous forces were at work here, for the hill literally opened up before them revealing a depositary much larger than the simple stone box familiar to most Latter-day Saints who visualize the scene in their minds' eye.

Brigham Young continued in his journal: "They laid the plates on ... a large table that stood in the room. Under this table there was a pile of plates as much as two feet high, and there were altogether in this room more plates than probably many wagon loads; they were piled up in the corners and along the walls." ("Readings in L.D.S. Church History," 1:326).

Other records have come to us "out of the ground." When the tomb of Mycerinus in the third of the three great Pyramids was opened, "all that was found in the tomb was a blue sarcophagus containing the decayed remains of a man, but no treasure, excepting some golden tablets inscribed with characters of a language which nobody could understand. The tablets were used to pay the workmen, and the gold in each of them was worth about two hundred dollars. We leave the reader to speculate on what might have been written on those plates of gold, which one of the mightiest of Pharaohs apparently regarded as the greatest treasure with which he could be buried." (Hugh Nibley, "Lehi in The Desert," p. 120).

Moroni was specific and pointed, when he wrote: "I speak unto you as if ye were present, and yet ye are not. But behold, Jesus Christ hath shown you unto me, and I know your doing." (Mormon 8:35). Surely, what The Book of Mormon prophets wrote, and what Mormon abridged from their records, is of inestimable value to us. As Nephi said: "I have written what I have written, and I esteem it as of great worth." (2 Nephi 33:3). We should too, because The Book of Mormon was preserved for our day.

Born Again Christians

"Because of the covenant which ye have made, ye shall be called the children of Christ, his sons, and his daughters; for behold, this day he hath spiritually begotten you; for ye say that your hearts are changed through faith on his name; therefore, ye are born of him and have become his sons and his daughters." (Mosiah 5:7).

"Now I say unto you that ye must repent and be born again; for the Spirit saith if ye are not born again ye cannot inherit the kingdom of heaven; therefore, come and be baptized unto repentance, that ye may be washed from your sins, that ye may have faith on the Lamb of God, who taketh away the sins of the world, who is mighty to save and to cleanse from all unrighteousness." (Alma 7:14).

To receive eternal life, we must be "born again" as we are transformed to become "new creatures in Christ," with a renewal of our determination to follow Him, wherever that journey make take us. (2 Corinthians 5:17). But without His sustaining influence of divine nourishment, it is inevitable that we will, sooner or later, die spiritually. Perhaps this is why the figurative counterpart to water is so dramatic, for except we "be born of water and of the spirit," there is no way we "can enter into the kingdom of God." (John 3:5). Of this flowing, self-sustaining, spiritual spring, Truman Madsen wrote: "If we do not drink, if we die of thirst while only inches from the fountain, the fault comes down to us. For the free, full, flowing, living water is there." ("Christ and The Inner Life," p. 31).

Being physically immersed in water symbolizes the burial of our past sins, and it is only when we emerge from the font that our new life begins. In fact, after King Benjamin's discourse exhorting his people to a renewed commitment to their covenants, they "all cried with one voice, saying: Yea, we believe all the words which thou hast spoken unto us; and also, we know of their surety and truth, because of the Spirit of the Lord Omnipotent, which has wrought a mighty change in us, or in our hearts, that we have no more disposition to do evil but to do good continually. And we, ourselves, also, through the infinite goodness of God, and the manifestations of his Spirit, have great views of that which is to come; and were it expedient, we could prophesy of all things. And it is the faith which we have had on the things which our king has spoken unto us that has brought us to this great knowledge, whereby we do rejoice with such exceedingly great joy. And we are willing to enter into a covenant with our God to do his will, and to be obedient to his commandments in all things that he shall command us, all the remainder of our days, that we may not bring upon ourselves a never-ending torment, as has been spoken by the angel, that we may not drink out of the cup of the wrath of God." (Mosiah 5:1-5).

This declaration of commitment set the stage for Benjamin to get to the very heart of the doctrine of his message. "Therefore, he said unto them: Ye have spoken the words that I desired; and the covenant which ye have made is a righteous covenant. And now, because of the covenant which ye have made, ye shall be called the children of Christ, his sons, and his daughters; for behold, this day he hath spiritually begotten you; for ye say that your hearts are changed through faith on his name; therefore, ye are born of him, and have become his sons and his daughters." (Mosiah 5:6-7).

The Lord told Alma what it means to be born again: "Marvel not," He said, "that all mankind, yea, men and women, all nations, kindreds, tongues, and people, must be born again; yea, born of God, changed from their carnal and fallen state to a state of righteousness, being redeemed of God, becoming his sons and daughters; And thus they become new creatures; and unless they do this, they can in nowise inherit the kingdom of God." (Mosiah 27:25-26).

So important did Alma consider the necessity of spiritual rebirth, that he was moved to declare: "This is the order after which I am called, yea, to preach unto my beloved brethren, yea, and every one that dwelleth in the land; yea, to preach unto all, both old and young, both bond and free; yea, I say unto you the aged, and also the middle aged, and the rising generation; yea, to cry unto them that they must repent and be born again." (Alma 5:49).

When Aaron had taught Lamoni's father, the king asked: "What shall I do that I may have this eternal life of which thou hast spoken? Yea, what shall I do that I may be born of God, having this wicked spirit rooted out of my breast, and receive his Spirit?" Then Aaron explained: "If thou desirest this thing, if thou wilt bow down before God, yea, if thou wilt repent of all thy sins, and will bow down before God, and call on his name in faith, believing that ye shall receive, then shalt thou receive the hope which thou desirest." (Alma 22:15-18).

Alma had asked the brethren of the church the same thing: "And now behold, I ask of you, have ye spiritually been born of God? Have ye received his image in your countenances? Have ye experienced this mighty change in your hearts?" (Alma 5:14). Then, he asked the $64,000.00 follow-up question: "If ye have felt to sing the song of redeeming love, I would ask, can ye feel so now?" (Alma 5:26). If not, all would not be lost as a result of their failure to maintain their forward momentum. A recommitment to their covenant of baptism would allow them to re-enter the fold, for being born again can be a process, as well as a point.

"And now," Nephi asked, "after ye have gotten into this strait and narrow path, I would ask if all is done? Behold, I say unto you, Nay; for ye have not come thus far save it were by the word of Christ with unshaken faith in him, relying wholly upon the merits of him who is mighty to save." After our baptism and receipt of the gift of the Holy Ghost, we must "press forward" with complete dedication and "steadfastness," or confidence and a firm determination in Christ, "having a perfect brightness of hope," or perfect faith, and charity, or "a love of God and of all men." If we do this, "feasting upon the word of Christ," or receiving strength and nourishment from the scriptures, and endure to the end in righteousness, we "shall have eternal life," that is the greatest gift that God can bestow. (2 Nephi 31:19-20).

Nephi's formula is, pure and simple, a statement of cold logic that has been made more savory by exposure to the warming tray of plain doctrine. "This is the way," he said, "and there is none other way nor name given under heaven whereby man can be saved in the kingdom of God. And now, behold, this is the doctrine of Christ, and the only and true doctrine of the Father, and of the Son, and of the Holy Ghost." (2 Nephi 31:21). Alma the Younger came to know this in the most intensely personal way possible. "I have seen my Redeemer," he testified, "and he shall come forth and shall redeem all mankind who believe on his name." (Alma 19:13). During a glorious manifestation, the Lord had told him: "Marvel not that all mankind, yea, men and women, all nations, kindreds, tongues, and people, must be born again, yea, born of God, changed from their carnal and fallen state, to a state of righteousness, being redeemed of God, becoming his sons and daughters." (Alma 27:25). He related how, after having been born again, his limbs had received their strength again, so that he might stand upon his feet to manifest unto the people that he "had been born of God." (Alma 36:23).

The scriptures do not record whether Nicodemus received the same infusion of holy element when Jesus "said unto him, Verily, verily, I say unto thee, Except a man be born again, he cannot see the kingdom of God … Marvel not that I said unto thee, Ye must be born again." (John 3:3 & 7). But we do know that Peter later taught the principle of "being born again, not of corruptible seed, but of incorruptible, by the word of God." (1 Peter 1:23). His fellow apostle John confirmed: "Whatsoever is born of God overcometh the world: and this is the victory that overcometh the world." (1 John 5:4). These are they who are insulated from the carnality, sensuality, and devilish nature of men, insomuch that "whosoever is born of God sinneth not." (1 John 5:18). These are they to whom Jesus Christ gave "power to become the sons of God, even to them that believe on his name: Which were born, not of blood, nor of the will of the flesh, nor of the will of man, but of God." (John 1:12-13).

The unconditional promise is that "every one that doeth righteousness is born of him." (1 John 2:29). "Every one that loveth is born of God, and knoweth God." (1 John 4:7). Immediately after his conversion, Alma sensed the transformation that had occurred, and declared: "Behold I am born of the Spirit." (Mosiah 27:24). He elaborated: "After wading through much tribulation, repenting nigh unto death, the Lord in mercy hath seen fit to snatch me out of an everlasting burning, and I am born of God." (Mosiah 27:28). Although he had been "saved," there was subsequently much work to do, as he patiently endured to the end in righteousness.

Alma later told his son Helaman: "I would not that ye should think that I know these things of myself, but it is the Spirit of God which is in me which maketh these things known unto me; for if I had not been born of God I should not have known these things." (Alma 36:8). He related to Helaman that following his spiritual rebirth, he had "labored without ceasing, that (he) might bring souls unto repentance; that (he) might bring them to taste of the exceeding joy of which (he) did taste; that they might also be born of God, and be filled with the Holy Ghost." (Alma 36:24). As a result of his ministry, he reported: "Many have been born of God, and have tasted as I have tasted, and have seen eye to eye as I have seen." (Alma 36:26). Similarly, Parley P. Pratt said of his own Pentecostal experience: "I have received the holy anointing, and I can never rest until the last enemy (that is, unresolved sin) is conquered, (spiritual) death destroyed, and truth reigns triumphant." (J.D., 1:15).

All who have thus been born again are set free by the perfect Law of Liberty to reach their potential. As Paul taught the Romans: "We are buried with him by baptism into death: that like as Christ was raised up from the dead by the glory of the Father, even so we also should walk in newness of life." (Romans 6:3). When we are born again we are as the acorns of a potential oak vitalized by a nurturing influence to reach the full stature of our spirits.

When we are not well-grounded, the very fibers of our being fail to hold us together coherently, and we lose our physical, emotional, and spiritual co-ordination. The synaptic activity within our ccentral nervous systems fires sporadically, and we respond to our environment ineffectively, without synchronization. At times, those who are not well-grounded need to be jolted out of their complacency, in the same way that defibrillator paddles are used to restore normal cardiac rhythm in a heart attack patient.

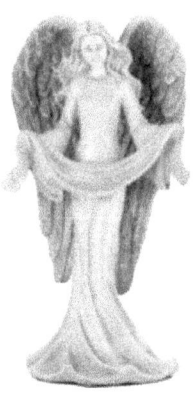

Brevity

*"I chose these things
to finish my record (which) I
shall take from the plates of Nephi;
and I cannot write the hundredth
part of the things of my people."
(Words of Mormon 1:5).*

"Brevity is the soul of wit." (Shakespeare, Polonius speaking, "Hamlet," Act 2, Scene 2). This essay is going to be brief, so let's get right to it. Actually, it would be 6 words long, if Shakespeare's advice were taken seriously.

Brevity is the economical use of words in speech or writing. As members of The Church of Jesus Christ of Latter-day Saints, we have many opportunities to develop clarity of thought, to practice being concise in conversation, and to be succinct in our written communication. When we invite the Spirit to guide us, it influences us to avoid loquacious speech. The scriptures reveal that when Jesus came to His disciples: They continued "without ceasing, to pray unto him and they did not multiply many words, for it was given unto them what they should pray." (3 Nephi 19:24). Their hearts were full, and they were "drawn out in prayer unto him continually" without being verbose, long-winded, rambling, chatty, effusive, loquacious, vociferous, or garrulous. (Oops!) (Alma 34:27).

Martin Luther advised: "The fewer the words, the better the prayer." For example, public prayer is not a discourse or exhortation that is given in a General Authority tone of voice, but is rather a simple expression of appreciation and an invitation of the Spirit. Likewise, opening prayers invoke the Spirit and closing prayers ask a benediction. We simply acknowledge God's influence in our lives, give thanks for our blessings and petition Him for our needs. Private prayers, to a degree, are the same, although there may be times when the hunger in our souls compels us to kneel down before our Maker and cry unto Him all the day long in mighty supplication. Even when the night comes, we may continue to raise our voices to the heavens. (See Enos 1:4). At other times, our petitions may be so great that they cannot be verbalized at all. As the Psalmist wrote: "Lord, all my desire is before thee; and my groaning is not hid from thee." (Psalms 38:9).

Whatever our circumstances when we pray, we must "use not vain repetitions, as the heathen do: for they think that they shall be heard for their much speaking." (Matthew 6:7). We learn to avoid pointless duplication of words that are to no avail, serve no useful purpose, and are an unnecessary reiteration. (Hmm!). Words can become a gratuitous reverberation and a cognitive irritation. However, internal parallelism that is poetically reinforcing and stirs our souls is a prominent exception to this rule: "He that findeth his life shall lose it, And he that loseth his life for my sake shall find it." (Matthew 10:39). "He will manifest the truth of it unto you by the power of the Holy Ghost, and by the power of the Holy Ghost ye may know the truth of all things." (Moroni 10:4-5).

Paul encouraged us to "shun profane and vain babblings" in our communication. (2 Timothy 2:16). Such thoughtless exercises are nothing more than prattle and are detrimental to our health. A good rule of thumb is that "any philosophy that can be put in a nutshell belongs there." (Branch Rickey). An example is this twelve-word encapsulation of the gospel: "I came into the world to do the will of my Father." (3 Nephi 27:13). God's mission statement is comparably brief: "This is my work and my glory, to bring to pass the immortality and eternal life of man." (Moses 1:39). Our challenge might be to come up with an equally powerful and comprehensive eighteen-word personal mission statement.

Howard W. Hunter came close. His wrote: "It is my aim to find pleasure and enjoyment in life by seeking after those things which are good and worthwhile, that I may gain knowledge and wisdom with each passing year; to carefully plan my allotted time so that none of it will be wasted; to give my family the benefits of education, recreation, and travel; to conduct my life in obedience to the gospel of Jesus Christ; to so manage my business affairs that I will have an income adequate to provide my family with their wants and advantages of some of the finer things of life; and to set aside a portion for investments to provide an income for retirement." (113 words).

My own dental practice mission statement stated: "We want you to enjoy a healthy mouth and pleasing smile. Through continuing dental education, we are constantly learning how to incorporate into our practice new equipment, materials, and methods that improve our skills. We strive to create and maintain an environment in which we provide oral health care of the highest quality in an atmosphere of mutual trust and acceptance. We value our reputation, which is built upon service, and invite your participation to help us to achieve our goals." (81 words).

The Preamble to our Family Constitution begins: "We, the Hudsons, in order to form a more Celestial Family, establish rules, rights, and privileges, ensure domestic tranquility, provide for the common needs of family members, promote their general welfare, and secure the blessings of liberty based on responsibility, do set forth and establish this Family Constitution. We agree that our family exists to provide a unique setting in which its members might individually and collectively pursue an abundant lifestyle, seek liberty through the full expression of agency, and find happiness by living in accordance with divine principles. To that noble end, we commit our fortunes, our talents, and our energies. We consider no sacrifice too great to guarantee these inalienable rights, among which are: righteous example, inspired teaching, unconditional love, mutual respect, understanding, education leading to self-sufficiency, privacy, and an orderly and comfortable home." Admittedly, it's a bit wordy, (136 words / 941 words in the entire document), but it's patterned after the U.S. Constitution, (4,500 words), so at least it's in good company. Winston Churchill put it this way: "Broadly speaking," he said, "short words are best, and the old words, when short, are best of all." (Speech on receiving the London Times Literary Award, 11/2/1949).

Given these asides, we must craft our language without giving "heed to fables and endless genealogies, which minister questions." (1 Timothy 1:4). Our speech and our written communications should be focused and purposeful. "The most valuable of all talents," declared Thomas Jefferson, "is that of never using two words when one will do." We've all heard someone say: "I would have to answer that in the affirmative," and thought to ourselves that a simple "Yes" would have done quite well, thank you! We are so accustomed to listening to political debaters skillfully dodging questions, however, that our brains frequently accept the chicanery as normal. The Savior could have been referring to us when He said: "This people's heart is waxed gross, and their ears are dull of hearing, and their eyes they have closed, lest at any time they should see with their eyes, and hear with their ears, and should understand with their heart." (Matthew 13:15).

Those who cleverly manipulate language sometimes do so to evade direct confrontations with issues. Rather than exerting ourselves and grappling with matters of concern and conquering difficulties, by exploiting (1) words, they hedge (2) their bets, sidestep (3) uncomfortable concerns, and skirt (4) around core issues. Their style is an artifice (5), a deception (6), a device (7), and a gimmick (8). It is a thinly veiled maneuver (9) or ploy (10), a stratagem (11), a subterfuge (12), and a shenanigan (13) designed to trick listeners into thinking they are in control, when in reality they are uncomfortably out of their league and skating (14) on thin ice. As a matter of fact, these three sentences have employed fourteen adjectives to describe the pitfalls of verbosity in an attempt to differentiate it from brevity. How easily we "fall into the pit which (we have) digged" for ourselves! (1 Nephi 22:14).

"Brevity is the best recommendation of speech, whether in a senator or an orator." (Cicero). "If any man teach otherwise, and consent not to wholesome words … he is proud, knowing nothing, but doting about questions and strifes of words, whereof cometh envy … railings, evil surmisings, perverse disputings of men of corrupt minds, and destitute of the truth, supposing that gain is godliness." (1 Timothy 6:3-5). Carelessness in our speech opens the floodgates of banality, leading to a rising tide of unremarkable words that are tedious, trivial, and predictable, and lack originality, interest, and excitement. They may even lead to the vices Paul described to Timothy.

Mormon similarly wrote: "Those who did not belong to their church did indulge themselves… in babblings, and in envyings and strife." (Alma 1:32). Regarding the churchmen in Palmyra, Joseph Smith lamented: "All their good feelings one for another, if they ever had any, were entirely lost in a strife of words and a contest about opinions." (J.S.H. 1:6). Words can be weapons when they are spit out in volleys, and the destruction they cause may be widespread precisely because they lack focus and miss the bullseye of their intended target. If we view our lexicon as an arsenal, we risk thinking that the armory of our thought is best utilized by waging an offensive war of words. But when they fail, Mutually Assured Destruction cannot be far off.

"Be not rash with thy mouth," cautioned the Preacher. (Ecclesiastes 5:2). Thoughtless or impetuous behavior that is a reaction to emotion or impulse is irresponsible because it does not consider the consequences. "Brevity," on the other hand, "is a great charm of eloquence." (Cicero). "If you bring that sentence in for a fitting," cracked Hawkeye Pierce, "I can have it shortened by Wednesday." (MASH, "The Gun"). Questions that have changed the world have been brief, articulate, and persuasively powerful. "If I sail west, will I fall off the edge of the earth?" "Why does an apple fall from a tree?" "What would the world look like if I were riding on a beam of light?" "Which church is right?" "Whom say ye that I am?"

Other questions, equally succinct, have changed and even transformed our lives, as well as the lives of those around us. "Have I made a good decision?" "Are these things true?" "What would You have me do?" "Is she the one?" "Am I my brother's keeper?" (Genesis 4:9). "What can I do to help?"

Some of the most profound statements are illuminating because of their brevity: "Come follow me." (Luke 18:22). "Jesus wept." (John 11:35). "Having been commissioned of Jesus Christ, I baptize you in the name of the Father, and of the Son, and of the Holy Ghost." (D&C 20:73). Even the scriptural expansion on the injunction to "Receive the Holy Ghost" is tightly wound: "Repent and be baptized every one of you in the name of Jesus Christ for the remission of sins, and ye shall receive the gift of the Holy Ghost." (Acts 2:38). Moroni's promise at the end of The Book of Mormon is brief and to the point: "When ye shall receive these things, I would exhort you that ye would ask God, the Eternal Father, in the name of Christ, if these things are not true; and if ye shall ask with a sincere heart, with real intent, having faith in Christ, he will manifest the truth of it unto you by the power of the Holy Ghost." (Moroni 10:4).

Even single words can penetrate to our deepest feelings or most private emotions. "The word of God is quick, and powerful, and sharper than any two-edged sword, piercing even to the dividing asunder of soul and spirit, and of the joints and marrow and is a discerner of the thoughts and intents of the heart." (Hebrews 4:12). "Repent!" "Obey!" "Sacrifice!" "Worship!" "Pray!" "Serve!" "Remember!"

When Joseph Smith "was laboring under the extreme difficulties caused by the contests of ... parties of religionists," he was "one day reading the Epistle of James, first chapter and fifth verse." (J.S.H. 1:11). Significantly, he was not reading the New Testament, or even the entire referenced epistle, but just one specific verse that jumped off the page and struck a raw nerve. In fact, he recalled: "Never did any passage of scripture come with more power to the heart of man that this did at this time to mine. I reflected on it again and again." (J.S.H., 1:12). Twenty simple words clearly defined both his present circumstances and the path that lay before him: "If any of you lack wisdom, let him ask of God, that giveth to all men liberally, and upbraideth not; and it shall be given him. But let him ask in faith, nothing wavering." (James 1:5-6). One wonders if James understood its ramifications, when he pondered how to best express this counsel embedded within his general epistle.

In his subsequent ministry, Joseph learned not to mince words. "I teach people correct principles and let them govern themselves," he declared on one occasion. Sometimes, though, rather than being a virtue, brevity, can be a poor substitute for a lack of forethought. Dullards, far from being incisive, are sluggish, lethargic, listless, distracted, inattentive, and literally absent-minded. Captain Moroni asked: "Can you think to sit upon your (living room couches) in a state of thoughtless stupor?" (Alma 60:7). As Hugh Nibley asked: "Why do people feel guilty about TV? What is wrong with it? Just this: It shuts out all the wonderful things of which the mind is capable, leaving it drugged in a state of thoughtless stupor." ("Zeal Without Knowledge").

Too many of us ask with glassy-eyed indifference: "And please bless us with all those things that we stand in need of." Or: "And please bless this food that it may be nourishing and strengthening to our bodies." Or: "And please bless us as we travel home, that we may do so safely." Or: "And please bless those who could not be with us, that they may be able to be with us next time." Or: "the letter is attached to this document as Exhibit A and incorporated by reference as if fully set out within this document." "Yada, yada, yada." ("Seinfeld," Episode 153). "Pleased to meet you." "How are you doing?" "Have a good day." Ad nauseum.

Helen Keller "asked a friend who had just returned from a long walk in the woods what she had observed. 'Nothing in particular,' she replied. (Three short words. Three dull, bland, insipid, unimaginative, featureless, uninspired words.) How was that possible, I asked myself? I, who cannot hear or see, find hundreds of things to interest me through mere touch. I feel the delicate symmetry of a leaf. I pass my hands lovingly about the rough shaggy bark of a pine. Occasionally, if I am very fortunate, I place my hand gently on a small tree and feel the happy quiver of a bird in full song." ("The Atlantic Monthly").

"The words of wise men are heard in quiet more than the cry of him that ruleth among fools." (Ecclesiastes 9:17). When we lower our voices, we strengthen our argument, and sometimes our rhetoric so resolutely marshaled can be a powerful force for good. During the dark days of World War II, when it had few other resources to resist the German Wehrmacht, Great Britain drew upon the verbal skills of its Prime Minister, Sir Winston Churchill. As no other could, he rallied the nation with stirring words. Who can forget listening to the defiant address wherein he promised: "We shall defend our island, whatever the cost may be, we shall fight on the beaches, we shall fight on the landing grounds, we shall fight in the fields and in the streets, we shall fight in the hills; we shall never surrender." (House of Commons Speech, 6/4/1940. See also his "This was their finest hour" speech of 6/18/1940). He said of the airmen who took to the skies over Britain and over the English Channel to meet the overwhelmingly superior numbers of the Luftwaffe: "Never in the field of human conflict was so much owed by so many to so few." Of his own assets, he apologetically declared: "I have nothing to offer but blood, toil, tears and sweat." (May 13, 1940). Later, he reflected on his efforts, saying: "It was the nation and the race dwelling all round the globe that had the lion's heart. I had the luck to be called upon to give the roar." (At his 80th birthday celebration, 11/30/1954). On that occasion, Clement Attlee paid tribute, calling him "the last of the great orators who can touch the heights."

Truly, "the words of a wise man's mouth are gracious; but the lips of a fool will swallow up himself. The beginning of the words of his mouth is foolishness: and the end of his talk is mischievous madness. A fool also is full of words: a man cannot tell what shall be." (Ecclesiastes 10:12-14). In the introduction of a letter to a friend, Blaise Pascal wrote: "I have made this letter longer than usual, because I lack the time to make it short." The effort expended to achieve brevity is brain sweat. When perspiration precedes inspiration, the spirit leads us to the four basic characteristics of interpersonal communication: clarity, simplicity, brevity, and humanity. "There is need of brevity, that the thought may run on." (Horace). Less is more. Seeds are small in comparison to the harvest.

Brevity can throw open the floodgates the mind. It can be the key that unlocks the door leading to the brightly lighted avenues of intellectual and spiritual inquiry. "Spartans, stoics, heroes, saints and gods use short and positive speech," declared Ralph Waldo Emerson. All the great things are simple, and many can be expressed in a single word: justice, code, honor, duty, mercy, hope, service, love, charity, sacrifice, and freedom.

Others require just a few words: "Semper fidelis." (U.S. Marine Corp motto). "Charity never faileth." (Moroni 7:46). "E pluribus unum." (Never codified by law, but the de facto motto of the United States of America, until 1956). "Citius, Altius, Fortius." (The Olympic motto, which is Latin for "Faster, Higher, Stronger"). "In God we trust." (Official motto of the United States of America, by an act of Congress, H.J. Resolution, 1956). "Do it! Do it right! Do it right now!" (A favorite motto of Spencer W. Kimball). "I'm sorry." "I love you."

Presidents John F. Kennedy and Ronald Reagan knew how to use just a few words to great effect. On June 26, 1963, Kennedy told a crowd of thousands of West Berliners: "Two thousand years ago the proudest boast was 'Civis Romanus sum' ("I am a Roman citizen"). Today, in the world of freedom, the proudest boast is 'Ich bin ein Berliner.' All free men, wherever they may live, are citizens of Berlin, and, therefore, as a free man, I take pride in the words Ich bin ein Berliner!" Twenty-four short years later, in a speech at the Brandenburg Gate commemorating Berlin's 750th anniversary, Reagan challenged Mikhail Gorbachev, the General Secretary of the Communist Party of the Soviet Union: "Mr. Gorbachev, tear down this wall!" In fact, it did come down, beginning on November 9, 1989, in a process leading to the reunification of Germany. The world remembers these events in a couplet of eight words: "I am a Berliner!" and "Tear down this wall!"

Dallin Oaks has enlarged upon this theme by offering the perspective of the young prophet Joseph Smith, who was "by his own admission, no writer. He felt imprisoned by what he called the 'total darkness of paper, pen, and ink." (Joseph Smith to William W. Phelps, 11/27/1832, B.Y.U. Press, 2002, p. 287). He thus considered it 'an awful responsibility to write in the name of the Lord'. (Joseph Smith Papers, 1:367).

He did not suppose that he could receive the revelations perfectly, and it is interesting that he was not generally verbose in his attempts. He represented the voice of God as he spoke in what he characterized as his own 'crooked, broken, scattered, and imperfect language'. (Joseph Smith to William W. Phelps, 11/27/1832, quoted in "Making Sense of the Doctrine & Covenants, a Guided Tour Through Modern Revelation," Steven Harper. "Personal Writings of Joseph Smith," p. 186-187).

At the end of the day, Joseph knew when his words, or the word of the Lord, had their desired impact. "Thus saith the still small voice, which whispereth through and pierceth all things," without belaboring the point, "and often times it maketh my bones to quake while it maketh manifest" without overanalyzing or exhausting the subject. (D&C 85:6). Is there a message here? The Golden Rule has 11 words. The Lord's Prayer has 50. The Ten Commandments have 297.

The Constitution of the United States of America has 4,500. The recorded words of Jesus in the Four Gospels total about 24,602 words. The New Testament contains about 138,020 words. The Book of Mormon has around 268,163 words. But The Affordable Health Care for America Act of 2010 is 1,990 pages long and contains 363,086 words, the IRS Tax Code has about 3,700,000 words, and the U.S. Code has around 42,000,000 words. (Brevity is not the strong suit of government). The eight volumes of essays in this series of Compendia contain around a million words. This essay, by the way, has 3,587 words. It had 1,911 as a rough draft before the editing process expanded the text by 88%. Perhaps I should have taken the advice of Polonius, after all.

Buddy, Can You Spare a Dime?

"Are we
not all beggars? Do
we not all depend upon
the same Being, even God,
for all the substance which we
have, both food and raiment,
and for gold, and for silver,
and for all the riches which
we have of every kind?"
(Mosiah 4:19).

Since Cain first made the inquiry, we have grappled with the question: "Am I my brother's keeper?" (Genesis 4:9). As true disciples, however, we actively practice our religion as John Taylor encouraged us. "There are some Christian people in this world," he declared, "who, if a man were poor or hungry, would say, let us pray for him. I would suggest a little different regimen for a person in this condition; rather take him a bag of flour and a little beef or pork. A few such comforts will do him more good than your prayers." (C.R., 10/1877). Such acts of quiet Christianity extended to the least of our brethren squarely address Cain's question. (See Matthew 25:40).

The bottom line is that when a child of God is down and out, an ounce of help is better than a pound of preaching. Socrates said, "Know thyself." Cicero urged, "Control Thyself." But the gospel teaches that we must give of ourselves. (1 Timothy 4:15). We establish our commitment to actively embrace the demands of discipleship by following His example. After all, "are we not all beggars? Do we not all depend upon the same Being, even God, for all the substance which we have, both food and raiment, and for gold, and for silver, and for all the riches which we have of every kind?" (Mosiah 4:19).

When we recognize our utter dependence upon Him, we are as Moses, who exclaimed: "Now, for this cause, I know that man is nothing, which thing I never had supposed." (Moses 1:10). In this regard, the confiscation of their earthly treasures was the best thing that could have happened to Lehi's family after they left Jerusalem. Divine tutorial training was woven into a seeming injustice when all the accumulated belongings of the family fortuitously fell into the hands of the unscrupulous Laban. Lehi's sons were being uncomfortably taught to put the value of the world's goods in its proper perspective. This teaching moment was created to emphasize the importance of relying on God's power alone and not on the extrinsic worth of telestial trinkets to accomplish His purposes.

We cannot allow ourselves to revert to stereotypes when considering the motives of God's children, allow our prejudices to determine the depth of our compassion, or debate the merits of the petitions of the impoverished. We can learn from those misguided priesthood leaders in Zarahemla who characterized the Lamanites to whom the Sons of Mosiah wished to minister as "a stiffnecked people, whose hearts delight in the shedding of blood, whose days have been spent in the grossest iniquity, whose ways have been the ways of a transgressor from the beginning." (Alma 26:23-25). This attitude was just as polarized as that of the Lamanites, and was a far cry from the feelings of pious Nephites barely a generation earlier, who had been ""filled with pain and anguish for the welfare of the souls of their brethren the Lamanites." (Mosiah 25:11).

As it turned out, the descendants of the very Lamanites whom the Sons of Mosiah subsequently served became the bulwark of the church. Later, Mormon reported the practice that had become engrained within Nephite society to be pro-gospel rather than anti-enemy. In the heat of battle, the Nephites had learned to act with compassion. After subduing their adversaries, they "cast their prisoners into prison, and did cause the word of God to be preached unto them; and as many as would repent of their sins and enter into a covenant that they would murder no more were set at liberty." (3 Nephi 5:4, see Helaman 6:37). By rediscovering the principle that ideology can be the most persuasive influence on earth, they had reinvented the practice of using truth and light as the only really effective weapons against evil and darkness.

The penitent Gadianton robbers who had "entered into a covenant to keep the peace of the land, who were (nevertheless) desirous to remain Lamanites," were given land to farm so that they might enjoy the fruits of their own labors. (3 Nephi 6:3). They were not compelled to become Nephites, nor were they pressured to join the church, but were instead given the means to provide for their own families so that their improving circumstances might not only stabilize their own self-esteem but also be a leavening influence upon the larger society in which they dwelt. It would have been critically important to give these former terrorists every opportunity to experience the success of working within the system, because only a dozen years earlier, Mormon had reported: "There was no way that they could subsist save it were to plunder and rob and murder." (3 Nephi 4:5). It had been the only way of life they had ever known, buts now they were eagerly focusing on rediscovered responsibilities and unforeseen opportunities as functioning members of Nephite society, and "there was great order in the land, and they had formed their laws according to equity and justice." As a matter of fact, "there was nothing in all the land to hinder the people from prospering continually, except they should fall into transgression." (3 Nephi 6:5).

In Dostoevsky's "The Brothers Karamazov," the Grand Inquisitor mused: "The ages will pass, and humanity will proclaim by the lips of their sages that there is no crime and there is no sin. There is only hunger." People need to be given opportunities to provide for themselves because the vast majority of the world's population votes with their stomachs and hundreds of millions go to bed hungry every night. This is an intolerable situation if mankind is to prosper.

Brigham Young was fond of repeating the aphorism: "Give a man a fish, and you have fed him for a day. Teach a man to fish, and you have fed him for a lifetime." He felt that "the first great principle that ought to occupy our attention, and which is the main spring of all action is the principle of improvement. No matter what their pursuits are, in what nation they were born, with what people they have been associated, what religion they profess, or what politics they hold, this embraces all the powers necessary in performing the duties of life. ("Discourses of Brigham Young," p. 87).

Abraham Lincoln famously declared: "I will prepare myself and some day my chance will come." In the land of the free and the home of the brave, he was given the tools to create a state of readiness for his day in the sun. He understood that if life has handed you a lemon, it's nice if you have the presence of mind, as well as the means, to make lemonade. Even a sidewalk concession selling cold drinks in Dixie cups for $0.25 apiece has more income producing potential than a person standing on a street corner with a crudely scrawled cardboard sign asking for a handout. J. W. Marriott turned a small refreshment stand in Washington, D.C., in 1927, into one of the world's largest hospitality, hotel, and food services companies, worth $18 billion in 2024. He did it with drive and initiative, but he could not have done it without a lot of quarters from generous strangers stopping by to purchase sodas.

B.Y.U. Coach Lavell Edwards felt that the most important quality his athletes could have, was not the will to win, but rather the will to prepare. He gave them the opportunities we all need, whether we are professional athletes or practiced panhandlers, living in the fast or the slow lane, whether we have rags or riches, are leaders or lepers, late bloomers or early prodigies, venture capitalists or welfare recipients. No matter our circumstances, we have been endowed with certain inalienable rights, and these include life, liberty, and the means to actively pursue happiness.

Helping hands are not synonymous with handouts and the sooner we recognize that we are all on the "dole," the faster we can get off it. We may not be standing in line at soup kitchens, and we may not be receiving free turkey dinners at the Union Gospel Mission, but we are all undeserving recipients of the largess of others. Whether it is in a Gospel Doctrine class, and the teacher spoon-feeds us doctrine (the scriptural dole), or we ask for "all other blessings that we stand in need of," (the prayerful supplication dole) it is still the dole. If we seek the solutions to our physical, emotional, or behavioral challenges in a bottle of pills, we are on the chemotherapeutic dole. If we are indiscriminate and neglectful in the care of our physical health we may find ourselves on the priesthood blessing dole. If we spread our assets too thin, so that we lack the resources to meet our temporal challenges head-on, we may be on the crisis-management dole, the debt-counselor dole, or the Church Welfare assistance dole. If we routinely go five miles per hour over the speed limit or run yellow lights, we may be on the playing the percentages dole. If we characteristically tweak the system to circumvent the delay of gratification of our appetites, we may be on the playing the angles dole. If we rationalize away behavior that is inconsistent with gospel principles, we may be on the self-denial dole. If we pay scant attention to our faith and testimonies until the moment when a pressing need arises, we are on the spiritual bank account dole, and we may find that it is habitually overdrawn. If we expect extensions on our contractual and financial obligations, we may be on the temporal treasure dole. If we seek greater and greater stimulation to receive the same level of emotional satisfaction, we may be on the sensory overload dole. If we consistently succumb to the pressure to keep up with the Joneses, we may be on a bonfire of the vanities dole.

Nature doesn't tolerate the dole, but instead provides the instinctive drive to survive. If butterflies are not allowed to struggle to free themselves from their cocoons, they will never fly. If sea turtles didn't run the gauntlet from the sandy nests in which they were born to the sea, they might never know the thrill of swimming with sharks and other predators. If squirrels did not gather acorns before winter's long night, they would starve to death in a short time. If bears did not fatten up on spawning salmon and on huckleberries before lumbering off to hibernation, they might shrivel away to nothing while slumbering in their dens. If Orcas did not hunt in cooperative pods their chances of success would plummet. In the wildebeest migration through the Serengeti Plain and Masai Mara National Park, vast herds cross the Mara River in a desperate gamble that they will be among the lucky ones to make it to the far bank without being eaten by a crocodile. But nature has endowed them all with the means and the adrenaline to take the risk and to unhesitatingly move forward.

We sink or swim, largely on our own. We hope and pray for "the serenity to accept the things we cannot change, the courage to change the things we can, and the wisdom to know the difference." (Reinhold Niebuhr). But it is nice to get a little help from our friends.

When we are not well-grounded, the very fibers of our being fail to hold us together coherently, and we lose our physical, emotional, and spiritual co-ordination. The synaptic activity within our ccentral nervous systems fires sporadically, and we respond to our environment ineffectively, without synchronization. At times, those who are not well-grounded need to be jolted out of their complacency, in the same way that defibrillator paddles are used to restore normal cardiac rhythm in a heart attack patient.

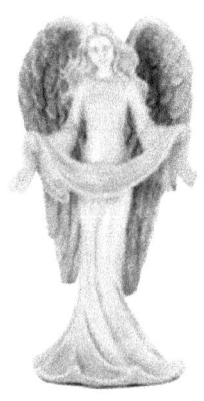

Caesar

(Mosiah Chapter 29)

"It is better that a
man should be judged of God than
of man, for the judgments of God are
always just, but the judgments of
man are not always just."
(Mosiah 29:12).

"There is no greater drama in the human record than the sight of a few Christians, scorned or oppressed by a succession of emperors, bearing all trials with a fierce tenacity, multiplying quietly, building order while their enemies generated chaos, fighting the sword with the word, brutality with hope, and at last defeating the strongest state that history has known. Caesar and Christ had met in the arena, and Christ had won." (Will Durant, "The Story of Civilization," 3:652).

Such was the assessment by the historian Will Durant, of the struggle that Christianity had with the pagan despots who ruled with an iron hand during the years of the infancy of the faith. The struggles of the cultures that are described in The Book of Mormon, that flourished in the New World at the same time Rome was exerting its influence in the Old World, can be differentiated from their Old-World counterparts and follow their own distinctive patterns. Mormon, who abridged the plates that chronicled the reign of the Nephite kings, went to great lengths to describe the process of the transition of power when Mosiah, the last of those rulers, died.

Book of Mormon history is distant from the time and place of its publication, but there is a consistency running through its pages. Although it is basically the record of a people inhabiting the New World, its attitudes have Old World precedents. Against that background, these patterns come into perfect focus. In the Old-World history of the Israelite nation, Book of Mormon prototypes are laid down perfectly, for its innermost structures are biblical. American political, historical, and social forms are conspicuously absent. The events chronicled in Mosiah Chapter 29 are faithful reflections of these ancient models.

When Mosiah had conferred upon Alma the Younger the emblems of authority, he sent messengers throughout the land of Zarahemla, desiring to know the will of the people concerning who should be their king. Mosiah was at this time about 62 years old and felt that the torch should be passed to a younger man.

The people preferred Aaron, the son of Mosiah first mentioned in the scriptures. He was probably the eldest, and so would have been the logical candidate. However, he was away on a mission to the Lamanites, that he and his 3 brothers felt was a more important responsibility than assisting in the affairs of state in the homeland.

Now King Mosiah recognized a potential crisis in the developing political stalemate, and he likely feared that, should another be appointed king, Aaron might one day return to claim the throne. The resulting division among the people could be the catalyst for much suffering. Additionally, Mosiah was probably concerned that his son, who had once been wayward, might again falter in his faith and force his claim and supposed right to the kingdom, which would create a spirit of contention in the land. Mosiah's was a literate society, and so he circulated a position paper among his subjects to justify to them his course of action and to educate them so that they might more responsibly exercise their agency in the future.

Mosiah decided to remain king for the rest of his life, which turned out to be just one more year. In anticipation of the end of his reign, he determined to appoint wise men to be judges, who would judge the people in accordance with the commandments of God. It has always been important to have leaders whose rule is founded on eternal law. The great American statesman and orator Daniel Webster recognized this when he declared: "If we and our posterity shall be true to the Christian religion, and if we and they shall live always in the fear of God and shall respect his commandments, we may have the highest hopes for the future fortunes of our country. It will have no decline and fall, but it will go on prospering. But if we or our posterity shall reject religious instructions and authority, violate the rules of morality and recklessly destroy the political constitution which holds us together, no man can tell how sudden a catastrophe may overwhelm us, that shall bury all of our glory in profound obscurity." (Address to The New York Historical Society, "Press of The Historical Society," 1852. See "Christian Life and Character of The Civil Institutions of the United States," p. 270).

During the same period of time that Webster gave his impassioned speech from the floor of the U.S. Senate, Alexis de Tocqueville was completing an extensive tour of America, and is purported to have written, in 1831: "I sought for the greatness and genius of America in her commodious harbors and her ample rivers, and it was not there; in her fertile fields and boundless prairies and it was not there; in her rich mines and her vast world commerce, and it was not there. Not until I went to the churches of America and heard her pulpits aflame with righteousness did I understand the secret of her genius and her power. America is great because she is good, and if America ever ceases to be good, America will cease to be great." (Quoted in Ezra Taft Benson, "God, Family, Country," p. 360).

Mosiah recognized the majesty and preeminence of divine justice, when he said that "it is better that a man should be judged of God than of man, for the judgments of God are always just, but the judgments of man are not always just." (Mosiah 29:12). He then vividly contrasted the reign of his righteous father Benjamin, with that of wicked King Noah.

The earlier Nephite kings, and the Chief Judges who were to follow Mosiah, were judicial, executive, and legislative branches all in one. We shall see, however, that there was a system of checks and balances built into the system of the Nephite Judges. More important than the type of government, though, was the obedience of those rulers to the unvarying laws and commandments of God. In such a situation, Mosiah said that it would be best to always have kings to rule over the people. Under these conditions, autocracy might even be preferable to democracy.

This principle might be startling to those who believe that democracy is ordained of God and is the best form of government. Actually, that form of government is best that allows man his agency to achieve his potential within the context of the gospel of Jesus Christ. Theocracy is the best form of monarchy; short of that, Mosiah believed that a righteous and God-fearing king is best. His own father, after all, had provided the classic example of enlightened leadership.

But a disciplined mind, by itself, is not enough. "If rationalism wishes to govern the world without regard to the religious needs of the soul, the experience of the French Revolution is there to teach us the consequences of such a blunder." (Renan, "The Apostles"). Religion is necessary to morality; otherwise, it would be possible to program a computer to be moral. The point is, that even in the best of circumstances, man cannot be left to his own devices without the guiding influence of the Spirit. Power tends to corrupt and absolute power corrupts absolutely. When our hearts are set upon temporal things, spirituality is weakened until the things that should be important to us are no longer a part of our daily lives.

Will and Ariel Durant wrote: "Since men love freedom, and the freedom of individuals in society requires some regulation of conduct, the first condition of freedom is its limitation; make it absolute and it dies in chaos." ("The Lessons of History," p. 68). The Lord declared of His own children: "We will prove them herewith, to see if they will do all things whatsoever the Lord their God shall command them." In other words, conditions and limitations were imposed upon the exercise of man's agency, so that he would be able to continue to progress. If men would be true to His divine nature, and nurture the characteristics of Heavenly Father, they would "have glory added upon their heads for ever and ever." (Abraham 3:25-26).

When we engage our agency, we automatically limit our options. If we choose the better alternative, we automatically have decided not to choose less attractive outcomes. Heavenly Father gives us commandments in order to help us to choose the better part, to allow us to grow through the exercise of agency, and to approach our potential.

Elder Neal A. Maxwell wrote, "Freedom wisely used to interact with the principles of the gospel of Jesus Christ, far from producing drabness and uniformity in disciples, produces not only more significant individuals but more interesting individuals. There is something about the gospel that makes personality more luxuriant, whereas, as Arthur Henry King has observed, sin robs us of our individuality.

What a great adventure most men decline when they choose not to know their Father. What great folly for the amateur climbing the rugged and strait and narrow way to decline the services of such an Experienced Guide. The unconfronted individual who persists in walking after his own way is clearly headed for a personality precipice." ("Freedom: A Hard Doctrine").

Freedom and security are incompatible. Security is at its zenith in prisons and hospitals, where every physical need is met. But the liability of freedom is risk. The tendency of Americans to look to the government for job security, social security, and even homeland security, speaks for itself. It is evidence of a desire to avoid risk. Caesar provides security, and assumes the risk. The danger lies in the persona of the power hungry individual eager to step into a vacuum to take control. All that is required is that the people give up their agency, which is generally done willingly, yet in blindness and ignorance, and in deceptively small and unnoticed increments.

"When God made the oyster, He guaranteed his absolute economic and social security. He built the oyster a house for shelter and protection from enemies. When hungry, the oyster simply opens his shell and food rushes in for him. He has freedom from want. But when God made the eagle He declared: 'The blue sky is the limit! Build your own house!' So, the eagle built on the highest mountain. Storms threaten him every day. For food he flies through miles of rain and snow and wind. But the eagle, and not the oyster, is the emblem of America." (Anonymous). Besides, whoever heard of an "Oyster Scout?"

To Mosiah, monarchy was a "type" of basic gospel principles, and was the antithesis of its unrighteous opposite. He taught that the ideal relationship of a king to his subjects is like that of parents to their children, and of God to all His children. The role of parents, of kings, and even of God Himself is ultimately to allow those within the sphere of their influence to exercise agency in order to strengthen commitment to personal responsibilities, and ultimately to help them to become co-inheritors of all our Father possesses.

Mosiah used the example of King Noah as a "type" of Satan, and his reign as a reflection of Lucifer's counterfeit plan. Noah's strategy was patterned after his mentor, the devil. Its centerpiece was to consciously avoid teaching correct principles, and to deny the people their freedom, thus leaving them ultimately disinherited, driven from their lands, and hunted; in short, they were left to physical and spiritual destruction. "And thus we see that the devil will not support his children at the last day, but doth speedily drag them down to hell." (Alma 30:60).

In Mosiah's view, men and women who would be free recognize the awesome responsibility of their stewardship. The last official words of President John F. Kennedy, that were to have been delivered at the conclusion of a speech he planned to give in Dallas, Texas, November 22, 1963, reflect his appreciation of this responsibility: "We in this country, in this generation, are - by destiny rather than by choice - the watchmen on the walls of world freedom. We ask, therefore, that we may be worthy of our power and responsibility; that we may exercise our strength with wisdom and restraint, and that we may achieve in our time and for all time the ancient vision of peace on earth, good will toward men. That must always be our goal, and the righteousness of our cause must always underlie our strength. For as was written long ago: 'Except the Lord keep the city, the watchman waketh in vain.'" (Psalms 127:1).

Lord Acton, a British observer of the Nineteenth Century American political scene, noted that "it was from America that the plain ideas that men ought to mind their business, and that the nation is responsible to Heaven for the acts of the State, burst upon the scene like a conqueror upon the world they were destined to transform, under the title of the Rights of Man; and the principle gained ground, that a nation can never abandon its fate to an authority it cannot control."

Mosiah pointed out that it was only because of their sincere repentance that the People of Limhi had been delivered from bondage. He recognized the importance of a foundation principle, that "when we obtain any blessing from God, it is by obedience to that law upon which it is predicated." (D&C 130:21). It is critical that we understand that blessings follow obedience to laws upon which those specific blessings are predicated.

Mosiah then taught his people that it is very difficult to dethrone a wicked king. Book of Mormon opposition to monarchy is not a matter of fixed principle. Mosiah's opposition to it was not advocated as a fundamental political truth. It was simply that wicked kings have the power to spread their iniquity. A good king, however, is quite another matter.

Apparently, King Mosiah condoned revolution as an acceptable alternative to corrupt government. "Ye cannot dethrone an iniquitous king," he said, "save it be thru much contention and the shedding of much blood." (V. 21). Even President Abraham Lincoln, who led the United States of America into its bloodiest conflict in order to preserve the Union, declared 13 years earlier that "any people, anywhere, being inclined and having the power, have the right to rise up and shake off the existing government, and form a new one that suits them better."

The issue of "independence" is charged with special emotion for Americans. The word, however, occurs only once in the scriptures, (D&C 78:14), and in that context describes the church as a body, and has no reference to individuals. The church, moreover, can "stand independent above all creatures" only because it is entirely dependent upon the providence of God. As Mosiah's father taught, when we serve God with our whole heart and soul, we are free from dependence upon any other being. Our indebtedness to God is transferred by Him to the poor, and it is through them that He asks us to pay our debt to Him. Thus is a Zion Society created from the raw material of righteous interdependency. (See "Government By The Voice of The People: A Witness and a Warning" in "The Book of Mormon: Mosiah, Salvation Only Through Christ," BYU Religious Study Center, 1991, p. 113-137).

No other religion, however, stresses so much the meaning and worth of the individual. It is the ultimate value, and the church is the instrument for its development. Not surprisingly, the family is the highest expression within the church of individual life. It is the foundation for individual and collective happiness on earth, and is the basic building block of eternal life.

Events in Zarahemla at the close of the reign of King Mosiah typify world events in the Twenty-First Century. Unrighteous rulers have had "friends in iniquity" and have maintained large armies and forces of secret police to protect their illegitimate rule and their selfish interests; they have torn up or disregarded the established laws of the land and have trampled under their feet the commandments of God. They have instead enacted laws to suit their own wicked purposes, and whoever has been so bold as to defy these laws has risked destruction. Rebellion against wicked rule has been violently suppressed. In this manner have unrighteous rulers dishonored their authority, that can ultimately be traced back to those whom they govern.

There is nothing intrinsically wrong with monarchy. It is not diametrically opposed to good government. It is inexpedient, or not suitable to most circumstances, simply because it is subject to abuse. The American patriot Patrick Henry delivered the following speech from the floor of the House of Burgesses, Williamsburg, Virginia, in March 1775. It is a stirring denunciation of an abusive monarchy.

"They tell us, Sir, that we are weak and unable to cope with so formidable an adversary. Sir, we are not weak, if we make a proper use of those means which the God of nature hath placed in our power. Three millions of people, armed in the holy cause of liberty, and in such a country as that which we possess, are invincible by any force which our enemy can send against us. Besides, Sir, we shall not fight our battles alone. There is a just God who presides over the destinies of nations, and who will raise up friends to fight our battles for us. The battle, Sir, is not to the strong alone; it is to the vigilant, the active, the brave. Besides, Sir, we have no election. If we were base enough to desire it, it is now too late to retire from the contest. There is no retreat but in submission and slavery! Our chains are forged! Their clanking may be heard on the plains of Boston! The war is inevitable, and let it come! I repeat, Sir, let it come!

It is vain, Sir, to extenuate the matter. Gentlemen may cry, 'Peace, Peace!' but there is no peace. The war is actually begun! The next gale that sweeps from the North will bring to our ears the clash of resounding arms! Our brethren are already in the field! Why stand we here idle? What is it that gentlemen wish? What would they have? Is life so dear, or peace so sweet, as to be purchased at the price of chains and slavery? Forbid it, Almighty God! I know not what course others may take; but as for me, give me liberty or give me death!"

Mosiah declared that, in their situation, in order to preserve their liberty, they must renounce monarchy and choose judges according to the voice of the people. To many, this may seem to refer to the democratic form of government desired by Patrick Henry, but the Lord's meaning may be different. The vote of the church is the voice of the people in church matters. This is the law of Common Consent. Before officers may serve in their positions, they must receive a formal sustaining vote of the people over whom they are to preside.

The Judges, however, could provide for the people a pattern of rule different and yet compatible with democratic government. In ancient Israel, the Judges were not simply legal advisers, but they were "deliverers," or men and women who redeemed tribe or nation from subjection to their neighbors, and who became local or national rulers. This is the same pattern that was to be established by Book of Mormon Judges.

Abraham Lincoln said that you can fool some of the people some of the time, and you can fool some of the people all of the time, but you cannot fool all of the people all of the time. Mosiah put it this way: "It is not common that the voice of the people desireth anything contrary to that which is right; but it is common for the lesser part of the people to desire that which is not right; therefore, this shall ye observe and make it your law - to do your business by the voice of the people." (V. 26).

The law of Common Consent recognizes that the righteous exercise of agency allows men and women to progress to ultimate salvation. This is the value of a democratic system. Inherent in this law is a warning, however. If the voice of the people chooses iniquity, the Lord will visit them with great destruction. Today, we recognize "iniquity" as legalized abortion, prostitution, pornography, institutional and state-supported gambling, Sabbath-breaking, filth on television and in motion pictures, corruption in the music industry, dishonesty in the marketplace, violence in society, a lowering of standards in the spoken and written word, and so on. "The world seeks not the Lord to establish his righteousness, but every man walketh in his own way and after the image of his own god, whose image is in the likeness of the world, and whose substance is that of an idol which waxeth old and shall perish in Babylon, even Babylon the Great, which shall fall." (D&C 1:16).

"Freedom does not mean the freedom to exploit law in order to destroy it. It is not freedom which permits the Trojan Horse to be wheeled within the gates, and those within it to be heard in the name of tolerating a different point of view." (Taylor Caldwell, "Pillar of Iron," p. 511). "No people can maintain freedom unless their political institutions are founded upon faith in God and belief in the existence of moral law. God has endowed men with certain inalienable rights and no legislature and no majority, however great, may morally limit or destroy those." (Ezra Taft Benson, "The American Challenge").

Mosiah then stressed that with Judges sustained by the voice of the people, individual accountability would prevail. One of the prices of monarchy is that the king must ultimately assume personal responsibility for many of the iniquities of his subjects. These include "the wars, and contentions, and bloodshed, and the stealing, and the plundering, and the committing of whoredoms, and all manner of iniquities which cannot be enumerated." (V. 36).

Mosiah desired that the vacuum of personal accountability among his subjects should be eliminated at the termination of his reign as King. Other scriptures reinforce the concept of equality among all the members of the Church. These scriptures focus on the philosophy of agency, accountability, individual liberty, and independence within the context of the gospel.

Mosiah knew well the difficulties facing even a righteous king, having personally experienced many challenges to the stewardship responsibilities of his office. "And he told them that these things ought not to be; but that the burden should come upon all the people, that every man might bear his part." (V. 34). Even though righteous individuals might lead the government, personal accountability would rule supreme.

These teachings, then, constituted the position paper Mosiah had sent forth among the people, and having read and studied it, "they were convinced of the truth of his words." (V. 37).

Joseph Smith was once asked how he managed to govern so many people. He responded, "I teach them correct principles, and they govern themselves." ("Life of Joseph Smith the Prophet," p. 496). Perhaps he was taught this valuable lesson by either Mosiah or Mormon, for he told John Taylor that he "not only had the principles of the gospel developed but was conversant with the parties who officiated as the leading men in former ages." (J.D., 20:174-175). He had communication "not only with the Lord, but with the ancient apostles and prophets." (J.D., 21:94). "Nephi and others of the ancient prophets who formerly lived on this continent came to him." (J.D., 17:374). George Q. Cannon said,

"If you read the history of the church from the beginning, you will find that Joseph was visited by various angelic beings. He doubtless also had visits from Nephi, and it may be from Alma and others." (J.D., 13:47).

In any event, as a result of the education in political science that Mosiah's people had received from him, they no longer desired to have another king succeed him, and instead they became anxious "that every man should have an equal chance throughout all the land." (V. 38). They assembled in bodies to cast their votes so that they might select a judge by common consent.

They recognized the wisdom of Mosiah's counsel, and were thrilled to have the opportunity to try the great experiment of self-determination in government. The leadership crisis threatening the Nephites, which had so troubled Mosiah, had been met head on. As is so often the case, after thoughtful consideration, a potential stumbling block had been turned into a stepping-stone. A crisis had become an opportunity for the people to incorporate a wonderful gospel principle into their lives. "Change comes like a flash of lightning and a clap of thunder. The people shrink in fear, but after the storm, flowers bloom." ("I Ching" - The Chinese "Book of Change").

One is reminded of Tom Paine's impassioned words: "These are the times that try men's souls. The summer soldier and the sunshine patriot will in this crisis, shrink from the service of his country; but he that stands it now, deserves the love and thanks of man and woman. Tyranny, like hell, is not easily conquered; yet we have this consolation with us, that the harder the conflict, the more glorious the triumph. What we obtain too cheap, we esteem too lightly; 'tis dearness only that gives everything its value. Heaven knows how to put a proper price upon its goods; and it would be strange, indeed, if so celestial an article as freedom should not be highly rated." ("The Political Works of Thomas Paine," p. 55).

The people loved Mosiah without reservation. He was esteemed for his uncompromised integrity. Another great prophet leader who has led the army of Israel during the battle for survival in the Last Days was Ezra Taft Benson, who declared: "I do not believe the greatest threat to our future is from bombs or missiles. I do not think our civilization will die that way. I think it will die when we no longer care, when the spiritual forces that make us wish to be right and noble die in the hearts of men, when we disregard the importance of law and order, and the basic principles upon which this nation has been built. Great nations are never conquered from outside unless they are rotten inside. Our greatest problem today is erosion of the national morality." ("The American Challenge"). Woven throughout the teachings of the prophets of all ages is the desire to instill in the people a sense of integrity that shines like a light through the eyes.

The prophets teach the principle that "You cannot believe in honor until you have achieved it. Better keep yourself clean and bright: You are the window through which you must see the world." (George Bernard Shaw). "This above all," declared Polonius. "To thine own self be true, and it must follow, as the night the day, thou canst not then be false to any man." (Shakespeare, "Hamlet," Act 1, Scene 3).

And so, Alma the Younger was appointed to be the first Chief Judge of the Nephite nation. As Senator Daniel Webster said of John Jay, first Chief Justice of the Supreme Court of the United States, so could we say of Alma the Younger: "When the spotless ermine of the judicial robe fell on (him), it touched nothing less spotless than itself." ("The Writings and Speeches of Daniel Webster," v. 2, p. 51).

Alma also held the position of Presiding High Priest, "his father having conferred the office upon him, and having given him the charge concerning all the affairs of the church." (V. 42-43). In the accounts of the affairs of both church and state that follow, we shall find "the beginning of philosophy: a recognition of the conflicts between men, a search for their cause, a condemnation of mere opinion ... and the discovery of a standard of judgment." (Epictetus).

Once again, there was peace in the land. The church enjoyed prosperity when its members lived in zealous harmony with gospel principles. After carefully observing The Church of Jesus Christ of Latter-day Saints, Leo Tolstoy was moved to predict: "If Mormonism could be true to its foundations and remain unchanged for four generations, it might well become the most powerful social influence in the world." (Reportedly, in a conversation with President Andrew White, of Cornell University).

When Alma was chosen by the voice of the people, the reign of the judges commenced in the land of Zarahemla. But note that the new order of Nephite government was no more resistant to monarchy in practice than it was in theory. The institution of judgeships, rather than beginning a republican era in Book of Mormon history, slid back at once toward monarchy. The Chief Judge much more resembled a king than an American President. Once elected, he never again submitted himself to the people. After being proclaimed Chief Judge by the voice of the people, Alma enjoyed life tenure. When he chose to resign because of internal difficulties, he selected his own successor. Thus, a dynasty seems to have begun, the judgeship passing "by right" to the successive sons of the judges.

At this point in the record, Mormon recorded that the elder Alma died, having lived a righteous life in harmony with the laws of the gospel. He was 82 years old. "How carefully most men creep into nameless graves, while now and again one or two forget themselves into immortality." (Philip Brooks).

"Thus ended the reign of the kings over the people of Nephi." (V. 47). The change in government initiated by King Mosiah was considered so significant that, from this point on, the Nephites recorded their time from the beginning of the Reign of the Judges, rather than from the year that Lehi had left Jerusalem, as had previously been the case. The duty and responsibility of government remained the same, that William Jennings Bryan declared "is to restrain those who would interfere with the inalienable rights of the individual, among which are the right to life, the right to liberty, the right to the pursuit of happiness and the right to worship God according to the dictates of one's conscience." This would prove to be the objective of government in Zarahemla during the next 400 years.

At Mosiah's retirement, perhaps he had thoughts similar to those of Thomas Jefferson, who mused: "If, in my retirement to the humble station of a private citizen, I am accompanied with the esteem and approbation of my fellow citizens, trophies obtained by blood-stained steel, or the tattered flags of the tented field will never be envied. The care of human life and happiness, and not their destruction, is the first and only legitimate object of good government and was my only objective." ("The Writings of Thomas Jefferson," 8:165).

Mosiah died that same year, being 63 years of age. Clearly, "Book of Mormon prophets considered Mosiah's reign a crucial episode in Nephite history, and abridged from a rich documentary tradition to give us as complete a picture as possible of what Mosiah accomplished. There are more than 20 texts, types of texts, and oral sources referred to in The Book of Mosiah, giving us a broad perspective of the events during his reign." (FARMS: "Mosiah: The Complex Symbolism, and the Symbolic Complex of Kingship in The Book of Mormon").

Cicero wrote, "The first law for the historian is that he shall never dare utter an untruth. The second is that he shall suppress nothing that is true. Moreover, there shall be no suspicion of partiality in his writing, or of malice." The accounts abridged by Mormon that we know as The Book of Mosiah were true to the mandate given by Cicero. Although, as Washington Irving brooded, it is the rule that "history fades into fable, fact becomes clouded with doubt and controversy, the inscription moulders from the tablet, the statue falls from the pedestal," and that "columns, arches, pyramids are but heaps of sand, and their epitaphs, nothing but characters written in the dust," yet The Book of Mosiah stands as a shining example of the divine model.

Truly, this book "is the witness that testifies to the passing of time; it illumines reality, vitalizes memory, provides guidance in daily life, and brings us tidings of antiquity." (FARMS: "Mosiah: Complex Symbolism"). It is "the evidence of time, the light of truth, the life of memory, the directress of life, the herald of antiquity, committed to immortality." (Cicero, "De Oratore," ii, 36). In its pages, "the centuries roll back to the ancient age of gold." (Horace, "Odes," IV, ii, 39)

"Combining so many records suggests a great deal of concern in writing. Mormon included more material in his abridgement from the reign of Mosiah, save any other king except Nephi. Yet Mormon gave us only some 100 verses dealing with Mosiah himself. This suggests that something very crucial took place at that time that went beyond the person of the king himself. While Mosiah was at the center of much attention, it seems that Mormon's concern was the process of bringing people to Christ." (FARMS: "Mosiah: Complex Symbolism"). Within the Book of Mosiah, we discern that "human history becomes more and more a race between education and catastrophe." (H.G. Wells, "The Outline of History," 2:594). But we are comforted to know that in it the Lord has provided a blueprint for our survival, in a time and in circumstances that are not so very different from our own.

The
Book of Mormon
is a blueprint for our
survival in The Last Days.
With it, under the direction of
the Spirit, we can become the
architects of our fate and
the masters of our
destiny.

(A) Change of Heart

"I ask of you, my brethren of the church, have ye spiritually been born of God? Have ye received His image in your countenances? Have ye experienced this mighty change in your hearts?" (Alma 5:14).

For whatever reason, it is the heart, and not the head, that is the repository of feeling. We have all felt the pain and anguish of heartache, something that is qualitatively and quantitatively different from a migraine headache. At special moments in our lives, our hearts leap for joy, but curiously, we never seem to describe the experience as if our heads were exploding with happiness. Our hearts race with excitement, even as our heads spin with dizziness. A particularly handsome young man may be described as a heartthrob, but rarely as a head case. Kindred spirits are closer to our hearts than to our heads. Instinct draws a baby close to a mother's nurturing breast, and little ones are comforted by the steady beat of her heart. The weak and timid, who are faint of heart, respond to the sweet influence of the Spirit better than to the analytical power of the rational mind. When we are broken-hearted, we are receptive to the teachable things of the kingdom, which is a far cry from the terrifying confusion of a mind that is out of synch with reality, or that lacks clarity because of a dim wit. A racing heart may be calmed by a strong will, but when a storm breaks loose in the head there may be no easy remedy for the ensuing nervous exhaustion or breakdown.

Those who listen to their hearts are sensitive, compassionate, empathetic, intuitive, caring, and considerate. When it is only our heads that influence us, we are too often callous, unfeeling, pitiless, harsh, cold-hearted, (brrr) or even (gasp) heartless. When we begin to lose our minds, others may first charitably describe us as eccentric, and only later harshly label us as demented. But when our hearts have been worn out in service, there is no such stigma. In fact, when we think of Mother Teresa, we recall the capacity of her heart, and not a numerical value that may be assigned to her intellect.

A pounding or racing heart may be the first sign of unbridled excitement. But unregulated stimulation of the brain is more commonly manifested as a grand mal seizure accompanied by foaming at the mouth. Endurance athletes may have enlarged hearts due to repetitive workouts involving aerobic exercise, while over-stressed business executives may only have dangerously enlarged heads due to misguided feelings of self-aggrandizement.

It is far better to have a troubled heart that leads us to repentance and reformed behavior, than it is to have a disturbed mind that can only be managed with antipsychotic medication. Those with wounded or broken hearts may heal slowly, but their prognosis is far better than those with irreversible brain injury. A heart may burst with the pride of accomplishment, but well-deserved achievement is easier to deal with than is the big head of one who is all wrapped up in himself. Those of us who have had our hearts stolen may be lucky enough to find our way back to happiness, but those who have lost their minds through trauma, disease, or the manipulation of others, are left with the irreversibility of a hollow core of existence from which there is no escape.

When we are light-hearted, we don't have a care in the world; but when we are lightheaded, we feel only dizziness and disorientation. With heart-felt sorrow, we experience empathy and compassion that cannot be described with words, and that cannot be explained by the rational mind. Some emotions touch our hearts in ways that could never penetrate our thick skulls. If our hearts are like flint, it is because they have become calcified through neglectful inattention and disuse. Sometimes, people are heartless because they are brainless.

We may have a gentle heart, but if we are soft in the head, it is because our brains have turned to mush; our hippocampus is no longer cranking out fresh neurons. A pounding heart may presage the excitement of new opportunities, but a throbbing head is often the symptom of poorly managed stress. A warm heart implies nurture, but a heart that is as cold as a lump of coal supposes neglect. A warm embrace draws people together, and in close proximity, hearts can be knits together as one. A sorrowful heart can also be a strong heart, but only when it is sustained by the Spirit.

The average heart contracts 80 times per minute, 4,800 times per hour, and 115,200 times per day. Over the course of a year, the heart beats over 42 million times. In 70 years, that's almost 3 billion beats. An adult heart pumps up to 2,000 gallons of blood daily, about 730,000 gallons per year, or up to 51,000,000 gallons in 70 years, through around 100,000 miles of vessels in a circulatory system that brings nourishment to the 37.2 trillion cells that make up the human body.

The ancients, who knew little about the anatomy or physiology of the circulatory system, mentioned the heart almost 1,500 times in the scriptures. Many, if not all, of the prophets have used the heart as a metaphor for the seat of our deepest emotions. For example, Joseph Smith described his revelatory experience when reading in the Book of James, in the New Testament: "Never did any passage of scripture come with more power to the heart of man than this did at this time to mine," he wrote. "It seemed to enter with great force into every feeling of my heart." (Joseph Smith History 1:12).

The book of Proverbs is a rich source of references to the heart, as in Proverbs 15:13: "A merry heart maketh a cheerful countenance: but by sorrow of the heart the spirit is broken." Or Proverbs 14:30: "A sound heart is the life of the flesh." Or Proverbs 16:23: "The heart of the wise teacheth his mouth, and addeth learning to his lips." Or Proverbs 2:2: "Apply thine heart to understanding." Or Proverbs 8:5: "Be ye of an understanding heart." Or Proverbs 15:14: "The heart of him that hath understanding seeketh knowledge." Or Proverbs 15:30: "The light of the eyes rejoiceth the heart." Or Proverbs 17:22: "A merry heart doeth good like a medicine." Or Proverbs 23:12: "Apply thine heart unto instruction, and thine ears to the words of knowledge." Or Proverbs 3:1: "Forget not my law; but let thine heart keep my commandments." Or Proverbs 3:5: "Trust in the Lord with all thine heart; and lean not unto thine own understanding." Or Proverbs 7:3: "Write (the law) upon the table of thine heart."

The Saints of all ages understand the feelings of the people of Zarahemla, who exclaimed to their prophet Benjamin: "We believe all the words which thou hast spoken unto us; and also, we know of their surety and truth, because of the Spirit of the Lord Omnipotent, which has wrought a mighty change in us, or in our hearts, that we have no more disposition to do evil, but to do good continually." (Mosiah 5:2).

Alma asked the brethren of the church: "Have ye spiritually been born of God? Have ye received his image in your countenances? Have ye experienced this mighty change in your hearts?" (Alma 5:14). Then, by extension, he asked each of us: "And now behold, I say unto you, my brethren, if ye have experienced a change of heart, and if ye have felt to sing the song of redeeming love, I would ask, can ye feel so now?" (Alma 5:26).

Sometimes, in the physical world, our hearts begin to falter. They may skip a beat or two, or we may suffer from arrhythmia (an abnormal heart rhythm), tachycardia (an abnormally rapid heart rate), or bradycardia (an abnormally slow heart rate). We may experience angina, or chest pain that is related to insufficient oxygenated blood reaching the heart muscle. When we experience the symptoms of heart disease, we are quick to initiate protocols designed to restore function. We make dietary changes, join a gym, habitually take the stairs instead of the elevator, and modify other patterns of behavior. We read everything we can about the subject, and follow the counsel of experts in the fields of medicine, physical therapy, and biofeedback. We seek inspiration from lifestyle coaches and self-help gurus. We learn to monitor our cardiovascular health, and we establish benchmarks to more easily gauge our progress toward the achievement of our goals. When we reach a sustainable level of fitness, we eschew lifestyle choices that would compromise our gains.

Although we have been told to "lift up (our) hearts and be glad," (D&C 29:5), scripture teaches us that in the Last Days, it is the heart that will bear the brunt of the consequences of wickedness. Amid signs in the sun, and in the moon, and in the stars, and upon the earth, men's hearts will fail them for fear. (See Luke 21:24-26). In fact, "all things shall be in commotion, and surely, men's hearts shall fail them." (D&C 88:91).

These scriptures, and others, suggest that there will be both physical and spiritual assaults on the integrity of the hearts of the children of men. On the one hand, significant cardiovascular disease may require medicine such as digitalis to treat a weakened heart. A pacemaker may be necessary to restore proper rhythm. In extreme cases, cardiomyopathy may necessitate a heart transplant to sustain life.

But it is a spiritual heart transplant that is of interest to those who have forsaken the world and embraced the lifestyle of a saint. Those who have had a physical heart transplant find it necessary to take a cocktail of immunosuppressant medication, according to a strict regimen, for the rest of their lives. The same prescriptions must be taken, in specific doses, at the same time every day. The routine must be followed without variation, in order to avoid the risk of failure of the surgical procedure. All doctor's appointments must be kept, every recommended laboratory test must be performed, medication side effects must be monitored, and drug interactions and the signs and symptoms of organ rejection must be controlled.

The same anti-rejection protocols must be followed after we have spiritually been given new hearts and have been born again. For, as the prophet Ezekiel declared: "A new heart also will I give you, and a new spirit will I put within you: and I will take away the stony heart out of your flesh." (Ezekiel 36:26). If we are not vigilant, our new hearts will surely fail us. We need to take a cocktail of immunosuppressant medication in the form of prayer, service, and temple attendance. We need to follow a strict regimen, in the form of regular spiritually aerobic church activity. We need to be diligent with medication that takes form and has substance in the ordinances of the gospel, including the bread and water that is offered on a weekly basis during our ward Sacrament services.

We must be diligent to maintain a schedule of regular accountability interviews with our spiritual physicians, and, in particular, to participate in the house calls that take the form of visits from our priesthood leaders. We must take our home and visiting teaching responsibilities seriously. We must be alert to our need for regularly recurring repentance and learn to self-monitor the spiritual promptings that assure us we have received forgiveness of our sins. If we sense that our organ transplant has begun to fail, or if we feel that it is being rejected because of the effects of carnality, sensuality, or devilishness, we must know to whom we can turn for triage, for guidance and direction, so that the destructive elements might be decisively addressed, in order to restore spiritual heart-health, and once again sing the song of redeeming love without experiencing shortness of breath.

We must strengthen our heart transplants by putting our shoulders to the wheel and pushing along. Cycling through the Standard works in Sunday School class every four years may seem repetitive, but it is one of God's favorite spin classes. It is no more pedestrian than is a spectacular sunset, no more dreary than a rainbow after a storm, and no more uninteresting than a flight of migratory geese passing overhead on a cold autumn evening. Studying the scriptures in Seminary every morning for four years may be daunting, but it establishes a habit pattern that can propel us over the summit of even the most daunting passes, those seeming obstacles to our progression.

Critics might see only frivolous repetition in our efforts to maintain spiritually aerobic health, mistaking repetition and reiteration for detachment from an active lifestyle that focuses only on instant gratification. In fact, sooner or later, there is for everyone who has had a spiritual heart transplant a moment in the sun, when the light of understanding illuminates the mind and confirms the divine potential of the new organ beating steadily in our chest. As the morning breaks over the eastern sky, and the sunrise heralds a new day, once again the self-evident truth is confirmed: We have been born again. The challenge before us has been met: We have received our new heart with gratitude, and have given ourselves completely to Him. With our new hearts, we enjoy a spiritual element that sustains our forward momentum as we push on into the unexplored reaches of eternity. Our new hearts not only expose us to an improved lifestyle, but also sustain our very lives. With all diligence, we keep them vital and healthy, knowing that it is from their steady beat that the fundamental issues of life flow, as in a revelatory stream. (See Proverbs 4:23).

(The) Character of God

"And thus
God bringeth about his
great and eternal purposes,
which were prepared from the
foundation of the world."
(Alma 42;26).

"There are but a very few beings in the world who understand rightly the nature of God (and) if men do not understand the character of God they do not comprehend themselves." (Joseph Smith, "Teachings," p. 343).

God the Father is in every sense perfect. He knows all things, "being from everlasting to everlasting." (D&C 132:20). He is eternal, which spans the time from uncreate intelligence, through our spiritual development as His children, on into mortality, and finally to our reunion with Him in the resurrection. He is absolutely perfect, and faith, hope and charity define His attributes. Of all those after whom we might model our behavior we should choose His Son Jesus Christ, Who is in every sense One with the Father. Thus, Mormon taught: "In Christ there should come every good thing." (Moroni 7:22).

All teaching of any worth is connected to the Savior. "All things which are good cometh of Christ." (Moroni 7:24). Quite simply, when He is the focus of our lives, we have the power to overcome our weaknesses. When our priorities are ordered and our lives are Christ-centered, we gain power. The Lord has revealed His gospel in the Dispensation of the Fulness of Times because He wants our perspective to be crystal clear so that we can clarify the principles of perfection that are emulated by His example and validated by the Spirit. Without His protective influence, we are vulnerable to the lethal storms initiated by the Destroyer that are sweeping the face of the earth and whose suffocating winds would suck the very life-sustaining marrow from our bones.

His power stems from love, in contrast to the elusive and transient power that is driven by greed, avarice, lust, and the unrighteous desire for dominion. It is easy to identify the fingerprints of Satan smeared all over the policies, pronouncements, politics, and parties that promote petty, provincial, and personal programs.

We are completely helpless to alter the progress or affect the outcome of any of God's activities. It was when Moses realized his utter dependence upon God that he exclaimed: "Now, for this cause, I know that man is nothing, which thing I never had supposed." (Moses 1:10). Our debt to God is total and complete. King Benjamin asked his people: "Can ye say aught of yourselves? I answer you, Nay. Ye cannot say that ye are even as much as the dust of the earth; yet ye were created of the dust of the earth; but behold, it belongeth to him who created you." (Mosiah 2:25).

Jesus Christ counseled: "Remember that it is not the work of God that is frustrated, but the work of men." (D&C 3:3). This led Joseph Fielding Smith, Jr. to declare: "No power on earth or hell can overthrow or defeat that which God has decreed. Every plan of the Adversary will fail; for the Lord knows the secret thoughts of men, and sees the future with a vision clear and perfect, even as though it were in the past." Jacob clearly understood "the holiness of our God. For he knoweth all things, and there is not anything save he knows it." (2 Nephi 9:20). Else He would cease to be God, and we could not have faith in Him.

Joseph Smith explained to John Wentworth: "No unhallowed hand can stop the work from progressing. Persecutions may rage, mobs may combine, armies may assemble, calumny may defame, but the truth of God will go forth boldly, nobly, and independent, until it has penetrated every continent, visited every clime, swept every country, and sounded in every ear; till the purposes of God shall be accomplished, and the Great Jehovah shall say 'The work is done.'" (H.C., 4:540). "The truth is, that after the thousands of attacks, and scores of books that have been published, not one criticism has survived, and thousands have borne witness that the Lord has revealed to them the truth of this marvelous work." (Joseph Fielding Smith, Jr.).

God is alive and well and is not living under an assumed name in Argentina, as some have supposed. He continues to enjoy tremendous popularity. His book is still on the best-seller list. In fact, it has enjoyed such publishing success that He has authored additional volumes. John Lennon was famously quoted as saying: "We're more popular than Jesus now." (For those of you who have forgotten, or never knew, Lennon was a member of a band called "The Beatles"). Oh, how foolish most men are when they get a whiff of fame or fancy themselves as celebrities, while all the time, the character of God remains unblemished. He, alone, deserves theatrical encores, and it is He who, in the end, will receive standing (or kneeling) ovations from His children.

Choose the Harder Right

"Helaman and his brethren
were no less serviceable unto the people
than was Moroni; for they did preach the
word of God, and they did baptize unto
repentance all men whosoever would
hearken unto their words."
(Alma 48:19).

Is it easier to choose wrong, and harder to choose the right? Is it easier to be wicked, and harder to be righteous? Is it easier to be sad, and harder to be happy? Is it easier to just put your life on cruise control, and harder to take the high road? Is it easier to go with the flow, and harder to swim upstream, against the current? Is it easier to walk with turkeys, and harder to soar with eagles? Is it easier to just throw in the towel and give up, and harder to continue the good fight? Is it easier to be mediocre or average, and harder to be exceptional? Is it easier to adopt the ways of the world, and harder to acknowledge the autobiographical thread within each of us that leads back to Deity? Is it easier to yield to temptation, and harder to resist sin? Is rebellion an easier alternative, and obedience a harder choice? Is it easier to live in a confusing fog of conflicting values, and harder to be grounded and principled?

Is it easier to be immoral, and harder to be virtuous? Is it easier to be slothful and indolent, and harder to be upright? Is it easier to be swayed by secular humanism, and harder to be faithful and submissive to the whisperings of the Spirit? Is it easier to be carnal and worldly, and harder to be holy? Is it easier to live in wanton defiance of God's laws, and harder to pattern our lives after obedience? Is it easier to yield to debauchery, and harder to have moral backbone? Is the pursuit of nobility akin to a quest to find the Holy Grail? Are those who attempt to follow the teachings of the Savior only tilting with windmills?

When Joan of Arc was carried to the stake, she was given the opportunity to obtain her freedom by denying her beliefs. Instead, she made this statement: "I know this now. Every man gives his life for what he believes. Every woman gives her life for what she believes. Sometimes people believe in little or nothing, and so they give their lives for little or nothing. One life is all we have, and we live it as we believe in living it, and then it is gone. But to surrender what you are and to live without belief is more terrible than dying, even more terrible than dying young." Resolutely, then, she faced death, still true to her faith and her beliefs. Her final acts on earth were consistent with her convictions. (Maxwell Anderson, "Joan of Lorraine," Act 2, Interlude 3).

In France during the Middle Ages, the successor to the throne was known as the Dauphin. During the reign of his father, unscrupulous and crafty counselors tried every means to corrupt the Dauphin, to thereby make him ineligible to inherit the throne. In all of their attempts, however, they were unsuccessful. Finally, in resignation, they asked him: "How is it that with all our enticements we have not been able to corrupt your high standards?" His reply was simple: "I am a King's son."

Both Joan of Arc and the Dauphin had established patterns of behavior that were consistent with their beliefs, and that allowed them to act in perfect harmony with their convictions. Many of us assume that all you need is 21 days to make or break a habit, be it good or bad, and that after that, unconscious mechanisms kick into gear, and we find ourselves on autopilot. This number comes from a popular book published in 1960 called "Psycho-Cybernetics" by Maxwell Maltz, a plastic surgeon who noticed his patients seemed to take about three weeks to get used to their new faces. However, the time it takes to make or break a habit may not be that clear-cut. More recent studies show that the average time it takes for a new habit to coalesce is about 10 weeks, but individual times varied from 18 days to almost 9 months. The bottom line is that if you want to internalize a new behavior, you shouldn't despair if three weeks doesn't do the trick. For most people, that's simply not enough time. Stick with it for a bit longer, and you'll end up with a habit you can keep without even thinking about it.

Along the way, as good habits are forged, there will be hurdles to surmount. We know that there needs to be opposition in order for the positive lifestyle promoted by the Plan of Salvation to succeed, and so, any habit formation, even the internalization of gospel principles, must grapple with this tricky phenomenon. Think, for example, of the predicament facing Adam and Eve in the Garden, before the Fall.

Not knowing the mind of God, that opposition is necessary for the enjoyment of eternal happiness, Satan sought what he thought would be the misery of all mankind, and with his congenital short-sightedness and his typical stratagem of promoting half-truths, he offered the forbidden fruit to Eve. "Ye shall be as God," he unwittingly promised, "knowing good and evil." (2 Nephi 2:18).

By innocently addressing this unfamiliar concept of opposition with a little help from Satan, Adam and Eve made the difficult choice to transgress God's law, having reached the conclusion that there was no other way for them to heed their Father's encouragement to embark upon the path of progress. They chose the harder right, rather than languishing in the moral stagnation of the easier wrong. Then, their Father visited them and gave them further instruction, including sacred covenants, in order to provide the nurturing matrix within which their newfound habit patterns could take root.

The Savior Himself explained: "It must needs be that the devil should tempt the children of men, or they could not be agents unto themselves; for if they never should have bitter they could not know the sweet. Wherefore, it came to pass that the devil tempted Adam, and he partook of the forbidden fruit and transgressed the commandment, wherein he became subject to the will of the devil, because he yielded unto temptation." (D&C 29:39-40). But Adam was not deceived. His was an intelligent, conscious decision, the result of a clear understanding of the requirements of the gospel Plan. Adam fell that his family might come to know true happiness and develop the moral fiber to consistently choose the harder right. Without understanding all the ramifications of his decision to partake of the fruit of the Tree of Knowledge of Good and Evil, he nevertheless believed that the change to a mortal condition would be necessary, even though it might come like a flash of lightning and a clap of thunder. In the end, though, he knew the storm would pass and that flowers would bloom. (See "I Ching," The Chinese Book of Change).

The decision made by Adam and Eve in the Garden to choose the harder right rather than the easier wrong obviated the paradox that lay before them, wherein they would have remained forever in "a state of innocence, having no joy, for they knew no misery; doing no good, for they knew no sin." (2 Nephi 2:23). To put it plainly, the Fall paved the way for the introduction of the very priesthood ordinances that had been individually crafted to develop good habit patterns within the crucible of opposition in the lone and dreary world.

Spencer W. Kimball observed: We often try to expel from our lives choices that are typified by the harder right, and that might result in "physical pain and mental anguish," and instead "assure ourselves of continual ease and comfort, but if we were to close the doors upon such sorrow and distress, we might be excluding our greatest friends and benefactors." Suffering can make saints of sinners as they learn patience and self-mastery. These are the very emotions that Adam and Eve must have appreciated, and that may actually have sustained them, as they forged a new life together in the telestial world outside the overly protective influences of the Garden, that might have ultimately proved to be suffocating.

President Kimball observed: "If we looked at mortality as the whole of existence, then pain, sorrow, failure, and short life would be calamity. But if we look upon life as an eternal thing stretching far into the pre-mortal past and on into the eternal post-death future, then all that happens may be put in proper perspective." This longitudinal view must have been adopted by our first parents, for it explains why they eagerly anticipated the opportunity to become mortal. "Blessed be the name of God," Adam had declared, "for because of my transgression my eyes are opened, and in this life I shall have joy, and again in the flesh I shall see God. And Eve, his wife, heard all these things and was glad, saying: Were it not for our transgression we never should have had seed, and never should have known good and evil, and the joy of our redemption, and the eternal life which God giveth unto all the obedient." (Moses 5:10-11).

The Plan was carefully crafted to create the conditions to come unto Christ within the crucible of the exercise of free will, as we are prompted and inspired to choose the harder right. Perhaps there is sense, after all, in the seeming chaos of existence, and there is a common thread underlying all experience. "For my thoughts are not your thoughts, neither are your ways my ways, saith the Lord. For as the heavens are higher than the earth, so are my ways higher than your ways, and my thoughts than your thoughts." (Isaiah 55:8-9).

We know that we cannot find "happiness in doing iniquity, which thing is contrary to the nature of that righteousness which is in our great and Eternal Head." (Helaman 13:38). We know by experience that if there be no righteousness, there be no happiness." (2 Nephi 2:13). Then, why do we sin, if "wickedness never was happiness?" (Alma 41:10). Why do we allow ourselves to form bad habits that reinforce negative behaviors and outcomes, and that can only lead to suffering, and spiritual death? Why does misery love company? Why can we not get it through our thick heads that it shall surely come to pass, that it is only "the spirits of those who are righteous (who) are received into a state of happiness, which is called paradise, a state of rest, a state of peace?" (Alma 40:12).

Alma the Younger is a good example of one who had seen life from both sides of the fence, and who, after his conversion, would never again look back. His abrupt change of habits was accompanied by indescribable suffering. His rehabilitation was accompanied by a detoxification from sin that we would wish upon ourselves or anyone else. His description to his son Helaman of his withdrawal symptoms is difficult even to read: "For three days and for three nights," he recounted, "was I racked, even with the pains of a damned soul." (Alma 36:26).

But he was able to measure his happiness against the discomfort of his former sinful life. "And oh, what joy," he wrote, "and what marvelous light I did behold; yea, my soul was filled with joy as exceeding as (had been) my pain!" (Alma 36:20). When he had been born again, his new life was illuminated by a personal witness that "the elements are eternal, and spirit and element, inseparably connected, receive a fulness of joy." (D&C 93:33). Having once made the harder decision to choose the right, it would become easier for him to sustain a lifestyle that was oriented to happiness. He had learned the hard way, as we all must to some degree, that specific blessings follow obedience to their related laws. For "there is a law, irrevocably decreed in heaven before the foundations of this world, upon which all blessings are predicated. And when we obtain any blessing from God, it is by obedience to that law upon which it is predicated." (D&C 130:20-21). Alma could now bear a personal testimony of Benjamin's counsel that the Lord "doth require that (we) should do as he hath commanded (us); for which if (we) do, he doth immediately bless (us)." (Mosiah 2:24).

Earlier, Benjamin had asked the people of Zarahemla to consider "the blessed and happy state of those that keep the commandments of God." (Mosiah 2:41). Nephi would later observe how "the Lord in his great infinite goodness doth bless and prosper those who put their trust in him." (Helaman 12:1). Satan is always slithering about in the shadows, offering an easier wrong that brings misfortune because it is only a caricature and an illusion of happiness. It is the norm that it is only after much tribulation that the promises of the Lord are fulfilled. (See D&C 58:4). Only our incessant labors in the kingdom, epitomized by the harder right, are worthy of His mighty blessings. (See D&C 21:9).

For example, it may be more convenient to skip our prayers, but it is only when we pray always that the Lord promises to pour out upon us his Spirit, and to bestow upon us His great blessings. (See D&C 19:38). Whether it takes three weeks or nine months, we will be like "the builder who first bridged Niagara's gorge. Before he swung his cable, shore to shore sent out across the gulf his venturing kite bearing a slender cord for unseen hands to grasp upon the further cliff and draw a greater cord, and then a greater yet, 'til at last across the chasm swung the Cable – then the mighty bridge in air. So may we send our little timid thoughts across the void, out to God's reaching hands, send our love and faith to thread the deep, thought after thought until the little cord has greatened to a chain no chance can break, and we are anchored to the infinite!" (Edward Markham).

If we want to develop the habit of choosing the harder right, instead of the easier wrong, we must not only say our prayers, but we must also be long suffering. Alma said of those "that did stand fast in the faith, (that) they were steadfast and immovable in keeping the commandments of God, and they bore with patience the persecution which was heaped upon them." (Alma 1:25).

If we want to develop the habit of choosing the harder right, instead of the easier wrong, we must "be humble, and be submissive and gentle," and be easily "entreated." (Alma 7:23). We must "call on his holy name, and watch and pray continually, that (we) may not be tempted above that which (we) can bear, and thus be led by the Holy Spirit, becoming humble, meek, submissive, patient," and "full of love." (Alma 13:28). If we are patient in all our sufferings (see Alma 20:29), and bear our afflictions with equanimity, the Lord will help us to succeed in our efforts. (See Alma 26:27).

If we want to develop the habit of choosing the harder right, instead of the easier wrong, we must guard ourselves against languishing in the comfort zones and aid stations that are scattered throughout Zion. (See 2 Nephi 28:24). As Benjamin warned the People of Zarahemla: "But this much I can tell you, that if ye do not watch yourselves, and your thoughts, and your words, and your deeds, and observe the commandments of God, and continue in the faith of what ye have heard concerning the coming of our Lord, even unto the end of your lives, ye must perish." (Mosiah 4:30).

If we want to develop the habit of choosing the harder right, instead of the easier wrong, we must endure to the end in righteousness. Only then will we be able to enjoy "eternal life, which gift is the greatest of all the gifts of God." (D&C 14:7). The Lord warned: "All those who will not endure chastening, but deny me, cannot be sanctified." (D&C 101:5). At the same time, Joseph Smith encouraged the Saints: "If thou endure it well, God shall exalt thee on high," and "thou shalt triumph over all thy foes." (D&C 121:8).

If we want to develop the habit of choosing the harder right, instead of the easier wrong, we will view our afflictions in a new light, and experience the epiphany that they really do work together for our good. (See D&C 98:3). During the process of the maturation of our good habit, the Lord will soften our hearts, inasmuch as he will bring us down into the depths of humility. (See Alma 62:41).

It may be that what doesn't make us stronger, kills us, in the sense that it destroys our drive and determination to improve our condition. It was the Dominican priest Henri Didón who, in the opening ceremony of a school sporting event in 1881, first expressed the words of the Olympic Motto: Citius, Altius, Fortius! (Faster, Higher, Stronger!) In this sense, it is the Lord Who, as our physical, mental, emotional, and spiritual fitness coach, "shall consecrate (our) afflictions for (our) gain." (2 Nephi 2:2). In other words, from His perspective, in the workout program He has designed for each of us, if there is no pain, there will be no gain.

It may take three weeks or three months, but after that, why should our hearts weep and our souls linger in the valley of sorrow, and our flesh waste away, and our strength slacken, because of our afflictions? (See 2 Nephi 4:26). During that initial period, when we are burning fat and building muscle, we need to be as Alma had been, to "be patient in (the) long-suffering and affliction" that often accompanies the formation of new habits. (Alma 17:11).

Edmund Dantès observed, in the concluding lines of Alexandere Dumas' "The Count of Monte Cristo," that "only a man who has felt ultimate despair is capable of feeling ultimate bliss. It is necessary to have wished for death, in order to know how good it is to live. Live, then, and be happy, and never forget that, until the day God deigns to reveal the future, the sum of human wisdom will be contained in these words: wait and hope."

In His infinite wisdom, He has designed all things to give us experience, and to be for our good. (See D&C 122:7). But he allows the anticipated change to hinge upon our desire and resourcefulness. Until we are committed and our agency kicks into high gear, "there is hesitancy, the chance to draw back, always ineffectiveness. Concerning all acts of initiative, there is one elementary truth, the ignorance of which kills countless ideas and splendid plans: That the moment we commit ourselves, then Providence moves too. All sorts of things occur to help us that would never have otherwise occurred. A whole stream of events issues from the decision, raining in our favor all manner of unforeseen incidents and material assistance, which no-one could have dreamed would have come our way." (Thomas Hornbein, "Everest - "The West Ridge," p. 100).

The process by which good habits are developed is that of testing the mettle of our convictions. We have no proof until we act on the basis of trust. Then comes the confirmation of the reality, as feelings of self-confidence grow, and purposeful actions replace tentative overtures. This is why the creation of good habits is so intimately tied to righteousness. The way of the Lord way is strait. Our tests during mortality are, ultimately, eminently fair. The rules are simple, and the rewards are unmistakably plain. Heavenly Father will not cause us to misplace our trust in ta program of spiritual fitness that cannot deliver on its promises.

Still, if we want to develop the habit of choosing the harder right, instead of the easier wrong, we must frequently take the road less traveled. As Robert Frost mused: "I shall be telling this with a sigh somewhere ages and ages hence: Two roads diverged in a wood, and I, I took the one less traveled by, and that has made all the difference." ("The Road Not Taken").

If we want to develop the habit of choosing the harder right, instead of the easier wrong, we must maintain unbridled optimism. Adversity may never end, even if we have a bright and cheerful outlook on life, but the journey will be much more pleasant if we have learned to channel hardship into constructive expressions that lead to positive outcomes.

If we want to develop the habit of choosing the harder right, instead of the easier wrong, we must take a few steps into the darkness before faith, the spiritual strong searchlight, illuminates the way before us. Then, as Helen Keller declared: "Although sinister doubts" may continue to "lurk in the shadow, (we will) walk unafraid towards the Enchanted Wood where the foliage is always green, where joy abides, where nightingales nest and sing, and where life and death are one in the presence of the Lord." ("Midstream").

If we want to develop the habit of choosing the harder right, instead of the easier wrong, we must not allow ourselves to be O.C.D. about it. In other words, we must not be Overly Concerned with Discipleship. At times, we need to just go with the flow of the Spirit, in the sense that we must "not run faster or labor more than (we) have strength." (D&C 10:4). Sometimes, we need to be content to enjoy glittering facets of the life of the Spirit, wherein we are receptive to flashes of insight as we are cast off into a stream of revelation and carried along in the quickening currents of direct experience with God.

So why, then, does it seem to be more difficult to choose the harder right than the easier wrong? Of all God's creations, is it not true that Satan is most miserable, and that our adoption of his tactics and counterproposal of democratization of the principles of the Plan without priesthood guidance and direction at the Council would have made us equally unhappy by denying agency, requiring obedience, relying on compulsion, and preventing progression? Although the plan he proposed in heaven was counterfeit, a fraud, inoperable, and ultimately rejected by the Council, basic elements have been transferred to the mortal battlefield, where a last-ditch effort for their acceptance is currently underway in the arena of agency. And that may explain a lot. A third part of the host of heaven, basking in celestial light, was drawn to Satan's ideology. Here on earth, with an impenetrable veil drawn across our minds, even with the light of Christ, and even with the gift of the Holy Ghost, and even though the curtains of His habitation have been extended, many of us are still swayed by his siren song.

Elements of his flawed ideology can be seen in social, political, cultural, and economic programs, and even in elements of religious ideology that pander to the natural man's innate insecurity, lack of initiative, and desire for undeserved entitlements. Those who voluntarily or involuntarily give up their agency in exchange for whatever transient pleasures poor choices may provide, have been snared by Satan and bound by his strong chains. They are enslaved by bad habits. When they feel the heavy cords of oppression around their necks, they realize too late that their poor choices have limited their options, restricted their actions, and fettered the expression of their righteous desires. Habitual sin creates a monotonous and mind-numbing conformity that is the antithesis of the artistic individuality proffered by the gospel. If we allow bad habits to limit our choices, often all that is left in the end is compromise that can leave a hollow core of emptiness in our gut.

Sometimes all too quickly, and sometimes agonizingly slowly, those who have sold their birthright for a mess of pottage are dragged down to a hell on earth that is of their own making. It is very hard to break the bad habits that are the result of repetitive poor choices precisely because agency must be surrendered in order to acquire them, and ironically, "we can never get enough of what we don't need, because what we don't need won't satisfy us." (Dallin Oaks). We exchange our noble birthright for a mess of pottage.

Heavenly Father does not operate this way. He always honors the eternal principle of agency. "Nevertheless," He counseled Adam in the beginning, "thou mayest choose for thyself, for it is given unto thee." (Moses 3:17). This is a riskier course of action, but it is the only way that eternal progression is possible. Choices and opposites are necessary as we stretch our spiritual muscles by reaching out to grasp the brass rings of immortality and eternal life. In the process, rather than enslaving us in good habits, God repeatedly gives us the opportunity to voluntarily recommit ourselves to covenants of obedience to true and eternal principles. Thus, church membership and meaningful participation in principled activities are vital to our spiritual well being, as is the renewal of the covenants we have made through the ordinances. God has unbridled confidence in our ability to choose the harder right, instead of the easier wrong, and as we do so, a miraculous transformation in our attitude takes place. The Prime Directive to which He adheres demands that we be free to choose, but the deck is fortuitously stacked in our favor because of the Light of Christ and the Gift of the Holy Ghost. And so, we are blessed with the physical and spiritual capacity to forge success strategies as we internalize the qualities of high achievers.

The Light of Christ exerts a nurturing influence. Although we must daily travel further from the East, we are nevertheless oriented toward a radiant glow emanating from that distant horizon. It provides us with the regularly recurring reassurance of a religious recalibration that autocorrects with celestial precision. It envelops us in an intuitive appreciation of where we came from, why we are here, and where we are going. As in a heavenly language that is rhythmical, melodious, soothing to our ears, and calming to our souls, when we hear the Spirit quietly whisper: "You're a stranger here," we are struck by the realization that we have "wandered from a more exalted sphere." (Eliza R. Snow). The Light of Christ personalizes what it means to be anxiously engaged, inspires us to plumb the depths of our commitment to the Savior, sensitizes us to the nobility of His work, and makes us more acutely aware of His glory, by bringing the visions of immortality and eternal life within our purview.

When we resolve to choose the harder right, instead of the easier wrong, we commit ourselves to the arduous process of spiritual rebirth. When we feel the urge to push His agenda instead of our own, the Light of Christ can be our labor coach, providing us with just the right amount of encouragement to successfully deliver our witness of the Savior without being overbearing.

One exciting element of our resolve to choose the harder right, instead of the easier wrong, is the constant stream of inspiration and revelation the subsequently cascades down from above. This ensures that we may walk along illuminated pathways, and allows us to use our faculties of mind, intellect, and spirit to our best advantage, that we might discern between truth and error, and more easily choose the right. It permits us to listen with sensitivity and to be receptive to the cries of the downtrodden and oppressed, to see with a clarity that allows us to be proactively responsive to our environment, and to be benevolently blind to the shortcomings of others who have not yet realized that the gospel is the perfect law of liberty.

When we resolve to choose the harder right, instead of the easier wrong, as fire in the sky, the air in the theater of life will be charged with an electricity that represents the inevitable merger of the universal encouragement of the Light of Christ, with the pointed and providential guidance provided by the Holy Ghost. When these influences streak in tandem across the heavens, their trajectories will coalesce to trace a flaming trail that sparkles over a vast cosmic ocean of thought. Over the ebb and flow of its tide, the Spirit will create an effectual bridge of understanding that is buttressed by the cohesive influence of the mighty foundation of faith. Then, the difficulty of making hard choices will melt away as the morning dew evaporates in the noonday sun.

Those who have chosen what they mistakenly believe to be the easier wrong, those who have voluntarily given up their agency to choose what they have perceived to be the harder right, will find themselves in the grip of bad habits, and will be snared by Satan and bound by his strong chains. The heavy cords he places around their necks will drag them down to hell. Once entrenched, it will have become very hard to consciously and purposefully break their bad habits precisely because agency itself has been surrendered in order to acquire them. Those who suffer from the resulting compulsions have reached this condition because of repeated actions, until a point is reached where, as William James explained, "unlimited freedom leads to unlimited tyranny."

Our habits, for better or for worse, are our constant companions. Completely at our command, they are our greatest helpers or our heaviest burdens. They push us onward and upward, or drag us down to mediocrity. Habits may be easily managed, but we must be firm with them as they become entrenched in our behavior patterns.

Habit is the servant of all, working with the precision of a machine, to be run for either profit or ruin. It really makes no difference to her, for she is coldly logical. Those who are firm with her will find that the world will come knocking at their door. But if she is treated carelessly or inattentively, she can easily become death, the destroyer of worlds. ("Bhagavad Gita").

Perhaps this is what President Monson had in mind, when he cautioned the Saints to choose the harder right, instead of the easier wrong.

Choose ye This Day

"Now there was no law against a man's belief;
for it was strictly contrary to the commands of God
that there should be a law which should bring men on to
unequal grounds. For this saith the scripture: Choose ye
this day, whom y will serve. Now if a man desired
to serve God, it was his privilege; or rather, if he
believed in God it was his privilege to serve
him; but if he did not believe in him,
there was no law to punish him."
(Alma 30:7-9).

During the 40-year sojourn of Israel in the wilderness of Sinai, Moses had served as its guide, given it God's law, and acted as His spokesman. He was the only leader an entire generation of Israelites had ever known. But the Lord took him at the end of their journey, just when they were about to face their greatest tests. The Lord had a contingency plan, however, to call Joshua to succeed Moses and to encourage him to fill the shoes of the great lawgiver by being strong, having courage, studying the scriptures, and being obedient. (See Joshua 1:6). Joshua rose to the occasion and allowed God to shape his nature. Similarly, as we allow God to mold our character, we can develop divine attributes and accomplish whatever He wants us to do.

Joshua faced great challenges when the Lord called him to lead the Israelites. He was not only taking the place of a great trailblazer, but he was also being asked to lead Israel in the conquest and colonization of Canaan. He may have felt as President Spencer W. Kimball did when he said: "This is my feeling for the work at this moment. There are great challenges ahead of us, and giant opportunities to be met. I welcome that exciting prospect and feel to say to the Lord: Give me this mountain! Give me these challenges!" (C.R., 10/1979).

Our own opportunities for growth require strength, moral courage, and the ability to prioritize our time so that we can cut to the quick and focus on matters of substance. Each of us has 168 hours each week, much of it discretionary time to do with as we please. As few as three of these hours are spent in church. We need to ask ourselves: How many hours are wasted "hanging out?" How many hours are squandered watching television, playing video games, or on our computers or our mobile devices? How many hours do we devote to social media?

Perhaps we should budget our time as carefully as we budget our money. Concentrating on the things that really matter endows us with a special capacity to manage the gift of time. We learn to take time with discipline, make time with diligence, find time with care, spend time with thoughtfulness, invest time with wisdom, and share time with pleasure. Turning our attention to the weightier matters of the law gives us a sense of independence, as we learn something new every day. Learning how to control our time can open our hearts and our minds to the breathtaking expansion of understanding. As we practice a learning style that embraces the Spirit, we will discover a pattern that will become our norm.

Heber J. Grant echoed the counsel of Ralph Waldo Emerson, when he declared: "That which we persist in doing becomes easier for us. Not that the nature of the thing has changed, but our power to do is increased." Spencer W. Kimball understood the powerful capacity of effective time management: "What I am asking for," he said, "is not a flashy, temporary change in performance, but a quiet resolve to lengthen our stride." ("Ensign, 12/1985, p. 26).

As Josiah Gilbert Holland pled: "God, give us men! A time like this demands strong minds, great hearts, true faith, and ready hands. Men whom the lust of office does not kill. Men whom the spoils of office cannot buy. Men who possess opinions and a will. Men who have honor; men who will not lie. Men who can stand before a demagogue and damn his treacherous flatteries without winking. Tall men, sun-crowned, who live above the fog in public duty and in private thinking. For while the rabble, with their thumb-worn creeds, their large professions, and their little deeds, mingle in selfish strife, Lo! Freedom weeps, Wrong rules the land, and Justice sleeps." ("God Give Us Men").

"It is not the critic who counts," declared Teddy Roosevelt, "and not he who points out where the strong man stumbled or where the doer of deeds could have done them better. The credit belongs to the man who is actually in the arena, whose face is marred by dust and sweat and blood, who tries and comes up short again and again, who knows the great enthusiasms, the great devotions and spends himself in a worthy cause; who, at best, if he fails, at least fails while daring greatly, so that his place shall never be with those cold and timid souls who know neither victory nor defeat." (Speech at the Sorbonne, Paris, 4/23/1910).

John F. Kennedy wrote, in a speech prepared for delivery on the afternoon of November 22, 1963: "We in this country, in this generation, are – by destiny rather than by choice – the watchmen on the walls of world freedom. We ask, therefore, that we may be worthy of our power and responsibility; that we may exercise our strength with wisdom and restraint, and that we may achieve in our time and for all time the ancient vision of peace on earth, and good will toward men. That must always be our goal, and the righteousness of our cause must always underlie our strength. For as was written long ago: 'Except the Lord keep the city, the watchman waketh in vain.'" (Psalms 127:1).

The Sons of Helaman "were all young men, and they were exceedingly valiant for courage, and also for strength and activity. But, behold, this was not all – they were men who were true at all times in whatsoever thing they were entrusted. Yea, they were men of truth and soberness, for they had been taught to keep the commandments of God and to walk uprightly before him." (Alma 53:20-21).

In order to be successful, the Lord commanded Joshua to study "the book of the law." (Joshua 1:8). Today, familiarity with the scriptures is important for us to succeed in our callings; indeed, in our lives. We cannot "wing it" in matters of substance, leave our fate to chance, or play it by ear in a world that has little to say. We must have proven protocols in place, study them, and apply them to our circumstances, in order to reach successful conclusions.

When Israel prepared to cross over Jordan, the flow of the river was halted, but not before the priests who carried the ark stepped into the current. (See Joshua 3:13-17). The Lord sometimes asks similar things of us. Boyd K. Packer said: "Shortly after I was called as a General Authority, I went to Harold B. Lee for counsel. He listened very carefully to my problem and suggested that I see David O. McKay. President McKay counseled me as to the direction I should go. I was very willing to be obedient, but saw no way possible for me to do as he counseled me to do. "I returned to Elder

Lee and told him that I saw no way to move in the direction I had been counseled to go. He said: The trouble with you is you want to see the end from the beginning. I replied that I would like to see at least a step or two ahead. Then came the lesson of a lifetime. You must learn to walk to the edge of the light, he said, and then take a few steps into the darkness. Then the light will appear and show the way before you." ("BYU Today," 3/1991, p. 22-23).

After crossing over Jordan, Israel set up a memorial of 12 stones as a testimony to future generations of the Lord's power, and to remind them that He would continue to bless them as He had their fathers. Today, we celebrate God's power through the ordinance of the Sacrament, by the example of the temple, and with the benchmarks of our own spiritual experiences. We remember the circumstances associated with our baptism, and our ordination to the priesthood is memorialized every time we exercise its power. The temple worthiness interview is commemorated with a personal recommend signed by our priesthood leaders and by ourselves. All of these experiences give us opportunities to commemorate God's influence in our lives.

In his final counsel to Israel, Joshua exhorted her to "cleave unto the Lord," or to join together with Him, rather than to "cleave unto the remnant of (the Canaanite) nations." (Joshua 23:8 & 12). Today, we sometimes "cleave unto" the world simply by tolerating its sins. "Vice," can be "a monster of such frightful mien, as to be hated needs but be seen. Yet seen too oft,' familiar with its face, we first pity, then endure, and then embrace." (Alexander Pope, "Essay on Man, Epistle 2").

We adopt the lifestyle of the world when we party and play in Idumea, rather than ponder and pray in Zion. We adopt coarse and profane speech. "Dude, we really do. I mean, its, like, normal." We adopt its manner of dress. Too frequently, the messages on our T-shirts, or even festooned on our bodies, reflect what we are thinking. But "this much I can tell you," Mosiah cautioned his people. "If you do not watch yourselves, and your thoughts, and your words, and your deeds ... you must perish." (Mosiah 4:30).

We sometimes adopt the values of the world, confusing them with the principles of the gospel. A neighbor of Marion D. Hanks came home with a new boat, and proudly showed it to Elder Hanks, asking for suggestions for a name. Elder Hanks said: "Why don't you call it 'Sabbath Breaker?" This might have been a little harsh, but illustrates the fact that we all need to be vigilant as we unconsciously establish our priorities.

Near the end of his life, Joshua gave important counsel. "Choose ye this day whom ye will serve," he declared. "But for me and my house, we will serve the Lord." (Joshua 24:15). We can't serve the true and living God and our worldly gods of wood and stone at the same time. The example of Joshua reminds us of the importance of commitment. "Not tomorrow, not when we get ready, not when it is convenient," taught Marvin J. Ashton, "but 'this day,' straightway, choose whom you will serve. He who invites us to follow will always be out in front of us with His Spirit and influence setting the pace. He has charted and marked the course, opened the gates, and shown the way. He has invited us to come unto Him, and the best time to enjoy His companionship is straightway." (C.R., 4/1983). We can best get on course and stay on it by making a total commitment, as Joshua did, to do the will of our Father.

Joshua's final counsel to the Israelites included the same charge to be strong and to have courage that the Lord had given when He had called him to be a prophet. (Joshua 23:1-6). Ezra Taft Benson echoed this injunction when he said that two principles are essential for security and peace: "First, trust in God; and second, a determination to keep the commandments, to serve the Lord, to do that which is right. The Lord has made it very clear in the revelations that even though times become perilous, even though we be surrounded by temptation and sin, even though there be a feeling of insecurity, even though men's hearts may fail them, and anxiety fill their souls, if we only trust in God and keep his commandments, we need have no fear." (C.R., 10/1950).

The
Book of Mormon
is a blueprint for our
survival in The Last Days.
With it, under the direction of
the Spirit, we can become the
architects of our fate and
the masters of our
destiny.

Christians

"Those who did
belong to the church were faithful;
yea, all those who were true believers in
Christ took upon them, gladly, the name
of Christ, or Christians as they were
called because of their belief in
Christ who should come."
(Alma 46:15).

There appeared in the Spokesman Review, on July 13, 1996, an article entitled: "Shaping a Word: Church people at odds over the meanings the word "Christian" should carry with it."

The article described "a widespread feeling that the word 'Christian' has been taken over by a particular community, namely evangelicals and other religious conservatives." On the other side of the coin, these same evangelicals "who have recently entered into theological dialogue with Roman Catholics are at times suspicious of Catholic references to the 'one true church.'"

Then there are the 'Mormons', who reportedly are "grappling more and more with what it means to be Christian even as some Christian groups continue to describe the nearly 10-million-member Church of Jesus Christ of Latter-day Saints as non-Christian."

Some even claim "the word 'Christian' would be more acceptable if we gave up our theological idea that the only way to salvation is through the cross of Christ. Of course, the ecumenical movement has long sought to open up the word 'Christian' to every church that confesses Jesus Christ, from the Roman Catholics to the Southern Baptists." Finally, the article concluded, "Only God ultimately knows who a true Christian is."

Latter-day Saints understand that the scriptures speak plainly about our relationship with Christ. They explain that "we talk of Christ, we rejoice in Christ, we preach of Christ, we prophesy of Christ, and we write according to our prophecies, that our children may know to what source they may look for a remission of their sins." (2 Nephi 25:26).

Emphatically, the doctrine of our church teaches that "there is no other name given whereby salvation cometh; therefore ... take upon you the name of Christ." (Mosiah 5:8). "Yea, come unto Christ, and be perfected in him," wrote the Prophet Moroni, "and deny yourselves of all ungodliness; and if ye shall deny yourselves of all ungodliness, and love God with all your might, mind and strength, then is his grace sufficient for you, that by his grace ye may be perfect in Christ." (Moroni 10:32)

The Book of Mormon is a powerful witness of Jesus Christ. Of 239 chapters in The Book of Mormon, 233 have references to Christ. Only Mosiah 9 & 22, Alma 51 & 52, and Helaman 1 & 2 do not. There are 88 name-titles of Jesus Christ found throughout the text, and 23 in First Nephi alone! Christ is referred to by name or inference 3,925 times in The Book of Mormon. Since the text has a total of 6,607 verses, it follows that some form of Christ's name is mentioned an average of every 1.7 verses in The Book of Mormon.

Clearly, we believe in Christ. We belong to The Church of Jesus Christ of Latter-day Saints. The Book of Mormon is Another Testament of Jesus Christ. We are Saints of the Most High God, in the truest biblical sense! In our meetings and conversations, we testify of His ante-mortal existence, and His foreordination to be the Redeemer of the world. The scriptures speak of His relationship with the Father, and of His divine investiture of authority. His appearances to His servants throughout history were many. The Book of Mormon, particularly, explains His condescension in taking a mortal body. Thus, we can better understand His temptations, and the power, might, dominion, and authority that typified His experience on the earth.

The scriptural accounts of His baptism demonstrate, by example, the way for all to follow. The stories of His ministry teach the truths of the gospel in simplicity. The events that transpired in the Garden of Gethsemane illustrate His strength and compassion. The path to Calvary, and the crucifixion, are reduced to a mere apostrophe; His death was but a pause that enables us to re-focus attention on His resurrection and ascension into heaven.

When He comes again, it will be in the clouds. He will be accompanied by The Church of the Firstborn, and His Second Coming will usher in His Millennial Reign. For a thousand years, His gospel will penetrate every soul and burn brightly in every bosom.

He is our Advocate with the Father, and the Bread of Life. He is the Cornerstone of our creation, the foundation of our existence. He is the Creator of worlds without number, and the Deliverer of the Covenant to all the children of the Father. He is Emmanuel: truly, in Him God is with us. The Firstborn of the Spirit Children of the Father, He is perfect in every detail. He is the Good Shepherd, and the Judge of both the quick and the dead. As Lord, King, and Jehovah, He has all power to act as a Mediator, and as the Messenger of the Covenant. The Lamb of God, He is the Messiah, the Anointed One, and the anticipated Redeemer of all mankind. He is our Rock, and our Savior, the Only Begotten Son of God in the flesh. He is the Son of Man of Holiness, and will be the Second Comforter to those who trust completely in His Holy Name.

Those who enter into the Covenant "are born of him." (Mosiah 5:7). This covenant is a binding contract, and since God is a party to every gospel covenant, it must come through revelation. No person may enter into such a covenant except on the basis of direct revelation from God. A "Born Again Christian" is one who is in a covenant relationship with the Lord, and since only members of Christ's true church can do that through the authority of the priesthood, it follows that the only real Born-Again Christians are Latter-day Saints! (See Bruce R. McConkie, "Mormon Doctrine," p. 166, Mosiah 15:10-11, 27:25, Alma 5:14, & 7:14, Alma 22:15 & 36:24).

In The Book of Mormon, King Benjamin told his people that because of their covenant with God, they would "be called the children of Christ, his sons and his daughters." (Mosiah 5:7). Even well-intentioned individuals use the term "Christian" in ways that are much less significant than its true meaning would convey. Christians recognize that "Jesus Christ (is) the Son of God, the Father of heaven and earth, the Creator of all things." (Mosiah 3:8). And so, they proudly take His name upon themselves.

Just as we are known by the name of our mortal parents, so too are we called by the name of Christ in a familial way. We are Christ's children in the sense that He united our body and spirit through the Resurrection: "For this day He hath spiritually begotten you," explained Benjamin. (Mosiah 5:7). There is a special family relationship reserved for the faithful that is in addition to the reality that we are all spirit children of the Father. (See D&C 34:3 & 121:7).

As the Lord revealed to Joseph Smith, the "greater priesthood administereth the gospel and holdeth the key of the mysteries of the kingdom, even the key of the knowledge of God. Therefore, in the ordinances thereof, the power of godliness is manifest. And without the ordinances thereof, and the authority of the priesthood, the power of godliness is not manifest unto men in the flesh." (D&C 84:19-21).

Only by making covenants with God and Christ can we break the bands of death, and are we made free. "There is no other name given whereby salvation cometh," said Benjamin; "therefore, I would that ye should take upon you the name of Christ, all you that have entered into the covenant with God." (Mosiah 5:8). Is it any wonder that The Church of Jesus Christ of Latter-day Saints is a missionary oriented church, and that the Lord Himself proclaims that it "is the only true and living church upon the face of the whole earth, with which I, the Lord, am well pleased?" (D&C 1:30).

The reality of the apostasy and the subsequent restoration of priesthood authority are well documented in the scriptures and in the history of the church. Today, no other church has the authority of the priesthood, which is necessary to bind and ratify the covenants we make with God. No other organization has the power to break the death grip of Satan, who would drag our souls down to hell in an instant, if he were given the opportunity to do so.

The attitude of the subjects of King Benjamin following his discourse was the same as that of true believers 50 years later who "took upon them, gladly, the name of Christ, or Christians, as they were called, because of their belief in Christ who should come." (Alma 46:15). They recognized the source of the only legitimate authority on earth with the power to sanctify man so that he can be brought into the presence of God.

In fulfillment of Benjamin's promise to them (See Mosiah 1:11), they were no longer "the people of Zarahemla" or "the people of Nephi," but "Christians." He who took upon himself the name of Christ would be found "at the right hand of God, for he shall know the name by which he is called; for he shall be called by the name of Christ." (Mosiah 5:9). As the Savior said: "My sheep hear my voice, and I know them, and they follow me." (John 10:27).

Benjamin pointed out that those who would not take upon themselves the name of Christ would find themselves in His disfavor, for their misplaced fealty would be manifest. "Whosoever shall not take upon him the name of Christ," Benjamin declared, "must be called by some other name; therefore, he findeth himself on the left hand of God." (Mosiah 5:10).

Alma asked: "If ye will not hearken unto the voice of the good shepherd, to the name by which ye are called, behold, ye are not the sheep of the good shepherd. And now if ye are not the sheep of the good shepherd, of what fold are ye? Behold, I say unto you, that the devil is your shepherd, and ye are of his fold; and now, who can deny this? ... Whosoever bringeth forth evil works, the same becometh a child of the devil, for he hearkeneth unto his voice, and doth follow him." (Alma 5:38-41). Benjamin also warned that through transgression the name of Christ would be blotted out of the heart. When this occurs, one no longer feels like a Christian (or Latter-day Saint). (Mosiah 5:11, See Mosiah 2:37). After all, the heart is the repository of feeling.

The invitation is extended by every missionary to those who are pure in heart: Deny the cares of the world and respond to a more noble calling. The discipline required of those who follow the Royal Law is alien to the natural man. After all, "urging self-restraints on hedonists is like asking Dracula to avoid hanging around the blood bank." (Neal Maxwell, C.R., 4/1995). But Christians know that it is only the redeeming blood of Jesus Christ that sanctifies the soul.

It is important to both hear and know "the name by which (Christ) shall call you." (Mosiah 5:12). Many hear, yet do not comprehend, "for how knoweth a man the master whom he has not served, and who is a stranger to him, and is far from the thoughts and intents of his heart?" (Mosiah 5:13, See K.J.T. & J.S.T. Matthew 7:23).

Baptism alone does not assure one of eternal life. Members of the church also need to be "steadfast and immovable, always abounding in good works." (Mosiah 5:15). They need to be sealed by the ratifying power of the Holy Spirit of Promise that is the Holy Ghost. (See D&C 88:3-4). One's calling and election is made sure only after the Lord has fully proven that individual. Then, when one receives "the other Comforter," Christ will appear and personally teach the visions of eternity.

What, then, is a Christian? No Latter-day Saint who is founded on the bedrock of faith, and is schooled in the grammar of the gospel, need grapple with this question.

(A) Christmas Miracle

"The voice of the
Lord came unto (Nephi), saying: Lift
up your head and be of good cheer; for behold, the
time is at hand, and on this night shall the sign be
given, and on the morrow come I into the world, to
show unto the world that I will fulfil all that
which I have caused to be spoken by the
mouth of my holy prophets."
(3 Nephi 1:12-13).

"It was always said of (Scrooge) that he knew how to keep Christmas well, if any man alive possessed the knowledge. May that be truly said of us, and all of us! And so, as Tiny Tim observed, God bless us, every one!" (Charles Dickens, "A Christmas Carol").

In Jerusalem, as the Meridian of Time approached, the angel of the Lord appeared in the temple to Zacharias and said: "I am Gabriel, that stand in the presence of God; and am sent to speak unto thee, and to shew thee these glad tidings." (Luke 1:19). He revealed that Zacharias and Elisabeth would have a son named John, who would turn many of the children of Israel to their God, "to make ready a people prepared for the Lord." (Luke 1:16-17).

At around the same time in the New World, angels appeared unto "wise men, and did declare unto them glad tidings of great joy; thus, in this year the scriptures began to be fulfilled" that had been spoken by the prophets. (Helaman 16:14).

Not long thereafter, the angel Gabriel was sent from the presence of God "unto a city of Galilee, named Nazareth, to a virgin espoused to a man whose name was Joseph, of the house of David; and the virgin's name was Mary … And the angel said unto her, Fear not, Mary: for thou hast found favour with God. And, behold, thou shalt conceive in thy womb, and bring forth a son, and shalt call his name JESUS. He shall be great, and shall be called the Son of the Highest: and the Lord God shall give unto him the throne of his father David. And he shall reign over the house of Jacob for ever; and of his kingdom there shall be no end." And the angel said unto Mary, "The Holy Ghost shall come upon thee, and the power of the Highest shall overshadow thee" and He which "shall be born of thee shall be called the Son of God." (Luke 1:26-35).

As Gabriel had foretold, less than a year later, Joseph "went up from Galilee, out of the city of Nazareth, into Judaea, unto the city of David, which is called Bethlehem with Mary his espoused wife, being great with child. And so it was, that, while they were there, the days were accomplished that she should be delivered. And she brought forth her firstborn son, and wrapped him in swaddling clothes, and laid him in a manger; because there was no room for them in the inn." (Luke 2:4-7).

On that same night in the New World "it came to pass also that a new star did appear, according to the word" that had been given by the prophets. (3 Nephi 1:21). And in the Old World, there were in Bethlehem "shepherds abiding in the field, keeping watch over their flock by night. And, lo, the angel of the Lord came upon them, and the glory of the Lord shone round about them … And the angel said unto them, Fear not: for, behold, I bring you good tidings of great joy, which shall be to all people. For unto you is born this day in the city of David a Saviour, which is Christ the Lord. And this shall be a sign unto you; Ye shall find the babe wrapped in swaddling clothes, lying in a manger. And suddenly there was with the angel a multitude of the heavenly host praising God, and saying, Glory to God in the highest, and on earth peace, good will toward men." (Luke 2:8-14).

In this same hour in the faraway land of The Book of Mormon, "the voice of the Lord came unto (Nephi), saying: Lift up your head and be of good cheer; for behold, the time is at hand, and on this night shall the sign be given, and on the morrow come I into the world, to show unto the world that I will fulfil all that which I have caused to be spoken by the mouth of my holy prophets." (3 Nephi 1:12-13).

To the Nephites there was given an additional sign, for "at the going down of the sun" on what turned out to be Christmas Eve, "the people began to be astonished because there was no darkness when the night came." (3 Nephi 1:15). Their world was filled with the light of Christ, "the light which is in all things, which giveth life to all things, which is the law by which all things are governed, even the power of God, who sitteth upon his throne, who is in the bosom of eternity, who is in the midst of all things." (D&C 88:13). How appropriate that the sign of the birth of the Savior should be the dissolution of the night. "And it came to pass that there was no darkness in all that night, but it was as light as though it was mid-day. And it came to pass that the sun did rise in the morning again, according to its proper order; and they knew that it was the day that the Lord should be born, because of the sign which had been given." (3 Nephi 1:19).

Later, "there came wise men from the east to Jerusalem, saying, where is he that is born King of the Jews? For we have seen his star in the east, and are come to worship him." (Matthew 2:1-2). When the Magi finally reached Bethlehem and "were come into the house, they saw the young child with Mary his mother, and fell down, and worshipped him: and when they had opened their treasures, they presented unto him gifts; gold, and frankincense, and myrrh." (Matthew 2:11).

Shortly thereafter, when the Holy Family traveled to Jerusalem to offer sacrifice, a just and devout temple patron named Simeon was moved to exclaim: "Mine eyes have seen thy salvation" for earlier it had been "revealed unto him by the Holy Ghost that he should not see death, before he had seen the Lord's Christ." (Luke 2:26). Later, as "the child grew and waxed strong in spirit, filled with wisdom," how inspiring it must have been to be His playmate, to work beside Him, or to be His friend or neighbor. (Luke 2:40).

None of us were actually there to hear the prophets and the angels speak of His birth. We did not see with our eyes the new star that appeared in the east, nor did we hear with our ears the heavenly host praising God. We were not dazzled by the light that pierced the darkness throughout the night before His birth. We know that as he grew to manhood "he spake not as other men, neither could he be taught; for he needed not that any man should teach him." (J.S.T. Matthew 3:25). But none of us witnessed these things first-hand.

Nevertheless, even after the story has been repeated over 2,000 times, His power is such that it reaches across the millennia to touch us as if we had been present when the drama first unfolded. Each Christmas season, the Holy Ghost bears witness with refreshing clarity that the babe born so long ago in Bethlehem is the Savior of the World.

When we open our scriptures to the book of Luke and we carefully unwrap our Nativity scene to gently place the carvings of Joseph, Mary, and the baby Jesus in the manger that is prominently displayed in our home, the Spirit confirms that Jesus is the Christ Child, the Son of God, and the Savior of the world, and we remember His gifts of peace on earth and good will toward all men. And that is our very own true Christmas miracle.

If we allow ourselves to succumb to our anxieties, and we permit faithlessness to handcuff the expression of our decision to accept The Book of Mormon as scripture, all that will be left in the end is a monochromatic and one-dimensional compromise that leaves us with a hollow core of emptiness in the pit of our stomachs and terror in our hearts. Faith, for a good reason, is fear that has said its prayers.

Christ's Church is Restored

"Thus saith the Lord God:
I will give unto the children of
men line upon line; precept upon
precept, here a little and there a little;
and blessed are those who hearken unto
my precepts, and lend an ear unto my
counsel, for they shall learn wisdom;
for unto him that receiveth I will give
more; and from them that shall say,
We have enough, from them shall
be taken away even that which
they have." (2 Nephi 28:30).

Jesus established His church so that His gospel could be taught, the priesthood could be organized, ordinances could be performed, and we could make covenants with God.

During the years after His mortal ministry, there was gradual but accelerating apostasy from the truth, culminating in a doctrinal free-fall that shattered any semblance of the church and resulted in the Dark Ages. "Whenever people choose to disregard, disobey, or distort any gospel principle or ordinance, whenever they reject the Lord's prophets, or whenever they fail to endure in faith, they distance themselves from God and begin to live in spiritual darkness. Eventually, this leads to a condition called apostasy. When widespread apostasy occurs, God withdraws His priesthood authority to teach and administer the ordinances of the gospel." ("Preach My Gospel," p. 33).

Long before, Amos had prophesied that there would be an apostasy. "Behold, the days come, saith the Lord God, that I will send famine in the land, not a famine of bread or a thirst of water, but of hearing the words of the Lord. And they shall wander from sea to sea, and from north even to the east, they shall run to and fro to seek the word of the Lord, and shall not find it." (Amos 8:11-12).

The Lord knew that, after His mortal ministry, there would be an apostasy, then a long night of darkness, followed by a renewal of faith. Speaking of the Last Days, His prophet Isaiah had written of the Restoration: "Behold I will proceed to do a marvelous work among this people, even a marvelous work and a wonder." (Isaiah 29:14). Joseph Smith became involved in that process simply because he had sought wisdom from God to know what he needed to do personally. "If any of you lack wisdom," the scriptures had instructed him, "let him ask of God, that giveth to all men liberally, and upbraideth not; and it shall be given him. But let him ask in faith, nothing wavering." (James 1:5-6). Many of us have done the same thing, as we have sought wisdom from God.

As a result of Joseph's petition, he related: "I saw a pillar of light exactly over my head, above the brightness of the sun, which descended gradually until it fell upon me." (JSH 1:16). Then, he said: "I saw two Personages, whose brightness and glory defy all description, standing above me in the air. One of them spake unto me, calling me by name, and said, pointing to the other – This is My Beloved Son, Hear Him!" (J.S.H. 1:17).

Joseph was told things about the churches that were then on the earth that must have really startled him, for his inquiry had been only to find out which among the churches was right. "I was answered that I must join none of them," he related, for they were all wrong, and the Personage who addressed me said that all their creeds were an abomination in his sight; that those professors were all corrupt; that they draw near to me with their lips, but their hearts are far from me, they teach for doctrines the commandments of men, having a form of godliness, but they deny the power thereof." (J.S.H. 1:19).

Today, there are a lot of churches in Spokane. Among them are the following: Jehovah's Witness, The Church of The Resurrection, The Cornerstone Pentecostal Church, Jesus is The Answer, The Living Truth Tabernacle, Amazing Grace Fellowship, The Assembly of God, The Crosswind Church , The Glad Tidings Church, The Trinity Lighthouse, The Baptist Church, The Living Water Community Church, The Shiloh Hills Fellowship, Christ Our Hope Bible Church, The Church of The Nazarene, The Catholic Church, The Christian Life Church, The Calvary Chapel, The Presbyterian Church, The Methodist Church, The Holy Temple Church of God in Christ, The Slavic Christian Church, The Refreshing Soaring Church of God in Christ, The Unity Church of Truth, The Life River Fellowship, The Cornerstone Pentecostal Church, The Northview Bible Church, The Lutheran Church, The New Beginnings Church, The Pentecostal Evangelical Church, The River of Life Open Bible Church, The Spokane Dream Center Women's Discipleship, The Unity Church of Truth, The New Hope Christian Reformed Church, The First Church of Christ Scientist, The Church of Christ, The Jesus Lord Church of the Living God International, The Holy Temple Church of God in Christ, The Church of Jesus Christ of Latter-day Saints, The Heritage Congregational Church, The First Covenant Church, The All Nations Christians Center, The Christ our Hope Bible Church, The Christ the Savior Orthodox Church, The First Church of The Open Bible, The Shalom Church, The Fellowship of The Messiah, A Fresh Start Ministries, Christ The Savior Orthodox Church, and The Unitarian Universalist Church of Spokane

Clearly, priesthood authority from God would need to be restored in order to establish His one true church. This occurred in May and June 1829, when Joseph Smith and Oliver Cowdery were first given the Aaronic Priesthood, and then the Melchizedek Priesthood. John the Baptist, a legal administrator, bestowed the Aaronic Priesthood. Peter, James, and John, also legal administrators, bestowed the Melchizedek Priesthood. Later more keys of the priesthood were restored by other messengers sent from God. (See D&C 110:11-16).

With the priesthood restored, so was the power to reorganize the church. This occurred on 4/ 6, 1830. (See D&C 20:1). On that day Joseph Smith was called by God to be a prophet and the first elder of his Church, and Oliver Cowdery was called as the second elder of the Church. (See D&C 20:2-4). Only the framework of the Church was set up at that time; it took several years for the church to be reorganized, in an ongoing process of restoration that continues even today.

The organization of offices within the church followed, as it had been in the primitive church (see the Sixth Article of Faith), with apostles, prophets, pastors, teachers, and evangelists. The first principles and ordinances were restored, which are faith in the Lord Jesus Christ, repentance, baptism by immersion for the remission of sins, and laying on of the hands for the gift of the Holy Ghost. (See the Fourth Article of Faith). Upon that humble foundation was built the great latter-day work we have today.

(The) Church

" Behold, there are
save two churches only;
the one is the church of the
Lamb of God, and the other
is the church of the devil."
(1 Nephi 14:10).

"We believe in the same organization that existed in the primitive church, (with) "apostles, prophets, pastors, teachers, evangelists, and so forth." (Sixth Article of Faith). When the Lord ministered among the Nephite Saints, He defined with greater clarity the name of His church, saying "if it be called in my name then it is my church, if it so be that they are built upon my gospel." (3 Nephi 27:8). That is the critical element upon which hangs the credibility of any church proclaiming to be the Lord's. Today, many churches have the name of Christ or a derivative in their titles, and so the substance of the issue is whether or not Church doctrine consisting of gospel principles that can be validated by the Spirit are taught by the Savior's earthly representatives who bear His priesthood authority. Thus, gospel principles can be put to the test in a very simple, uncomplicated way.

The way of the world is to scrutinize from every rational angle, to form committees charged with the responsibility to analyze data, compile reports, develop hypotheses and paradigms, reach compromise, and finally publish conclusions. But "O that cunning plan of the evil one! O the vainness, and the frailties, and the foolishness of men! When they are learned they think they are wise, and they hearken not unto the counsel of God, for they set it aside, supposing they know of themselves, wherefore, their wisdom is foolishness and it profiteth them not. And they shall perish. But to be learned is good if they hearken unto the counsels of God." (2 Nephi 9:29-30).

An appeal to vanity is Satan's way of turning the minds of men against gospel principles. "I" and "Mine" are usually accompanied by an unbended knee. Neal Maxwell wrote that "to the humble, the simpleness and the easiness of the way are glad realities; to the crowded, ego filled minds of proud men, the sudden burst of light from a spiritual sunrise is irritating rather than awesome, and causes them to blink rather than to stare in reverent awe." ("That My Family Should Partake," p. 82).

We come to a knowledge of the truth of church doctrine through meekness, lowliness of heart, and humility. Moroni's formula was to "ask God, the Eternal Father, in the name of Christ, if these things are not true; and if ye shall ask with a sincere heart, with real intent, having faith in Christ, he will manifest the truth of it unto you, by the power of the Holy Ghost. And by the power of the Holy Ghost ye may know the truth of all things." (Moroni 10:4-5).

The best venue in which to study gospel principles is within the programs of The Church of Jesus Christ. Interestingly, of all the churches in the world when the Lord restored His church in this dispensation, there was not a single one that bore the name of Jesus Christ. To Joseph Smith, He declared: "For thus shall my church be called in the last days, even the Church of Jesus Christ of Latter-day Saints." (D&C 115:4, recorded 4/26, 1838). Before this revelation was received, the church was variously called The Church of Christ, The Church of Jesus Christ, The Church of God, and The Church of The Latter-day Saints. Even today, it is sometimes inaccurately called The Mormon Church, or The L.D.S. Church.

But "there is no valid reason why the Latter-day Saints should speak of themselves as "Mormons," or of the church as "The Mormon Church." Missionaries should persuade people to believe in Christ, the Son of God, and to become members of His Church - The Church of Jesus Christ. We should all emphasize that we belong to The Church of Jesus Christ of Latter-day Saints, the name the Lord has given by which we are to be known and called." (Joseph Fielding Smith, Jr., "Answers to Gospel Questions," 4:174-175).

Members of the Lord's church call themselves "saints," which "is a translation of a Greek word also rendered 'holy,' the fundamental idea being that of consecration or separation for a sacred purpose; but since what was set apart for God must be without blemish, the word came to mean 'free from blemish,' whether physical or moral. In the New Testament, the saints are all those who by baptism have entered into the Christian covenant." ("Bible Dictionary," p. 768).

Thus, the epistles of Paul often begin with familiar salutations: "To all that be in Rome, beloved of God, called to be saints." (Romans 1:7). Or, "Unto the church of God which is at Corinth, to them that are sanctified in Christ Jesus, called to be saints." (1 Corinthians 1:2). Or, "Paul and Timotheus, the servants of Jesus Christ, to all the saints in Christ Jesus which are at Philippi." (Philippians 1:1).

The prophet Jacob was inspired by the same spirit, describing the righteous in the New World as "the saints of the Holy One of Israel, they who have believed in the Holy One of Israel, they who have endured the crosses of the world, and despised the shame of it, they shall inherit the kingdom of God, which was prepared for them from the foundation of the world, and their joy shall be full forever." (2 Nephi 9:18).

The righteous are they who yield to the enticings of the Holy Spirit, and put the natural man out of their minds. Focusing on the solemnities of eternity, they become saints through the atonement of Jesus Christ. They follow His admonition to become as little children, and emulate the qualities of these innocents; they are "submissive, meek, humble, patient, full of love, and willing to submit" to the will of their Father. (Mosiah 3:19).

The church offers baptism to the repentant for "the remission of sins (which) bringeth meekness, and lowliness of heart; and because of meekness and lowliness of heart cometh the visitation of the Holy Ghost, which Comforter filleth with hope and perfect love, which love endureth by diligence unto prayer, until the end shall come, when all the saints shall dwell with God." (Moroni 8:26).

The church is identified with the principles of the gospel, and is in harmony with the doctrine of Christ. When reviewing these, it is important to remember that God's work is progressive; it changes its appearance, but never its principles. Practices may change with circumstances, but doctrine remains constant.

Church doctrine addresses the issue of continuing revelation from God. "We believe all that God has revealed, all that He does now reveal, and we believe that He will yet reveal many great and important things pertaining to the Kingdom of God." (Ninth Article of Faith). As Paul explained, God "at sundry times and in divers manners spake in time past unto the fathers by the prophets." (Hebrews 1:1-2). Thus, did Daniel declare "there is a God in heaven that revealeth secrets." (Daniel 2:28). For "surely He "will do nothing but he revealeth his secret unto his servants the prophets." (Amos 2:7).

"Whom say ye that I am?" the Savior asked His Chief Apostle. " And Simon Peter answered and said, Thou art the Christ, the Son of the living god. And Jesus answered and said unto him, Blessed art thou, Simon Bar-Jona, for flesh and blood hath not revealed it unto thee, but my Father which is in heaven. And I say also unto thee, that thou art Peter, and upon this rock (of revelation) I will build my church." (Matthew 16:15-18).

Such revelation in the church often comes quietly. "But the Comforter, which is the Holy Ghost, whom the Father will send in my name, he shall teach you all things, and bring all things to your remembrance, whatsoever I have said unto you." (John 14:26). When this voice comes, wrote Truman Madsen, "as a flow of pure intelligence attended by a burning in the center self, it is of God. Our search for external warrant is really the confirmation and application of what is already, and more certainly, known." ("Eternal Man," p. 73).

The doctrine of priesthood authority from God is at the foundation of The Church of Christ. Paul taught "no man taketh this honour unto himself, but he that is called of God, as was Aaron." (Hebrews 5:4). As the Savior explained: "For the Son man is as a man taking a far journey, who left his house, and gave authority to his servants, and to every man his work, and commanded the porter to watch." (Mark 13:34).

Clearly, in the church, we do not take these honors upon ourselves, but we are called by those file leaders who hold the keys of authority to administer the ordinances of the gospel. "Ye have not chosen me," said the Savior, "but I have chosen you, and ordained you, that ye should go and bring forth fruit." (John 15:16). Later, in the apostolic church, leaders "ordained them elders in every church, (after having) prayed with fasting." (Acts 14:23).

The organization of the church is today "built upon the foundation of the apostles and prophets, Jesus Christ himself being the chief corner stone." (Ephesians 2:20). Paul gave us some insight into the organization of the primitive church, when he wrote to the Ephesian Saints: "And he gave some, apostles; and some, prophets and some, evangelists; and some, pastors and teachers; For the perfecting of the saints, for the work of the ministry, for the edifying of the body of Christ: Till we all come in the unity of the faith, and of the knowledge of the Son of God, unto a perfect man, unto the measure of the stature of the fulness of Christ." (Ephesians 4:11-13).

The first principles and ordinances of the gospel identify the true church, as well. Those who hold the priesthood first teach for doctrine the two basic principles of faith and repentance. Then, they explain the necessity of the ordinances of baptism and receiving the Holy Ghost. The Savior affirmed, "Except a man be born of water and of the Spirit, he cannot enter into the kingdom of God." (John 3:5).

On the Day of Pentecost, Peter and others taught over three thousand people. When this multitude heard their message, "they were pricked in their heart, and said unto Peter and to the rest of the apostles, Men and brethren, what shall we do? Then Peter said unto them, repent, and be baptized every one of you in the name of Jesus Christ for the remission of sins, and ye shall receive the gift of the Holy Ghost." (Acts 2:37-38). After joining with the body of the church through the waters of baptism, "they continued steadfastly in the apostles' doctrine and fellowship, and in breaking of bread, and in prayers." (Acts 2:42).

Ordinances for the dead, as well as for the living, are found in the doctrine of the true church. The Savior, after all, preached to the dead, between His death and resurrection. "For Christ also hath once suffered for sins, the just for the unjust, that he might bring us to God, being put to death in the flesh, but quickened by the Spirit: By which also he went and preached unto the spirits in prison, which sometime were disobedient." (1 Peter 3:18).

Peter elaborated "for this cause was the gospel preached also to them that are dead, that they might be judged according to men in the flesh, but live according to God in the spirit." (1 Peter 4:6). Paul justified this doctrine by asking rhetorically "else what shall they do which are baptized for the dead, if the dead rise not at all? Why are they then baptized for the dead?" (1 Corinthians 15:29).\

The manifestation of spiritual gifts is found in the doctrine of the true church. (See 1 Corinthians 12:4). Those who have the image of God engraven upon their countenances enjoy these gifts. "Who shall ascend into the hill of the Lord," asked the Psalmist, "or who shall stand in his holy place" to partake of the Divine Nature? "He that hath clean hands and a pure heart; who hath not lifted up his soul unto vanity, nor sworn deceitfully." (Psalms 24:4-5).

The doctrine of the true church is supported and sustained by the ardor and conviction of its members. Marion G. Romney observed that "having a testimony (of the principles of the gospel) and being converted are not necessarily the same thing. A testimony comes when the Holy Ghost gives the earnest seeker a witness of the truth (of one or more specific principles). A moving testimony vitalizes faith, that is, it induces repentance and obedience to the commandments. Conversion, on the other hand, is the fruit or the reward for repentance and obedience." (C.R., 10/1963). Spiritual gifts follow conversion to the true doctrine and are received on the foundation of testimony.

Apostasy from true principles is itself evidence of the Restoration. If spiritual gifts are not found in the church, then there must have been an apostasy. Isaiah foresaw such a day, when "the earth also is defiled under the inhabitants thereof; because they have transgressed the laws, changed the ordinance, broken the everlasting covenant." (Isaiah 24:5).

Later, Paul wrote to the Thessalonian Saints, cautioning them to be "not soon shaken in mind, or be troubled, neither by spirit, nor by word, nor by letter as from us, as that the day of Christ is at hand. Let no man deceive you by any means: for that day shall not come, except there come a falling away first," in an apostasy from the doctrine of Christ. (2 Thessalonians 2:2-3).

Nephi saw in vision that "they have taken away from the gospel of the Lamb many parts which are plain and most precious; and also many covenants of the Lord have they taken away." (1 Nephi 13:21-29). The Lord affirmed to Joseph Smith "in the ordinances (of the Melchizedek Priesthood) the power of godliness is manifest. And without the ordinances thereof, and the authority of the priesthood, the power of godliness is not manifest unto men in the flesh. For without this no man can see the face of God, even the Father, and live." (D&C 84:20-22). The true doctrine of Christ has the power to bring us into the presence of God.

The Reformation that necessarily preceded the Restoration came about as a result of an initial apostasy from the true doctrine. Martin Luther justified his actions by declaring: "I have sought nothing beyond reforming the church in conformity with the Holy Scriptures. I simply say that Christianity has ceased to exist among those who should have preserved it."

Roger Williams flatly stated that "there is no regularly constituted church on earth, nor any person authorized to administer any church ordinance; nor can there be until new apostles are sent by the Great Head of the church for Whose coming am seeking." One is reminded of the prophecy of Amos, who wrote: "Behold, the days come, saith the Lord God, that I will send a famine in the land, not a famine of bread, nor a thirst for water, but of hearing the words of the Lord." (Amos 8:11).

John the Revelator "saw another angel fly in the midst of heaven, having the everlasting gospel to preach unto them that dwell on the earth, and to every nation, and kindred, and tongue, and people." (Revelation 14:6). These angels include not only Moroni, but also John the Baptist, Peter, James and John, Moses, and Elijah who, as messengers and servants of the Lord Jesus Christ restored true doctrine and priesthood keys of authority after a long night of apostasy.

The Bible itself promised that there would be a Restoration when Peter declared: "He shall send Jesus Christ, which before was preached unto you: whom the heavens must receive until the times of restitution of all things, which God hath spoken by the mouth of all his holy prophets since the world began." (Acts 3:20-21).

The Savior told the Nephites that when the Latter-day Restoration bursts upon the world stage, it will be of such significance "that kings shall shut their mouths." (3 Nephi 21:8). Its destiny is to become the greatest power the world has ever known. "For in that day," declared the Savior, "shall the Father work a work, which shall be a great and marvelous work among them." (3 Nephi 21:9).

When members of the Lord's church zealously live in harmony with gospel principles and the true doctrine of the Kingdom, the character of society can change. After carefully observing The Church of Jesus Christ of Latter-day Saints, Leo Tolstoy was moved to predict: "If Mormonism could be true to its foundations and remain unchanged for four generations, it might well become the most powerful social influence in the world." (Reportedly, in a conversation with President Andrew White, of Cornell University).

When we open our scriptures
to the book of Luke and we carefully
unwrap our Nativity scene to gently place the
carvings of Joseph, Mary, and the baby Jesus in
the manger that is prominently displayed in our
home, the Spirit confirms that Jesus is the Christ
Child, the Son of God, and the Savior of the
world, and we remember His gifts of peace
on earth and good will toward all
men. And that is our very
own true Christmas
miracle.

(The) Church of Jesus Christ in Former Times

"Behold, the righteous, the saints of the Holy One of Israel, they who have believed in the Holy One of Israel, those who have endured the crosses of the world, and despised the shame of it, they shall inherit the kingdom of God, which was prepared for them from the foundation of the world, and their joy shall be full." (2 Nephi 9:18).

"We believe in the same organization that existed in the primitive church, namely, apostles, prophets, pastors, teachers, evangelists, and so forth." (Sixth Article of Faith)

During the Lord's ministry among the Nephite Saints, He defined with greater clarity the name of His church, teaching: "If it be called in my name then it is my church," with the qualifying prerequisite that its foundation be "built upon my gospel." (3 Nephi 27:8). That is the critical point upon which hangs the credibility of any church proclaiming to be the Lord's. Today, many organizations have the name of Christ or a derivative in their titles, and so the substantive element that identifies the true church is its adherence to gospel principles that are taught by the Savior's earthly representatives who bear His priesthood authority.

Interestingly, of all the churches in the world when the Lord restored His church in this dispensation, there was not a single one that bore His name. It must have been very satisfying for Him to declare to Joseph Smith: "For thus shall my church be called in the last days, even The Church of Jesus Christ of Latter-day Saints." (D&C 115:4). Before this revelation, the church was variously called The Church of Christ, The Church of Jesus Christ, The Church of God, and The Church of The Latter-day Saints. Even today, it is sometimes inaccurately called The Mormon Church, or The L.D.S. Church. But in 1830, this revelation from the Lord resolved the issue once and for all.

Today, "there is no valid reason why the Latter-day Saints should speak of themselves as 'Mormons,' or of the church as 'The Mormon Church,' taught Joseph Fielding Smith, Jr. We emphasize that we belong to The Church of Jesus Christ of Latter-day Saints, the name the Lord has given by which we are to be known and called." ("Answers to Gospel Questions," 4:174-175). But did the members call themselves 'Saints' in former times? "The word 'saint' is a translation of a Greek word also rendered 'holy,' the fundamental idea being that of consecration or separation for a sacred purpose; but the word came to mean 'free from blemish,' whether physical or moral. In the New Testament, the saints are all those who by baptism have entered into the Christian covenant." ("Bible Dictionary," p. 768).

Hence, Paul addressed "all that be in Rome, beloved of God, called to be saints." (Romans 1:7). He saluted "the church of God, which is at Corinth, to them that are sanctified in Christ Jesus, called to be saints." (1 Corinthians 1:2). He introduced himself and his missionary companion Timothy as "the servants of Jesus Christ, to all the saints in Christ Jesus which are at Philippi." (Philippians 1:1).

Book of Mormon prophets also characterized the members as 'saints.' "Behold, the righteous," Nephi declared, "the saints of the Holy One of Israel." Then he described saints as those "who have believed in the Holy One of Israel, (and) who have endured the crosses of the world." (2 Nephi 9:18).

Benjamin taught: "The natural man is an enemy to God, and has been from the fall of Adam, and will be, forever and ever, unless he yields to the enticings of the Holy Spirit, and putteth off the natural man, and becometh a saint through the atonement of Christ the Lord." He characterized the Saints as children, "submissive, meek, humble, patient, full of love, willing to submit to all things which the Lord seeth fit to inflict upon him, even as a child doth submit to his father." (Mosiah 3:19).

Moroni explained that "the remission of sins bringeth meekness, and lowliness of heart; and because of meekness and lowliness of hearth cometh the visitation of the Holy Ghost, which Comforter filleth with hope and perfect love, which love endureth by diligence unto prayer, until the end shall come, when all the saints shall dwell with God." (Moroni 8:26).

Revelation was one of the principles of the gospel with which the Saints in former times were blessed. Paul spoke of "God, who at sundry times and in divers manners spake in time past unto the fathers by the prophets, (and who) hath in these last days spoken unto us by his Son." (Hebrews 1:1-2). "Whom say ye that I am?" the Savior asked. "And Simon Peter answered and said, Thou art the Christ, the Son of the living god. And Jesus answered and said unto him, Blessed art thou, Simon Bar-jona, for flesh and blood hath not revealed it unto thee, but my Father which is in heaven. And I say also unto thee, That thou art Peter, and upon this rock" of revelation "I will build my church." (Matthew 16:15-18). This is "the Comforter," taught the Savior, "which is the Holy Ghost, whom the Father will send in my name, he shall teach you all things, and bring all things to your remembrance, whatsoever I have said unto you." (John 14:26).

Institutional revelation came to those who had divine authority, for as Paul correctly understood it, "no man taketh this honour unto himself, but he that is called of God, as was Aaron." (Hebrews 5:4). "For the Son man is as a man taking a far journey, who left his house, and gave authority to have not chosen me," Jesus explained, "but I have chosen you, and ordained you." (John 15:16). Following His ministry, the Apostles "ordained them elders in every church." (Acts 14:23). Their authority came through a formal church organization that was "built upon the foundation of the apostles and prophets, Jesus Christ himself being the chief corner stone." (Ephesians 2:20). Accordingly, "he gave some, apostles; and some, prophets, and some, evangelists; and some, pastors and teachers; For the perfecting of the saints, for the work of the ministry, for the edifying of the body of Christ: Till we all come in the unity of the faith, and of the knowledge of the Son of God, unto a perfect man, unto the measure of the stature of the fulness of Christ." (Ephesians 4:11-13).

With this authority, the organization administered the first principles & ordinances. Those who held the priesthood in former times taught the two basic principles of faith and repentance, and then, the two basic ordinances of baptism and receiving the Holy Ghost. For "except a man be born of water and of the Spirit, he cannot enter into the kingdom of God." (John 3:5). On the Day of Pentecost, over three thousand people "were pricked in their heart, and said unto Peter and to the rest of the apostles, Men and brethren, what shall we do? Then Peter said unto them, Repent, and be baptized every one of you in the name of Jesus Christ for the remission of sins, and ye shall receive the gift of the Holy Ghost." (Acts 2:37-38). "And they continued steadfastly in the apostles' doctrine and fellowship, and in breaking of bread, and in prayers." (Acts 2:42). These ordinances of salvation and exaltation were not only for the living, but were for the dead, as well. The scriptures plainly teach that Christ preached to the dead, between His death and resurrection. "For Christ also hath once suffered for sins, the just for the unjust, that he might bring us to God, being put to death in the flesh, but quickened by the Spirit: By which also he went and preached unto the spirits in prison. Which sometime were disobedient, when once the longsuffering of God waited in the days of Noah, while the ark was a preparing, wherein few, that is, eight souls were saved by water." (1 Peter 3:18-20).

As Peter further explained: "For this cause was the gospel preached also to them that are dead, that they might be judged according to men in the flesh, but live according to God in the spirit." (1 Peter 4:6). "Else what shall they do which are baptized for the dead," asked Paul, "if the dead rise not at all? Why are they then baptized for the dead?" (1 Corinthians 15:29).

The ordinances exposed the Saints to a multitude of spiritual gifts. Paul told the Corinthian Saints: "Now there are diversities of gifts." (1 Corinthians 12:4). With these gifts, the image of God was engraven upon their countenances. "Who shall ascend into the hill of the Lord," asked the Psalmist, "or who shall stand in his holy place" to partake of the Divine Nature? "He that hath clean hands and a pure heart; who" is a partaker of spiritual gifts, and "hath not lifted up his soul unto vanity, nor sworn deceitfully." (Psalms 24:4-5).

Spiritual gifts were accompanied by conversion and testimony. Regarding our comprehension of the different manifestations of the Spirit, Marion G. Romney said that "having a testimony and being converted are not necessarily the same thing. A testimony comes when the Holy Ghost gives the earnest seeker a witness of the truth. A moving testimony vitalizes faith, that is, it induces repentance and obedience to the commandments. Conversion, on the other hand, is the fruit or the reward for repentance and obedience." (C.R., 10/1963). Spiritual gifts follow conversion that is built on the foundation of testimony.

When the Saints in former times closed their hearts and minds to the Spirit, darkness superseded the light. The loss of these gifts was precipitated by apostasy. Isaiah prophesied: "The earth also is defiled under the inhabitants thereof; because they have transgressed the laws, changed the ordinance, (and have) broken the everlasting covenant." (Isaiah 24:5). Paul counseled the Thessalonian Saints: "Be not soon shaken in mind, or be troubled, neither by spirit, nor by word, nor by letter as from us, as that the day of Christ is at hand. Let no man deceive you by any means: for that day shall not come, except there come a falling away first." (2 Thessalonians 2:2-3). "For behold," an angel taught Nephi, "they have taken away from the gospel of the Lamb many parts which are plain and most precious; and also many covenants of the Lord have they taken away." (1 Nephi 13:26).

As in former times, a restitution was eagerly anticipated by visionaries seeking to redress the wrongs resulting from the corruption of basic principles relating to the covenants. "I have sought nothing beyond reforming the Church in conformity with the Holy Scriptures," declared Martin Luther. "I simply say that Christianity has ceased to exist among those who should have preserved it." Roger Williams concluded: "There is no regularly constituted church on earth, nor any person authorized to administer any church ordinance; nor can there be until new apostles are sent by the Great Head of the church for Whose coming am seeking." (Ernest Schweibert, "Luther and His Times").

After the Reformers had paved the way, it was only natural that a Restoration would burst upon the scene. It had been prophesied that the Lord Himself would come again. Luke had written: "He shall send Jesus Christ, which before was preached unto you: whom the heavens must receive until the times of restitution of all things, which God hath spoken by the mouth of all his holy prophets since the world began." (Acts 3:20-21). John saw in vision the angel Moroni, who would "fly in the midst of heaven, having the everlasting gospel to preach unto them that dwell on the earth, and to every nation, and kindred, and tongue, and people." (Revelation 14:6). The everlasting gospel included the ordinances of the Melchizedek Priesthood, in which "the power of godliness is manifest. And without the ordinances thereof, and the authority of the priesthood, the power of godliness is not manifest unto men in the flesh. For without this no man can see the face of God, even the Father, and live." (D&C 84:20-22). The history of the church that administers these ordinances speaks for itself, and is a seamless continuation of the history of the church in former times.

(The) Circle of Knowledge

"I have showed thee new
things ... even hidden things,
and thou didst not know them."
(1 Nephi 20:6).

Does anyone really know how all the pieces of the puzzle of life fit together? Does anyone have all the answers? "My life is but a weaving between the Lord and me," wrote the poet. "I cannot choose the colors; He worketh steadily. Oft-times, He weaveth sorrow, and I, in foolish pride, forget that He seeith the upper, and I, the underside. Not 'til the loom is silent, and the shuttles cease to fly, shall God unroll the canvas and explain the reasons why. The dark threads are as needful in the Weaver's skillful hand, as the threads of gold and silver, in the pattern He has planned." (Benjamin Malachi Franklin).

As Alice asked the Cheshire Cat: "Would you please tell me which way I ought to go from here?" Replied the cat: "That depends a good deal on where you want to go." "I admit," responded Alice, "I don't much care where." Said the cat: "Then it doesn't matter which way you go." "Just so I go somewhere!" cried Alice. "Oh," responded the cat, "you are sure to do that if you walk far enough." (Lewis Carroll, "Alice's Adventures in Wonderland").

The Lord's intriguing explanation, entirely unsatisfactory, uncomfortable, and unfathomable to most of us, is: "My thoughts are not your thoughts, neither are your ways my ways." (Isaiah 55:8). Frustratingly, as our circle of knowledge expands, so do the borders of darkness. The more we know, the more we need to learn. It should do no violence to our faith to realize that, with a greater understanding of doctrinal truth, there might be additional questions to ponder.

The Lord told Alma what it means to be born again: "Marvel not that all mankind, yea, men and women, all nations, kindreds, tongues, and people, must be born again; yea, born of God, changed from their carnal and fallen state to a state of righteousness, being redeemed of God, becoming his sons and daughters; And thus they become new creatures; and unless they do this, they can in nowise inherit the kingdom of God".
(Mosiah 27:25-26).

Citizenship in The Church and Kingdom

"It is better that a man
should be judged of God than
of man, for the judgments of God
are always just, but the judgments of
man are not always just. Therefore, if it
were possible that you could have just men to
be your kings, who would establish the laws of
God, and judge this people according to his
commandments ... then it would be
expedient that you should always
have kings to rule over you."
(Mosiah 29:12-13).

December 7, 2013, a Women's World Cup Downhill ski race was held at Lake Louise, Alberta, Canada, with the temperature dipping to 14 degrees F. below zero, and with a wind chill factor dropping that to 31 degrees F. below zero. The course was two miles long, and the racers completed the run in just under two minutes, which means they averaged over 60 miles per hour in the face of arctic conditions. My questions were: "How in the world could they prepare for such a demanding event, held is such pitiless conditions? How could they even "warm up" beforehand, so their muscles could withstand the brutal punishment and their exposed skin the chilling cold?" The only answer I could come up with, was that having been through similar trials before, they must have relied upon a strict and comprehensive protocol that had, aforetime, been rigorously tested, and was now meticulously followed.

We all have conscious and unconscious protocols in place that we need to follow in order to achieve desired results. I have a protocol that works for me each morning when I wake up. I take a hot shower to limber up my muscles and work out the kinks before I begin my day. I know that if I don't slowly work up to my established physical capacity, if I try to take shortcuts, I will pay in spades later on and it will take quite a while for me to even get back to my original starting point.

We also have spiritual protocols or proven formulas to follow, in order to achieve envisioned results. If we want to perform at a level that compliments the full stature of our spirits, but don't follow the protocols required to do so, we could entirely miss our mark.

In 1952, while serving in the Quorum of the Twelve Apostles, Ezra Taft Benson was asked by Dwight D. Eisenhower, then President of the United States, to serve as the nation's Secretary of Agriculture. With the encouragement of church President David O. McKay, Elder Benson accepted the assignment and served well. In his first General Conference address after becoming Secretary of Agriculture, he said: "I have been happy in the privilege to serve, in a small way at least, this great country and the government under which we live. I am grateful to the First Presidency and my brethren that they have been willing, not only to give consent, but also to give me their blessing as I responded to the call of the Chief Executive." (C.R., 4/1953).

As of 2023, there were 3 members of the church serving in the Senate, and 6 in the House of Representatives of the Congress of the United States of America. It was almost 180 years ago (1835) that the church unanimously approved a declaration of beliefs about government. This declaration is recorded in D&C Section 134. It was a protocol, or a formula, given by God, about how to be good citizens. This protocol was articulated just 48 years after the ratification of the U.S. Constitution, in September 1787.

48 years is not a long time. Some of us can still remember when a postage stamp cost a nickel, and "The Sound of Music," with Julie Andrews singing in high alpine meadows, hit the theaters. In 1965, The Big Bang Theory was experimentally confirmed by Penzias and Wilson. Winston Churchill died, and the Beatles were at the height of their popularity. The Boatmobile was created, and the Gateway Arch in St. Louis was completed. Sandy Koufax pitched a perfect game for the Los Angeles Dodgers. Likewise, in context, the Declaration of Beliefs about Government came shortly on the heels of the U.S. Constitution. The Founding Fathers were still fresh in the minds of many citizens in 1835.

That Declaration of Beliefs had a lot to say about the purposes, or role, of civil government in the lives of private citizens. It declared that government was instituted "for the good and safety of society." (D&C 134:1). It promoted the postulate that government was created "for the protection of the innocent and the punishment of the guilty." (D&C 134:6). It endorsed the belief that government existed "for the protection of all citizens in the free exercise of their religious belief" and "for redress of all wrongs and grievances." (D&C 134:7 & 11).

To support and sustain the Declaration of Beliefs, we each need our own personally prepared protocol to help fulfil the purposes of government. L. Tom Perry said that we need to be "actively engaged in supporting and defending the principles of truth, right, and freedom" (C.R. 10/1987). To do so, we should turn to the scriptures for guidance, as we seek to uphold leaders who "administer the law in equity and justice." (D&C 134:3). "Honest men and wise men should be sought for diligently, and good men and wise men ye should observe to uphold; otherwise, whatsoever is less than these cometh of evil." (D&C 98:10).

When we do not observe this protocol, "the wicked rule, (and) the people mourn." (D&C 98:9). Having said that, the church itself "is politically neutral. It does not endorse political parties, platforms, or candidates. Candidates should not imply that they are endorsed by the church or its leaders. Church leaders and members should avoid any statements or conduct that might be interpreted as church endorsement of political parties or candidates." ("Church Handbook of Instructions").

This is interesting, in light of our understanding of the political atmosphere in heaven surrounding the events that transpired at the Council and shortly thereafter. It seems that even though the political spectrum is not black and white, politics can be. Our challenge is to work within the Lord's protocol to achieve a spiritual resolution to the issue of how we can meaningfully participate in the process of government in a republic.

To that end, we must ask ourselves: "What is our responsibility regarding the laws of the land?" The scriptures teach: "Let no man break the laws of the land, for he that keepeth the laws of God hath no need to break the laws of the land. Wherefore, be subject to the powers that be, until he reigns whose right it is to reign, and subdues all enemies under his feet." (D&C 58:21-22). In addition: "That law of the land which is constitutional, supporting that principle of freedom in maintaining rights and privileges, belongs to all mankind, and is justifiable before me. Therefore, I, the Lord, justify you, and your brethren of my church, in befriending that law which is the constitutional law of the land." (D&C 98:5-6). "We believe in being subject to kings, presidents, rulers, and magistrates, in obeying, honoring, and sustaining the law." (Twelfth Article of Faith).

About 20 years after the Declaration of Beliefs about Government was written, Abraham Lincoln asserted: "To sin by silence, when words should be spoken, makes cowards of men." (Attributed to Ella Wheeler Wilcox). So, even as we practice our religion, we must nurture within ourselves an active, participating relationship with our civil government. The Declaration of Beliefs clearly states: "We believe that religion is instituted of God; and that men are amenable to him, and to him only, for the exercise of it, unless their religious opinions prompt them to infringe upon the rights and liberties of others; but we do not believe that human law has a right to interfere in prescribing rules of worship to bind the consciences of men, nor dictate forms for public or private devotion; that the civil magistrate should restrain crime, but never control conscience; should punish guilt, but never suppress the freedom of the soul." (D&C 134:4). It goes on to say: "We do not believe it just to mingle religious influence with civil government, whereby one religious society is fostered and another proscribed in its spiritual privileges, and the individual rights of its members, as citizens, denied." (D&C 134:9).

Joshua drew a line in the sand, when he declared: "Choose you this day whom ye will serve; whether the gods which your fathers served that were on the other side of the flood, or the gods of the Amorites, in whose land ye dwell: but as for me and my house, we will serve the Lord." (Joshua 24:15). Today, members of the church "should do their civic duty by supporting measures that strengthen society morally, economically, and culturally." Latter-day Saints "are urged to be actively engaged in worthy causes to improve their communities and make them wholesome places in which to live and rear families" ("Handbook of Instructions"). The "Proclamation to The Word" regarding the Family (1995), that has been adopted and internalized by members of the church attests to their commitment to these worthy causes.

We can begin to strengthen our communities by ministering to the needs of others, by serving in elected or appointed public service positions, and by supporting worthy activities. We should always "be anxiously engaged in a good cause, and do many things of (our) own free will, and bring to pass much righteousness. For the power is in (us), wherein (we) are agents unto (ourselves). And inasmuch as (we) do good (we) shall in nowise lose (our) reward." (D&C 58:27-28).

To be anxiously engaged, we need to influence more than we are influenced by others, lead and not follow, and light candles rather than curse the darkness. When it rains, we need to open up our umbrellas, rather than stand around complaining about the foul weather. We need to stem the tide rather than allow ourselves to be passively swept up in it, solve problems rather than ignore them, and pay it forward more than we watch our own backs. We need to have protocols in place that will allow us to fulfil the measure of our creation. We need to recognize that the ultimate power to change rests within ourselves, and then let go and let God.

Victor Frankel declared: "Everything can be taken from us but one thing: the last of the human freedoms – to choose our attitude in any given set of circumstances, to choose our own way. The one thing you can't take away from me is the way I choose to respond to what you do to me. The last of one's freedoms is to choose one's attitude in any given circumstance. Between stimulus and response, there is a space. In that space is our power to choose our response. In our response, lies our growth and our freedom. Forces beyond your control can take away everything you possess except one thing, your freedom to choose how you will respond to the situation."

He continued: "We who lived in concentration camps can remember the men who walked through the huts comforting others, giving away their last piece of bread. They may have been few in number, but they offer sufficient proof that everything can be taken from a man but one thing: the last of the human freedoms - to choose one's attitude in any given set of circumstances, to choose one's own way." ("Man's Search for Meaning").

In June 1965, President David O. McKay spoke to a group from the Physical Facilities Department of the Church." He said: "Let me assure you, brethren, that some day you will have a personal Priesthood interview with the Savior, Himself. If you are interested, I will tell you the order in which He will ask you to account for your earthly responsibilities. First, He will request an accountability report about your relationship with your wife … Second, He will … request information about your relationship to each and every child. Third, he will want to know what you have personally done with the talents you were given in the pre (earth) existence. "Fourth, He will want a summary of your activity in your church assignments… Fifth … if you were honest in all your dealings. Sixth, He will ask for an accountability on what you have done to contribute in a positive manner to your community, state, country, and the world." Let us make sure that each of us has protocols in place, so that we can prepare for that joyful occasion when we can sit down one-on-one with the Savior and recount the story of our life.

Civil Liberties

(Alma Chapters 50 & 51)

"Those who were desirous that
Pahoran should be dethroned from the
judgment-seat were called king-men, for
they were desirous that the law should be altered
in a manner to overthrow the free government and to
establish a king over the land. And those who were
desirous that Pahoran should remain chief judge
over the land took upon them the name of
freemen." (Alma 51:5-6).

In the land of Zarahemla, around 70 B.C., there began to be a warm contention within the ranks of the Nephites. The situation quickly deteriorated until bloodshed seemed inevitable. As the fabric of their society disintegrated, escalating civil disobedience exposed them to the scourge of aggression from the Lamanites, who hated everything about Nephite culture. Only decisive action by a young military officer named Moroni averted disaster, and it is noteworthy that his humane policy toward his Lamanite brethren insured a happy ending to the episode, with the original political antagonists once again joined in friendship.

Shortly after this threat to Nephite security had been averted, their Chief Judge died. It was critically important to quickly replace him with another leader who would continue the tradition of nonpartisanship, righteous judgment, and peace keeping. Ideally, he would become the type of leader who would grant unto the people "their sacred privileges to worship the Lord their God, yea, to support and maintain the cause of God all his days, and to bring the wicked to justice according to their crime." (Alma 50:39).

The examples of righteous judges in Zarahemla dramatically illustrate the power of even a handful of inspired government leaders to hold evil in check and positively influence an entire culture. Pahoran "was appointed chief judge and governor over the people, with an oath and sacred ordinance." (Alma 50:39). He began his reign in 67 B.C., and for the next fifteen years guided the Nephites through perilous days. The history of their nation is interesting to latter-day readers for its relevance to our times.

Characteristically, when a financial crisis or terrorism threat shakes the foundations of a society, there is a strident call for strong leadership and instant response. Think of the knee-jerk reaction in the immediate aftermath of 9/11: The Patriot Act, and the subsequent erosion of civil liberties and constitutional guarantees. Recall the banking and market "reforms," and the bailouts and stimulus packages that were rushed through Congress in the aftermath of the worldwide economic meltdown in 2009. The more grave the circumstances, the more the people look for security from leaders who typically respond in an uncomfortably dictatorial fashion, usurping powers not specifically vested in them by the law of the land. Nevertheless, the people have historically applauded their actions even as they have surrendered their own civil liberties.

The typical unfolding of events, then, is from democracy to imperialism that destroys the earlier republican institutions. Inequality is first rationalized, then validated, and finally accepted as a given. Liberty suffers as society becomes less egalitarian, even as Conventional Wisdom justifies the requisite attitude adjustments. What is often misunderstood about Caesarism is that it is not a dictatorship nor is it a covert action. It is done with the tacit approval of Congressional oversight. In fact, the people demand it! They embrace Caesar, and he is welcomed for dinner and a fireside chat. Caesarism is the result of a natural progression by a free people who no longer desire to carry the burdens of responsibility or personal accountability, and who enthusiastically relinquish their rights and privileges to one branch of government, or even to one man within that branch, with a big sigh of relief. The road to Caesarism is so practical and pragmatic that the abuse of checks and balances is barely noticed and soon forgotten. But concentrated power and centralized authority are escapes from freedom, nevertheless. The situation in Zarahemla in 67 B.C. is a chilling reminder that history does tend to repeat itself. The question always boils down to this: "Can our collective consciousness be so traumatized that we eagerly sacrifice our individual liberties in exchange for an authoritarian central government that guarantees security?"

Today we have charismatic leaders whose specialty is to capitalize on our distress and bang the drums of war in order to whip us into a nationalistic fervor. We allow their rhetoric to reach a fever pitch, causing our blood to boil with prejudice, suspicion, doubt, misgivings, mistrust, and even hatred of those whom we have not taken the time to understand. We face the spectre of voluntarily surrendering our rights and responsibilities to leaders who realize they do not need to work very hard to centralize and consolidate their authority, concentrate their power, and usurp our privileges. Infused with a fear that is fueled by a frenzied media that castigates rational approaches to problem-solving as outmoded, outdated, and out of touch, we give up our rights not only to the highest bidder, but also to the loudest and most persistent jingoist.

Perhaps we can learn from past mistakes, after all. In a reflexive reaction to the Lamanite threat, the spectre of such a dictatorial government reared its ugly head in the Land of Zarahemla. The members of a faction called the king-men "were desirous that the law should be altered in a manner to overthrow the free government and to establish a king over the land." (Alma 51:5). Those who opposed this action were called freemen.

Freedom cannot be confused for the security afforded by a prison cell, where armed guards are at the ready to quell every disturbance to the status quo, or mistaken for the sanctuary of an intensive care unit, where life-support devices are always available to countermand a DNR order. Life entails the assumption of risk, and our tendency to look to the government for job security, financial security, and social security speaks for itself. It is the evidence of our desire to avoid risk. Caesar provides our security and assumes the risk, but at a prohibitive price. Ultimately, we will be asked to pay in spades, with a pound of flesh thrown in for good measure. Because the freemen in Zarahemla understood the danger, they responded quickly and decisively.

They would have agreed with the American Declaration of Independence that unequivocally formalized the principle for which men have been willing to die: "Governments are instituted among men, deriving their just powers from the consent of the governed." Among the Nephites, it came to pass that "this matter of their contention was settled" in a similar fashion, "by the voice of the people in favor of" the chief judge Pahoran, and "the freemen." (Alma 51:7). The Lord has similarly instructed the Latter-day Saints: The "law of the land which is constitutional, supporting that principle of freedom in maintaining rights and privileges, belongs to all mankind, and is justifiable before me. Therefore, I, the Lord, justify you, and your brethren of my church, in befriending that law which is the constitutional law of the land; and as pertaining to law of man, whatsoever is more or less than this, cometh of evil." (D&C 98:5-7).

Alistair Cooke observed: "We can make one fairly certain generalization. When the people in power can neither keep the consent of the governed, nor keep down the dissent of the governed, then there will be a revolution." ("America," p. 122). Indeed, in Zarahemla "this was a critical time for such contentions to be among the people of Nephi; for behold, Amalickiah (note the similarity of his name to "Al Qaeda") had again stirred up the hearts of the people of the Lamanites against the people of the Nephites, and he was gathering together soldiers from all parts of his land, and arming them, and preparing for war with (coldly methodical) diligence." (Alma 51:9). He intuitively knew that time could be his ally, and that if the moral fiber of the Nephite nation weakened, it could be more easily defeated.

Even though the desires of the king-men had been nullified by the voice of the people, they still "were supported by those who sought power and authority over the people." (Alma 51:8). Their hidden agenda was to wrest control of the government in Zarahemla, so that they could exercise unrighteous dominion over the People of Nephi. Furthermore, their foreign policy was one of appeasement, for "they would not take up arms to defend their country" against the external threat of the Lamanites. (Alma 51:13).

When Moroni learned of these treasonous acts, he immediately sent a petition to the governor, requesting authorization to institute special military powers to "compel those dissenters to defend their country or to put them to death." (Alma 51:15). Under the circumstances, his request "was granted according to the voice of the people." (Alma 51:16). This was no small group of rabble-rousers. In the ensuing confrontation, four thousand of the dissenters were killed, and "those of their leaders who were not slain in battle were taken and cast into prison, for there was no time for their trials at this period." (Alma 51:19). The emergency was so acute that they were sent to the Nephite equivalent of Guantanamo Bay to be interred. The rest "yielded to the standard of liberty ... and thus Moroni put an end to those king-men." (Alma 51:20-21).

Abraham Lincoln, in his first Inaugural Address in March 1861, envisioned the preservation of a latter-day Zarahemla with these stirring words, relevant also to the Twenty-first Century: "The mystic chords of memory, stretching from every battlefield and patriot grave to every living heart and hearthstone all over this broad land, will yet swell the chorus of the Union when again touched, as surely they will be, by the better angels of our nature." President Lincoln was urging his fellow Americans to look beyond the animal instincts that so often blur our vision.

That vision requires our domestic and foreign policies to be indistinguishable from our ecclesiastical example. In 1852, Daniel Webster declared: "If we and our posterity shall be true to the Christian religion, and if we and they shall live always in the fear of God and shall respect his commandments, we may have the highest hopes for the future fortunes of our country. It will have no decline and fall, but it will go on prospering. But, if we or our posterity shall reject religious instructions and authority, violate the rules of morality, and recklessly destroy the political constitution which holds us together, no man can tell how sudden a catastrophe may overwhelm us, that shall bury all of our glory in profound obscurity." (Address to The New York Historical Society, Press of The Historical Society, 1852. See Christian Life and Character of The Civil Institutions of the United States," p. 270).

At close hand, we must recognize that the looming tragedy is not what may happen to our society, but what we may have already done to ourselves. The Savior admonished us to hold our ground. "Stand in the office which I have appointed unto you," He said: "Succor the weak, lift up the hands which hang down, and strengthen the feeble knees." (D&C 81:5). There is in the world today a flight from that level of responsibility. Ours is the age of passing the buck, the half- done job, and of mediocre effort. Our citizenship requires a higher standard and correspondingly greater effort. The damage may have already been done, but it is not irreversible.

We must remain steady, even when the world is in chaos and teetering on the precipice of destruction. As Josiah Gilbert Holland (1819-1881) wrote: "God, give us Men! A time like this demands strong minds, great hearts, true faith, and ready hands. Men whom the lust of office does not kill. Men whom the spoils of office cannot buy. Men who possess opinions and a will. Men who have honor; men who will not lie. Men who can stand before a demagogue and damn his treacherous flatteries without winking. Tall men, sun-crowned, who live above the fog in public duty and in private thinking. For while the rabble, with their thumb worn creeds, their large professions, and their little deeds, mingle in selfish strife, Lo! Freedom weeps, Wrong rules the land, and Justice sleeps." ("God, Give us Men!").

We must be an informed electorate, familiar with the vital issues of the day, and ready to stand up and strengthen family values and then move out of our comfort zones into our communities and countries, in order to stem an advancing tide that would erode the very foundations of the pillars of our society that secure our future. We must remember that it is better to light a candle than to curse the darkness. A thousand points of light, taken together, cast a very long shadow. Abraham Lincoln offered a sage observation that has never been more true: "To sin by silence, when words should be spoken, makes cowards of men." (Attributed to Ella Wheeler Wilcox).

Since the attrition of civil liberties cannot be summarily eliminated, we must initiate damage control protocols as quickly as possible to try to contain the problem, so that sustained countermeasures may then be initiated. It is easier to hold up an umbrella than it is to turn off the rain. At the same time, let us not forget: "Vice is a monster of so frightful mien, as to be hated needs but to be seen. Yet seen too oft, familiar with her face, we first endure, then pity, then embrace." (Alexander Pope, "Essay on Man, Epistle 2").

Dictatorial policies can take on a legitimacy they do not deserve when they are openly discussed in a society accustomed to the exercise of free speech. These may be the very "times that try (our) souls. Yet we have this consolation with us, that the harder the conflict, the more glorious the triumph. What we obtain too cheap, we esteem too lightly. 'Tis dearness only that gives everything its value. Heaven knows how to put a proper price upon its goods; and it would be strange, indeed, if … celestial article(s) … should not be highly rated." ("The Political Works of Thomas Paine," p. 55).

When government has immense power to siphon off our productivity, when our creativity is stifled, and when we give involuntarily for the support of entitlement programs from which we receive no benefit, the chains of slavery begin to tighten around us. We can learn a lesson from The Book of Mormon wherein the rulers "were supported in their laziness, and in their idolatry, and in their whoredoms, by the taxes which King Noah had put upon the people; thus did the people labor exceedingly to support iniquity. Yea, and they also became idolatrous because they were deceived by the vain and flattering words of the kings and priests; for they did speak flattering words unto them." (Mosiah 11:6-7).

Aristotle cautioned that we should "be on our guard against those who mislead the multitude. Their actions prove what sort of men they are. Spies and informers are the principal instruments of the tyrant. War is his favorite occupation, for the sake of engrossing the attention of the people, and making himself necessary to them as their leader. The tyrant, who in order to hold his power, suppresses every superiority, does away with good men, forbids education and light, controls every movement of the citizens and, keeping them under a perpetual servitude, wants them to grow accustomed to baseness and cowardice, has his spies everywhere to listen to what is said in the meetings, and spreads dissension and calumny among the citizens and impoverishes them, is obliged to make war in order to keep his subjects occupied and impose on them permanent need of a chief." These are sobering words, indeed, as they speak out of the dust, but they are as true today as they were when they were first uttered over 2,300 years ago.

Fortunately: "Men's and nations' finest hours are those when extraordinary challenge is met with extraordinary response." (Winston Churchill). Our courage to stand against demagogues can be the catalyst that transforms timidity and temerity into powerful presence of mind, which then acts as a platform for assertive action. It is not bravado, but boldness. Unlike a paper tiger, it is an intense and compellingly positive response to threat. In the fight or flight scenario, it is the launch pad for the anticipated adrenalin rush that will carry us through the challenge. It is the foundation quality on which is built our defense.

In our day, many churches bear the name of Christ or a derivative in their titles, and so the substance of the issue becomes whether or not church doctrine is taught by ministers who bear the authority of God's priesthood. Is their message composed of gospel doctrine that can easily be validated by the Holy Ghost? Can the validity of the principles which they purport to be true withstand the scrutiny, and ultimately receive the unqualified approbation, of the Spirit?

(A) Coat of Many Colors

"And it came to pass
that he rent his coat; and he
took a piece thereof, and wrote upon
it – In memory of our God, our religion,
and freedom, and our peace, our wives, and
our children – and he fastened it upon the
end of a pole." (Alma 46:12).

It is interesting to think of Joseph's coat of many colors as an allegory for the fabric of our own lives, sewn by our Heavenly Father Himself, with each thread individually tailored to suit our circumstances, and representing, not the drab monotone of the world, but a true Technicolor DreamCoat signifying the glories and riches of eternity. To do so helps us to put the day-to-day elements of the Plan of Salvation in perspective, and to more clearly discern the grey-toned obstacles to our progression so that they may stand out in sharp contrast to the polychromatic backdrop of the design that God has created for each of us.

Joseph's coat was a wonderful expression of his father's love for him, and to wear it must have given him a great deal of pleasure, but it did get him into serious trouble. Had this impressionable youngest son of Jacob kept his counsel to himself after he had received visions of his brethren paying him obeisance, he might have mitigated their growing envy and avoided their subsequent conspiracy against him. "For although a man may have many revelations, and have power to do many mighty works, yet if he boasts in his own strength, and sets at naught the counsels of God, and follows after the dictates of his own will and carnal desires, he must fall and incur the vengeance of a just God upon him." (D&C 3:4).

We all know what happened next: "And the Midianites sold him into Egypt unto Potiphar, an officer of Pharaoh's, and captain of the guard." (Genesis 37:36). Joseph's physical garment was gone, and he would find himself falsely accused and in bondage in Egypt, ostensibly left in rags in a dark and hopeless dungeon. It would be up to him to seek God's guidance in reconstructing the coat, if only in his mind's eye, that he might learn to appreciate the significance of each thread that had been so thoughtfully and carefully provided.

I think of Joseph when I read the dialogue between Edmund Dantès and the priest Abbé Faria that occurred deep within the walls of the prison of the Chateau d'If, in Alexandere Dumas' novel "The Count of Monte Cristo." "What are you thinking?" asked the Abbé smilingly, imputing the deep abstraction in which his visitor was plunged to the excess of his awe and wonder. "I was reflecting, in the first place," replied Dantès, "upon the enormous degree of intelligence and ability you must have employed to reach the high perfection to which you have attained. What would you not have accomplished if you had been free?" "Possibly nothing at all," replied the priest. "The overflow of my brain would probably, in a state of freedom, have evaporated in a thousand follies; misfortune is needed to bring to light the treasures of the human intellect. Compression is needed to explode gunpowder. Captivity has brought my mental faculties to a focus; and you are well aware that from the collision of clouds electricity is produced - from electricity, lightning, and from lightning, illumination."

Finally, at the end of the tale, Dantès observes: "Only a man who has felt ultimate despair is capable of feeling ultimate bliss. It is necessary to have wished for death, in order to know how good it is to live. Live, then, and be happy, and never forget that, until the day God deigns to reveal the future to man, the sum of human wisdom will be contained in these words: wait and hope."

As the poet sagaciously observed: "My life is but a weaving between my God and me. I cannot choose the colors. He weaveth steadily. Oft' times He weaveth sorrow, and I in foolish pride, forget He sees the upper, and I, the underside. Not 'til the loom is silent and the shuttles cease to fly, will God unroll the canvas and reveal the reason why. The dark threads are as needful in the weaver's skillful hand, as the threads of gold and silver in the pattern He has planned." (Benjamin Malachi Franklin).

Joseph's coat of many colors teaches us that every cloud has a silver lining. As Helen Keller wrote: "I believe that no good shall be lost, and that all man has willed or hoped or dreamed of good shall exist forever. I believe in the immortality of the soul because I have within me immortal longings. I believe that the state we enter after death is wrought of our own motives, thoughts, and deeds. I believe that my home there will be beautiful with color, music, and speech of flowers and faces I love. Without this faith, there would be little meaning in my life. I should be a mere pillar of darkness in the dark. Observers in the full enjoyment of their bodily senses pity me, but it is because they do not see the golden chamber in my life where I dwell delighted; for dark as my path may seem to them, I carry a magic light in my heart. Faith, the spiritual strong searchlight, illuminates the way, and although sinister doubts lurk in the shadow, I walk unafraid towards the Enchanted Wood where the foliage is always green, where joy abides, where nightingales nest and sing, and where life and death are one in the presence of the Lord."

Joseph received his coat as a gift from his father, just as surely as we receive our coats from our Heavenly Father. We can be sure that the bolts of cloth have been carefully selected and cut to address every exigency in our lives. As Mark E. Petersen observed: "Shall we not be willing to sacrifice our ordinary desires when necessary, and cut our cloth to fit the pattern of revised circumstances" that unfolds before us, with the intention of maximizing our life experiences? Those evolving circumstances provide for us coats of many colors with enough room to allow us to grow into the full stature of our spirits. They are not tailored to be contemporary or fashionable or form fitting. They have not been designed to emphasize our physical form, or to impress the world. Rather, they are of enduring quality, and their fitting has been carefully customized to be comfortably motivating, subtly inspiring, quietly elegant, gently refining, spiritually uplifting, and unobtrusively sophisticated, with an easy grace that belies the power that is intrinsic to the material. The purpose of our Father's careful selection of material, meticulous tailoring, and almost obsessive attention to detail, protects us from both the winds of adversity and the wiles of the adversary.

Just as Joseph's siblings were jealous of Jacob's gift, and were likely envious of their younger brother's evolving spiritual maturity, so too are our contemporaries sometimes resentful of the accomplishments that are facilitated by our own coats of many colors. No matter what other outfits may be in our closets, however, and especially if their design is after the likeness of the world, we must have the courage to brush them aside and instead choose modestly uplifting and complementary ensembles. If we then wear our coats with dignity, they can make statements equivalent to that of the cape worn by Superman. The fabric of our coats will have come, not from Krypton, but from Kolob, and the powers thereby derived will not only be otherworldly, but they will also be supernatural. If we see in their vibrant colors the Lord and his strength, (and) seek his face continually," (1 Chronicles 16:11), our coats will transform us. They will allow us to be faster than speeding bullets, more powerful than locomotives, and empower us to leap tall buildings in a single bound. Our coats will bestow upon us the power of God, to give strength to the poor and to the needy in his distress, and to be "a refuge from the storm, (and) a shadow from the heat," even when the blast from the unrighteous and unworthy is as a storm against the fortress of our spiritual security. (Isaiah 25:4).

If we desire the attention and adoration of the world, and are tempted to leave our coats of many colors hanging unused and unattended in the back of our closets, hidden behind our more contemporary outfits, we should attune our ear to our Father, Who quietly reassures us: "Be still, and know that I am God" (D&C 101:16). From the Book of Exodus, Aaron's example teaches that each of us may enjoy the protection afforded by the special clothing that complements, as an ensemble, our coat of many colors. "And thou shalt bring Aaron and his sons unto the door of the tabernacle of the congregation, and wash them with water. And thou shalt put upon Aaron the holy garments, and anoint him, and sanctify him." (Exodus 42:12-13). From time immemorial, the coats of many colors that have been provided by God for His children to wear have shielded them against the power of the destroyer, and have been designed to protect them from his evil influence until they have finished their work on the earth.

As we care for and maintain our coats by repenting and by humbling ourselves sincerely, through faith, God will minister unto us through His holy angels, whose own garments will be pure and white above all other whiteness, whose countenances will be as lightning, and whose personages will be glorious beyond description. (See D&C 20:6 & J.S.H. 1:32).

Like spiritual swaddling clothes, our coats will resonate with intrinsic light that does not resound from pigment and dye. Their power will be evident to even the most hardened skeptics, such as Belshazzar, who summoned Daniel to his court, and said: "I have even heard of thee, that the spirit of the gods is in thee, and that light and understanding and excellent wisdom is found in thee." (Daniel 5:14). The king did not realize it, but the power that he sensed in Daniel came from the prophet's own coat of many colors.

The light of the Spirit will give each thread in our own coats a vibrancy, vitality, and vivacity that is unique to holy vestments. Their colors are fast, and can only fade if we neglect to properly care and maintain them. Inasmuch as we do not defile them, however, but are true and faithful to the care instructions that are clearly printed on their labels, they will be shields of protection to us. But if we inadvertently or carelessly wash our coats with other garments that have been soiled with the stain of sin, their powers of enchantment will be neutralized.

Each of our individual coats has many colors that make it unique. Psychophysicists tell us that the human eye can distinguish around 10 million different colors, which is really quite remarkable, since there are only three primary colors in the visible light spectrum (red, green, and blue). Isaac Newton, who was the first to use a prism to separate white light (at wavelengths between 390 – 700 nm) into its individual colors, divided the spectrum into seven named colors (red, orange, yellow, green, blue, indigo, and violet). So, the arrangement of colors in our individual coats has plenty of latitude to be unique, to fit our individual circumstances.

In general, though, the color red calls us to action, and reminds us that the Savior trod the winepress alone. Orange is a warning to take care that we conform our lives to the Lord's design. Yellow encourages us to seek the light that is gathering in the east. Green brings to mind the power of envy, and our requirement to observe and keep the 10th commandment, and to be content with the cards in the hand that God has dealt us. Blue reminds us to mourn with those that mourn, and to comfort those that stand in need of comfort. Indigo is a color whose depth and brightness represent the profundity of the gospel, and its ability to illuminate truth wherever it may be found. Violet is the color of amethyst, lavender, and beautyberries, and reminds us of the garlands festooning the walls of the celestial city of God. (See Revelation 21:20).

Grey (black and white) is associated with neutrality, conformity, uncertainty, and indifference. It prompts us to choose whom we will serve, and encourages us to stand on the Lord's side. Purple (red and blue) urges us to remember the royal robes of Christ our King. Black (blue, red, and yellow) underscores the necessity of opposition that paves the way to our progression. White (red, orange, yellow, green, blue, indigo, and violet) solemnly suggests the totality of the ordinances of the priesthood, our temple covenants, and the purity of the Spirit, all of which are necessary if we are to regain the glory of our former home.

From ultraviolet to infrared, our coats of many colors will incorporate into their pattern and design every color of visible light, but they will also resonate with radiation from a spectrum that can only be seen with eyes that have been touched by the hand of God. If we were able to break down that energy with a spiritual prism, we would look beyond the limited horizon of our sight, and see the visions of eternity. "By the power of the Spirit our eyes (would be) opened and our understandings (would be) enlightened, so as to see and understand the things of God." (D&C 76:12).

Cogito, Ergo Sum

"And now, my sons,
I would that ye should look to
the great Mediator, and hearken unto
his great commandments; and be faithful
unto his words, and choose eternal life,
according to the will of his Holy
Spirit." (2 Nephi 2:28).

I will describe non-linear thinking shortly, and in greater detail, but let me first tease you with this possibility. Maybe Joseph Smith was one of the first non-linear thinkers. His unconventional view of the world helps to explain why he would look back on his life, and muse: "I stood alone, an unlearned youth, to combat the worldly wisdom and multiplied ignorance of eighteen centuries, with a new revelation, which ... would open the eyes of more than eight hundred millions of people, and make plain the old paths." (H.C., 6:74). Or: "When we understand the character of God, He begins to unfold the heavens to us, and to tell us all about it. When we are ready to come to Him, He is ready to come to us." (H.C. 6:308). Or, "It is my meditation all the day, and more than my meat and drink, to know how I shall make the Saints of God comprehend the visions that roll like an overflowing surge before my mind. Oh! How I would delight to bring before you things which you never thought of." (H.C. 5:362). Or, "The best way to obtain truth and wisdom is not to ask it from books, but to go to God in prayer, and obtain divine teaching." ("Teachings," p. 191).

Now let me turn to linear thinking, that has been defined as "a process of thought following known cycles or step-by-step progression, where a response to a step must be elicited before another step is taken." This is the conventional way most of us think, most of the time, and in most situations it actually works quite well. However, there is always the danger of relying too heavily on the sheer logic of linear thinking, for once we have settled upon a starting point in our inquiry, there are only a limited number of avenues that lead to logical conclusions. Additionally, there is no guarantee that our starting point relies on truth, or on what I would call eternally valid principles. If we are lucky, and it does, we are certainly going to be much better off than if we had chosen a starting point that was either blatantly false, or that was so narrowly defined that it would limit our exposure to the rich variety of alternatives that might just be the best ones to provide the answers to our inquiry. In any event, we risk being led astray right from the beginning, and then finding ourselves in unfamiliar, indefensible territory from which there is no easy avenue of escape. Linear thinking is dangerous when it takes us down the road of expediency that leads to ethical and moral dilemmas, and to conundrums that can be of cosmic proportions.

Non-linear thinking, as opposed to linear thinking, is a relatively new term, which means that there is a lot of obfuscation going on when attempting to articulate its definition. But, for the sake of simplicity, let's describe it as human thought that is characterized by cerebral expansion in multiple spatial and even temporal directions, rather than in just one pre-determined linear direction. It is based on the concept that there exist multiple starting points from which the basic principles of logical thought may be applied to a problem. Consider, once again, my characterization of Joseph Smith as the quintessential non-linear thinker of the Nineteenth Century.

We do not have to stretch our minds very much to be immediately struck with the realization that God Himself must be the quintessential non-linear thinker, that the Plan of Salvation is its best expression, and that it might be consistent with His design to view the gospel through the clarifying lens of similar unconventional thought processes.

Non-linear thinking is expansive, and it lets creative juices run wild precisely because it is not dependent upon a self-limiting structure. It increases the sheer number of possible outcomes because it encourages multiple starting points for any endeavor. There is enough room in the world for an infinite number of non-linear thinkers, which allows us to segue right into the basic premises of the Plan of Salvation. The Plan, too, is flexible enough to accommodate those of every persuasion and inclination, for God "inviteth them all to come unto him and partake of his goodness; and he denieth none that come unto him, black and white, bond and free, male and female; and he remembereth the heathen; and all are alike unto God, both Jew and Gentile." (2 Nephi 26:33).

Non-linear thinkers who happen to lucky enough to consciously appreciate the elasticity of the Plan of Salvation have flexible testimonies. To them, the veil is almost transparent. They are spiritually sensitive and prepared to act. As their powers expand, they experience the glittering facets of the life of the Spirit. They find themselves cast off into a stream of revelation, as if they were being carried along in the quickening currents of direct experience with God. Non-linear thinking sets them free to be creative, and sets them creative, that they might be free. In a sense, we all enter this world as non-linear thinkers. We are "born free," as it were. If that is true, from the very beginning, the stage is set for the inauguration of the perfect law of liberty. We are nurtured from our birth to master the ability to generate higher-level non-linear thought processes, that the quiet spiritual stirrings that underlie our experience might be amplified, and become a catalyst with the ability to propel us into the presence of God.

Non-linear thinkers have no privileged frames of reference, which opens up almost unlimited options for them. They jump around, forward and backward, and side to side, when working through a problem. They literally see the big picture, as they move at will from one point on the canvas of life to another, focusing with greater sensitivity on areas that have demanded their attention. This sounds a lot like how we envision that God must govern His creations.

Think of a linear slide show, contrasted with the comprehension of a huge canvas that illustrates the entire story, not from start to finish, but all at once, the beginning and the end at one and the same time, with the additional capacity to zoom in and out, to fast forward, reverse, and freeze frame. If you can visualize that, you can see why God must be a non-linear thinker. With a little practice, we can be, too.

We all experience situations where we employ the best techniques of both liner and non-linear thinking. Ultimately, both are useful and important cognitive devices to be mastered. Non-linear thinking, however, is at its best when we re-examine our potential starting points, because doing that increases the possibility of selecting the right option from all the alternatives available. But somewhere during the process of inquiry, after that critical starting point has been fixed in our crosshairs, we might also want to employ linear thinking because of its efficient logic-based reasoning. Once we have embarked upon the journey, linear thinking might help us to get to the finish line in a more timely manner. How effectively we use both devices depends upon how thoroughly we have read the play book, how vigorously we exercise our gift of free will along the way, and how often we rely upon powers greater than ourselves to make necessary course corrections, in order to re-align ourselves with our envisioned goals and recalibrate our efforts to achieve them.

As you face new challenges, look to both linear and non-linear thinking, and decide for yourself how to best incorporate them into your own style of inquiry.

"My thoughts are not your thoughts," Jehovah told his prophet, "neither are your ways my ways." (Isaiah 55:8). Frustratingly, as our circle of knowledge expands, so do the borders of darkness. The more we know, the more we need to learn. It should do no violence to our faith to realize that, with a greater understanding of doctrinal truth, there might be additional questions to ponder.

Cognates in The Book of Mormon

"I have dreamed a dream"
(1 Nephi 8:2).

Cognates are related words that come from the same root. For example, the English noun 'student' is cognate to the verb 'study' and to the adjective 'studious'. In Hebrew, a verb is sometimes followed by a noun that is a cognate, such as "wrote upon it a writing" (Exodus 39:30) and "she vowed a vow," and sometimes, the verb and the noun are the same word. (1 Samuel 1:11).

When writing in English, cognates are used infrequently, because they are considered awkward or in elegant in their style. For example, someone writing in English would be more likely to use "thy servant vowed" or "he made a vow," rather than "thy servant vowed a vow." (1 Samuel 15:8).

A cognate accusative is a device that arises from the similarity between related Hebrew words. For example, the words Jershon, inheritance, and possession, that are found in Alma Chapter 27. "And they went down into the land of Jershon, and took possession (YRS) of the land of Jershon" (yarsôn) "for an inheritance" (yarsôn, Alma 27:22). This is a remarkable example of the cognate accusative in the underlying Hebrew text of The Book of Mormon.

In many ways The Book of Mormon sounds like a Hebrew text. John A. Tvedtnes has pointed out that The Book of Mormon employs cognates more than one would expect if the original language of the book had been English. These cognates illustrate the book's Hebrew influence. One of the most widely recognized examples is the familiar "I have dreamed a dream" (1 Nephi 8:2). That is exactly the way the same idea is expressed in literal translation from Old Testament Hebrew. It looks like Joseph Smith has scored another bullseye! (See Genesis 37:5 & 41:11).

Cognates in The Book of Mormon include the following 23 examples, each followed by the more normal expression as it might typically be rendered in English.

"I will curse them even with a sore curse" (1 Nephi 2:23), instead of "I will curse them sorely."

"I have dreamed a dream" (1 Nephi 3:2), instead of "I have had a dream."

"I have dreamed a dream" (1 Nephi 8:2), instead of "I have had a dream."

It "yoketh them with a yoke of iron," (1 Nephi 13:5), instead of "it burdens them with a yoke of iron."

"I will work a great and a marvelous work" (1 Nephi 14:7), instead of "I will perform a great and marvelous work."

"Arise from the dust …that ye may not be cursed with a sore cursing " (2 Nephi 1:22), instead of "Arise from the dust …that ye may not be cursed sorely."

"I did teach the people to build buildings" (2 Nephi 5:15), instead of "I did teach the people to construct buildings."

"They are cursed with a sore cursing " (Jacob 3:3), instead of "They are sorely cursed."

"This was the desire which I desired of him" (Enos 1:13,) instead of "This is what I desired of him."

"Succor those that stand in need of your succor" (Mosiah 4:16), instead of "Comfort those that stand in need of your succor."

"(We are) taxed with a tax" (Mosiah 7:15), instead of "We are "taxed."

"And we began to build buildings (Mosiah 9:8), instead of "And we began to construct buildings."

"He also caused that his workmen should work all manner of fine work" Mosiah 11:10), instead of " He also caused that his laborers should create all manner of fine work."

"He caused many buildings to be built" (Mosiah 11:13), instead of "He caused many buildings to be constructed."

They began "to build buildings" (Mosiah 23:5), instead of "They began to erect buildings," or simply "They began to build."

"Judge a righteous judgment" (Mosiah 29:29), instead of "Make a righteous judgment."

"He did judge righteous judgments" (Mosiah 29:43), instead of "He judged righteously" or "He made righteous judgments."

"Have ye felt to sing the song of redeeming love?" (Alma 5:26), instead of "Have ye felt to sing of redeeming love?"

"Limoni began to fear exceedingly, with fear" (Alma 18:5), instead of "Limoni began to fear exceedingly."

"We will give up the land of Jershon, which is on the east by the sea, which joins the land Bountiful, which is on the south of the land Bountiful; and this land Jershon is the land which we will give unto our brethren for an inheritance" (Alma 27:22), instead of ""We will give up the land of Jershon, which is on the east by the sea, which is on the south of the land Bountiful; and this is the land which we will give unto our brethren for an inheritance."

"They went down into the land of Jershon, and took possession of the land of Jershon" (Alma 27:26), instead of "They went down into the land of Jershon, and took possession of it."

"This people is a free people" (Alma 30:24), instead of "These people are free."

"And they did work all manner of fine work (Ether 10:23), instead of "And they did complete all manner of fine work."

Weak and insipid claims that Joseph Smith composed The Book of Mormon by simply imitating King names while inventing others, typically exhibit insensitivity and ignorance relating to its myriad linguistic nuances. The use of cognates scattered throughout the text would render the fabrication of the book an overwhelming challenge for anyone in Joseph Smith's day, let alone for an untutored lad such as he.

The example of righteous judges in Zarahemla illustrates the power of even a handful of inspired government leaders to hold evil in check and positively influence an entire culture.

Combating Evil

"The captives of the mighty
shall be taken away, and the prey
of the terrible shall be delivered; for I
will contend with him that contendeth
with thee, and I will save thy children."
(1 Nephi 21:25).

A hundred and fifty years ago, Daniel Webster declared: "If we and our posterity shall be true to the Christian religion, and if we and they shall live always in the fear of God and shall respect his commandments, we may have the highest hopes for the future fortunes of our country. It will have no decline and fall, but it will go on prospering.

But, if we or our posterity shall reject religious instructions and authority, violate the rules of morality and recklessly destroy the political constitution which holds us together, no man can tell how sudden a catastrophe may overwhelm us, that shall bury all of our glory in profound obscurity." (Address to The New York Historical Society, "Press of The Historical Society," 1852. See "Christian Life and Character of The Civil Institutions of the United States," p. 270).

What can we do today to strengthen the values of our country, stem the advancing tide of immorality and secure our future? We must remember that it is better to light a candle, than to curse the darkness. A thousand points of light, taken together, cast a very long shadow. Abraham Lincoln said that "to sin by silence, when words should be spoken, makes cowards of men." (Attributed to Ella Wheeler Wilcox). That sage observation was never more true than it is today.

Since wickedness cannot be summarily eliminated, we must initiate damage control protocols as quickly as possible, to try to contain the problem, so that sustained countermeasures may be set in place. It is easier to hold up an umbrella than it is to turn off the rain.

Often, in our communities, it seems that immorality is legislated. When this happens, it takes on a legitimacy it does not deserve. As Alexander Pope cautioned: "Vice is a monster of so frightful mien, as to be hated needs but to be seen. Yet seen too oft, familiar with her face, we first endure, then pity, then embrace." ("Essay on Man, Epistle 2").

Better to be counted a Christian, and to demand legislation that promotes family values and demands personal accountability. Better to be labeled as a member of the "religious right" and insist on personal integrity and high moral standards of our elected representatives. "Go ye out from Babylon," declared Jesus Christ. "Be ye clean that bear the vessels of the Lord. Go ye out from among the nations, even from Babylon, from the midst of wickedness, which is spiritual Babylon." (D&C 133:5 & 14).

Love your enemies, and do good, and lend, hoping for nothing again; and your reward shall be great." (Luke 6:35). Revenge, the "get even" mentality that is popularized in books and film and is reinforced in everyday interpersonal relationships in business and societal settings, is antithetical to the gospel of Jesus Christ. It may be true that in business, you don't get what you deserve, you get what you negotiate. But when the earth is cleansed to receive its paradisiacal glory, a higher standard will prevail and each of us will get exactly what he deserves. In the meantime, the Saints' responsibility is to conduct their affairs in a conscious anticipation of the millennial day.

"If," instead, "we go on lusting after the groveling things of this life which perish with the handling, we shall surely remain fixed with a very limited amount of knowledge and like a door upon its hinges, move to and fro from one year to another without any visible advancement or improvement" like flotsam and jetsam on the sea of life. (Brigham Young).

Daddy Warbucks told Annie: "You don't have to be nice to those you climb over, or step on, on your way up the ladder of success, if you don't plan on coming back down again." But the Savior said: "Whosoever will be chief among you, let him be your servant." (Matthew 20:27).

Satan's Golden Question is "Do you have any money?" He would have us believe that you can have anything in this world for money. Does a personal need exist? Solve the problem with a generous application of money, to be repeated in escalating doses for life. This is the prescription upon which the world relies.

"Babylon has never wanted for dedicated and highly paid apologists to justify the ways of those who 'seek for power, and authority, and riches' (3 Nephi 6:15), at the expense of the public at large." (Hugh Nibley, "On the Timely and Timeless," p. 96). The number one task of any bureaucracy, after all, is to justify its own existence. Any residual benefit to the public is only a bonus.

The Savior illustrated a very different success formula for those who would negotiate the minefields of mortality. "Then shall the King say unto them on his right hand, Come ye blessed of my Father, inherit the kingdom prepared for you from the foundation of the world. For I was an hungered, and ye gave me meat; I was thirsty, and ye gave me drink; I was a stranger, and ye took me in; Naked, and ye clothed me; I was sick, and ye visited me; I was in prison, and ye came unto me ... Verily I say unto you, inasmuch as ye have done it unto one of the least of these my brethren, ye have done it unto me." (Matthew 25:34-36 & 40).

"Stand in the office which I have appointed unto you," He admonished. "Succor the weak, lift up the hands which hang down, and strengthen the feeble knees." (D&C 81:5). There is in the world today a flight from that level of responsibility. Ours is the age of passing the buck, the half-done job, and of mediocre effort. Discipleship requires a higher standard and correspondingly greater effort.

It is antithetical to the way of the world that every worthy young man should serve a mission. Service to God and country today meet with stiff opposition. These qualities are a mystery to Spiritual Babylon, which caters instead to the lowest common denominator in human behavior. Only the righteous who have tried the virtue of the word of God, know that he "doth grant unto you whatsoever ye ask that is right, in faith, believing that ye shall receive. O then, how ye ought to impart of the substance that ye have one to another." (Mosiah 4:21). The Church Welfare System offers a wonderful opportunity for the practice of active, meaningful brotherhood. Government assistance and entitlement programs, on the other hand, too often offers only detached, disinterested, and ineffectual paternalism without personal accountability.

Hugh Nibley has talked of the "Mahan Principle," which he defined as the great secret of converting life into property. There is, we discover, an economic baseline to every government action that unfortunately ignores or trivializes the worth of souls.

How has the Lord countered this Satanic twisting of the principle of consecration? Even though the early Saints were in the most straitened of circumstances, He declared to them: "And this shall be the beginning of the tithing of my people." (D&C 119). This Law has remained a foundation principle in this Dispensation. Tithing is paid with faith, more than it is with currency, and when the Saints are obedient, they are blessed beyond measure. On the other hand, when government has immense powers to siphon off the productivity of people, when creativity is stifled, and when taxpayers give involuntarily for the support of entitlement programs from which they receive no benefit, the roots of evil become entrenched.

We should learn from the lesson illustrated in The Book of Mormon wherein the rulers "were supported in their laziness, and in their idolatry, and in their whoredoms, by the taxes which King Noah had put upon the people; thus did the people labor exceedingly to support iniquity. Yea, and they also became idolatrous because they were deceived by the vain and flattering words of the kings and priests; for they did speak flattering words unto them." (Mosiah 11:6-7).

"Take heed," cautioned the Savior, "that ye do not your alms before men; to be seen of them; otherwise ye have no reward of your Father which is in heaven. Thy Father which seeth in secret himself shall reward thee openly." (Matthew 6:1 & 6). Ralph Waldo Emerson lamented that "once we had wooden chalices and golden priests. Now we have golden chalices and wooden priests." As Alvin R. Dyer cautioned: "We must not be caught in the bind of building a church and killing the articles of its faith, or permitting form to triumph over spirit. The church and kingdom of God is built by the ardor and conviction of its members. We must be alert to the expansion of its assets at the cost of lost conviction. When buildings or institutions grow bigger and bigger, let us be fearful lest the Spirit will thin out." ("A Foundation For Education").

One problem is that "when we undertake to cover our sins, or to gratify our pride, our vain ambition ... behold the heavens withdraw themselves, (and) the Spirit of the Lord is grieved." (D&C 121:37). Without the temple, for example, any civilization becomes an empty shell, a structure of custom and convenience only. Speaking of those who are patrons of the temple, Hugh Nibley wrote: "Here is a band of mortals who are actually engaged in doing something which has not their own comfort, convenience, or profit as its object. Here, at last, is a phenomenon that commands respect in our day and could safely be put forth among the few valid arguments we now have to induce Deity to spare the human race; thousands of men and women putting themselves out for no ulterior motive." ("On The Timely and Timeless," p. xxvii).

Ultimately, every individual will have to ask: "Am I going to follow the prophet, or follow the profit?" On the one hand the Lord has assured us that "the earth is full, and there is enough and to spare; yea, I prepared all things, and have given unto the children of men to be agents unto themselves. Therefore, if any man shall take of the abundance which I have made, and impart not his portion, according to the law of my gospel, unto the poor and the needy, he shall, with the wicked, lift up his eyes in hell, being in torment." (D&C 104:17-18).

On the other hand, collective bargaining to gain advantage over another is the norm in our society. Caveat emptor - let the buyer beware - is the rule of business. The world makes a religion of economic programs ostensibly designed to improve the quality of our lives, but which really have a personal profit motive as their basis. Truly, Spiritual Babylon has a perverted conception of equality.

Aristotle cautioned that we should "be on our guard against those who flatter and mislead the multitude. Their actions prove what sort of men they are. Of the tyrant, spies and informers are the principal instruments. War is his favorite occupation, for the sake of engrossing the attention of the people, and making himself necessary to them as their leader. The tyrant, who in order to hold his power, suppresses every superiority, does away with good men, forbids education and light, controls every movement of the citizens and, keeping them under a perpetual servitude, wants them to grow accustomed to baseness and cowardice, has his spies everywhere to listen to what is said in the meetings, and spreads dissension and calumny among the citizens and impoverishes them, is obliged to make war in order to keep his subjects occupied and impose on them permanent need of a chief."

The world desperately needs the gospel because it has tried nearly everything else, and still, Satan rules in the land. The Book of Mormon itself is a record of recurring cycles and we should view it as a mirror of our times, and as a blueprint for survival in the Last Days. Within its pages, when the people were righteous the Lord blessed them and they began to prosper. Temporal security led the people, especially the rising generation, to pride. Then, apostasy brought a loss of spiritual power and God's protection. Resulting warfare and suffering humbled the people, who then turned to the Lord, and the cycle began anew.

Generally, only when we are chastened by afflictions are we "awakened to a remembrance of (our) duty." (Alma 4:3). The purpose of chastisement is to bring people to a condition of repentance. God wants all His children to rely on the Atonement of His Son, rather than on their own energies, intellect, or abilities, so that they might qualify for eternal life. That is why the Lord reproves those whom He loves. As a result of our chastisements, we begin "to establish the church more fully." (Alma 4:4).

There is a timelessness to the question: How does one help to establish the church? Elder Neal Maxwell said that in "the Last Days, discipleship will be lived in crescendo." The actions of each individual member of the church will swell the chorus of voices shouting "Hallelujah," and can significantly hasten the millennial reign of the Lord. B.H. Roberts once said that "the Latter-day Saints are the white-hot sparks struck off the Divine Anvil of God," destined to kindle a fire which will burn so brightly that it will celestialize the earth so that it might receive its rightful King.

True disciples commit the Thirteen Articles of Faith to life, as well as to memory, and actively practice their religion. John Taylor observed that "there are some Christian people in this world who, if a man were poor or hungry, would say, let us pray for him. I would suggest a little different regimen for a person in this condition; rather take him a bag of flour and a little beef or pork. A few such comforts will do him more good than your prayers." ("Companion to The Old Testament," p. 192). As Edward Bulwer-Lytton observed: "When a person is down in the world, an ounce of help is better than a pound of preaching." Socrates said, "Know thyself." Cicero said, "Control Thyself." Jesus said, "Give of thyself." Those who establish the church are committed to actively embrace the demands of discipleship in just this way.

These demands require a revision of commonly accepted standards of qualification. In the Kingdom of God, it is not ability, or inability, but availability that is important when His servants are called to the work. Brigham Young once declared, "I never count the cost of anything. I just find out what the Lord wants me to do, and I do it." It is this kind of total commitment and dedication that establishes the church.

When Joan of Arc was carried to the stake in circumstances similar to the Prophet Abinadi's, she was given the opportunity to obtain her freedom by denying her beliefs. Instead, she made this statement: "I know this now.

Every man gives his life for what he believes. Every woman gives her life for what she believes. Sometimes people believe in little or nothing, and so they give their lives for little or nothing. One life is all we have, and we live it as we believe in living it, and then it is gone. But to surrender what you are and live without belief is more terrible than dying, even more terrible than dying young." ("Speeches of The Year," l 975, p. 428). Resolutely, then, she faced death, still true to her faith and her beliefs. Her final acts on earth were consistent with her convictions. (Maxwell Anderson, "Joan of Lorraine," Act 2, Interlude 3).It is this quality of total commitment and dedication that establishes the church.

In 1820, in Western New York State, a spirit of religious revivalism flared brightly among the people, and Joseph Smith sought diligently to establish the Church. His efforts are carried on today by those to whom the torch has been passed.

In 85 B.C. in the Land of Zarahemla, that same spirit burned among the people of Nephi, "who sought diligently to establish the church." In addition to those of the faith, there were surely many nonmembers living in Zarahemla, for in the 109 years since the reign of Mosiah 1, People of Zarahemla, People of Limhi, and other descendants of Zeniff, might not yet have had the benefit of baptism. Additionally, Lamanites, as well as non-Book of Mormon peoples, might have co-existed in the land.

Mention of pride is made more than sixty times in The Book of Mormon. Some call it the parent sin out of which all others come. The sad fact is that "I" and "Mine" are usually accompanied by the unbended knee. Pride robs one of the wide-eyed wonder of innocence, kills the spirit of inquisitiveness, and substitutes callous arrogance for teachability. Dante, speaking of the souls in the hellfire of his vision of Inferno, revealed that Pride, Envy, and Avarice were the three sparks that had set their hearts on fire. Indeed, "Pride breakfasted with plenty, dined with poverty, and supped with infamy." (Benjamin Franklin)

We are given two of a lot of things, and can generally do without one of them: for example, eyes, ears, arms, legs, and kidneys. But we are only given one heart. Everyone needs a heart, and it is best to keep it softened. Spiritual sclerosis, or hardening of the spiritual arteries, can be an eternally fatal heart condition. Left undiagnosed and untreated, this disease ravages the soul and is always terminal.

The chastening hand of the Lord prompts us to repent of our sins and to focus on the infinite. But ensuing prosperity can distort our vision, leaving us spiritually shortsighted. "To the humble, the simpleness and the easiness of the way are glad realities. To the crowded, ego filled minds of proud men, the sudden sunlight from a spiritual sunrise is irritating rather than awesome, and causes them to blink rather than to stare in reverent awe." (Neal Maxwell, "That My Family Should Partake," p. 82). We suffer temporal trauma when our concern is for telestial toys and trinkets, rather than for celestial sureties. Our myopia can be the classic lack of vision that has so often inspired the observation that "having eyes they do not See" (See Mark 8:18).

Lyman Abbott said: "The brotherhood of man is an integral part of Christianity no less than the Fatherhood of God; and to deny the one is no less infidel than to deny the other." Truly, there is no brotherhood of man without the fatherhood of God. "The mystic bond of brotherhood makes all men one." (Thomas Carlyle). "The universe is but one great city, full of beloved ones, divine and human, by nature endeared to each other." (Epictetus).

Another way to stem the rising tide of evil is to abase ourselves to the benefit of those who need both physical and spiritual nourishment. We must never allow ourselves to be caught up in the machinery of the church, without making contact with the Savior, and without being spiritually begotten of Him. For such, life can be a treadmill. The gospel is dynamic, and its ordinances can be a springboard to new spiritual heights. Church experiences can be a springboard providing sunbursts of sensitivity to fill our spiritual reservoirs. For without the Savior, we cannot enjoy God's Rest, or "that peace which surpasseth understanding." (Philippians 4:7).

As our powers expand, we experience the glittering facets of the life of the Spirit. "To use the careful preparation and training we receive as a springboard, to be capable of disciplined, controlled procedure and to be receptive to flashes of insight, is what solid Latter-day Saints should have going for them in their inner lives. The gospel sets us free to be creative, and sets us creative to become more free. It is the perfect law of liberty," freeing us from the evil that surrounds us. ("My Religion & Me," Lesson #9).

We use the scriptures as a powerful weapon against evil, and we use them to stir up our people "in remembrance of their duty." (Alma 4:19). We use the scriptures to encourage our brethren to mend their ways, and to guide them toward greater obedience based on a clearer understanding.

We use testimony to combat evil. "A word about testimony. In one sense a testimony is a wholly private thing. It is part of your life, your conscience, your experience, but you cannot show it to anyone else. That, of course, is why it is valuable to you. It is your personal comfort and warrant for your faith. No matter what happens to anyone else, you have something you know for sure about spiritual matters. You and the Lord have a functioning, ongoing relationship and companionship." (Chauncy Riddle, "The Pillars of Testimony," B.Y.U. Devotional, 6/30/1970).

But in another sense, a testimony lives to be "borne." In the initial stages of a spiritual awakening, a testimony is born in the classical sense, with physical and emotional struggle. Then it must be developed through constant labor and careful attention, with significant nurturing and careful pruning, so that it might have the strength to stand independently with no external witness.

To bear testimony is to carry it with you at all times. Thus, it establishes one standard of conduct for all circumstances. When church members bear their testimonies with responsibility, others may know with certainty where those members stand. They take the Lord's side on all issues, and uphold righteousness in all situations.

One also bears testimony by giving it to another, when the Spirit dictates such an action. Testimony, like love, can grow only by unconditionally giving it away. When one bears the gift of testimony to another, oft-times the name of one more soul is added to the membership rolls of the Kingdom of God.

Although testimony is born of foundation faith in Jesus Christ and the principles of the gospel, it is itself the necessary prerequisite to sustained saving faith. It is the driving force behind acting on faith. One has a testimony that the gospel is true. Knowing that, one can then exercise great faith by acting on the saving principles, and by participating in the ordinances of the gospel, beginning with baptism. Faith, without works of righteousness and obedience to the commandments, which are the tangible expression of testimony, is dead, being alone. (See James 2:17).

We also use the priesthood to combat evil. "Priesthood" is only directly mentioned 8 times in The Book of Mormon, but evidence of the power of God permeates all the canonized texts dealing with His relationship with mankind. Karl G. Maeser illustrated our total dependency upon God, and the wisdom of relying on the power of His priesthood. Many years ago, he was leading a party of young missionaries on foot across the Alps. As they slowly climbed the steep slope, he looked back and saw a row of sticks thrust into the glacial snow to mark the one safe path through the treacherous mountains. Something about those sticks impressed him, and halting the company of missionaries he gestured toward them and said, "Brethren, there stands the priesthood. They are just common sticks like the rest of us. Some of them may even seem to be a little crooked, but the position they hold makes them what they are. If we step aside from the path they mark, we are lost."

By righteously exercising his priesthood, Alma sought to influence the people of the Land of Zarahemla with the power of the word of God. He hoped that bearing testimony might fire their faith and make them spiritually self-sustaining. Alma recognized that "seeing, even the Savior, does not leave as deep an impression in the mind as does the testimony of the Holy Ghost. The impressions on the soul that come from the Holy Ghost are far more significant than a vision. It is where spirit speaks to spirit, and the imprint upon the soul is far more difficult to erase." (Joseph Fielding Smith, Jr.).

Surely, Heber C. Kimball echoed Alma when he warned the Saints in 1856 that many trials would test their faith, and that the time would come when no man or woman would be able to endure on borrowed light. Our day is the time of which he spoke. But Heavenly Father has purposely stacked the deck in our favor. While allowing us our agency, He is not indifferent to our tests of faith, nor is He an impartial observer, distanced from our struggles in mortality. He never asks us to walk alone, and if at times, it seems that there is only one set of footprints in the sands of time, it is because Christ carries us on His shoulders when our own burdens seem so heavy that we lose the desire to carry on.

"Every member of the church is entitled to know that God our Heavenly Father lives. They are also entitled to know that our elder brother, Jesus Christ, is the Savior and Redeemer of the world, and that he has opened the door for us, that we, through our individual acts, may receive salvation and exaltation and dwell once again in the presence of our Heavenly Father." (Henry D. Taylor).

This assurance and witness must be earned, but when it is finally recognized it has the power to change lives and the ability to overcome evil. First, we must have the desire, or spiritual thirst that awakens "the true light that lighteth every (one) that cometh into the world." (D&C 93:2). Secondly, we must study and search the scriptures; for in them, Jesus assured us, "ye think ye have eternal life; and they are they which testify of me." (John 5:39). Thirdly, we must pray. Alma testified: "Behold, I have fasted and prayed many days that I might know these things of myself. And now I do know of myself that they are true; for the Lord God hath made them manifest unto me by his Holy Spirit; and this is the spirit of revelation which is in me." (Alma 5:46). Lastly, we must be obedient to the principles, for the Savior said: "Unto (those) that keepeth my commandments I will give the mysteries of my kingdom." (D&C 63:23). It is of these "mysteries" that faithful members of the church regularly bear testimony.

When our lives conform to the pattern established by the Savior, and scales of darkness fall away, the eyes of our spiritual understanding are opened. The nature of entire societies can change as spiritual fluency is developed, and hearts swells with the pure love of Christ. It could be again, as it was in the years following the ministry of the Savior in the New World, when "it came to pass that there was no contention in the land, because of the love of God which did dwell in the hearts of the people. And there were no envyings, nor strifes, nor tumults, nor whoredoms, nor lyings, nor murders, nor any manner of lasciviousness; and surely there could not be a happier people among all the people who had been created by the hand of God. There were no robbers, nor murderers, neither were there Lamanites, not any manner of -ites; but they were one, the children of Christ, and heirs to the kingdom of God." (4 Nephi 1:15-17).

"When we understand the character of God, He begins to unfold the heavens to us, and to tell us all about it. When we are ready to come to Him, He is ready to come to us."
(Joseph Smith).

Commitment

"Listen to the words
of Christ, your Redeemer,
your Lord and your God."
(Moroni 8:8).

In the church, our hands-on training teaches us that if we plan our work, and then work our plan, we will enjoy success in our endeavors. We know that proper prior planning prevents poor priesthood performance. We dream big, and by establishing deadlines, we create realistic goals. We know by our own experience that work without vision is drudgery, and vision without work is dreamery, but work with vision is destiny. It is because of our commitment to the cause that we know these things.

I also know that there is a God in heaven, because I have witnessed the universality of commitment. I believe it is a characteristic with which God has blessed both men and beasts. High energy levels of commitment are found within those who are members of The Church of Jesus Christ of Latter-day Saints, but they do not have a lock on the no noble character trait. Commitment is not even found solely within the human family; it is also common among those with whom we share the rungs on the evolutionary ladder. I have gotten between an agitated cow moose and her calf. I have seen momma bears aggressively protecting her cubs. I have witnessed bald eagles riding updrafts relentlessly looking for food for their chicks back in the nest. Commitment runs deeply; it is not only in our blood, but it also drives the behavior of countless other species. This cannot be happenstance. It must be that the apple does not far fall from the tree.

Commitment is not something that we consciously cultivate. We seldom say: Today, I think I'll work on commitment. Instead, it seems to come naturally, but it is actively nurtured by the settled conviction in our minds that we are the acorns of a mighty oak; the offspring of deity. John K. Edmunds, who also served as the President of the Salt Lake Temple, enjoyed a long and distinguished legal career in Chicago. One day, a widow came to him for advice, and when they were finished, she apprehensively asked: "How much do I owe you?" Gently, he responded, "Why don't you pay me what you think it's worth. Greatly relieved, she got out her coin purse, fished around for a quarter, and pressed it into his hand. He looked at the quarter, looked at her, and then got out his own coin purse, and gave her ten cents change. Howard W. Hunter must have been referring to this level of commitment, when he counseled: "We need to walk more resolutely and more charitably the path that Jesus has shown. We need to pause to help and lift another, and surely we will find strength beyond our own. If we would do more to learn the healer's art, there would be untold chances to use it, to touch the wounded and the weary, and to show to all a gentle heart."

Commitment begins with a strong sense of intention or focus, but that is only half the equation. The second half defines a statement of purpose or a plan of action. The difficulty is that we make promises about behaviors and outcomes with the sense of intention or focus, but we ignore the process necessary to achieve the goal. Envisioned outcomes are simply the byproducts of that dynamic flow of process. If we learn to commit fully to the process, then the outcomes will be what they should be. But, if we commit merely to the outcomes and ignore the process, we sabotaged both. Wobble and instability will be created by the unequal demands of intention on the one hand, and our lack of purpose or a plan of action on the other, that will condemn any hope of success.

The principle of commitment is ingrained within us from earliest childhood, even before we are capable of understanding. Think of the promises that were articulated when we received our first blessing as babies, for example. By the authority of the priesthood, blessings were pronounced that contained promises linked to anticipated high levels of future commitment. Later, we had baptismal interviews before we turned eight years of age, preparatory to making a series of commitments related to our membership in the church and kingdom. We reinforce the commitments we have thus made when we participate in the ordinance of the Sacrament, and we make additional covenants in the temple that are directly related to a divinely inspired statement of purpose and a plan of action, all of which are buttressed by the powerful spiritual intervention of our Father in Heaven, Who stands ever ready to minister to our needs. Ever time we receive a calling in the church, it is accompanied by a priesthood blessing that sets us apart with a statement of purpose and plan of action that vitalizes the utilization of resources related to the successful execution of our responsibility.

Day in and day out, our success is largely determined by our capacity to make and keep commitments. Each time we take the road less traveled, we keep a date with destiny, as we reach greater heights of achievement. As Robert Frost wrote: "I shall be telling this with a sigh somewhere ages and ages hence: Two roads diverged in a wood, and I, I took the one less traveled by, and that has made all the difference." ("The Road Not Taken").

It is easy to take for granted the blessing that activity in the church teaches us about commitment. As we study the scriptures, we learn to be more patient in our insistent desire for the instant gratification that can neutralize dedicated discipleship. But it is only after we "have done the will of God, (that we) receive the promise." (Hebrews 10:36). As we learn to recognize the Lord's timetable, our commitment level is protected and shielded from the erosive influence of impatience. We quietly go about out business, "and do the things which the Lord hath commanded, for (we) know that the Lord giveth no commandments unto the children of men, save he shall prepare a way for them that they may accomplish the thing which he commandeth them (1 Nephi 3:7). We learn to "trust in the Lord with all (our) heart; and lean not unto (our) own understanding." (Proverbs 3:5). "Then shall (our commitment) wax strong in the presence of God." (D&C 121:45).

When we learn how to focus our commitment, and to engage "the Lord (as our) helper, (we) will not fear what man shall do unto (us)." (Hebrews 13:6). We learn about the follow-through element of commitment; that "it is God which worketh in (us) both to will and to do of his good pleasure." (Philippians 2:13). We have proven Him in times past, and can testify: "If any man will do his will, he shall know of the doctrine." (John 7:17). We establish a habit pattern of obedience, and follow the admonition of Paul, to "perform the doing of it; that as there was a readiness to will, so there may be a performance also out of that which (we) have." (2 Corinthians 8:11).

We persevere in the plan of action born of our resolve, in part because we know that "reason and experience both forbid us to expect that morality can prevail in exclusion of religious principle." (George Washington). We are concerned because of society's problem keeping its commitments. In a cover story entitled "The Me, Me, Me Generation," in "Time" magazine, (5/20/2013), Joel Stein wrote: "Millennials are lazy, entitled, narcissists, who still live with their parents."

He continued: "Here's the cold, hard data: The incidence of narcissistic personality disorder is nearly three times as high for people in their 20s as for the generation that's now 65 or older, according to the National Institutes of Health. 58% more college students scored higher on a narcissism scale in 2009 than in 1982. Millennials got so many participation trophies growing up, that a recent study showed that 40% believe they should be promoted every two years, regardless of performance. They are also fame-obsessed: Three times as many middle school girls want to grow up to be a personal assistant to a famous person as want to be a Senator, according to a 2007 survey. They're so convinced of their own greatness that the National Study of Youth and Religion found the guiding morality of 60% of Millennials in any situation is that they'll just be able to feel what's right. Their development is stunted: More people ages 18 to 29 live with their parents than with a spouse, according to the 2012 Clark University Poll of Emerging Adults. And they are lazy. In 1992, the nonprofit "Families and Work Institute" reported that 80% of people under 23 wanted to one day have a job with greater responsibility. 10 years later, only 60% did."

Many young adults who fall within the parameters of the Me Generation are active, faithful Latter-day Saints. But precisely because they have been schooled in obedience to the principles of the gospel, they are not counted as flotsam and jetsam on the sea of life, "tossed to and fro, and carried about with every wind of doctrine, by the sleight of men, and cunning craftiness." (Ephesians 4:14). Instead, the gospel has taught them how to stem the tide; they no longer just go with the flow. Their standard of behavior towers above the lowest common denominator that is the norm in society. They are "fellowcitizens with the Saints, and with the household of God. (Ephesians 2:19).

Latter-day Saints are assisted in their ability to internalize commitment to true principles when they receive their temple endowment, and when they return to the temple to perform vicarious work for the dead. The garment they wear reinforces their commitment with the promise that it will be a shield and a protection to them, as long as they do not defile it.

They receive divine assistance when they are called to positions of responsibility within the church. When they are uniquely set apart to do a particular work in the church, the position becomes theirs. Under priesthood direction, it is clearly stated that the position doesn't belong to anyone else, and no-one else has a right to it. They know that if they do not do the job, it will not be done. Therefore, they accept callings with the intention to carry out the associated responsibilities as though their lives depended on it. Their commitment level becomes unassailable.

Those who have committed their lives and fortunes to the Lord are amazed by what can happen when they set their mind to a task. They have learned that the secret of their success is to accept positions of responsibility without reservation and to perform their labors with a strong heart. They have found that when the spirit of the gospel flows in their bloodstream, they are energized with a spiritual power that defies description; and it is then that things really begin to happen. A burning zeal to serve God lifts them to greatness. It gives them authority over their weaknesses, and over the defeats of life.

Latter-day Saints have learned how to recognize the process that is necessary to follow in order to achieve envisioned outcomes. They know that "a successful life requires commitment - whole-souled, deeply held, eternally cherished commitment to the principles they know to be true." (Howard W. Hunter). Disciples have learned to make the distinction between a total commitment and a vapid contribution to the cause. They remember the story of the chicken and a pig who were invited to a breakfast, and how the chicken said that he would bring some eggs. He asked the pig if he would provide bacon, to which the pig replied: Yours is a contribution, but mine is a sacrifice. Latter-day Saints know that, ultimately, "what our Father in Heaven will require of us is more than a contribution; it is a total commitment, a complete devotion; all that we are and all that we can be." (Howard W. Hunter).

When Joan of Arc was carried to the stake, she was given the opportunity to save her life and to obtain her freedom by simply denying her beliefs. Instead, she made this statement: "I know this now. Every man gives his life for what he believes. Every woman gives her life for what she believes. Sometimes people believe in little or nothing, and so they give their lives for little or nothing. One life is all we have, and we live it as we believe in living it, and then it is gone. But to surrender what you are and live without belief is more terrible than dying, even more terrible than dying young." Resolutely, then, she faced death, still true to her faith and her beliefs. Her final acts on earth were consistent with her convictions. (Maxwell Anderson, "Joan of Lorraine," Act 2, Interlude 3).

In France at around the same time that Joan of Arc became a martyr to the cause, the successor to the throne was known as the Dauphin. During the reign of his father, unscrupulous and crafty counselors tried every means to corrupt the Dauphin, to thereby make him ineligible to inherit the throne. In all of their attempts, however, they were unsuccessful. Finally, in resignation, they asked him, "How is it that with all our enticements we were not able to corrupt your high standards?" His reply was simple: "I am a King's son." The implications of that statement are eternal in scope.

Both Joan of Arc, and the Dauphin had established patterns of behavior that were consistent with their beliefs, and that allowed them to act in perfect harmony with their convictions. Many of us assume that all you need is 21 days to make or break a habit, be it good or bad, and that after that, unconscious mechanisms kick into gear, and we find ourselves cruising along on autopilot. This number comes from a popular book published in 1960 called "Psycho-Cybernetics" by Maxwell Maltz, a plastic surgeon who noticed his patients seemed to take about three weeks to get used to their new faces. However, the time it takes to make or break a habit may not be that clear-cut. More recent studies show that the average time it takes for a new habit to coalesce is about 10 weeks, but individual times varied from 18 to 254 days. The bottom line is that if you want to internalize a new behavior, you shouldn't despair if three weeks doesn't do the trick. For most people, that's simply not enough time. Stick with it for a bit longer, commit to one standard of behavior, and you'll end up with a habit you can keep without even thinking about it. You will have successfully internalized your commitment, so that it may run on autopilot, with only periodic preventive maintenance.

Choose you this day whom ye will serve," declared Joshua, "but as for me and my house, we will serve the Lord." (Joshua 24:15). President Hunter once remarked during a General Conference address: "There is good reason to make our decision now to serve the Lord. On this Sunday morning, when the complications and temptations of life are somewhat removed, and when we have the time and more of an inclination to see from an eternal perspective, we can more clearly evaluate what will bring us the greatest happiness in life. We should decide now, in the light of the morning, how we will act when the darkness of night and when the storms of temptation arrive." (C.R., 10/1982).

In that day of decision, belief alone will not be sufficient; we will also need to do Heavenly Father's will with a ready heart. Belief is nothing more than the mental assent to a proposition, but without the critical element of moral responsibility that we call faith. As such, belief alone may very well lack the power to generate positive outcomes. Commitment may very likely be absent, because it simply does not spontaneously follow belief. But, if belief is nurtured by faith, commitment can transform knowledge into the blossoming of testimony. Finally, obedience to the Celestial Law of Consecration just might be the noblest expression of commitment. As Joseph Smith said: "A religion that does not require the sacrifice of all things never has power sufficient to produce the faith necessary (to lead) unto life and salvation." ("Lectures on Faith," p. 58.)

Disciples are committed to live according to active religious principles that immerse them in the gospel every day of the week. As a Church Welfare Program pamphlet stated long ago: "The church cannot hope to save a man on Sunday if during the week it is a complacent witness to the crucifixion of his soul." ("Helping Others to Help Themselves: The Story of the Mormon Church Welfare Program," 1945, p. 4). The gospel nurtures commitment with an energetic program that gives vitality to every waking moment.

The Lord revealed something very special about His children, in His preface to the Doctrine and Covenants. He stated that The Church of Jesus Christ of Latter-day Saints is the "only true and living church upon the face of the whole earth." (D&C 1:30). This begs the question: Are we "living members" of the church? If the Lord put His finger to our pulse, would He be able to detect the quickening influence of the Spirit? If He measured our core testimony temperature, would it reflect a burning zeal to embrace the principles of the gospel? Would our actions betray our commitment to do everything we could do to come unto Christ? Would we love God and our neighbors as ourselves? Would our actions reflect who we are and what we believe? If we were on trial, would there be enough evidence to convict us of being Christians?

Are we pressing forward with complete dedication and steadfastness, with confidence and a firm determination in Christ, having a perfect brightness of hope and perfect faith; with charity, or a love of God and of all men. If we do this, if our commitment level is such that we are feasting upon the word of Christ, receiving strength and nourishment from the scriptures, and if we endure to the end in righteousness, we shall have eternal life, which is the greatest gift that God can bestow. (See 2 Nephi 31:20).

Do we listen to the Spirit and constantly seek its direction? Do we pray for the strength to meet our challenges? Do we set our hearts upon the riches of eternity, rather than the things of the world? Do we recognize that spiritual renewal will always trump physical gratification? Have we made a choice regarding whom we will serve? Do we strengthen our brethren? Are we anxious to share our joy? Do we put into action our beliefs? Are we anxiously engaged in bringing to pass many good things of our own free will? Do we love one another? Do we keep ourselves unspotted from the world? Do we stand firm, and are we true and living members of the church? Does our level of commitment betray the reality that we have received the promise to be among those "who are come unto Mount Zion, and unto the city of the living God, the heavenly place, the holiest of all?" (D&C 76:66).

The Book of Mormon will point us
to other resources that will instruct and inspire us
to seek out the ordinances of the gospel. These allow us to
immerse ourselves in the three-fold mission of the church; to
perfect the Saints, to preach the gospel, and to cement family
relationships in both time and eternity. As we become
unified in our faith, we will strengthen each other's
testimonies of the mission of the Author
of Salvation, of Whom the book
repeatedly testifies.

Conditional Sentences in The Book of Mormon

"And if ye shall ask with a sincere
heart with real intent having faith in Christ
and he will manifest the truth of it unto
you by the power of the Holy Ghost."
(Moroni 10:4, 1830 Edition).

The Book of Mormon was received and translated under miraculous circumstances, and has been a topic of scholarly debate ever since its publication. Joseph Smith, the first prophet of The Church of Jesus Christ of Latter-day Saints, was led to the plates by a heavenly messenger named Moroni. Joseph Smith had very little formal education and, at the time of the translation, "could neither write nor dictate a coherent and well-worded letter, let alone dictate a book like the Book of Mormon," according to his wife, Emma. ("Last Testimony of Sister Emma," "Saints' Herald, 11/1/1879). Almost all of the present-day text of the Book of Mormon was translated during a three-month period between April and June of 1829, with a schoolteacher named Oliver Cowdery acting as Joseph Smith's scribe. The manuscript that was created is called the "Original Manuscript," of which only 28% survives today.

To assist in the printing of the book, Oliver Cowdery made a handwritten copy of the manuscript, which is known today as the "Printer's Manuscript." In the nearly 200 years since the first printing of The Book of Mormon, there have been 20 published editions of the book, 15 of them by The Church of Jesus Christ, 4 by the Reformed Church of Jesus Christ of Latter-day Saints (now the Community of Christ, which is a separate church established by former members, years after the death of Joseph Smith) and one private edition published in 1858 by James Wright, in New York City.

The Book of Mormon was written by ancient prophets in a language called "the reformed Egyptian." (See 1 Nephi 1:1 & Mormon 9:42). The use of the Hebraic "if/and" construction in the text reflects the linguistic heritage of the authors of The Book of Mormon. As a young man with limited formal education, Joseph Smith would have had no knowledge of this archaic grammatical sentence structure.

Nor would he have encountered the Hebrew "if/and" construction in the King James Bible. Yet, in the original dictation manuscript of the Book of Mormon, 1 Nephi 17:50 reads "if he should command me that I should say unto this water be thou earth, and it shall be earth." That "and" was removed when Oliver Cowdery produced the so-called "Printer's Manuscript," but similar constructions persisted, and appeared in the 1830 first edition.

In grammar, these "conditional sentences" are used when describing hypothetical situations and their consequences. Languages use a variety of constructions and verb forms to form such sentences. A common form of a conditional sentence in English is the "if/then" construction, such as "'If you don't study, then you will fail the test." Or "If you don't eat your vegetables, then you will not get dessert." Or "If you go near the ledge, then you will fall off the cliff."

In biblical Hebrew, however, conditional clauses are emphasized by an "if/and" format, such as "If you don't study, and you will fail the test." Or "If you don't eat your vegetables, and you will not get desert." Or "If you go near the ledge, and you will fall off." While "if/and" conditional clauses sound wrong to an English speaker's ear, they are perfectly acceptable to those who speak or read biblical Hebrew.

Native speakers of English simply don't use the "if/and" construction. Consequently, when it is used in Hebrew, it never survives an English Bible translation, such as in the King James Bible. Nevertheless, over the years, scholars have identified a number of Hebraisms, or unique Hebrew rhetorical or literary devices commonly used in the ancient Near East, such as the use of conditional sentence construction in the in the original manuscript and the 1st edition of the Book of Mormon.

The original manuscript and 1st edition of The Book of Mormon contain several examples of conditional sentences, which often follow the structure of "if/and." For example, Mosiah 2:21 states, "I say if ye should serve him with all your whole soul, and yet ye would be unprofitable servants". The word "and" was removed from this passage in the 1837 edition, resulting in the current version,: "I say, if ye should serve him with all your whole souls, yet ye would be unprofitable servants".

Other passages in the original manuscript and 1st edition had similar "if/and" conditional clauses. One such instance can be found in Helaman 12:13-21 (on page 440 in the 1830 edition), which reads: "Yea and if he saith unto the earth move and it is moved. Yea if he say unto the earth thou shalt go back that it lengthen out the day for many hours and it is done. And behold also if he saith unto the waters of the great deep be thou dried up and it is done. Behold if he saith unto this mountain be thou raised up and come over and fall upon that city that it be buried up and behold it is done. And if the Lord shall say be thou accursed that no man shall find thee from this time henceforth and forever and behold no man getteth it henceforth and forever. And behold if the Lord shall say unto a man because of thine iniquities thou shalt be accursed forever and it shall be done. And if the Lord shall say because of thine iniquities thou shalt be cut off from my presence and he will cause that it shall be so."

Another occurrence is in Moroni 10:4, in Moroni's oft quoted promise. In the 1830 edition of the Book of Mormon, it reads: "And if ye shall ask with a sincere heart with real intent having faith in Christ and he will manifest the truth of it unto you by the power of the Holy Ghost."

Beginning with the 1837 edition, the examples of the extra "and" in Helaman 12:13-21 and Moroni 10:4-5 were edited out of the text. These examples of a Hebraic "if-and" construction in the original text provide evidence that Joseph Smith received the text word for word, when translating the plates. If he had received only ideas, there would have been no logical reason to have added the non-English use of "and" in these verses.

Such expressions were good Hebrew, but poor English, and as such, they were eliminated by Joseph Smith wherever they were found, in the second printing of the Book of Mormon. Though an unlettered young man, he was nevertheless a native speaker of English who knew that these constructions felt wrong. Today, we might say that they are examples of 'language contamination,' or leakage from the text's original language into the translation language, in the way that Spanish/English interpreters sometimes inadvertently slip into "Spanglish." Perhaps their inclusion in the manuscript and 1st edition copies of The Book of Mormon subtly hint that the original language of the Book of Mormon wasn't English.

These "if/and" conditional clauses in The Book of Mormon are impressive enough on their own, but the fact that Joseph Smith edited them out is further evidence of the divine authenticity of the record and of the fidelity with which he translated the record by "the gift and power of God." (Preface to The Book of Mormon, 1830 Edition). Had he intentionally inserted them into a fraudulent record, then surely he would have left them in the text for future scholars to discover, inasmuch as they would constitute literary evidence on behalf of his claims. But the fact that he innocently edited them out simply to correct the English grammar of the book lends support to the thesis that he was not aware of the reinforcing ramifications of these "if/and" conditional clauses to support the claim that the book was the miraculous translation of an ancient Hebrew document. (See "Book of Mormon Translation," The Church of Jesus Christ of Latter-day Saints).

"If/and" conditional clauses in The Book of Mormon are impressive enough on their own, but the fact that Joseph Smith edited them out is further evidence of the divine authenticity of the record and of the fidelity with which he translated the record by "the gift and power of God." Had he intentionally inserted them into a fraudulent record, then surely he would have left them in the text for future scholars to discover, inasmuch as they would constitute literary evidence on behalf of his claims. But the fact that he innocently edited them out simply to correct the English grammar of the book lends support to the thesis that he was not aware of the reinforcing ramifications of these "if/and" conditional clauses to support the claim that the book was the miraculous translation of an ancient Hebrew document.

Connections

"I speak unto you as if ye were present, and yet ye are not. But behold, Jesus Christ hath shown you unto me, and I know your doing."
(Mormon 8:35).

No one would argue that we are bound to each other by more than genetics. With few exceptions, for example, in the case of monastic ascetics and agorophobics, we are social creatures. Many years ago, it became apparent to social scientists that our connections can be viewed as a hierarchy. In 1943, Abraham Maslow described a pyramid of need, in a paper entitled "A Theory of Human Motivation." In an ascending order of significance, he described the pattern of our connections as if they were on a path leading to self-transcendence beginning with physiological configurations, and then safety, belongingness, love, esteem, and then self-actualization. The order of his hierarchy remains a popular framework in sociological research and management training.

I believe that it is even more useful if our connections are viewed in the context of the gospel of Jesus Christ. I believe there are levels of interconnectivity that transcend the behavioral sciences to reveal the core of existence and to bind us to Him Who "hath also sealed us, and given the earnest of the Spirit in our hearts." (2 Corinthinans 1:22). These are concepts that are foreign to behaviorists who attempt to explain interpersonal conduct by utilizing only tangible terms while skirting metaphysical abstractions.

The first category I would suggest is what I call Type 0 or human genome connections. Within this class are the associations that exist only because our species shares the same D.N.A. sequences. Consequently, Type 0 connections relegate us to be as ships passing in the night. We may appear to be similar in construction and in purpose, but at the end of the day there is more of a disconnect between us than anything else. Type 0 human genome connections do not require eye to eye contact, and rarely establish bonds with others because they are really nothing more than nameless faces in the crowd. There is little or no evidence of the emotion that is really the glue that binds us to each other.

The second category is what I call Type 1 connections. These are real, and allow us to relate to each other through common interests like sports, schools, jobs, cars, and hobbies. But, at the same time, they are casual connections. For example, how many times has each of us said to ourselves: "I know that face; I just can't put a name to it." Type 1 connections are neural in origin, and owe their existence to the molecular basis of memory, but they too often develop along the pathways of short-term, and not long-term, memory. They may initially be powerful, but their intensity often fades with time.

The third category is what I call Type 2 connections, those that are forged through the commanding chemistry of shared experiences, especially those that elicit intense emotion. These visceral connections can last for years, because they trace their foundations to the crisis of uncommonly positive or negative experience that catalyzes our nervous systems with electrifying consequences. We have close associates, life-long friends, and even blood-brothers with whom we have established Type 2 connections that seem unassailable.

But Type 2 connections, like Type 1 connections, can and often do fade with time. Think of the unity that gripped America in the aftermath of 9/11. We can all still visualize members of the U.S. Congress standing on the steps of the Capitol, with arms linked together, singing God Bless America. How quickly are our Type 2 connections smothered in the marsh gas emitted by our scramble for scarce resources and telestial trash!

Somewhere beyond Type 2 connections, there may come a moment when we "see the light." We may have an A-ha! moment, an instant of sudden realization, inspiration, insight, recognition, or comprehension. We might even feel that we have been "born again!" Nicodemus asked: "How can a man be born when he is old? Can he enter the second time into his mother's womb, and be born? Jesus answered, verily, verily, I say unto thee, except a man be born of water and of the Spirit, he cannot enter into the kingdom of God. That which is born of the flesh is flesh; and that which is born of the Spirit is spirit." (John 3:4-6). The Savior used this occasion to teach Nicodemus about Type 3 connections that can only be appreciated in the context of deeply moving spiritual experiences.

The Sons of Mosiah had such a moment, when they felt compelled to "impart much consolation to the church, confirming their faith, and exhorting them with long-suffering and much travail to keep the commandments of God." (Mosiah 27:33). Thereafter, their developing connection with the Lamanites motivated them to embark upon a mission in the Land of Lehi that lasted fourteen long years. (See Mosiah 28:9). Ironically, the Lamanites among whom they ministered did not initially understand the power of Type 3 connectivity. But in each of these instances cited, their Type 2 connections evolved into Type 3 connections with the missionaries, with each other, and with the Lord.

There follows in The Book of Mormon a description of what we might do, in order to have and sustain Type 3 connections. Mormon reported that at the conclusion of their mission, the Sons of Mosiah were still the brethren of Alma "in the Lord; yea, and they had waxed strong in the knowledge of the truth; for they were men of a sound understanding and they had searched the scriptures diligently, that they might know the word of God. But this is not all; they had given themselves to much prayer, and fasting; therefore, they had the spirit of prophecy, and the spirit of revelation, and when they taught, they taught with power and authority of God." (Alma 17:2-3). Their mission had given them the perspective to allow them to experience Type 3 connectivity.

Type 3 connectivity can last forever; examples include the bond that can exist between a mother and child, or between "soulmates" whose match was made in heaven. Both birth and death experiences can generate the intensity to power Type 3 connections. Veil experiences in the temple can compellingly and convincingly communicate connections between the living and the dead. In our everyday interpersonal relationships, when we have taken the time to nurture Type 3 connections, we feel comfortable addressing each other as "Brother" or "Sister" even though no actual familial bond exists.

Type 3 connections are enduring because with them we touch the face of God. Think of the genius of the advertising executives who coined the phrase: "Reach out and touch someone." Perhaps without realizing it, they were tapping into our universal need to establish connections with eternity. Paul clearly recognized our desire to establish connectivity with each other and with our Heavenly Father when he wrote to the Ephesians that, by obedience to gospel principles, they would be "no more strangers, but fellowcitizens with the Saints, and with the household of God." (Ephesians 2:19).

From the beginning of time, the traditional family has provided a milieu in which Type 3 connections are generated. Alarmingly, today many families do not have the tools or recognize the need to consciously cultivate these connections. Rather, they subsist on a meager diet of Type 1 or Type 2 connections, mistakenly thinking that they are experiencing the pinnacle of achievement in human interrelationships. Or, perhaps they just do not care, either way. Sometimes, they simply have no interest in expanding their horizons, and they are content to just go with the flow. For whatever reason, they are either unwilling or unable to generate the intrinsic power necessary to create what Latter-day Saints would call "forever families."

With this in mind, we can better appreciate the purpose behind the dissemination since 1995 of The Church of Jesus Christ of Latter-day Saints' statement of belief entitled: "The Family: A Proclamation to The World." We also better understand the meaning of Joseph Smith's teaching that, at every age in the world, the main object of gathering the people of God "was to build unto the Lord a house whereby He could reveal unto His people the ordinances of His house and the glories of His kingdom, and teach the people the way of salvation," which has primarily been to develop Type 3 leading to Type 4 connections. (See below). (H.C., 5:423, June 1843). We are enjoined: "Thou shalt lay aside the things of this world, and seek for the things of a better." (D&C 25:10).

In essence, both Joseph Smith and the Lord taught that we could not completely nurture our spiritual connections "until the Temple (was) completed, where places (could) be provided for the administration of the ordinances of the Priesthood." (H.C., 4:603.) When we neglect our religious opportunities, we jeopardize our eternal souls. Sometimes, individuals are baptized after Type 2 connections have propelled them along on their journey toward Type 3 experiences. At other times, those investigating the merits of the church and of Christ may have already had fleeting Type 3 connection experiences, have strongly felt the Spirit, and have then determined to be baptized in order to capture those wonderful feelings with the confident anticipation of enjoying them on a regular basis. These are the pathways along which testimony is nurtured and strengthened.

But, in order to maintain their momentum, new members, as well as established members, of the church need to have sustaining spiritual experiences that foster Type 3 connectivity, in order to make it enduring. As Gordon B. Hinckley said: "Every convert needs a friend, a responsibility, and nurturing with the good word of God." ("Liahona," 2/1999). If they do not find the resources that are necessary to sustain Type 3 connections, they risk sliding back into Type 2 interconnectivity. They cannot endure for long if they rely only upon the light emitted by Type 1 and 2 connections. They need an external power source in order to become members of the Second Mile Club of Type 3 Interconnectivity, a select group to which they will be invited to join soon after their baptisms. (See Matthew 5:41).

Paul knew what it meant to go the second mile. He ministered among the Corinthian Saints, whom he was pleased to discover had a working relationship with the laws of the gospel, whose expression he characterized as being written upon "tables of stone." He explained the connectivity the Saints had with each other in terms of their second mile commitment: "Ye are manifestly declared to be the epistle of Christ ministered by us, written not with ink, but with the Spirit of the living God; not in tables of stone, but in fleshy tables of the heart." (2 Corinthians 3:3).

Sooner or later, every member of the church is a second miler, who is encouraged to become perfect in Type 3 commitment, and to so live to be worthy of Type 4 commitment. During His mortal ministry, the Savior said: "He that shall endure unto the end, the same shall be saved." (Matthew 24:13). Going a step further, He explained to Joseph

Smith: "If you keep my commandments (the first mile / Type 3 commitment) and endure to the end (the second mile / Type 4 commitment) you shall have eternal life, which gift is the greatest of all the gifts of God. (D&C 14:7).

Our Type 3 connections are solidified with service, particularly with service that is directed at those who cannot provide of their own means to generate equivalent connections. Service in the temple comes to mind. In the ordinances performed by patrons in the temple on behalf of the dead, the expression "for and in behalf of" is uttered in baptisms, confirmations, ordination to the priesthood, washing, anointing, in clothing ordinances, in the endowment, and in the sealing together of spouses and children. Temple ordinances give substance to the expression that "no man is an island." The Designer of the Plan created opportunities for us to perform vicarious work, that we might comfortably surround ourselves with Type 3 connections to both the living and the dead, as we establish bonds between all those who have been strengthened by covenants made with God. These can seal us to our forbearers all the way back to Father Adam and Mother Eve, and to our descendants, forging an unbreakable chain leading all the way to the I. We can use Type 3 connections to redeem the dead as well as to pay it forward.

But that is not all we can do. Our Type 3 connections have the power to establish a platform upon which we can build an even more ambitious milieu of connectivity. After the Flood, the ancients built ziggurats that were towers specifically designed to reach all the way to heaven. The Tower of Babel is a good example of these exaggerated church steeples. (See Genesis 11:4). But their architects and builders missed the point. Instead of creating physical structures, they would have more profitably spent their time if they had built relationships or connections with each other. Starting with Type 1 connections, they could have rapidly advanced through Type 2, and on to Type 3. Then, they would have figuratively reached the stars with what I will call the Type 4 level of connection that is described in the scriptures as having one's "Calling and Election" made sure. This is not a relationship that is well understood by either theologians or scriptorians. It requires a profound spiritual comprehension that can only be built upon the foundation of Type 1, 2, and 3 connections.

By design, this essay has purposely saved the best for last. When we achieve Type 4, we shift our focus, and our mystical connection with God becomes a permanent part of our spiritual identity. That is how members of The Church of Jesus Christ of Latter-day Saints have the presumption to declare that it is our destiny to one day rule as kings and queens, and priests and priestesses, in the house of Israel forever, to reign with authority over kingdoms, thrones, principalities, powers, dominions, and exaltations.

But we can't get there if we begin at Type 0, but expect to skip the intermediate steps. That's where the experiences of mortality in the learning laboratory of life come into play. No man is an island unto himself, and when we hear the bell, we need not wonder for whom it tolls, for it tolls for us.

When designing the Plan, God knew that, with only nine months of preparation, we would transition from our eternal world where we had enjoyed the warmth of hearth and home in heaven, to the bleak atmosphere of the lone and dreary world here on earth, and that when we did so, there would be an immediate disconnect that would be brutal and unrelenting in its intensity. The Plan requires that we take this labor of love and somehow postpone our Type 4 pre-mortal proclivities, as we emerge on the world stage surrounded by Type 0 mortal experiences.

In order to counteract that unforgiving reality check, God made it instinctively possible for us to enjoy Type 1 and Type 2 connections that would gently lead us toward Type 3 connections, so that we could eventually have Type 4 connections. He provided a blueprint for survival, and inserted within its many pages of instruction enough information to organize ourselves and prepare every needful thing, so that we might establish a house of prayer, fasting, faith, learning, glory, and order; even a house of God where dreams come true; where connectivity would not only be magical, but also entirely possible. (See D&C 88:119).

That is why Adam and Eve, who were living in innocence in a Garden setting, were told that it had been patterned after the order of heaven. When Adam fell that men might be, their physical surroundings in the lone and dreary world were designed to provide a hint of familiarity. If they would be sensitive to the Spirit, they would be able to re-establish their celestial connectivity and have joy. (See 2 Nephi 2:25). They would enjoy communication with the heavens. Adam fell so that God could teach him and his posterity how to re-establish Type 4 eternal connections.

Truly, "the universe is but one great city, full of beloved ones, divine and human, by nature endeared to each other." (Epictetus). Heavenly Father is the Grand Architect of the design that establishes the brotherhood of man even as it confirms His fatherhood, so that "in him we live, and move, and have our being; as certain also of (our) own poets have said. For we are also his offspring." (Acts 17:28).

When Cain asked his father Adam if he was his brother's keeper (see Genesis 4:9), he did so not really know the answer to the question. But it did expose his failure to comprehend his Type 3 connection with his brother Abel. When the Savior posed the question to the lawyer: "Which now of these three, thinkest thou, was neighbour unto him that fell among the thieves?" He was asking the young man to recognize the spiritual handwriting on the wall and acknowledge the Type 3 connections he should have had with someone so despised as a Samaritan. (Luke 10:36). Moroni's challenge to come unto Christ was an invitation to us to establish with Him a Type 3 connection, and to stretch our minds and our spirits, that the way might be paved for us to envision a Type 4 connection that would allow Him to perfect us. (See Moroni 10:32).

Joseph Smith asked the Saints if they could somehow establish a Type 3 connection with each other that was founded on charity. (See D&C 121:45-47). Similarly, Moses instructed all of Israel to regard its neighbors not with Type 0 connectivity, but as Type 3 brothers and sisters. He taught: "And if a stranger sojourn with thee in your land, ye shall not vex him. But the stranger that dwelleth with you shall be unto you as one born among you, and thou shalt love him as thyself." (Leviticus 19:33-34). In short, we establish covenant relationships with God so that we can establish Type 3 connections, leading to Type 4 eternal joy in the kingdom of heaven.

Ruth felt this connectivity, when she implored her mother-in-law Naomi: "Entreat me not to leave thee, or to return from following after thee, for whither thou goest, I will go, and where thou lodgest, I will lodge. Thy people shall be my people, and thy God my God. Where thou diest, will I die, and there will I be buried. The Lord do so to me, and more also, if ought but death part thee and me." (Ruth 1:16-17). Ruth established a profound connectivity that eleven hundred years later allowed the Savior to come through her lineage.

The mission statement of our Father in Heaven is to establish Type 4 connections with His children. (See Moses 1:39). Peter taught: "Brethren, give diligence to make your calling and election sure; for if ye do these things, ye shall never fall." (2 Peter 1:10). The Savior likewise taught His disciples: "Then shall the King say unto them on his right hand, Come, ye blessed of my Father, inherit the kingdom prepared for you from the foundation of the world. For I was an hungered, and ye gave me meat. I was thirsty, and ye gave me drink. I was a stranger, and ye took me in; naked, and ye clothed me. I was sick, and ye visited me. I was in prison, and ye came unto me. Then shall the righteous answer him, saying, Lord, when saw we thee an hungered, and fed thee; or thirsty, and gave thee drink? When saw we thee a stranger, and took thee in; or naked, and clothed thee? Or when saw we thee sick, or in prison, and came unto thee? And the King shall answer and say unto them, Verily I say unto you, Inasmuch as ye have done it unto one of the least of these my brethren, ye have done it unto me." (Matthew 25:34-40).

With disappointment, He said to others who never went to the effort to establish Type 3 or 4 connectivity: "I never knew you: depart from me, ye that work iniquity." (Matthew 7:23). Or, as the Joseph Smith Translation puts it: "Ye never knew me." (J.S.T. Matthew 7:33). Similarly, the J.S.T. changed the wording: "Verily I say unto you,

I know you not," (Matthew 25:12), to "Ye know me not." (J.S.T. Matthew 25:11). In both instances, the ball is clearly in our court.

Modern-day revelation speaks of those who, during their mortal probation, establish an unshakable bond with our Father in Heaven and with the Lord Jesus Christ, through unfettered access to the Holy Ghost. "Then shall they be gods, because they have no end; therefore, shall they be from everlasting to everlasting, because they continue; then shall they be above all, because all things are subject unto them. Then shall they be gods, because they have all power, and the angels are subject unto them." (D&C 132:20).

Sooner or later, every member of the church will encounter a line drawn in the sand. Those who "endure unto the end, the same shall be saved." (Matthew 24:13). Or, as the Lord explained to Joseph Smith: "If you keep my commandments" by fostering Type 3 connections, "and endure to the end," and establish Type 4 connectivity "you shall have eternal life, which gift is the greatest of all the gifts of God. (D&C 14:7).

Construction Zone: Proceed with Caution

"I give it as my opinion…"
(Alma 40:20).

A better understanding of the principles of the gospel and of the doctrines of the kingdom can help us to better negotiate the minefields of mortality, conceptual cul de sacs, doctrinal dead-ends, religious roundabouts, one-way roads that lead to hell, spiritual stop signs and yield to temptation signs, dangerous curves, blind intersections, cross traffic, and speeders on the excess express. Properly identifying these ten pitfalls can help us to internalize the principles of the gospel and doctrines of the Kingdom of God, that each of us "may act in doctrine and principle pertaining to futurity, according to the moral agency" that the Lord has given each of us, that we may be accountable for our own sins in the day of judgment. (D&C 101:78).

Principles are laws that definitively explain how things work and why things happen as they do. They form the foundation of doctrine. They have a basis in truth, and so they give definition to doctrine. Principles establish the ideal as the standard to which all should strive. Our testimonies are founded on principles rather than on values, and so our witness of truth bridges cultural, economic, political, and social boundaries that might otherwise segregate the Saints. Principles speak to our spirits because everyone is entitled to guidance from the Light of Christ. Our understanding of principles provides immunity to conventional wisdom, and resistance to the twisted influence of private interpretation.

Principles become the torch of truth, as if a homing beacon. They help us to avoid being caught in the bind of building the church while killing the articles of its faith, or permitting form to triumph over spirit. Principles have vitality because they are alive with interactive communication with God. They are the substance of the currents that are part of the flowing fountain of the church. Principles quicken us to recognize the source of the life-giving water that is ultimately expressed in doctrine.

Doctrine relates to specifics, but it also encompasses the collective foundation of principles. It describes an interrelated system of teachings that provide context for particular subjects. In this milieu, justice and mercy are principles that relate to the doctrine of Atonement. Repentance is the principle that relates to the doctrine of Forgiveness. Faith and repentance are principles that relate to the doctrine of baptism for the remission of sins. Vicarious work is a principle that relates to the various doctrines that form the basis of temple work. Moral behavior is a principle that relates to the doctrines founded on the Law of Chastity. Free will is a principle that relates to the doctrine of self-determination. Service in the kingdom is a principle that is related to foreordination. Guidance by the Spirit is a principle that is related to the doctrine of revelation. Making correct choices is a principle that is related to the doctrine of eternal progression.

Henry B. Eyring said: "We must be cautious and careful not to go beyond teaching true doctrine." This requires that we be sensitive to the whisperings of the Holy Ghost. "His confirmation is invited as we avoid speculation or personal interpretation. One of the surest ways to avoid even getting near false doctrine is to choose to be simple in our teaching. Safety is gained by that simplicity, and little is lost." (C.R., 4/2009).

Jeffrey Holland addressed a similar theme in another General Conference. "The scriptures are not the ultimate source of knowledge for Latter-day Saints," he said. The living God is the ultimate source, and His teaching comes as vibrant revelation. This doctrine is central to the message of the Restoration. "God is engaged in our lives," said Elder Holland, and "continues to speak His word and reveal His truth." (C.R., 4/2008). This basic belief demands that we maintain an open canon of scripture, including continuing revelation.

As we learn about both principles and doctrine, we receive the mysteries of the kingdom of heaven, and have the heavens opened unto us. We "commune with the general assembly and church of the Firstborn, and enjoy the communion and presence of God the Father, and Jesus the mediator of the new covenant." (D&C 107:18-19). We learn how to teach correct principles that relate to doctrine when we are asked, as Antionah asked of Alma: "What does the scripture mean...?" (Alma 12:21).

1). We learn how to avoid conceptual cul-de-sacs. We carefully and cautiously follow the example of Alma, who told Corianton: "Now, my son ... I give it as my opinion." (Alma 40:20). As the High Priest and leader of the church, we can cut him some slack, as he taught his own son.

Written in an era of limited resources, the first issue of the Times and Seasons contained a lead editorial to the elders of the church: "Be careful that you teach not for the word of God, the commandments of men, nor the doctrines of men. Study the word of God and preach it and not your own opinions, for no man's opinion is worth a straw." We have been repeatedly counseled to trust in the Lord with all our heart and lean not unto our own understanding. (Proverbs 3:5). This is why B.H. Roberts "said after a coherent and vigorous presentation that he loved books; indeed, that in some degree books had made him. But then, in a most vehement way, he said 'But I am not dependent on books. I am dependent for what I really know and really trust, on the direct experience of God.'" ("Defender of The Faith" p. 374).

It is our teaching, with all of its wonderful resources, that brings those within the sphere of our influence into the realm of direct experience with God. In fact, "we save ourselves by our teaching, and we save those who will get in tune with the same Spirit that we have, when we teach those truths." (Bruce R. McConkie, "The Foolishness of Teaching"). We remember the wise counsel of Paul to Timothy: "And the things that thou hast heard of me among many witnesses, the same commit thou to faithful men, who shall be able to teach others also." (2 Timothy 2:2).

2). We learn to identify the paths leading to doctrinal dead ends. We remember the observation of B.H. Roberts, who believed that the religions of his day were often simply multiplying mirrors and studying angles without actually increasing the light. The restoration of the gospel, he felt, had done just the opposite.

Dallin Oaks taught: "Latter-day Saints know that learned or authoritative commentaries can help us with scriptural interpretation, but we maintain that they must be used with caution. Commentaries are not a substitute for the scriptures any more than a good cookbook is a substitute for food. When I refer to commentaries, I refer to everything that interprets scripture, from the comprehensive book-length commentary to the brief interpretation embodied in a lesson or an article, such as this one."

"One trouble with commentaries," he continued, "is that their authors sometimes focus on only one meaning, to the exclusion of others. As a result, commentaries, if not used with great care, may illuminate the author's chosen and correct meaning but close our eyes and restrict our horizons to other possible meanings. Sometimes those other less obvious meanings can be the ones most valuable and useful to us as we seek to understand our own dispensation and to obtain answers to our own questions. This is why the teaching of the Holy Ghost is a better guide to scriptural interpretation than even the best commentary." ("Ensign," 1/1995).

3). We learn how to get off religious roundabouts. We follow the simple and straightforward counsel offered by Moroni, to "come unto Christ, and be perfected in him, and deny (ourselves) of all ungodliness; and if (we) shall deny yourselves of all ungodliness, and love God with all (our) might, mind and strength, then is his grace sufficient for (us), that by his grace (we) may be perfect in Christ; and if by the grace of God (we) are perfect in Christ, (we) can in nowise deny the power of God." (Moroni 10:32).

If we suddenly and without warning find our heads spinning on telestial turntables, we don't fret, because experience has thrown us a curve more than once. We know how to get back on the strait and narrow. We also know that worry is interest on a debt that never comes due, so we are optimists who see opportunity in every difficulty, rather than pessimists who see difficulty in every opportunity.

4). We learn that it is a one-way road, that leads to hell. Our ears often ring with the lyrics of popular music that may be pleasing to the ear, but promote half-truths. "Living easy, living free; season ticket on a one-way ride. Asking nothing; leave me be. Taking everything in my stride. Don't need reason; don't need rhyme. Ain't nothing that I'd rather do. Going down; party time. My friends are gonna be there too. I'm on the highway to hell. No stop signs, speed limit. Nobody's gonna slow me down. Like a wheel, gonna spin it. Nobody's gonna mess me around. Hey, Satan, paying my dues, playing in a rock band. Hey, mamma, look at me. I'm on the way to the promised land. I'm on the highway to hell, and I'm going down all the way. I'm on the highway to hell." ("The Highway to Hell," Lyrics by AC/DC).

The Lord communicates differently with His children. Gordon B. Hinckley said: "I think the best way I could describe the (communication) process is to liken it to the experience of Elijah as set forth in the book of First Kings. Elijah spoke to the Lord, and there was a wind, a great wind, and the Lord was not in the wind. And there was an earthquake, and the Lord was not in the earthquake. And there was a fire, and the Lord was not in the fire. And after the fire a still, small voice, which I describe as the whisperings of the Spirit." (C.R., 10/1996).

Ezra Taft Benson asked if we take time to listen to the promptings of the Spirit. "Answers to prayer," he said, "come most often by a still voice and are discerned by our deepest, innermost feelings. I tell you that you can know the will of God concerning yourselves if you will take the time to pray and to listen." (C.R., 10/1977). We will be comforted and guided if we put God first, and heed the whisperings of the Holy Ghost.

5). We learn not to yield to the signs of temptation. When dealing in the currency of faith, particularly in large denominations, we always make sure that we have enough cash in our wallets. We make regularly recurring deposits into our spiritual bank accounts, so that in times of emergency or adversity, there will always be enough in reserve to make adequate withdrawals.

We seek divine direction, and have learned how to focus the powers of heaven in our behalf. Because we are on an errand of the Lord, we take advantage of the opportunity to be cast off into a stream of revelation as we are carried along in the quickening currents of direct experience with God. We find examples from our daily experiences that will support our thesis on life. We recognize and act upon moments when the Spirit leads us along the path of principles and the direction of doctrine, remembering that President Kimball said: "Seeking the spectacular, we often miss the constant flow of revealed communication that comes."

6). We learn that there may be dangerous curves ahead of us on the path of progression. When our faith is tested, and we feel inadequate to meet the demands of those who would challenge our beliefs, we take courage in the example of Alma, who on at least one occasion took the 5th. In response to a difficult question from his son Corianton, he simply said: "Now these mysteries are not yet fully made known unto me; therefore, I shall forbear." (Alma 37:11).

The Psalmist wrote of those who, trying to make sense of life, "reel to and fro, and stagger like a drunken man, and are at their wits' end." (Psalms 107:27). Daniel described the crisis of confidence of his king, whose "thoughts troubled him, so that the joints of his loins were loosed, and his knees smote one against another." (Daniel 5:6). When we are not well-grounded in principle and doctrine, the very fibers of our being fail to hold us together, and we lose our physical, emotional, and spiritual coherence. If synaptic activity within our central nervous systems fires sporadically, we can only respond inappropriately and ineffectively to a palsy of principles and a dilemma of doctrine, without a hope of spiritual synchronization or expectation of religious recalibration.

Sometimes, those who are not well-grounded need to be jolted out of their complacency in the same way that defibrillator paddles are used to restore normal cardiac rhythm in a heart attack patient. We remember the relevance of the Lord's instruction to Nephi: "Stretch forth thine hand again unto thy brethren, and...I will shock them, saith the Lord, and this will I do, that they may know that I am the Lord their God." (1 Nephi 17:53).

7). Sometimes, when we are approaching blind intersections, we take a deep breath, hold tightly to our faith, and keep quiet. For example, when someone points out that Justice and Mercy have picked a gender, we offer no opinion, but secretly hope for personal enlightenment: "For behold, justice exerciseth all his demands, and also mercy claimeth all which is her own." (Alma 42:24).

We are clear about our purpose. "We "make no small plans, for they have no magic to stir men's souls." (Spencer W. Kimball). Whatever we do, we do it well, remembering the words of Abraham Lincoln, who declared: "I will prepare myself, and someday my chance will come." We emphasize the positive aspects of gospel principles and doctrines. We don't shirk our responsibilities or leave our understanding to the whims of fate. We all know about those four people named Everybody, Somebody, Anybody, and Nobody. An invitation to explain doctrine had been extended, and Everybody was sure that Somebody would prepare well ahead of time. Anybody could have done it, but Nobody did. Somebody got angry about it because, although it was Everybody's responsibility, he thought that Anybody could do it, but Nobody realized that not Everybody would take it seriously. It ended up that Everybody blamed Somebody when Nobody did what Anybody could have done. (Anonymous).

8). If we encounter cross traffic during our journey, we learn to be especially vigilant. We are alert to those who would try to trip us up, particularly by wresting the scriptures. (See Alma 41:1). Those who kick against the pricks often have only a weak foundation of doctrinal understanding of the gospel, and risk falling into transgression in consequence of their shallow comprehension of principles. As they pick apart the scriptures or the words of the Lord's servants, doctrine can be distorted into meaningless fragments without any coherent connection. As Alma declared to the inhabitants of Ammonihah: "Behold, the scriptures are before you; if ye will wrest them it shall be to your own destruction." (Alma 13:20).

The Lord told Joseph Smith: I "shall bring to light the true points of my doctrine...that I may establish my gospel, that there may not be so much contention; yea, Satan doth stir up the hearts of the people to contention concerning the points of my doctrine; and in these things they do err, for they do wrest the scriptures and do not understand them." (D&C 10:62-63).

9). We learn to avoid the overzealous behavior of speeders on the excess express. The world simply does not recognize the value of balanced nutrition from the good word of God. Instead, it embraces the fleeting rush of artificial sweeteners, the empty calories of convenience, and the hypoglycemia of hypocrisy. The world jostles to and fro on a platform of platitudes before boarding the Excess Express in a vain attempt to take a shortcut to perfection. But the day will come when the worldly-wise will look in the mirror and see themselves as they really are; "that their spiritual bodies have become one sorry sight; no more than skeletons, covered with skin. They will get up to heaven, but never get in. "Another soul's mine!" they will hear Satan scream. "Give man something nice, and he'll take the extreme!" OK, I'll admit it; I'll outright confess. For the fast way to hell, take the Excess Express." (Anonymous).

In our own pre-mortal life, we must have recognized that strenuous spiritual exercise would give us vigorous vitality and leave us stronger, and so we surely learned to use our recovery time wisely. We must have developed the capacity to carefully monitor the vital signs of our bodies; to feel the spiritual equivalents of oxygen-debt and lactic acid buildup; to monitor the efforts of our minds to keep pace with our spiritual development. We surely experienced brief bursts of energy resulting in spectacular achievement, but more importantly, we discovered that sustained effort would be more effective in carrying us further along the road leading to eternal life. In that setting, we must have learned the value of developing endurance, so that when the time would come to turn the other cheek, instead of embracing the carefree lifestyle of the rich and famous, it would be easier to go the second mile simply because of the force of habit.

10). We learn to recognize and to heed the spiritual stop signs that the Holy Ghost strategically places along the crooked path that lies before us. In a very real sense, each of us is confined to a world of our own making, and most of us are trapped within the narrowly defined perceptual prisons we have created for ourselves. The walls of that world are reinforced with the razor-wire of limiting beliefs, those stories we tell ourselves that cause us to sabotage our own best efforts. They can damage and even cripple our lives, diminish our abilities, compromise our progress, and prevent us from attaining our goals. Although all of us have limiting beliefs, everyone has the power to change them. Most people, however, don't realize it's possible, and for that matter, aren't even aware that they have made conscious decisions about what they choose to believe and not to believe.

If we learn to let go and let God, and allow His principles and doctrines to govern our lives, surely He will bless our efforts, and we will feel better about ourselves and about our contributions to the kingdom, no matter how large or small they may be. We will learn that the only way we can increase our strength is to give away that which we have received. We will learn that when we serve our hearts out, we will feel rejuvenated.

We will hear the voice of the Lord, asking: "Hast thou not known? Hast thou not heard that the everlasting God, the Lord, the Creator of the ends of the earth, fainteth not, neither is weary? There is no searching of His understanding. He giveth power to the faint; and to them that have no might, He increaseth strength... They that wait upon the Lord shall renew their strength; they shall mount up with wings as eagles; they shall run, and not be weary; and they shall walk, and not faint." (Isaiah 40:28 & 30-31).

A better understanding of the principles of the gospel and of the doctrines of the kingdom can help us to better negotiate the minefields of mortality, and the conceptual cul de sacs, doctrinal dead-ends, religious roundabouts, one-way roads that lead to hell, spiritual stop signs and yield to temptation signs, dangerous curves, blind intersections, cross traffic, and speeders on the excess express. Properly identifying these ten hazards can help us to internalize the principles of the gospel and doctrines of the Kingdom of God, so that each of us "may act in doctrine and principle pertaining to futurity, according to the moral agency" that the Lord has given each of us, that we may be accountable for our own sins in the day of judgment.
(D&C 101:78).

Conversion

"Return unto me
and repent of your sins,
and be converted, that I may
heal you." (3 Nephi 9:33).

One can be fully committed and still have repetitive moments of confirmation, when we can say, as did members of the church in Zarahemla, that our "hearts are changed through faith on his name, for this day [we] are born of him and have become his sons and his daughters." (Mosiah 5:7). These reconfirmations may come in the temple, where we carry thoughts or concerns that needs a special kind of resolution. For we have discovered that His house is not only a house of prayer, of fasting, and of faith, but also of learning. (See D&C 88:119).

They may come during a ministering visit, when those with whom we are leaving a message instead give us new insight into the scriptures. They may come when talking with our children, from whom we catch glimmers of truth thanks to their fresh and untinctured perspectives. We may gain new insight when listening to those speaking in Sacrament meeting. This is one of the reasons we always take our scriptures, pen, and paper to our church services.

When reading the scriptures, we often think of the Lord's counsel: "These words are not of men nor of man, but of me; wherefore, you shall testify they are of me and not of man; For it is my voice which speaketh them unto you; for they are given by my Spirit unto you, and by my power you can read them one to another; and save it were by my power you could not have them. Wherefore, you can testify that you have heard my voice, and know my words." (D&C 18:34-36). These words are given, He explained, "to ponder in your hearts, with this commandment which I give unto you, that ye shall call upon me while I am near. Draw near unto me and I will draw near unto you." (D&C 88:62-63).

"Motivation," Steven Covey taught, "is a fire from within." Christopher Columbus recounted the motivation for his voyage of discovery by simply saying: "The Holy Spirit gave me fire for the deed." Our hearts burn within us when God gives us "knowledge by His Holy Spirit, yea, by the unspeakable gift of the Holy Ghost ... when nothing shall be withheld." (D&C 121:26 & 28). Thus did Jeremiah describe his feelings: "His word was in mine heart as a burning fire shut up in my bones, and I was weary with forbearing, and I could not stay." (Jeremiah 20:9). The Spirit worked on Belshazzar's troubled conscience to the extent that "the king's countenance was changed, and his thoughts troubled him, so that the joints of his loins were loosed, and his knees smote one against another." (Daniel 5:6). Joseph Smith was moved to declare of his revelatory experiences: "Thus saith the still small voice, which whispereth through and pierceth all things, and often times it maketh my bones to quake while it maketh manifest." (D&C 85:6).

As the process of our conversion unfolds, and our discipline matures, we recognize the wisdom in the observation of

Hans Christian Anderson, who said: "Every man's life is a fairy tale waiting to be written." A number of the chapters in our story have already been set to paper, and we don't know how many yet remain to be written. But we do know this: God has set the standard, and we must follow the course He has established. We cannot start over and make a new beginning, but we can begin now and make a new ending.

We believe Him when He says: "If your eye be single to my glory, your whole bodies shall be filled with light, and there shall be no darkness in you; and that body which is filled with light comprehendeth all things." (D&C 88:67). For "that which is of God is light; and he that receiveth light, and continueth in God, receiveth more light; and that light groweth brighter and brighter until the perfect day." (D&C 50:24). In marvelous ways, the Holy Ghost has confirmed the words of Heber J. Grant, who said that as we gain spiritual maturity, "by doing our duty, faith increases until it becomes perfect knowledge." (C.R., 4/1934).

And as the seasons of our lives unfold, we learn that "Life is a sheet of paper white, where each of us may write a line or two, and then comes night. Greatly begin! If thou hast time for but a line, make that sublime. Not failure, but low aim, is crime." (James Russell Lowell).

Observations

The Book of
Mormon describes
how we are intertwined
with Heavenly Father, Jesus
Christ, and with the Holy Ghost,
in palpable connections. It reassures
us that They take note when sparrows
fall from trees, and on cold winter nights
They turn our attention to the explosion of
supernovas in distant galaxies. They do not
play dice with Their creations; We can be sure
that They will leave nothing to chance. In
particular, when we sit quietly and
study the scriptures, we can
be at-one with Them.

What we call
"coincidence" is
often simply our
Heavenly Father Who
is working behind the
scenes. Every moment we
study The Book of Mormon
is influenced by His divine
design. We need to be in tune
with the Spirit, however, to
recognize it and act
upon them.

It will be difficult for
those who have lived a telestial existence
to justify their behavior before God, angels,
and witnesses, in the face of the many signs
and wonders He has revealed in The Book of
Mormon as both warnings and blessings.
Those of us who have witnessed any or
the least of these has seen God
moving in his majesty
and power.

The mortal ministry
of Jesus Christ among
the Nephites and Lamanites
may be the greatest miracle of
all, but those who deny His power
cannot be saved on His merits alone,
simply because they have not generated
faith with enough energy to carry their
progression onward. Only a profound
attitude adjustment will jump-start
their forward momentum along
the pathway leading to the
Kingdom of God.

Those who have lived a telestial existence will find it extremely difficult to justify their behavior before God, angels, and witnesses, in the face of the many signs and wonders He has revealed in The Book of Mormon as both warnings and blessings. Those of us who have witnessed any or the least of these has seen God moving in his majesty and power.

The ministry of Jesus Christ among the Nephites and Lamanites may be the greatest miracle of all, but those who deny His power cannot be saved on His merits alone, simply because they have not generated faith with enough energy to carry their progression onward. Only a profound attitude adjustment will jump-start their forward momentum along the pathway leading to the Kingdom of God.

Our Lord and Savior Jesus Christ told the Prophet Joseph Smith that He would reveal to all of His followers the unmistakable signs of His Second Coming. He said: "Be not troubled, for, when all these things shall come to pass, ye may know that the promises which have been made unto you shall be fulfilled." (D&C 45:34-35). Prior to that event, it will once again be as it was just before the birth of the Savior, when great signs were given in Zarahemla "to the intent that there should be no cause for unbelief," and also "to the intent that whosoever" would muster the faith to "believe might be saved." (Helaman 14:18-19). Finally, at His Second Coming, He will reveal Himself "from heaven with power and great glory" to those who have faithfully waited for the dawn of the millennial day, and He will dwell in righteousness with them on the earth for a thousand years. (D&C 29:11).

Those who have tried the virtue of the word of God - see Alma 31:5 - have the image of God engraven upon their countenances. They shall ascend into the hill of the Lord, stand in holy places, and partake of His divine nature, because they have clean hands and pure hearts, and have not lifted up their souls unto vanity, nor have they sworn deceitfully.

We are reinvigorated to share th gospel with our neighbors as we read the account in the Book of Alma, wherein Ammon metaphorically described a harvest, in an effort to illustrate how thousands and thousands of wicked Lamanites had been gathered through the missionary efforts of his brethren, known as the Sons of Mosiah. "Behold, the field was ripe," he said, "and blessed are ye, for ye did thrust in the sickle, and did reap with your might, yea, all the day long did ye labor; and behold the number of your sheaves!" (Alma 26:5). His party had come up out of the Land of Zarahemla into the highlands of Nephi to bring a message of peace to the Lamanites. In its absence, their kinsmen "would still have been racked with hatred (directed toward their brethren the Nephites), and they would also have (remained) strangers to God." (Alma 26:9).

We think of Abinadi when we read about Joan of Arc, who stood before the stake and was offered her freedom by denying what she believed. Instead, she declared: "Every man and woman gives their lives for what they believe. Sometimes, when people believe in little or nothing, they give their lives for little or nothing. One life is all we have, and we live it as we believe in living it, and then it is gone. But to surrender what you are, and to live without belief, is more terrible than dying. It is even more terrible than dying young."

When the Lord taught the Nephites the Law of Tithing (see 3 Nephi 24:8), He inferred that nothing that is short of the very best that we can provide is good enough, and so our tithe is no more than a token. We consecrate that which we are, for God requires more than an uncommitted gesture of faith. Our offering before his throne is found within ourselves; it is in our hearts. It is not just a tenth part, but is our complete devotion to the will of our Father, Who is our Benefactor and the Provider of, not what we ever hope to have, but what we ever hope to be.

Echoing the Bard of Avon, ("Hamlet," Act 3 Scene 1), Lehi declared that he would "soon lay down in the cold and silent grave, from whence no traveler can return." (2 Nephi 1:14). The two most important days of our lives, that should be commemorated with celebration and joy, are the day we were born, and the day we find out why. After we have come to understand our purpose, our lives will never again be the same, until the day we die, when we really discover why we lived. When we comprehend the grammar of the gospel, we see, as Neal A. Maxwell observed, that "death is a mere comma, and not an exclamation point!" The light has not been extinguished; rather, the lamp has been put out because the dawn has arrived. Death is only an artificial horizon that limits our sight.

There will soon
come a time when all of the
inhabitants of the earth "shall see
my face and know that I am," declared
the Lord. (D&C 93:1). "The veil shall be rent
and you shall see me, not with the carnal neither
natural mind, but with the spiritual." (D&C 67:10).
Our Father gives us this clarity "to the intent that there
should be no cause for unbelief," and also "to the intent
that whosoever will believe might be saved, and that
whosoever will not believe, a righteous judgment
might come upon them; and also, if they are
condemned, they bring upon themselves
their own condemnation."
(Helaman 14:28-29).

When the Nephites
violated God's laws, their
conscience encouraged them to
recognize the shortcomings of their
spiritual insecurities, and it prompted
them to experience feelings of penitence
for having yielded to temptation, to right
the wrong if it were within their power to do
so, to refrain from repeating it, to repent of
their errant behavior, to receive forgiveness,
and then move on with their lives. It was in
the Atonement of Christ, and it alone, that
their stumbling blocks were miraculously
transformed into stepping-stones. Only
then could mortality, with its potholes
and pitfalls, become the growth
experience that the heavens
designed it to be.

Elder Mark E. Petersen declared that in the midst of the trials and tribulations that will become even more commonplace in the Last Days, "God will send fire from heaven if necessary to destroy our enemies while we carry forward our work." The Master of the Universe would never permit Satan or his lieutenants to thwart His purposes, no matter how hard they try. As a matter of fact, those who have "perverted the right ways of the Lord, yea, that great and abominable church, shall tumble to the dust, and great shall be the fall of it." (1 Nephi 22:14).

The emotional, physical, mental, and psychological abuse that typified the conflict between the Nephites and Lamanites, not to mention Lucifer's deception, was an all-out rebellion, a struggle for our minds, as conflicting ideologies grated against each other. The misery caused was profound, with souls not a few cut off from God's presence. So many bright lights were dimmed in the struggle! With weeping, and wailing, and with gnashing of teeth, those who fell forfeit both their birthright and the promise of increase, as their final expression of free will destroyed both their desire and their ability to comply with the equitable laws of heaven.

Every society that has ever existed on the face of the earth has always paid a heavy price for its lack of vision, as it closes its minds and hearts to an expansion by the Spirit. The Dark Ages remain the worst-case scenario, but in many respects we are once again living in that stifling era. Every time a culture loses its spiritual equilibrium, it seems to re-adjust its values in an expedient realignment with worldly coordinates. Today, worship of gods of wood and stone is justified as multiculturalism. Perversion is embraced and legitimized as an alternative lifestyle. The poor are exploited under the guise of programs sponsored by government. Unborn children are torn from their mother's wombs, and the collective conscience is assuaged by calling it pro-choice. The gross abuse of power is justified as the means to an end, and every obscenity pollutes the media, but new-speak characterizes it as freedom of speech. The target has been moved so often that self-congratulatory pundits believe that they are scoring bulls-eyes when they are really far from the mark. The prophet Isaiah saw our day, when he warned the Nephites: "Wo unto them that call evil good, and good evil; that put darkness for light, and light for darkness; that put bitter for sweet, and sweet for bitter."
(2 Nephi 15:20).

As we read The Book of Mormon and we ponder its message, a spiritual sixth sense that is unimpeachable invites us to reach out and touch the face of God. As we seek the truth, both the Light of Christ and the Holy Ghost will manifest their incorruptible expression deep inside us, in a place within our hearts.

Lehi, Nephi, and Jacob were aware
that Heavenly Father always honors
our free will, which they recognized as the
guiding principle of heaven. They understood
that its exercise would entail risk, but they also
knew that it was tied to their progression. Rather
than enslaving them in good habits, He repeatedly
gave them the opportunity to recommit themselves to
true and eternal doctrines and to covenants of action.
Agency allows each of us to enjoy all of the privileges
of church membership, empowers us to remain active,
and is a principle that sanctions our commitment to
baptismal promises, all of which are essential if we
are to nourish our spiritual wellbeing. Only with
agency can we gyroscopically maintain our
spiritual equilibrium and hope to manage
the mercurial fluidity of a world whose
only constant seems to be its harsh
and unrelenting proclivity to
continually reinvent itself
in both good and bad
ways.

The Lord revealed this great truth to
His prophet Moses: "I made the world, and all
men before they were in the flesh." (Moses 6:51).
To Jeremiah, He explained: "Before I formed thee in the
belly I knew thee; and before thou camest forth out of the
womb I sanctified thee, and I ordained thee a prophet unto the
nations." (Jeremiah 1:4-5). Moses was asked to "remember the
days of old … when the most High divided to the nations their
inheritance. When he separated the sons of Adam, he set the
bounds of the people according to the number of the
children of Israel." (Deuteronomy 32:7-8). The
Lord clearly testified that we lived before
we were born. (See Ether 3:15-16).

Our comprehension of the truth that is found within the pages of The Book of Mormon is made possible by the irreproachable influence the Holy Spirit. Our knowledge expedites the application of moral agency, that is just suitably channeled free will. It provides us with the tools to hammer out our salvation with both fear and trembling before the Lord. Gaining wisdom is critical to the successful implementation of the Plan, and is another of the spiritual gifts that has been providentially provided by the Source of all wisdom, Who is the embodiment of God the Father, Jesus Christ, and the Holy Ghost.

We know that our weaknesses are a part of the tapestry that has been woven by God to be the fabric of our lives. We simply turn to the inventory of thread that have been provided within the pages of The Book of Mormon, that enables us to weave imaginative new patterns that are reflections of the celebration of our faith in our Savior's ability to turn stumbling blocks into stepping stones.

"We who lived in the concentration camps remember those who walked thru the huts comforting others, giving away their last pieces of bread. They may have been few in number, but they offer us sufficient proof that everything can be taken away from us but the one thing that is the last of our freedoms, which is to choose what our attitude will be," said Victor Frankel. We do this no matter how hard our circumstances may seem. (See Moroni 1:3). We keep our own counsel, are our own guides, and we determine that we will follow our own path, firm in the faith that our steps will safely guide us to the peace and rest that are the sanctuary of the Lord.

Whenever they fell into the habit of neglecting to quickly repent of their sins, it was the Nephites' inclination to feel uncomfortable when they were in proximity to spiritual experiences, and so they withdrew to lifestyles devoid of such associations. Thus, began a downward spiral that gained momentum as they became entrenched in sin. "Thus, saith the Lord concerning all those who know my power, and have been made partakers thereof, and suffered themselves through the power of the devil to be overcome, and to deny the truth and defy my power. They are they who suffer spiritual death," or life without light and truth. (D&C 76:31-32). This explains why, all too often, those that doeth this, come out "in open rebellion against God." (Mosiah 2:37).

Laman
and Lemuel's murmuring
focused on mind-numbing chatter
and speaking without real purpose. (See
1 Nephi 2:11). It was damaging because it
voraciously fed on vanity, hearsay, rumor and
inuendo. When it was left unchecked, it built into
a self-perpetuating chain reaction leading to a whole
series of unfortunate, and yet inevitable, consequences.
In its myriad iterations, murmuring has consequences.
Words that are so carelessly spoken cannot be gathered up
later on. Like feathers left on the doorsteps of those with
whom one has engaged in idle conversation, they will
scatter to the four winds and cannot be recalled.
Words so thoughtlessly bantered about imply
that the mouth has been put in motion
before the heart and the brain have
been brought on-line.

Over and over, the
Nephites were enjoined by their
prophet-leaders to put things in their
proper perspective; that they should not seek
to obtain riches, but wisdom (see Alma 39:14),
and that in order to have a working understanding
of spiritual things, they must have discernment, which is
guidance from the Holy Ghost. (See Alma 30:46). Nephites
who inquired in sincerity were taught by the Spirit, and the
confirmation of their faith was a manifestation of the special
gift of the Holy Ghost. The Lord's mission has always been
to shepherd the covenant faithful through the power of
baptism, along the strait and narrow path to the
other ordinances that are necessary for
them to obtain eternal life.

God's inspired
solution for dealing
with the revolting filthiness of
our sins is to wash them away both
figuratively and literally in the healing
waters of baptism. Although it could have
been lifted right out of The Book of Mormon,
The Manual of Discipline from the Serek Scroll
found at Qumran reads: "His sin is forgiven him
and in the humility of his soul he is for all the laws
of God. His flesh is cleansed shining bright in the
waters of purification, or the waters of baptism,
and he shall be given a new name in due
time, to walk perfectly in all the
ways of God."

The Book of
Mormon's prophets
ask that we push beyond
our perceived limitations, and
they instill within our hearts a
quiet determination to lengthen
our stride. To avoid the ugly fate of
those who would greet the restoration
of truth with skepticism, to ensure
that our faith will be animated by
energy, and to have no regrets as
we move along on our own Via
Dolorosa, we have been given
the Light of Christ, as well
as the supernal gift of
the Holy Ghost.

The mind-numbing tedium
and unrelenting monotony of the years
between 400 and 1000 A.D., a period of time
that coincided with the aftermath of the destruction
of the Nephite civilization, has been characterized as the
Dark Ages. It was stark in every dimension. Intellectual
life had vanished from Europe (and we might say, from the
Americas, as well). Even Charlemagne, the first Holy Roman
Emperor and the greatest of all medieval rulers, was illiterate.
In all those static centuries, absolutely nothing of consequence
had either improved or declined. With the sole exception of the
introduction of waterwheels in the 800s there were very few
inventions of note. A creative vacuum existed, where
everything remained as it had been for as long
as anyone could remember.

Conditions
in Book of Mormon society
illustrated the contraries that always
exist between Zion and Babylon. Those in
Zion see with wide-eyed wonder while Babylon
squints at every sunburst that heralds a spiritual
awakening. She would rather wear designer sunglasses
than adjust her eyes to the increased illumination of the light
of truth. Zion abases the wealthy in order to exalt the poor while
Babylon emphasizes earthly treasure, worships the almighty dollar,
trades in counterfeit currency, destroys initiative thru a misguided
sense of entitlement, allows ambition to replace righteous desire, and
suppresses upward mobility and progress while maintaining the
status-quo and subjugating the interests of those who are no
less deserving, but who, through no fault of their own,
find themselves in much less fortunate
circumstances.

When
our razor
sharp focus is on
gaining a testimony
of The Book of Mormon,
we do not get in the thick
of thin things. We cultivate
an equilibrium that is centered
far from the madding crowd, at a
safe distance from the ego-filled
minds of mediocre men. We are
insulated from the tumult, the
confusion, and the cares of
the world, and enjoy an
unshakable firmness
in our quest for
truth.

Familiarity
with the teachings of
The Book of Mormon can
protect us from the false sense
of carnal security experienced by
the world, as well as from indifferent
complacency. We view our weaknesses
in positively constructive ways, and are
grateful for our conscious awareness of
opportunities for personal improvement
and for the tools that we have been
given to accomplish our mortal
mission assignments.

It would have been of great comfort to him if Lehi could have heard the words of a modern-day prophet, that "if we were to close the doors upon sorrow, we might very well be excluding our greatest friends and benefactors. Suffering can make saints of us as we learn patience and self-mastery. If we looked at mortality as the whole of existence, then pain, sorrow, failure, and short life would be calamity. But if we look upon life as an eternal thing stretching far into the pre-mortal past and on into the eternal future, then all happenings may be put in proper perspective." (Spencer W. Kimball).

In a lesson that could have been taken from the pages of The Book of Mormon, J. Reuben Clark, Jr. declared that "ravening wolves are amongst us from our own (people), and they, more than any others, are in sheep's clothing, because they wear the habiliments of the priesthood. We should be careful of them." Ezra Taft Benson agreed: "There are some in our midst," he declared, "who are not so much concerned about taking the gospel into the world, as they are about bringing worldliness into the gospel."

As
we embrace
the teachings of
The Book of Mormon,
we're able to increase our
metaphysical metabolism,
to burn away as much of the
fat of faithlessness as we can
when our hearts are broken in
the fiery crucible of contrition.
We remain unable, ourselves, to
remove the stain of sin, for only
as long as we remain incapable
of maintaining unequivocal
subservience to the celestially
crafted doctrine that we call
the Atonement that is so
unambiguously and
incontrovertibly
taught by the
prophets.

As
we follow
the numerous
admonitions from
The Book of Mormon
to repent, we can learn
to be humble as we receive
chastisement and counsel, by
being forgiving to those who have
offended us, by our service, and by
being good examples that teach others
to follow the pattern that was set by
the Lord during His ministry.

The inherent power of Jesus Christ is manifest by the instruction that He gave to the Nephites in Bountiful. The process of sanctification described in a fifth Gospel (3 Nephi Chapters 9 - 30) beckons us to draw nearer to God's throne in heaven, and we realize from His teachings, and especially as he recounted the Beatitudes to his faithful children, that He will bestow upon our heads the blessings we need, instead of those that we thought we had wanted.

Studying the Book of Mormon will bless us with a pure form of focus that transforms our five natural senses into something that is wonderful, by a heaven-sent sixth sense that defies description. Physical and spiritual resources work in tandem to compound each other, and to condition us through the patience of faith, the miracle of repentance, the diligence of baptism, the sweet spirit of the Holy Ghost, and our soul-sustaining renewal through the Sacrament of the Lord's Supper.

Weakness
can seed the
atmosphere of
our inspiration, to
nurture and moisten
our tender testimonies
as well as to germinate
our budding desire to
repent of our wicked
ways. (See Ether
12:27).

When we find ourselves
in the company of those who turn to
the prophets from The Book of Mormon to
be their labor coaches, we are able to deal with
weaknesses in the contractions that push forward
the Lord's agenda. We learn to rely on the pitocin of
the Atonement and to utilize the therapy of repentance
to quicken our efforts, that we might bear down with
renewed conviction on our solemn witness, unto
the convincing of both Jews and Gentiles
that Jesus is the Christ. (See 1 Nephi
13:41-42 & 19:18).

The Liahona guided Lehi's family to the Promised Land. The transliteration from Hebrew suggests that the term "Liahona" means "God gives light, as does the sun." Whereas a magnetic compass shows the way one may go, the Liahona is a spiritual compass that points the way we should go. God has provided for each of us a celestial compass of gospel principles that are founded on truth, to guide us to a safe haven at the day of reckoning. It is also there for those of us who have lost our way, to bring us back to the fold of the Good Shepherd.

As Alma counseled his son Helaman, "It is as easy to give heed to the words of Christ" Who is our compass, "which will point you to a straight course to eternal bliss, as it was for our fathers to give heed to this compass," the Liahona, which would point unto them a strait course to the promised land. Do not let us," then, "be slothful," or move slowly, "because of the easiness of the way." Instead, as if our very lives depended upon it, we must "look to God, and live!" (Alma 37:44 & 46-47).

"When thou hurtest not thy neighbors, then art thou sure that God's Spirit worketh in thee and that they faith is no dream nor any false imagination." (William Tyndale). "Blessed are the merciful," the Savior taught, "for they shall obtain mercy." (3 Nephi 12:7). "For with what judgment ye judge, ye shall be judged, and with what measure ye mete, it shall be measured to you again." (Matthew 7:2). What goes around, comes around, and if we cast our bread upon the waters, we can be sure that after many days, it will return to us.

We remember the account in the scriptures that describes how the Savior overthrew the tables of the moneychangers at the temple in Jerusalem. How cheaply do we sell that which seems most dear to us. "That for which all virtue is sold, and almost any vice - almighty gold!" (Ben JonsOon). How ironic that it is all for nothing. The world's covetous passion to hoard telestial trash leads to societal bickering that paves the way for "the destruction of nearly all the people of the kingdom." (Ether 12:9).

How rapidly are we "lifted up in pride; yea, how quick to boast." (Helaman 12:5). And yet, how great an example were the Zoroastrian Magi? They may have worn the trappings of wealth and position, and borne costly gifts, but it was their humility that compelled them to undertake the arduous journey to Bethlehem. Significantly, 2,000 years later, we still refer to them as "wise men."

As the Magi plodded thru desert wastes during their long journey from the East, they were guided by a new star that appeared over Bethlehem, so that the mighty and high-born might also stand as witnesses of the heavenly choir and the babe who lay in the manger. But they took no honor unto themselves, and after leaving their gifts of gold, frankincense, and myrrh, they discreetly left Judea by another way. Just as Isaiah had foreseen, so it had come to pass: Those who had "walked in darkness (had) seen a great light." (2 Nephi 19:2).

Jacob used The
Book of Mormon to testify
that the Savior knows us better
than anyone else. He knows when
we've been sleeping, and He knows when
we're awake. he knows when we've been good
or bad, so we need to be good for goodness' sake.
There is no one else who knows our thoughts, or the
intent of our hearts. "O how great the holiness of
our God!" cried Jacob. "For he knoweth all things,
and there is not anything save he knows it."
(2 Nephi 9:20).

"And behold,
there shall a new star
arise, such an one as ye never
have beheld, and this also shall be
a sign unto you." (Helaman 14:5). Even
the Zoroastrian priests from the East saw the
light, and perceived, its significance. Arriving in
Jerusalem after the Savior's birth, they inquired of
Herod: "Where is he that is born King of the Jews?
For we have seen his star in the east, and are
come to worship him." (Matthew 2:2).

Our Lord and Savior Jesus Christ is our Rock of Revelation. (See Matthew 16:18). He is the personification of the "one eternal God." (Alma 11:44). We accept His counsel as "the doctrine of Christ, and the only and true doctrine of the Father, and of the Son, and of the Holy Ghost, which is one God, without end." (3 Nephi 18:12). The morning stars and all the sons of God were mustered out of heaven itself to come to earth, to shout for joy as they bore testimony to shepherds who had been quietly tending their flocks by night in the fields outside the little town of Bethlehem. (See Luke 2:13-14).

Although first-time readers may find it difficult to understand, God's condescension is beautifully illustrated in The Book of Mormon. (The First Book of Nephi Chapter 11). It required that Jesus Christ atone for the sins of the world, to bring about the Plan of Redemption, while meeting the demands of Justice. This allowed our Heavenly Father, at one and the same time, to be both just and merciful.

The Book of Mormon sets us free to be creative, while it is our creativity that sets us free to properly plan before we come face to face with the crises of life. Our obedience prevents our poor performance or mitigates its consequences. As we learn to rely upon the doctrine of Christ that is taught in the Book of Nephi, we internalize its elements, which permits us to surrender ourselves to infinite possibilities. Therein, we find our individuality, and avenues for personal expression open up before us. At last, we discover the noblest expression of our free will, which is manifest in a breathtaking opportunity to "become."

Sooner or later, each of us will ideally reach a point in our lives where we've read The Book of Mormon frequently enough that it's motivated us to persevere with determination and discipline to make lifestyle changes that bring us into conformity with the character of our Father in Heaven. We will enjoy that realm of spirit as our natural environment and we'll understand that it's more vibrantly real than anything we've ever known. In the meantime, we must beware, lest we strangle ourselves with illusions of reality, and with things whose opacity obstructs our ability to see what is really there.

We will all be tested by trial and temptation and we will make mistakes. But we will rise above our failures because of the love of the Savior and His Atonement. It's in the next act that all the mysteries will be solved, every piece of the puzzle will be put in its proper place, all the confusion that often tormented us will put to rest, and everything will be made right. If that is to occur, we need to be up and about, starting now, by making our way through The Book of Mormon.

Joseph Smith "has shown unto us the plates ….. which have the appearance of gold; and as many of the leaves as ….. Smith has translated we did handle with our hands; and we also saw the engravings thereon, all of which has the appearance of ancient work, and of curious workmanship." (Testimony of The Eight Witnesses).

The
Atonement, that is
thoroughly explained in
The Book of Mormon, allows
us to be liberated from the mire
of sin, and to be cleansed in the
redeeming blood of Jesus Christ;
to stand firmly on gospel sod.
Our faith separates us from
those who precariously hop
about on the flotsam and
jetsam that bobs up and
down and tosses them
to and fro upon the
unpredictably
roily sea of
life.

We live in the
midst of spiritual
Babylon, and recoil as
we encounter the sprawling
wasteland of worldliness that
reeks of the rotting stench of sin.
But we mustn't allow our faith in
the cleansing power of the Lord's
infinite and eternal Atonement
(see 2 Nephi Chapters 2 and 9)
to be contaminated by the raw
sewage that is unleashed by
Satan's servants, who are
often thinly disguised
as sanitation
workers.

Those who have been
blessed with a testimony
of The Book of Mormon are
witness to the Savior's power.
They are sanctified in Him by
the grace of God, and thru the
shedding of His blood which is
in the covenant of His Father
unto the remission of their
sins. They are consecrated
unto righteousness, and
to become holy and
without spot.

While
the desire
to obtain gold
can corrupt us, as
has been so vividly
described by Book of
Mormon prophets, that
bright, shiny metal that
can't be corroded may be
a symbol of purity that
turns our thoughts to the
Celestial Kingdom, where
gilded streets will dazzle
our eyes, as the opening
gates of heaven invite
us to enter into the
presence of the
Lord.

Inspirational counsel from
the pages of The Book of Mormon
encourages an interrelationship between
our physical and spiritual well-being and
obedience that must exist if we hope to nurture
the faith to obey the divine design of God during
the assembly of our mortal tabernacles. Its purpose
after all, is to facilitate our transformation into
holy temples that, in His wisdom, have been
designed to exist contemporaneously
with our immortal spirits.

The Book of Mormon
teaches us that the Atonement
can be a powerful financial device
providing over-draft protection as we
invest our resources in the theater of life.
It stands as our guardian, or our personal
asset manager, to make certain that when
our foolish debts become due and payable,
our checks that have been co-signed by
the Savior can only be cashed by a
creditor who goes by the name
of Justice, but only if they
have been previously
endorsed by
Mercy.

Book of
Mormon prophets
describe the Atonement
as if it were some sort of a
kidney dialysis machine,
which, as we know, it is not!
Still, there are similarities, for
it's a mechanism that removes
impurities from our hearts, so
that we might enjoy the faith
necessary to build the holy
accommodations that are
worthy of the habitation
of our spirits.

In his
dream, Lehi
saw the attention
and adoration of the
world as nothing more
than a satanic seduction
attempting to influence
him to abandon his faith
in Jesus Christ and leave
his coat of many colors
hanging unattended
and unused in the
closet in the back
of his tent.

It is within The
Book of Mormon that
we learn how the Atonement
can become infinite and eternal
in its scope and dimension. From
Nephi, Abinadi, Alma, Samuel the
Lamanite, and the Savior Himself,
we learn basic mathematics; that the
legal tender of the Atonement is all
the currency we will ever need to
purchase a golden ticket that
ensures our safe passage
back to our home in
heaven.

The
influence of
faith extends only
as far as our deeds.
Alma said that works
that reflect reliance on
our Savior Jesus Christ
become an important
companion not only
to faith, but also to
testimony and
conversion.

The brilliant
doctrine of The
Book of Mormon
was designed as a
celestial thermostat
that easily measures
the volatility of the
telestial tempests
that regularly
sweep across
our lives.

When we get up off our knees to
study The Book of Mormon, we feel as if
we have entered the precincts of a revelatory
observatory. The Spirit blesses us to see things
as they really are, through the clarifying lens of
eternity. There is an aura surrounding us that is
crystal clear, and its uncontaminated atmosphere
blesses us with discernment, with the ability to
make the distinctions between good and evil,
and right and wrong; to make choices that
are based on celestial certainties, free of
the distortions of darkness, temporal
improbabilities, or any sort of
pollutions whatsoever.

In The Book of Mormon,
it is not too difficult to see Satan's
fingerprints that are smeared all over the
programs and pronouncements that are promoted
by parties that pander to provincial policies and politics.
With perseverance and preoccupation, he props up paltry, petty,
and personal plans that lack piety or a palpably proven priesthood
purpose or perspective, and he persistently persuades people who
are unprincipled, and from whom patience has plummeted,
to pursue perilous pathways that can only lead to one
inevitable outcome, and that is punishment,
pure and simple.

The
Book of Mormon
shepherds us through
the growing pains and the
mental, emotional, physical,
and spiritual unsteadiness that
are related to our early childhood
development. Nevertheless, unless
our behavior matures so that it is in
harmony with Christ's Atonement,
the freedom that exists outside of the
sphere harboring the moral element
of responsibility that is faith will
inevitably forge our fetters and
lead us into bondage. It is only
within His gospel that we will
discover the perfect law
of liberty.

Sometimes all too quickly, and at other times agonizingly slowly, those who have sold their souls to the Devil for a mess of pottage are dragged down to a hell on earth that is of their own construction. Their bad habits are the result of repetitively impulsive behaviors that, in a rising tide of wickedness, continually erode away at the foundations of agency. They are fettered by the chains of compulsions. They realize too late that unlimited freedom leads to tyranny. The Book of Mormon has the power to lead the most vile sinners to the Atonement's path of safety, and to the Savior's perfect law of liberty.

As imperfect mortals who are struggling to believe what we have not seen, the reward of our maturing faith is to see what we believe. Some things just have to be believed to be seen, before our emerging faith in the doctrine of The Book of Mormon has been shaped by our experience, and we can say, as did the believing man who had been blind from his birth, but was healed by the Savior: "One thing I know, whereas I was blind, now I see." (John 9:25).

Our testimony of the divine authenticity of The Book of Mormon requires the moral element of responsibility that we call faith. Of those to whom much is given, however, much is expected. The discharge of faith presupposes action. Thus, without the works to back up our faith, we fall short of the mark. As James taught in his epistle to all the House of Israel, stripped of attendant works, our faith "is dead, being alone." '(James 2:17).

During our journey of faith that leads to an appreciation of The Book of Mormon, it is necessary to take a few halting steps into the darkness in order to let the spiritual strong searchlight of truth illuminate the way. Only after the trial of our faith, will it be confirmed to us by the Spirit that its prophet-historians were inspired by the One Who is both the Author and Finisher of our faith.

When
cultural collapse
is imminent, external
controls are often imposed
to manipulate behavior in order
to maintain at least a semblance
of societal steadiness. An escalating
dependence upon laws to regulate moral
discipline and to conform our conduct
to something that, at least, resembles
integrity says something about us,
and about our critical need for
the principles elucidated in
The Book of Mormon to
step in and provide
stability in our
lives.

No matter
that we may live
in the frigid reaches of
the Arctic or in the stifling
heat of the Tropics, it is with our
invigorating study of The Book of
Mormon that we catch a religious fever
that elevates our testimony temperature
enough to get our juices flowing with an
appreciation of Who the Savior really is. It
is at this moment that we prepare ourselves
to experience the earth shaking and mind
bending theophany that we who once were
the children of men, have become His
spiritual offspring. We are born
of Him Who lives in heaven
on the right hand of the
throne of God.

Alma the Younger is a stellar example of a repentant sinner who fasted and prayed many days to receive the spirit of revelation, and to know and understand the things of God. (See Alma 5:45-46). As we fast, the spiritual and temporal sides of our nature slowly harmonize. Our physical desires, held in check by an expanding spiritual awareness, strengthen our resolve to discipline our nature. We transcend forces pulling us one way or the other, and enter a metaphysical state of euphoria where virtue garnishes our thoughts unceasingly, as the doctrine of the priesthood distills upon our souls as the dews from heaven because our confidence begins to wax strong in the presence of God. As this process unfolds, the Holy Ghost becomes our constant companion, our scepter an unchanging scepter of righteousness and truth, and our dominion a God centered and focused protectorate. Under these conditions, all that is good begins to freely flow like an artesian well from the fountain of heaven, in an unending stream.

Nephites who became mired in the bonds of iniquity knew despair very well. It was the hopelessness they felt when they had to deal with the sense of futility that came from having to choose between alternatives that were equally disappointing because they were fruitless, or devoid of value.

Those of weak will, who are swift in running to mischief, forfeit their capacity to learn, although they may not even be consciously aware of it. They lose their focus, just as eyesight may be lost over time. First they will squint, and then they may position the page a bit closer or a little further away, compensating for their inability to see clearly. It could be either the printed page or their integrity that they can't read. But without clarity, there may result a compromise of crippling proportion as they neglect to poke and prod The Book of Mormon in the spirit of inquiry.

The Book of Mormon teaches us that when life throws us a curve, and we go south when the trail goes north, we'll need to remember to "just get back on the bike." When we do, we'll find that, in no time we will forget the spill, as we twist the throttle to get back up to speed, anticipating our next chance to get serious air. When another rock in the trail looms before us, we will be the wiser for our experience, and we will be less intimidated and better prepared to avoid another close encounter of the dirt kind.

Limiting beliefs deafen us to the
guidance of The Book of Mormon, that
might have otherwise helped us to monitor
our progress along the pathway to perfection.
They also foster insensitivity to the standards
to which we might, in other circumstances, have
turned. They can corrode the iron rods running
straight and true that would have otherwise led
us to the waters of baptism, and they weaken
our focus on the absolutes in which its
prophets have asked us to place
our implicit trust.

Historically, and sadly,
organized religion has become magical in
the eyes of many devout believers because the power of
the church has been transferred from God to those who have
only professed to be His earthly representatives, but who are, in
reality, only competing for market share. Priesthood has acquired
the standing of an office that mechanically bestows both blessings
and grace, regardless of the moral or spiritual qualifications of its
possessor. The Bible then appears to convey power and knowledge
without the need for revelation. Moroni saw that there would be
many in the Last Days, who had "transfigured the holy
word of God," or who had wrested the scriptures, by
changing their appearance and substance
to meet their profane needs.
(Mormon 8:33).

As a bright beacon
of hope twinkling optimistically
in the night sky, The Church of Jesus
Christ in the New World became a third class
of witnesses to the birth of the Savior, joining the
Wise Men and the shepherds in their fields. As a result,
His people in Zarahemla began "to have peace in the land,
and there were no contentions." (3 Nephi 1:23-24). The star
in the East was symbolic of their focus on the Savior. His
gospel was their fortification, obedience to their covenants
was their sanctuary, and reliance upon the light was
their protection against the prince of darkness,
whose murky influence would soon enough
be sweeping across the land like a
suffocating wind.

Every day, we are 24 hours closer
to the Pleasing Bar of Christ (Moroni 10:34),
if we have patterned our lives after the 13th Article
of Faith. We strive to "be honest, true, chaste, virtuous,
and in doing good to all men. Indeed, we may say that we
follow the admonition of Paul: We believe all things, we hope
all things, we have endured many things, and hope to be able to
endure all things. If there is anything that is virtuous, lovely, or
of good report or praiseworthy, we seek after these things." In fact,
"at the banquet of consequences, there will not be much that is
satisfying at the table, unless we are able to bow our heads in
reverence, and not hang them in shame, in the presence of
God, who will be there." (Marion D. Hanks, "B.Y.U.
Devotional Address," 10/3/67).

It is
only thru the
phenomenon of the
infinite, continuing,
enduring, immeasurable,
uncorrupted, unfathomable,
uninterrupted, and unspoiled
grace that is embodied within
the principles and doctrine of
The Book of Mormon that we
find ourselves "swallowed
up in the joy of God to
the exhausting of our
strength." (Alma
27:17).

The
ways of the
world can leave us
vulnerable to a spiritual
sickness that imitates the
symptoms of those who have
advanced diabetes. When our
peripheral circulation has been
compromised, we will become
numb to the better angels of
our nature and we can lose
our capacity to feel the
power of The Book
of Mormon.

Of all the holy sanctuaries that have been created by the hand of God to be as safe havens from the follies of the world, it is The Book of Mormon that stands out as one of the least understood. It reminds us that the natural man does not receive the things of the Spirit of God, for they are foolishness unto him. He cannot know them, for they are discerned spiritually.

Nothing stifles the guiding Spirit faster than the stubborn self-confidence that has mutated into vanity, unbridled pride, selfishness, and haughtiness. These are the character crippling traits that are antithetical to the expansion of understanding that is found in the revelatory atmosphere of The Book of Mormon.

The meager substitutes for the rewards that are found in the humility of faith include wealth, affluence, authority, style, influence, position, fashion, and dominion. When lumped together, these become the holy grail of those who engage in a blind quest for the power and control that are the antithesis of the humble lifestyle that is illustrated by faithful Nephites and Lamanites within the narrative of The Book of Mormon.

By making covenants with God we can break the bands of death and we are made free to enjoy His grace. "There is no other name given whereby salvation cometh," said Benjamin; "therefore, I would that ye should take upon you the name of Christ, all you that have entered into the covenant with God." (Mosiah 5:8).

In our busy
and complex world,
we often see through a
glass darkly. This makes
it difficult to discover how to
harness the power of the elusive
equations that drive the majestic
clockwork that is found within
the mathematics of The Book
of Mormon.

It is to The Book of
Mormon where we turn
for triage, if we have been
wounded by the adversary's
fiery darts. It is a safe haven,
where we confidently regroup,
as we take hold of the horns of
sanctuary. Within its pages
we learn about the order of
heaven and how to honor
our covenants.

The Book of Mormon gives us the chance to catch a glimpse of heaven. "Abundance is multiplied unto (us) thru the manifestations of the Spirit" that we feel so profoundly that they seem to overflow. D&C 70:13). These stay in focus because the book's spiritual guideposts provide us with an orientation that is centered on eternity. They bless us with the only proven perspective in a world that is overflowing with so many voices that are in competition for our attention.

For those whose behavior is not in harmony with Book of Mormon doctrine, there will come a time when a readjustment of their attitude must obliterate their façade of hypocrisy that has been thrown up as defensive dross. As painful as that process of reformation might be, it will be necessary, if there is to be the cultivation of a more nurturing and receptive lifestyle that embraces the special promises they have been invited to make with God. (See Moroni 10:30 - 33).

When
we are at one
with God, and we
have been spiritually
born of Him to the point
that we have internalized
His divine nature, we receive
His image in our countenances.
That blazing aura, in tandem with
His likeness, will bridge the barriers of
time and space to leave an indelible marker
as a reminder of our noble birthright. The
Book of Mormon will be as a Rosetta Stone,
the key to our interpretation of a genetic
code that links our lives to that of God,
with the bond of an intertwined
double helix that remains
unbreakable.

"My thoughts are not your thoughts,"
said the Lord, "neither are your ways my
ways … For as the heavens are higher than the
earth, so are my ways higher than your ways,
and my thoughts than your thoughts." (Isaiah
55:8-9). His thoughts are loftier, broader, more
visionary, and infinitely more expansive. His
ways circumscribe the sum of our reality
and encompass more than we have ever
dared to dream. But we get a hint
of His mighty omniscience in
The Book of Mormon.

On the Day of Pentecost, the manifestation of the Holy Ghost appeared to the people as "a sound from heaven as of a rushing mighty wind, and it filled all the house where (the multitude was) sitting." (Acts 2:2, see also, 3 Nephi 11:3). So dramatic was its appearance, that "there appeared unto them cloven tongues like as of fire, and it sat upon each of them." So spectacular was the presence of the Spirit that "they were all filled, and they began to speak with other tongues as (it) gave them utterance." (Acts 2:3).

When we neglect our opportunities to expand our faith to make the connections that can only be envisioned when we maintain an eternal perspective, we neutralize the magical capability of The Book of Mormon to get our juices flowing and stir our souls by raising our testimony temperature. That body of scripture is as a human growth hormone for our spirits.

God
pronounced
all things good,
and even very good,
that He had made at the
creation. Then He gave it
into our care, to be dressed,
nurtured, and protected. But it
remains His handiwork, and the
earth, together with all its flora and
fauna, is His footstool, and not ours to
be used according to our whim. (See 3
Nephi 12:34). Ours is a sacred trust,
and the manner in which we carry
out our stewardship is not open
to discussion, argument,
or interpretation.

Those who internalize
The Book of Mormon's doctrine
are as lights unto the world. They are
as beacons to those who are seeking the
truth. They are saviors on Mount Zion
to both the living and the dead, and
are as missionary companions to
the Author of salvation, Who
embedded its principles
within His gospel
Plan.

Whenever the Nephites allowed themselves to be enveloped within the Lord's watch care they would begin to enjoy the glimmering facets of the light of the Spirit. With enhanced vision, they could see as clearly as did Hans Christian Anderson, who knew that our lives can be as fairy tales "waiting to be written by the finger of God."

It was at the very instant when their unsatisfied desire for the praise and popularity of the world began to control their actions that the Nephites found themselves in the awkward position of bending their character, when they supposed they were only taking a bow. It was especially at these times when they needed the softening influence of the Holy Ghost, the healing touch of our Lord and Savior Jesus Christ, and finally the loving encouragement of our Father in Heaven, Who looked over them every day of their lives, from heaven above.

By its very own description and definition, it was the gospel that encouraged the Nephites to be enthusiastic. After all, it is the good news practically begging them to experience the feeling of being possessed by a god, to have supernatural inspiration, and even a prophetic frenzy. The definition found in the dictionary is unmistakable. If we are charged with enthusiasm, our actions are no longer ours; for it is God Who has taken control of our destiny with kindness and benevolence.

The Nephites' leaders pricked their hearts with the word, and stirred them up to repentance. Their mission was to heal their brethren of their deafness and their blindness, and at the same time to apply a curative balm that was necessary to soothe their throbbing spiritual muscles and joints.

"Truth,
as well as error,
may be recognized by its
effects. The claims of the Book of
Mormon may be tested by rendering
obedience to their principles of action.
Practicing our religion is the most
direct method of gaining a
testimony of the truth."
(John Widtsoe).

"The scriptures are laid before thee, yea,
and all things denote there is a God; yea
even the earth, and all things that are upon
the face of it, yea, and its motion, yea, and
also all the planets which move in their
regular form do witness that there
is a Supreme Creator."
(Alma 30:44).

The Nephites had a mutually nurturing relationship with God as they helped Him to bring to pass their immortality and eternal life within the biological broth whose secret spice was unbridled free will. As we look back on their experiences that are recounted in The Book of Mormon, it is unthinkable that He would focus His energies and concentrate His powers on an activity that was doomed to failure because of flaws in the instruments that were not only the very center of His attention, but also critical to its success.

Many times in the holy scriptures, the prophets utilized the word "mountain" both allegorically and figuratively, to refer to a high place of God, a place of revelation, and perhaps to the temple of the Lord. In some cases it refers to Mount Zion, or Jerusalem. In the Last Days, "the Lord's house will be established in the tops of the mountains." (Isaiah 2:2) This may be a reference to the intermountain west, but that interpretation may be too narrow, because the Lord warned Joseph Smith: "Let them who be of Judah flee unto the mountains of the Lord's house." (D&C 133:13). Clearly, the eternal city of Jerusalem must be considered when this scripture is being interpreted.

As we read The Book of Mormon and we reflect upon our lineage and birthright, we may want to consider the covenant consciousness of the members of The Church of Jesus Christ in the latter days. Sometimes, we forget that Latter-day Saints are also of the House of Israel, either literally or by adoption, and that they too may claim the covenant blessings promised by God so long ago, not only to Abraham, but also to all of his seed.

The righteous Nephites were sure of God's power, strength, and support when the arm of the Lord was made manifest. On the other hand, the arm of flesh was unstable, and it was prone to uncontrollable spasm, atrophy, and paralysis, that are all symptoms of clumsy outbursts of behavior that is destructive and ineffectual.

The actions of the
Nephites were "in vain" when they
lacked value. For example, when they tried
in vain, they struggled without the expectation
of success. Taking the name of the Lord "was in vain"
blasphemous because it was using His name improperly and
without authority. Those who did so were imposters, invoking the
name of God in a false, misleading, and counterfeit way. So too,
the Nephites' sinful behavior was in vain. Too often, they caved to
pressure to follow the path of least resistance. They did one thing,
when something else of far greater consequence could have been
accomplished with a little more blood, soul sweat, and tears. It
was settling for mediocrity rather than following the more
difficult road that would lead to greater heights. It was
a capitulation to spiritual stagnation rather than
acceptance of the effort required to surmount
obstacles in a quest for enlightenment. It
was akin to trading their eternal
birthright for a mess
of pottage.

Because the word of God was
generally foreign to the Lamanites,
they often resorted to violence in a vain
attempt to bolster their position. But power
and violence were mutually exclusive; where
one was present the other was absent. Even today,
those who are least prepared for positions of trust and
responsibility seem to be those who are the most inclined
to abuse their authority. Measured against the standard of
heaven, violence can never be justified when exercising
the power of one's position. It is contrary to the order
of the Celestial Kingdom, and it abrogates the
rights of the governed, hiding behind the
cloak of supposed authority.

The consciousness of victory over ourselves and our communion with the infinite is the hallmark of spirituality. As The Book of Mormon so amply illustrates, the terrifying jungle of worldliness is always close at hand, but we can't allow ourselves to compromise our standards or yield to the siren song of Satan's seductive sentinels. Ours must always be a non-negotiable standard of celestial bound disciples. We must be firm and resolute, for as Alexander Pope pointed out, the risk of accommodation is high, and vice can be "a monster of so frightful mien, as to be hated needs but to be seen. Yet seen too oft, familiar with her face, we first endure, then pity, then embrace."

When we have made covenants with God, only to then conspicuously compromise the standard to which we have pledged our undeviating allegiance, we may thereafter "wax strong in wickedness and abominations." (3 Nephi 2:3). It is one thing for an ignorant people to live in opposition to the laws of God, but it is quite another for those who have had the light, to turn from it, willfully rebel, and consciously seek an alternative path of darkness. That is a course of action which is an abomination, because it represents unfaithfulness to God. It is not easy for those who repudiate His gifts to obtain forgiveness. Those who perish in such circumstances must die in their sins. They cannot be saved in God's kingdom.
(See Moroni 10:26).

Those penitent Nephites who entered the fold at the waters of Mormon may not have realized at the time that Alma's presence there denoted greatness. His ministry foreshadowed that of St. Patrick, who only a few centuries later would "convert the Irish with the resolute confidence of his belief, as well as the passionate persistence of his work. He ordained priests, built churches, established monasteries and nunneries, and he left strong spiritual garrisons to guard his conquests at every turn. He surrounded himself with men and women of courage and devotion who endured every privation to spread the good news that man was redeemed. He did not convert all Ireland; some pockets of paganism and its poetry survived, and leave traces to this day. But when he died in 461 A.D., it could be said of him, as no other, that one man had converted a nation." (Will Durant).

The Nephites' firm and unshakable testimony of the great Plan of Deliverance from Death govern ignorance, and became the catalyst of their purposeful action. As they sought to gain an understanding of both the temporal and eternal worlds, they developed the power to exercise moral agency. Awakening comprehension came "line upon line and precept upon precept." (D&C 98:11-12). Their life beyond the veil offered them the promise of an exponential expansion of their knowledge accompanied by an awakening re-acquaintance with heaven itself.

The decay of our physical bodies is necessary to satisfy the requirements of the merciful Plan of our Father. But our spiritual death is far more serious, because it happens when we die "as to things pertaining unto righteousness." (Alma 12:16). The first spiritual death occurs when we commit sin after the age of accountability. We can be spiritually born again, however, through the sanctifying influence of the Holy Ghost, after repentance and baptism by immersion. But there is also a second spiritual death, which is eternal separation from God's presence that transpires after we have passed from mortality to immortality without having beforehand received all of the ordinances of the priesthood, and when we thereafter deny the Lord a second time, by willingly declining the ordinances of the priesthood that have been performed on our behalf in the House of the Lord.

The Book of Mormon spectacularly responds to our needs. With a clear vision, its instruction sees the clouds before they appear on our horizons, and issues weather bulletins.

Alma asked his brethren if they had received the image of the Lord in their countenances? He wondered if their faces naturally reflected the Light of Christ? Because of the change in their hearts, had they become new creatures in Christ, thereby able to reach their potential in both the image and likeness of God their Father? Were their testimonies the foundation for a sustained saving faith that gave them confidence to stand tall before the pleasing bar of God, to bask in the embrace of His holy presence, to be weighed in the balances, and by His good grace to receive His approbation, as well as their inheritance in His kingdom?

We need the wise counsel of The Book of Mormon now, as much as we ever have, because we have exponentially increased the odds that we will destroy ourselves if we are careless; if we do not obey the covenants whose importance is explained in the book.

When the Nephites were obedient, and listened to the Spirit, they were careful to avoid squandering resources, or wasting precious energy by becoming preoccupied with what was missing in their lives. Focusing attention on what they lacked could have become a paralyzing fear, and that flawed strategy would have ultimately defeated them. Instead, they needed to focus on their available assets, capitalize on them, and turn them into forces for positive, substantive, and significant change. They needed to pray as if everything depended upon the will of God, as it surely does, but then get to work, as if the ultimate success of their joint ventures with Him hinged upon their own initiative and determination.

How fitting it is that our study of The Book of Mormon is accompanied by guidance received from the Spirit, that is beyond our limited understanding, but that directs us as we face challenges, as we make important decisions, and as we grapple with the greatest questions relating to our faith.

"Ye are no more
strangers and foreigners,
but (are) fellow citizens with the
saints, and of the household of God"
(Ephesians 2:19), sounds like Mormon's
characterization of the Saints in 4 Nephi. The
recipients of Paul's epistle were congregants of one of
the seven churches in Asia, who might have heretofore
viewed themselves as privileged members of an exclusive
ecclesiastical country club situated on a narrow theological
terrace. They may have been accustomed to giving each other
high-fives and gracious compliments, while at the same time
treating those outside their inner circle in a deprecating way.
But Paul hoped that, if foreigners from Sardis, Smyrna,
Philadelphia, or Pergamum, or strangers from Thyatira or
Laodicea arrived in Ephesus, they would be welcomed in
the bonds of fellowship, and be warmly received by
the Saints into the household of God. They were
not to be mistreated as undocumented illegal
immigrants, or as if they were on a "no
fly" watch list of subversives, that
was maintained by the local
authorities.

Because they are
unable to recognize the thunder,
lightning, and burning bush of Sinai,
the enthusiastically ignorantly endeavor to
drag communication from the heavens down to
their level so that it is in harmony with their myopic
view of life. The world ridicules revelation and
disparages its delivery. This is why it is
unable to comprehend The Book of
Mormon.

If it were not possible
to regularly repent of our sins,
our misdeeds of the past would forever
compromise our future and hold it hostage,
extort our best efforts, and thwart the Great Plan
of Redemption. As Nephi exclaimed: "Rejoice, O my
heart, and give place no more for the enemy of my soul.
Do not anger again because of mine enemies. Do not
slacken my strength because of my afflictions."
(2 Nephi 4:28-30).

When the Savior ministered among the Nephites
in the New World, they enjoyed a Pentecostal experience,
for "they had been "encircled about as if it were by fire; and it
came down from heaven, and the multitude did witness it, and
did bear record; and angels did come down out of heaven and
did minister unto them." (3 Nephi 19:14). It was as it had
been during the Exodus when Moses was commanded:
"Put off thy shoes from off thy feet, for the place
whereon thou standest is holy ground. For
I am the God of thy fathers, the God
of Abraham, the God of Isaac,
and the God of Jacob."
(Exodus 3:5-6).

An interesting account of the discovery of the Bar Kokhba Documents that were hidden in caves near Ein Gedi on the western shore of the Salt Sea, about 31 A.D., speaks of records that were buried deeply in the dry dirt of the cave floor. When they came to light, choking clouds of dust required the archaeologists to wear masks to breathe. Truly, the prophets speak to us out of the ground, and their speech is low out of the dust, even as it were out of the ground, and they whisper to us out of the dust. (See 2 Nephi 26:16).

At the moment of our birth, we are only recently removed from our spiritual kindergarten. We barely skip a beat as we recommence our education in our Primary classes, but we are trailing clouds of glory from God, who is our Home. Years pass, and the graduation ceremony commemorating the conclusion of our course of study on earth draws closer. It comforts us to know that when we cross the bar to enter the kingdom of God, our bodies will be "full of light." (3 Nephi 13:22). But we might be surprised to discover that we will enjoy no more luminosity then, than any three-year old Sunbeam pupil now has. As the Savior taught: "Suffer the little children, and forbid them not, to come unto me, for of such is the kingdom of heaven." (Mark 10:14).

We've all
witnessed those
who have vacationed
in Babylon to celebrate
the festival of free will and
the carnival of carefree living.
But we also remember Alma, who
willingly shed his temporal trappings
and telestial tendencies, that he might
experience a greater comprehension
of his eternal identity.

Without The Book
of Mormon, we are free
to negotiate our way thru
the minefields of mortality.
However, as we do, forsaking
help where it may be found,
we may very well look and
feel like an octopus on
roller skates.

How many times in
The Book of Mormon have
we read about cultural collapse
because a faithless society decayed
from within? In every case, destruction
followed those who surrendered themselves
"unto the power of Satan." (3 Nephi 7:5). The
world does not seem to be able to understand
that Lucifer was a first-grade dropout whose
influence was the companion of anarchy. As
his disciples do today, from the beginning,
he denied the power of the Atonement and
he demeaned the idea that the intelligent
application of knowledge could help
us to work out our salvation
before God, angels, and
witnesses.

The Book of Mormon
clearly explains that after the Fall
of our First Parents, the portal to Eden
swung shut, but as it did so, another door
opened that introduced Adam and Eve to a
secret garden that was accessible only to those
who would exercise the power of the Atonement,
thru baptism by immersion for the remission of
their sins. They would be able to have successful
interactions with evil as well as with good, with
vice as well as with virtue, with sickness as
well as with health, with darkness as well
as with light, and not only with pain,
but also with pleasure, in the
white-hot crucible of
experience.

As we
read The Book
of Mormon, and
as our testimonies of
the Savior swell in our
hearts, faith intensifies
our desire to repent, and the
effort we've made to maintain
our worthiness centers our lives,
bringing us into harmony with
true principles. As we endeavor to
be obedient, we find ourselves in a
constant state of improvement. We
begin to believe in ourselves, and in
Heavenly Father, too. Our hearts race
as we realize that His promise is true,
and that we are really headed in the
direction of perfection, after all. As
it turns out, life is amazing,
and our God awesome!

Our Savior
is the Lord God
Omnipotent. We can
know Him on the terms
He has established, or we
can know Him not at all.
The Book of Mormon
becomes our key
to theology.

The
Book of Mormon
assures us that we will
be resurrected and will live
forever. But the gospel asks us
to do a bit more. We must organize
ourselves, and "prepare every needful
thing; and establish a house, even a house
of prayer, a house of fasting, a house of faith
a house of learning, a house of glory, (and) a
house of order." (D&C 88:119). In fact, we must
create and then maintain a house that has been
dedicated to God, that we might inherit not
only immortality, which has been freely
given to all, but also the greater gift of
eternal life, which is reserved for
the obediently faithful.

We
may be very
surprised to find
that our enduring to
the end simply involves
our mastery of two principles
that are tied to the Atonement
of the Savior, that are powerfully
taught in The Book of Mormon:
Repentance for our own sins,
and our forgiveness of
the trespasses of
others.

The Book of
Mormon blesses us
with the currency of
faith that accrues with
interest. We persevere as
disciples of Christ, because
we know that the wages of sin
is death. Gaining a testimony
of the principles of the gospel is
the only venture on earth whose
retirement benefits are out
of this world.

We feel
that we are as lights
that are set on a hill, when
we publish peace with The Book of
Mormon. Our discipleship is built up
with dignity and is made honorable. We
enlarge and strengthen our callings, and
we simply perform the service that pertains
to them. We are like a pair of old shoes, to
be worn out as we follow the path of the
Savior thru the Galilee, to Jerusalem
and the Via Dolorosa, and then on
to Gethsemane, to Calvary,
and to empty tomb.

The Book of
Mormon anchors our
faith on a foundation of
rock, rather than sand. Our
testimonies are composed of
three essential elements. First
is our conscious recognition of
gospel principles. Second is our
understanding of the Lord's word
concerning the principles. Lastly
is our direct experience with those
principles, which is what we call
"the fruits of faith." Some have
explained this experience as a
mystical rapture that occurs
when our hearts have been
touched by the
Spirit.

The Book
of Mormon
fans our fire of
resolve with a faith
to hope and pray for
the courage to change
the things we can, for the
serenity to accept what we
cannot change, and for the
wisdom to be able to know
the difference between
the two.

The Book
of Mormon teaches
us how to consecrate to
the Savior our time, our
talents, our means, and
all else with which He
has providently
blessed our
lives.

The tangible token
of our participation in our
Father's work and glory, which
is to bring to pass our immortality
and our eternal life, is the ordinance
of baptism. (See Mosiah Chapter 18).
Some may consider the commitment
too costly, but countless witnesses
have testified how obedience has
become, for them, not only a
bargain at half the price,
but also the perfect
law of liberty.

We proclaim our
testimonies of The Book
of Mormon, that we might
rejoice in our characterization
by the world as peculiar people,
for, in our eyes, that positive
expression means we have
become witnesses to the
vitalization of the
Merciful Plan of
our Creator.

The steadiness of The
Book of Mormon stands out
as the polar opposite of the moral
ambiguity, the cultural confusion,
intellectual instability, and spiritual
schizophrenia that we witness in the
world today. Because there is no
stable ground anywhere else,
we stand in holy places,
and we are not
moved.

The Book of Mormon and
the doctrine of Christ that is
found therein are little quanta
of energy that contribute just the
right amount of illumination
that is critically needed by
a world that has become
enveloped in thick
darkness.

During our Book of
Mormon study, when our
souls have been illuminated
by the glow that emanates from
the burning Spirit of God, we can
no longer remain passive. There is
a flickering fire of faith that warms
our souls as we begin to recognize the
upward reach within ourselves. We are
sensitized to truth, to beauty, and to
a goodness above and beyond our
our own attainment. If we're very
fortunate, we'll even experience
faint stirring of the golden
quality of gratitude
in our hearts.

In our
approach
to The Book
of Mormon, we
adopt a culture of
faith that embraces us,
helping insulate us from
worldly influences. It alerts
us to Satan's misdirection that
attempts to lead us from brilliant,
dazzling white, through every shade
of grey, to that fathomless black which,
by subtraction, is the absence of every
uplifting thought, word, deed, and
sustaining principle.

When we embrace
The Book of Mormon,
we have little inclination
to look back, as we flee from
Sodom and Gomorrah. We leave
the ranks of those who comfortably
maintain their summer residences in
Babylon, even though God's love letters,
and in fact everything but junk mail,
will be providentially delivered to their
permanent home addresses back
in Zion.

When
we are tempted to
curse the darkness, it
is The Book of Mormon
that will invite us to pause
and, instead, quietly
light a candle.

Every time
a child of God accepts The
Book of Mormon, the advancing
tide of wickedness slows just a bit
and the future looks brighter. A
thousand points of light, when
gathered as one, cast a very
long shadow, and extend
the promise of sunny
days ahead.

The Book of
Mormon provides
a metric to measure
the distance to heaven in
faith, rather than in miles.
It is not a question of dollars
and 'cents', but rather of casting
our lot with our Father in Heaven,
and trusting our fortunes to Him
and in His omniscient
'sense.'

The Book of Mormon
gives us the means to unite
ourselves with the mechanism
by which eternal principles are
communicated. Its lessons are a
manifestation of the practical
application of the ability of
the Holy Ghost to be a
Revelator and a
Testator.

We embrace The
Book of Mormon in the hope that
we might no longer be carried about by
every wind of doctrine, which are worldly
influences that play mind-games with
us as they jockey for position in a
competition for market share,
in the swap meets of
Babylon.

The Book of
Mormon is the great
equalizer. Its ordinances
that illuminate the Plan will
always stand ready to save our
souls, but in the meantime, the
children of God may worship
Him according to the dictates
of their own conscience. He
will force no one to go to
heaven. Water will
always seek its
own level.

The Book of Mormon is a
catalyst that propels us upward
toward our discovery of the personal
levels of our experience with the Savior.
For when we talk of knowing Him, we are
referring to a special sense of the word. It is
not enough to know about Him by reading
the book, or by listening to others speak of
Him. We must know Him thru the bonds
of common experience and feeling, and
therein lies the beauty and the power
of the Holy Ghost to touch our
lives with the fire of
faith.

Our
Father in Heaven
never envisioned that
a testimony of The Book
of Mormon would follow the
receipt of signs from heaven.
Our faith precedes the miracle.
We must take a few steps into the
darkness, and then the spiritual
strong searchlight illuminates
the way. Confirmation always
flows along the pathway
that has been created
by faith.

In The Book of Mormon, we are taught that it is the Holy Ghost Who will bestow upon us responsibility, whereas it is the devil who hoards power. The Lord revealed: he "rebelled against me, saying, Give me thine honor, which is my power; and also a third part of the hosts of heaven turned he away from me because of their agency." (D&C 29:36). Cain, who was only his lackey, "said: Truly I am Mahan, the master of this great secret, that I may murder and get gain. Wherefore Cain … gloried in his wickedness." (Moses 5:31). It was the Savior Who said: "Father, thy will be done, and the glory be thine forever." (Moses 4:2). The Book of Mormon teaches accountability so that we "may stand independent above all other creatures beneath the celestial world." (D&C 78:14). For the Plan to operate smoothly and as it was intended, "it is required of the Lord, at the hand of every steward, to render an account of his stewardship, both in time and in eternity." (D&C 72:3). Therefore, said the Lord, it is incumbent to "make use of the stewardship which I have appointed unto you." (D&C 104:63).

In general, throughout most of The Book of Mormon's history, the Lamanites remain a bad example of the fact that wickedness is the companion of frailty, friability, and futility. It is the bedfellow of despondency, distress, and desperation. Poor lost souls of any age who abound in iniquity have no hope of progression, forgiveness, redemption, or salvation. Without hope, they must despair; for spiritual death is the wages of sin. (See Romans 6:23).

When we have been blessed by the Holy
Ghost to "tingle with the consciousness of our
kinship with the infinite, (when) all the petty
trials, sorrows, and sufferings of this life"
that sometimes accompany our study of
The Book of Mormon "will fade away
as temporary, harmless visions,
seen (only) in a dream."
(David O. McKay).

We have determined to search the
scriptures, and in particular, to study The
Book of Mormon. In the face of competing
activities, we persevere. Although there
are many influences that attempt to
weaken our resolve, yet we will
continually turn to the
word of the Lord for
inspiration.

The Book of Mormon reaffirms that our Father in Heaven is mighty to save! The hearts of those with strong testimonies of its teachings ache for those who walk in darkness, who don't yet know where or how to find gospel truth. They pray for ways to reach out to those who helplessly endure the night and suffer the pain of spiritual blindness.

From the lands of The Book of Mormon, the righteous have cried "hallelujah!" Before the millennial day, when the signs of the times proclaim that the Second Coming of Jesus Christ is nigh at hand, the faithful and true will once again shout: "Praise ye the Lord!" (See 2 Nephi 4:30 & 22:2).

A fire with dancing flames, (see 2 Nephi 31:13), billowing clouds of smoke (see 2 Nephi 14:5), as well as an ethereal light (see 2 Nephi 20:17), a sharp and penetrating spirit (see Alma 19:13), and deeply penetrating burnings (see 2 Nephi 20:16), are symbolic of the presence of the Lord and of the glory of God. They frequently depict the grandeur of celestial realms. In the words of Joseph Smith: "God Himself dwells in eternal fire." ("Teachings," p. 367).

Many of us are carrying heavy loads as we approach our Book of Mormon study. There is a silent prayer in our hearts: "O Lord, promise to care for me in Bethesda, as I come to Thee in great need, for the weight of my burdens seems too much to bear. In Thy word, may I find rest, and a tabernacle of peace in Thy house of grace."

The life-long learning laboratory
within which we find ourselves immersed
while we tarry upon the Earth has provided us
with a grand opportunity to mold ourselves to
more closely resemble the nature of our Father
in Heaven. He initiated the ordinance of
the Sacrament (see Moroni Chapters
4 & 5), to make that difficult
transformation easier for
us to experience.

The Book
of Mormon coherently
stitches foundation principles
together into an easily recognizable
pattern, so that the power of the word
and the witness of truth might be
conveyed without the need
for external warrant.

We can have no proof
of Moroni's promise to bless
us with the Spirit of truth until
we act on the basis of our awakening
belief. Then comes the ratification that
is manifest as a spiritual confirmation,
but only after we have exercised faith.
This is why James taught: "Faith,
if it hath not works, is dead,
being alone." (James
2:17).

Every day,
we choose to receive
the word of God, or to
reject it. That's a decision
that will be determined by
the quality of our devotion to
the Savior. Sometimes, though,
it can be negatively defined by
our adoration of the prince of
darkness, in a process of
subtraction.

Without the blessing of the Atonement
of Jesus Christ, and devoid of the gifts that
might have otherwise flowed unto us following
our obedience to the covenants that are described
in The Book of Mormon, we must forever remain
miserable, living in an unrelenting state of
separation from the presence of Heavenly
Father, His Only Begotten Son
Jesus Christ, and the
Holy Ghost.

The
portal
to Eden
may have
swung shut
for us, but as
it did, another
door opened that
introduced us to a
a secret garden that
is only accessible to
those who grasp The
Book of Mormon's
awesome power.

The
invitation
to forgive and
to be forgiven is
juxtaposed against
the sense of distress,
despondency, despair,
and desolation that is
frequently a part of our
mortal schooling when
we've chosen to ignore
the blessing that are
found in The Book
of Mormon's
messages.

Reading The Book of
Mormon is a definitive step
that we all must take during
our journey to Christ. The path
ahead leads all the way to the Tree
of Life. It is not a freeway, but a toll
road. Until we have paid the requisite
levy, we cannot hope to comprehend
with fluency the language of the
Spirit that clearly explains what
we must do to make our way
to the tree, that we might
harvest its delicious
fruit.

Nephite baptism was witnessed by the Spirit of Sanctification. It asked them to consider the possibility that, one day, they might actually be holy and without spot, as is our Exemplar.

The raw wounds and ugly contamination of sin among the Nephites were incompatible with the uncompromising standard of spiritual hygiene required of those who desired baptism, who one day would hope to inhabit heaven and live in the holy company of God and angels.

When the
Nephites were dealing with
weakness in the contractions that
pushed forward the Savior's agenda,
relying on the power of His Atonement
quickened them to bear their witness
with renewed conviction, unto the
convincing of their brethren the
Lamanites of the truthfulness
of the gospel. (See Mosiah
Chapter 28).

Moroni understood
that worthily partaking of the
Sacrament could be the fuel firing the
determination of the Saints to follow the
Savior. (See Moroni Chapters 4 & 5). His
Atonement, upon which the ordinance was
founded, would charge their spiritual
batteries and energize their vision
with an infinite perspective.
They could become holy
and without
spot.

When we read
The Book of Mormon,
we sometimes will have a
striking experience when light
and truth distil upon our souls.
Just so, in the Sacred Grove, light
"descended gradually," entering the
quiet grove slowly enough that Joseph
was able to gauge its approach, until it
finally reached him and enveloped him
within a dazzling brilliance. It was only
then that he "saw two Personages, whose
brightness and glory (were beyond all)
description," and who stood suspended
in the air within the encircling light.
(J.S.H. 1:17). We may not see Them
as we contemplate the scriptures,
but we receive inspiration and
revelation when we are in the
presence of those from the
unseen world, and we
can be sure that we
stand in holy
places.

The revelation of The Book of
Mormon is as a mortar that binds
together the building blocks of our
testimony. It becomes the footing of
our conversion. These foundation
cornerstones of our conviction
are continually bathed and
washed clean in living
water.

As long as the hard-hearted choose
to remain in a state of rebellion against
the Spirit, a Book of Mormon testimony must
remain just beyond their reach. If they never raise
their eyes to search eternal horizons, the world will
appear to them as nothing more than a barren desert
devoid of refreshing oases, the welcoming shade of
trees, and an abundance of well-watered gardens.
Without faith in nourishing revelation, the
bread of life will be to them as stale
and moldy leftover crumbs.

The revelation that
we revere as The Book of
Mormon speaks a language
that is universally understood
without ambiguity. It leaves little
room for discussion as to its meaning
because it is spiritually discerned. Even
more remarkably, it unifies us even as it
recognizes our diversity. It quickly moves
us away from dependence and independence,
to interdependence. However, it blesses us with
unity and conformity without asking us to give
up our individuality, or those things that make
us unique. It invites us to come unto God and
to "partake of his goodness; (reminding us
that) he denieth none that come unto him,
black and white, bond and free, male
and female; and he remembereth the
heathen; and all are alike unto
God, both Jew and Gentile."
(2 Nephi 26:33).

All around us, it is not difficult to
see the fulfillment of the prophecy of The Book of
Mormon that we are living in the Last Days, when the
hearts of men shall fail them as their shields of faith
begin to crumble. When heaven closes, the revelatory
voice of warning is silenced, and all is quiet from
pulpits that had aforetime been aflame with faith.
The rebellious rant and rave against that which
is good, but the righteous can also be pacified
and lulled away into a false sense of carnal
security, until they believe that all is well
in Zion. None of us can have the luxury
of being able to take our foot off the
gas pedal during our journey
along the highway that
leads to the gate of
heaven.

We can be sure we are on the Lord's
errand, because the messages of The Book
of Mormon will flow easily and poetically to
our minds. Our persistence will lead to practiced
fluency in the language of the Holy Ghost, that
is the result of the inspiration that will come as
we approach our study with faith, fasting, and
prayer. As our minds are enlightened, we will
be cast off into streams of revelation and
swept up in the quickening currents of
direct experience with our Heavenly
Father, His Son Jesus Christ,
and the Holy Spirit.

Revelation from
God releases us to be creative,
and our creativity sets us free to
properly plan before we come face to
face with the crises of life. It prevents
our poor performance and it mitigates
consequences. As we learn to rely upon
the doctrine of Christ that is taught in
The Book of Mormon, we internalize its
elements. This allows us to surrender
ourselves to its infinite possibilities.
Therein, we discover avenues for our
personal expression and, finally,
we encounter our freedom to
'become.'

If we wish to follow the
divine design of God during
the complicated construction of
the fortress of our spiritual symmetry,
we will need to turn our undivided attention
to His counsel that can be found in The Book of
Mormon. We can only do so if we have the faith to
believe all that He has revealed and all that He now
reveals. If, finally, the eyes of our understanding are
opened to believe that He will yet reveal many great
and important things that relate to our progression,
we will be up and moving on a journey that leads
to the successful completion of the fabrication
of our proper and perfect frames. We will be
blessed with certificates of occupancy,
so that we might freely invite the
Spirit to dwell with us.

As we embrace the creative
expression of revelation that is found
within The Book of Mormon, we'll recognize
how its energy can help us to comprehend our
Heavenly Father. We'll feel our divine potential
welling up within us, and have the confidence
to ask seemingly innocent questions that will
have profound answers and implications that
shake our world, spreading like ripples that
radiate outward from rocks thrown into
the still water of our perceptual ponds.
The answers to our humble petitions
will come to us as if in a revelatory
machine that has been created
for the making of Gods.

Darkness is the conjoined twin of misery.
Therefore, the obedience of faith when we turn to
The Book of Mormon for the answers to life's most
important questions frees us to embrace the truth, to
make intelligent choices, and to perform purposefully; to
carry on convincingly, and to persistently progress; to
dismiss the cares of the world through the Atonement of
Jesus Christ; to ascend into the rarified atmosphere
of the Spirit that invites us to inhale deeply; that
we might be powerfully reinvigorated by
refreshing communication from
our Heavenly Father.

Those who are ignorantly unenlightened can become argumentive; they exercise unrighteous dominion, while the humble invite the Spirit to guide them as they work their way thru The Book of Mormon. They acknowledge revelation from God as the fruit of the faith that has driven their inquiry.

If we thoughtlessly postpone our quest for the holy grail of the revelation that is The Book of Mormon until we've become spiritually blinded to the Light of Christ, we'll become subjected to the spirit of the devil. When he captures our hearts, they will mutated to become stony and cold, and we'll lose the capacity to distinguish good from evil and light from darkness. When we exchange the sunshine that is generated by the whisperings of the Spirit for the wintry weather of worldliness, it will withdraw and move on to warmer climes. Satan's icy breath will consequently be sucked into the vortex.

Without
knowledge,
there can be no
faith; without faith,
there can be no light,
and without the light of
revelation from the heavens
there can be no recognition of
religious truth; and without the
enlightenment of the Spirit, if just
one of these elements is missing, all
must be lost. Our fortunes rest on the
basis of how we embrace our intuition,
inspiration, and the revelation of
The Book of Mormon.

As our expanding
testimonies of Christ swell in our
hearts, it is our faith that intensifies
our desire to receive the revelation of The
Book of Mormon. It centers our lives, by
bringing them into harmony with true
principles. We endeavor to be obedient to
God, that we might find ourselves in a
constant state of improvement. As we
begin to believe in ourselves, we find
it is that much easier to believe our
Father in Heaven, too. It is with a
quickening pulse that we realize
that our progress is headed in
the direction of perfection.
Our Father doesn't deal
in knock-offs. We are
the right stuff!

We are at a
crossroads, for our
decision to believe The
Book of Mormon could
deify us, just as our choice
not to believe can destroy us.
How we respond to the massive
lightning, thunder, and burning
bush of Sinai, that summon us to
acknowledge the Savior of the world
will delineate our dreams and will
define our destiny. Ultimately, it
will determine how, where, and
with whom we will spend
all of eternity.

When the
Saints cannot
find resources within
the church to sustain their
connection to God that had been
established by revelation, such as
that which can be found in The Book of
Mormon, they'll be at risk of sliding back
into marginalized relationships that may
even brand them as 'less active,' or 'inactive.'
They'll lose direction, power, and purpose when
they've lost the means to nourish, support, and
sustain their testimony of a book that is
driven by the revelatory principles
that had, at one time, been
their guiding lights.

Revelation from God leaves a distinct afterglow from our pre-mortal lives and establishes an undeniable connection between ourselves and The Book of Mormon. A simple yet uncommitted recognition of Jesus will not qualify us to inherit the Celestial Kingdom. Christians of convenience lack the revelatory fire that is ignited by faith. Many honorable people who accept the Savior will still inherit the Terrestrial Kingdom. According to the scriptures, these are they who "received not the gospel, neither the testimony of Jesus, neither the prophets, neither the everlasting covenant. Last of all, these are all they who will not be gathered with the Saints, to be caught up unto the Church of the Firstborn, and received into the cloud." (D&C 76:101-102).

Without the power that is manifest in The Book of Mormon, we must remain ever learning, while never coming to the knowledge of the truth that would have made us free. We grasp at straws, failing to recognize that nothing will kill our creativity more quickly than the self-assurance that poisons our ability to recognize the revelatory influence of awesome powers that are greater than ourselves.

The effects of sin are inevitable and inescapable, but for the intercession thru faith of the Atonement. The Builder and Fashioner of the universe must intervene in our behalf by implementing His Plan to engage laws that were designed to restore equilibrium. The Book of Mormon helps us to understand that "in the heavens, there is a "better and an enduring substance." (Hebrews 10:34). It is guidance from above that makes it possible for us to blend that substance into the elixir of the gods.

Those who are ignorant among us will be forever attempting to drag communication from the heavens down to their own level so that it is in harmony with their myopic view of life. The world ridicules revelation and disparages its delivery, and scorns The Book of Mormon. These feeble exertions ring hollow, however, when compared to the thunder, lightning, and burning bush that was not consumed, on Sinai.

The Book
of Mormon
nudges us off
our complacency
plateaus as we steer
away from the trendy
cafés situated along the
broad avenues of Idumea.
We are transported as upon
the wings of eagles beyond the
boundaries of our self-imposed
limitations, along a different
highway that leads to
heaven.

With The
Book of Mormon, we are
enabled to envision a magical
place of innocence. We realize
that it is only if we can return
to our psychological, spiritual,
and emotional childhood that
we may rediscover the place
where dreams really do
come true and all of
God's children live
happily ever
after.

The Book of Mormon would characterize us as Mr. Rogers. He was without guile. There were no strangers in his neighborhood. He was less judgmental and was more accepting of our differences. He was less suspicious and was friendlier.

Our Father tenders the currency of revelation to purchase golden tickets for our passage back Home. He is reimbursed with soul-sweat, as it works on our sense of duty, on our conscience, and on our scruples, to nurture our faith to believe. We no longer see things as they are and wonder: 'Why?' Instead, we dream about things that never were, and ask: 'Why not?' The Book of Mormon helps us to push thru our problems rather than working around them.

Isn't it interesting that
we nearly universally celebrate the
miracles of the birth and resurrection of
our Savior, but we somehow find it difficult
to recognize the reality of His post-mortal
ministry among the Nephites. Should
we not all "fear the Lord and ...
stand in awe of him?"
(Psalms 33:8).

During Christmas and then at
Easter, the Word is again revealed to all of God's
children, to those who are both literate and untutored in
the grammar of the gospel. The Book of Mormon joins these
celebrations as a primer that brings us unto Christ. Continual
guidance from the Holy Ghost, known as revelation, is critical
to the process, for a vital religion "cannot be maintained and
preserved on the theory that God dealt with our human race
only in the far past ages, and that the Bible is the only
evidence we have that our God is a living, revealing,
communicating God. If He ever spoke, He is still
speaking. He is the great I Am, not the great
He was." (Rufus Jones).

The testimonies of the witnesses of The Book of Mormon suggest that the book is meant to be devoured as if it were literally the bread of life. Those who read feast upon the book and feel exhilaration as it speaks to them from the dust. We seek, we yearn, we strive, and we wrestle for our blessing, realizing that "unto some it is given by the Holy Ghost to know that Jesus Christ is the Son of God," while "to others it is given to believe on their words, that they also might have eternal life if they continue faithful." (D&C 46:13-14).

When we read and study The Book of Mormon, we find ourselves in supporting roles to the Star of David, whose name appeared in lights on the heavenly marquee above Bethlehem. The book prepares us to embrace the faith to believe by introducing us to fast-scale runs thru more than half a dozen octaves on all 88 of the glistening black and white ivory keys of experience. As we rehearse in our minds the expression of our witness of the Savior, of Whom the book testifies, we are accompanied by the rising tenor of a celestial symphony that has been scored for every imaginable instrument. But most of all, the orchestration of life prepares us for a Senior Recital that will showcase our familiarity with the pitch, rhythm, dynamics, timbre, and texture of the book. Our effort will become an oeuvre that is worthy of the approbation of God. Along the way, the Spirit will guide us back to the Source of our inspiration. It will be there that we will kneel at the feet of the Maestro, to enjoy master classes from Him Who first created musicality by matching movement and form to the melody and mood of The Book of Mormon.

Time and again, intemperance and gluttony impaired the judgment of weak-willed Nephites and Lamanites. Of those who were mesmerized by physical impairment and were blinded to the path of progress, Isaiah wrote: "They regard not the work of the Lord, neither consider the operation of his hands." (2 Nephi 15:12). Too often, the Nephites were held captive because their character had been crippled and they could no longer receive insight, intuition, inspiration, or revelation. Their indulgence required greater intensities of validation for the same level of gratification. They had not only lost their traction on gospel sod, but they were also spinning their wheels and slipping backward toward the precipice of destruction.

Our Book of Mormon study demands that we pause in our frenzied pursuit of temporal treasure to stretch our spiritual muscles, brush the cobwebs from our minds, and crane our necks as we look up to heaven.

Those who are stiff-necked lack the pliancy, flexibility, and perspective of faith. (See Jarom 1:4). This prevents them from looking up to Heavenly Father for guidance, over to priesthood leaders for counsel, around to seek out those in need, or down in an attitude of humility. The Book of Mormon has the power to soften our telestial tendencies, assuage our secular skepticism, and blur the lines distinguishing mortality from eternity. It leaves us eager to respond to the questions that loom before us all: "What think ye of Christ?" and "Whose Son is He?" (See Alma 5:14 & 26). It nudges us off our complacency plateaus, as we steer away from the trendy cafés situated along the broad avenues of Babylon. It carries us to the edge of eternity, to the portals of heaven, and paints a portrait of "forever" that stands revealed before us in a breath-taking panorama.

The prophets of The Book of Mormon warn us in no uncertain terms that a day of judgement is coming for every one of us, when we will no longer be able to fabricate lies, either to ourselves or our Heavenly Father. We will have written the record of our lives in the sinews of our bodies and the tablets of our minds. In that coming day, both will be unfolded before God and angels, who will read that record as easily as we read the book. At that moment, if we have aforetime embraced its principles and doctrine, we will be swept up by quickening currents into the rapture of direct experience and a holy communion with God. His thoughts will have somehow become our thoughts, and His ways will have become our ways. (See Isaiah 55:8). Legions of angels will confirm the truth that the universe has become "a machine for the making of gods." (Henri Bergson).

When we harden our hearts against the glad
tidings and the message of salvation that are found in The
Book of Mormon, the flow of living water will slow to a trickle
to leave us defenseless against the suffocating desert winds of
the devil. The Book of Mormon helps us to put all the pieces of the
puzzle of life together. It answers the question Alice posed to the
Cheshire Cat: "Would you please tell me which way I ought to go
from here?" Replied the cat: "That depends a good deal on where
you want to go." "I admit," responded Alice, "I don't much
care where." Said the cat: "Then it doesn't matter which
way you go." "Just so I go somewhere!" cried Alice.
"Oh," responded the cat, "you are sure to do
that, if you walk far enough."
(Lewis Carroll).

When we read and study The
Book of Mormon, we determine to
accomplish fluency in the language of
the scriptures that testify of Christ. Only
if we have paid the price will the words of the
prophets in that book flow easily and poetically
to our minds. Confidence will come after practice
that is manifested by memorization, recitation,
individual and cooperative study, comparison
with companion scriptures, expansion of
understanding by critical analysis
of supportive commentaries, as
well as by faith, fasting,
and prayer.

When the Fall is considered in conjunction with the birth, ministry, atonement, death, and resurrection of Christ, it is clear that all are part of God's Plan of Eternal Progression. When Lehi wrote that "Adam fell that men might be, and men are that they might have joy" (2 Nephi 2:25), he understood that we are "spirit, the elements are eternal, and spirit and element, inseparably connected, receive a fullness of joy." (D&C 93:33).

In the midst of the persecution that would seven years later take his life, William Tyndall confidently wrote of his testimony of Christ, that "it declares that we are safe already, and certifies our hearts and makes us feel that our faith is right and that God's spirit is in us." (William Tyndall). Knowledge from The Book of Mormon that is received through the exercise of faith is the mortar that binds together the building blocks of conversion and testimony. A wise Teacher counseled that knowledge is received by faith. (See D&C 26:2). He taught: "As all have not faith, seek ye diligently and teach one another words of wisdom; yea, seek ye out of the best books words of wisdom; seek learning, even by study and also by faith." (D&C 88:118).

The Book of Mormon will now and forever be 'published' by the authorized and inspired servants of the Lord, called to preach faith and repentance to "every nation, kindred, tongue, and people." (Alma 37:4). Knowledge of the truth will increase in the world "by hearing those who are sent from God and preacheth His promises."
(William Tyndall).

The Savior said that we must be perfect in our hope to inherit the kingdom of God. (3 Nephi 12:48). Perhaps He meant that we should try to be perfect in our repentance. After explaining to his people the great Plan of Redemption that solved the doctrinal dilemma created by God's demand for perfection coupled with our inability to lead sinless lives, the prophet Jacob simply concluded: "O be wise; what can I say more?" Moroni echoed his message: "Be wise in the days of your probation: strip yourselves of all uncleanness (and) ask with a firmness unshaken, that ye will yield to no temptation, but that ye will serve the true and living God."
(Mormon 9:28).

As the spiritual sons and
daughters of our Heavenly Father,
we are the heirs of His spiritual gifts and
joint-heirs with His Son Jesus Christ, when we
follow the covenant path. (See Romans 8:17). It's
when we're on that course that the bands of death will
be broken, and we'll be set free by His matchless grace.
There is no other name given whereby salvation cometh,"
said King Benjamin; "therefore, I would that ye should
take upon you the name of Christ, all you that have
entered into the covenant with God."
(Mosiah 5:8).

We pray for a unity of the faith,
and for a time when we will "talk of
Christ, rejoice in Christ, preach of Christ,
prophesy of Christ, and write according
to our prophecies, that our children may
know to what source they may look
for a remission of their sins."
(2 Nephi 25:26).

When The Book of Mormon has finally penetrated the hearts of men and women all over the world, "every man shall be his own priest, to whom the Lord God shall incline His ear. Young men shall prophesy, and old men shall dream dreams. There shall be no "confession in the ear. For neither the Apostles, nor they that followed many hundred years after, knew of any such whispering."
(William Tyndall).

The Book of Mormon boldly testifies to all the world: "And behold, there shall a new star arise, such an one as ye never have beheld; and this also shall be a sign unto you." (Helaman 14:5). Even Zoroastrian priests beheld the star and recognized its significance. Making haste, they traveled to Jerusalem after the Savior's birth, bearing gifts of gold, frankincense, and myrrh, to inquire of King Herod: "Where is he that is born King of the Jews? For we have seen his star in the east, and are come to worship him."
(Matthew 2:2).

The Book of Mormon
is able to confound "the worldly wise,
enemies to the wisdom of God, our deep and
profound wells without water, our clouds without
moisture of rain, natural souls without the Spirit of
God." (William Tyndall). To even the most hardened
skeptics, the book is just one of many signs and
wonders in heaven and on the Earth that have
been given as additional testimony of
the divinity of the Savior.

The messages of The Book of Mormon
reach to the very core of our spiritual center, where
we feel in our hearts that we have consented unto the law
of God. Under such circumstances, "we feel ourselves meek,
patient, courteous, and merciful to our neighbours, altered
and fashioned like unto Christ. Why, then, should
we doubt but that God hath forgiven us, and
chosen us, and put his Spirit in us?"
(William Tyndale).

When we are reading The Book of
Mormon, we listen to the sound of trumpets
speaking to us from out of the heavens, and we
hear their clarion call, not with our ears, but with
our hearts. Sometimes, the gulf between the secular
and the sacred cannot be bridged with profane speech.
When the Lord communed with His Father in the presence
of Nephite Saints, "so great and marvelous were the words
which he prayed, that they cannot be written, neither can
they be uttered by man." (3 Nephi 19:34). Nevertheless,
the spiritual preparation of the multitude permitted
them to receive those things, and so "they did
understand in their hearts the words which
he prayed." (2 Nephi 19:33).

In the land Bountiful, near the precincts of the temple,
the Saints brought their children to the Savior, that He might
minister to them. After taking them "one by one, (He) blessed them,
and prayed unto the Father for them." (3 Nephi 17:21). The Spirit was
overwhelming and as the multitude raised their eyes, "they saw the heavens
open, and they saw angels descending out of heaven, as it were, in the midst
of fire; and they came down and encircled those little ones about, and they
were encircled about with fire. And the angels did minister unto them."
(3 Nephi 17:24). Truly, they were "one, the Children of Christ,
and heirs to the kingdom of God." (4 Nephi 1:3 & 17).

The morning stars are able to see at once the beginning and the end. They witnessed the coming forth to the world of The Book of Mormon, and they were, and are, and forever will be singing together and shouting for joy. (See Job 38:7). As Alma taught his son: "All is as one day with God, and time only is measured unto men." (Alma 40:8). Albert Einstein was right; time is relative. Joseph Smith revealed: "The great Jehovah contemplated the whole of the events connected with the earth ... before it rolled into existence, or ever the morning stars sang together for joy; the past, the present, and the future were and are, with him, one eternal now." (Teachings," p. 220). The Savior exists, as well, in the past, present, and future tense; He is "the Great I AM, Alpha and Omega." (D&C 38:1). His "course is one eternal round, the same today as yesterday, and forever." (D&C 35:1).

At the very end of The Book of Mormon, the invitation is extended to "come unto Christ, and (to) be perfected in Him." (Moroni 10:32). We are invited to move off the telestial turf that is Satan's territorial treasure, and to grasp the horns of sanctuary where the "covenants and ordinances (of the book) will fill us with faith as a living fire. In a day of desolating sickness, scorched earth, barren wastelands, sickening plagues, disease, destruction, and death, we as a people will rest in the shade of trees. We will drink from the cooling fountains. We will abide in places of refuge from the storm; we will mount up as on the wings of eagles; we will be lifted out of an insane and evil world. We will be as fair as the sun and clear as the moon." (Vaughn Featherstone).

As our testimonies of The Book of Mormon grow
and mature into bastions of spiritual solidarity, we sense
that "no unhallowed hand can stop the work from progressing;
persecutions may rage, mobs may combine, armies may assemble,
calumny may defame. But the truth of God will go forth boldly,
nobly, and independent, until it has penetrated every continent,
visited every clime, swept every country, and sounded in every
ear, 'til the purposes of God shall be accomplished and
the Great Jehovah shall say 'The work is done.'"
(Joseph Smith).

The time when we are initially handed a copy of
The Book of Mormon and invited to try the virtue of the word of God will
test our souls. The summer soldier and the sunshine patriot, as they initially
engage the book, may shrink from their worship of God, but those who prayerfully
undertake its study deserve the love and thanks of men and women. Ignorance of the
meaning of the book, like hell, will not be easily conquered; yet we have this consolation,
that the harder our divine commission, the more glorious the triumph. What we obtain too
cheap, we esteem too lightly. 'Tis dearness only that gives everything its value. Heaven
knows how to put a proper price upon its goods; and it would be strange, indeed, if so
celestial an article as a testimony of The Book of Mormon, Another Testament
of Jesus Christ, should not be highly rated. (See Tom Paine's pamphlet
entitled, "The Crisis," published on 12/23/1776).

When we initially read The Book of Mormon, many
of us have had an experience akin to that of George Frideric
Handel. When, in just 24 days, he composed the 259 pages of
musical score that comprise "The Messiah," the notes came to him so
quickly that he could barely keep up, as he furiously scratched out
the oratorio on whatever paper was handy. After he had written
the "Hallelujah Chorus" in a fervor of divine inspiration, he
exclaimed that he had "seen all heaven before him." At the
end of the manuscript, in acknowledgement of his
own puny efforts, he wrote the letters "SDG"
that stood for "Soli Deo Gloria" or
"To God alone the glory."

If we will
allow The Book of Mormon to work its
magic, and to accomplish what it promises
it can do, we will be blessed with a continuing
endowment of the Holy Spirit, which is enough
to bring us into the presence of God. It will be
as if we were kneeling at the manger
ourselves, to adore and worship
the Newborn King.

There is an interesting account of Eve's directions to her children following the death of her husband Adam, that bears on the subject of the plates of ore upon which the record of the Nephites and Lamanites was written. It reads: "Listen to me, my children. Make ye tables of stone and others of clay, and write on them all my life and your father's, and all that ye have heard and seen from us. If, by water, the Lord judge our race, the tables of clay will be dissolved and the tables of stone will remain; but if, by fire, the tables of stone will be broken up, and the tables of clay will be baked hard." ("Christ's Eternal Gospel," p. 97, the "Pseudepigraphic Book of Adam and Eve"). Paper and ink and even tablets of stone or metal may not survive the ravages of time, but God will be able to read the record of our lives engraved in our very sinews. For Him who created us, that tapestry woven into our souls may be read as easily as any printed text. Our Heavenly Father "knows when (we've) been bad or good, so be good for goodness' sake!" (John Frederick Coots and Haven Gillespie, "Santa Claus is Coming to Town").

As we read and study The Book of Mormon, we hear the music of heavenly choirs and discern the voices of angelic messengers testifying that the Son of God has come in righteousness "to declare the glad tidings of great joy." (Mosiah 3:3). It will seem to us that it is "in the dark recesses of memory, in unbidden suggestions, in trains of thought unwittingly pursued, in multiplied waves and currents all at once flashing and rushing, in dreams that cannot be laid to rest, in the force of instinct, in the obscure, but certain, intuitions of the spiritual life, that we will have glimpses of a great tide of life ebbing and flowing, rippling and roiling and beating about where we cannot see it." (E.S. Dallas).

If we reject the invitation of heaven to enjoy an intimate association with the Divine, we damage our eternal selves, for the Lord warned, "in an hour when ye think not the summer shall be past, and the harvest ended, and your souls not saved." (D&C 45:2). In fact, whether we acknowledge it or not, every second of every day, we are one tick of the clock closer to "the undiscovered country, from whose bourn no traveler returns." (Shakespeare, Hamlet, Act 3, Scene 1). The Book of Mormon invites us to make every one of those seconds count for something.

Telestial treasures are the counterfeit blessings that have been tailor-made for those whose undisciplined minds are easily swayed by a siren song so seductively sent by Satan. Unprincipled character crumbles in the face of temptations that are tantalizing and yet traumatizing. The more those who are covetous focus on the idols of the day, the less will they be influenced by the power of doctrine in The Book of Mormon.

Commentary, Compendia, & Observations Index

Moroni taught:
Those who believe "in Christ, doubting nothing, whatsoever he shall ask the Father in the name of Christ it shall be granted him; and this promise is unto all" who have faith in the power of God to reveal His will.
(Mormon 9:21).

Commentary Volume One
Born in The Wilderness

- 1 Nephi
- 2 Nephi
- Jacob
- Enos
- Jarom
- Omni
- Words of Mormon
- Observations
- Author's Note
- Addendum – A Sampling of Scriptures

Commentary Volume Two
Voices From The Dust

- Mosiah
- Alma
- Observations
- Author's Note
- Addendum – A Sampling of Scriptures

Commentary Volume Three
Journey to Cumorah

- Helaman
- 3 Nephi
- 4 Nephi
- Mormon
- Ether
- Moroni
- Observations
- Author's Note
- Addendum – A Sampling of Scriptures

When situational ethics guide our behavior, and when every man walketh in his own way, and after the image of his own god, the erosion of our capacity to accept Latter-day scripture will be met by the chaotic collision of cultural disintegration with the stability of the gospel.

Compendium
Volume One

- Introduction
- Questions Answered by The Book of Mormon
- Topical Index
- Observations
- A few of my favorite things
- Familiar Scriptures
- Commentary & Compendium Index

Compendium
Volume Two

- Introduction
- Questions Answered by The Book of Mormon
- Topical Index
- Without The Book of Mormon
- Observations
- Introduction to the Isaiah Chapters
- "And it came to pass in The Book of Mormon
- "Ad thus we see" in The Book of Mormon
- "Behold" in The Book of Mormon
- "Wherefore" and "Therefore in The Book of Mormon
- The Appearance of Gold
- The Use of The Name of Christ
- Pragmatism in The Book of Mormon
- Dry Humor in The Book of Mormon
- A Book of Mormon Timeline
- Commentary and Compendium Index

Compendium
Volume Three

- Compendia Index
- Essays That Relate to Teachings in The Book of Mormon
- Observations
- Commentary, Compendium, & Observations

Compendium
Volume Four

- Compendia Index
- Essays That Relate to Teachings in The Book of Mormon
- Observations
- Commentary, Compendium & Observations Index

Compendium
Volume Five

- Compendia Index
- Essays That Relate to Teachings in The Book of Mormon
- Observations
- Commentary, Compendium & Observations Index

Do we really think it is
easier to yield to temptation,
and more difficult to resist sin?
Is rebellion easier because it is more
difficult to acknowledge and then to
act upon the revelations of God that are
found in The Book of Mormon? Can it be
easier to live in disorienting and swirling
fog of conflicting values, and harder to
be guided by what He has written
with His finger on the fleshy
tables of our hearts?

Compendium
Volume Six

- Compendia Index
- Essays That Relate to Teachings in The Book of Mormon
- Observations
- Commentary, Compendium & Observations Index

Compendium
Volume Seven

- Compendia Index
- Essays That Relate to Teachings in The Book of Mormon
- Observations
- Commentary, Compendium & Observation Index

Compendium
Volume Eight

- Introduction
- Hebrew Poetry in The Book of Mormon
- Synonymous Parallelism
- Antithetical Parallelism
- Synthetic Parallelism
- Climactic Parallelism
- Chiasmus
- Book of Mormon Scriptures Illustrating

Observations
Volume One

- 550 Observations

Observations
Volume Two

- 550 Observations

Observations
Volume Three

- 550 Observations

Observations
Volume Four

- 550 Observations

Often, it
is only when
we have enrolled
in the graduate school
of hard knocks, and have
pre-paid the required tuition,
that we obtain the credits that
are earned by our obedience to
the promptings of the Spirit that
are the form and the substance of
revelation. If we will take the time to
read The Book of Mormon, we will be
at our best. w\We will find ourselves
particularly sensitive to the comfort
that can come thru the revelatory
whisperings of the Spirit.

Observations Volume 5

- 550 Observations
- Commentary, Compendium & Observations Index

Observations Volume 6

- 550 Observations
- Commentary, Compendium & Observations Index

Heavenly Father tenders the currency of revelation to purchase the golden tickets for our passage back Home. We reimburse Him with soul-sweat, as it works on our sense of duty, on our conscience, and on our scruples, to nurture our faith to believe. We no longer see things as they are and wonder: 'Why?' Instead, we dream about things that never were, and ask: 'Why not?' The Book of Mormon helps us to work thru our problems rather than working around them.

A Book of Mormon Commentary
Volumes One – Three

Compendia
Volumes One – Eight

Observations
Volumes One – Six

www.ingramcontent.com/pod-product-compliance
Lightning Source LLC
Chambersburg PA
CBHW061400010526
44107CB00012B/1003